ISLAM IN TRANSITION

ISLAM
IN TRANSITION
MUSLIM PERSPECTIVES

Edited by
John J. Donohue
and
John L. Esposito

New York   Oxford
OXFORD UNIVERSITY PRESS
1982

Copyright © 1982 by Oxford University Press, Inc.

198 Madison Avenue, New York, New York 10016-4314

Library of Congress Cataloging in Publication Data
Main entry under title:

Islam in transition.

    I. Islam—20th century—Addresses, essays, lectures.
I. Donohue, John J.   II. Esposito, John L.
BP163.1754   297'.1978   81-11015
ISBN 0-19-503022-2   AACR2
ISBN 0-19-503023-0 (pbk.)

Printing (last digit): 9 8

Printed in the United States of America

For
Elizabeth (Donohue) Scavone
and
Jeanette P. Esposito

PREFACE

Our greatest and most frustrating challenge in assembling this volume has been making these selections. We have tried to provide a broad spectrum of positions that reflects the issues and diversity of thought that characterize modern Islam. Emphasis has been placed on currents of thought rather than on significant personalities. Therefore, some individuals have been omitted because their general position was already represented. Space limitations have forced us to cut our original manuscript by one third. Reluctantly, selections from Turkey, Southeast Asia, and Soviet Central Asia have been omitted.

Transliteration and diacritical markings are always a vexing problem. With few exceptions, we have standardized the transliteration throughout the volume and followed a limited system of diacritical markings.

The prospectus for this volume was circulated among many colleagues for suggestions. We are grateful to each of them for their encouragement and assistance. We would especially like to thank Charles J. Adams, Khurshid Ahmad, Shaul Bakhash, L. Carl Brown, Hamid Enayat, Ismail Ragi al-Faruqi, Howard Federspiel, Albert Hourani, Nikki Keddie, Bernard Lewis, Gail Minault, James P. Piscatori, Wilfred Cantwell Smith, John O. Voll, and Farhat Ziadeh. Special thanks are due to those who assisted in the typing and related tasks: Sandra Froment, Jean Heffernan, Kathleen Lauring, Jennifer Carey, and Joanne Klocker. William Darrow wishes to acknowledge the assistance of N. Safa-Isfehani in preparing his translations.

We gratefully acknowledge the College of the Holy Cross and the Center for the Study of the Modern Arab World, Beirut, for their support for this and other projects throughout the years.

Unless otherwise indicated, we assume responsibility for translations as well as the editing of all the selections. We are grateful to the following publishers, editors, and authors for permission to reprint materials:

George Allen & Unwin for Muhammad 'Abduh's *The Theology of Unity*, translated by Kenneth Cragg, 1966, pp. 103–4, 107–8, 133–35, 145–46, 148–50.

American Council of Learned Societies for Sayyid Qutb's *Social Justice in Islam*, translated by John B. Hardie, 1970, pp. 7–9, 13–16, 24–28; and Tāhā Husayn's *The Future of Culture in Egypt*, translated by S. Glazer, 1954, sections 2–5, 7, 10.

Sh. Muhammad Ashraf for Afzal Iqbal, ed., *Selected Speeches and Statements of Maulana Mohamed Ali*, 1963, II, pp. 33–45.

Asia Publishing House, Inc., for S. 'Ābid Husain's *The Destiny of Indian Muslims*, 1965, pp. 170, 174–75, 195–202; and A.A.A. Fyzee's *A Modern Approach to Islam*, 1962, pp. 85–96, 98–108.

A.K. Brohi for *Islam in the Modern World*, pp. 93–98.

Frank Cass & Co. Ltd., London, for Shaykh Fazl Allāh Nūrī's "Refutation of the Idea of Constitutionalism," translated by Abdul Hadi Ha 'iri, *Middle Eastern Studies*, 13:3 (Oct. 1977), 327–39.

Éditions du Seuil for Hichem Djait's "La personnalité et le devenir arabo-islamiques," in *Collections Esprit—La Condition Humaine*, 1974, pp. 126–35.

Paul Geuthner, S.A. for "L'Islam et Les Bases Du Pouvoir," *Revue Des Études Islamiques*, VIII (1934), pp. 171–73, 185–87, 190–91, 200–08, 211–13, 218–22.

Hartford Seminary Foundation for Subhī Mahmasānī's "Muslims: Decadence and Renaissance" in *Muslim World* 44 (1954), pp. 186–91, 196–97, 199–201.

Humanities Press, Inc., New Jersey 07716, and Vikas Publishing House for Christian W. Troll's *Sir Sayyid Ahmad Khān: A Reinterpretation of Muslim Theology*, 1978, pp. 311–19.

Indian Institute of Advanced Study for Mushīr ul-Haq's *Islam in Secular India*, 1972, pp. 6, 8–9, 14–16, 19–21, 85–86.

Islamic Council of Europe, London, for Khurshid Ahmad's "Islam and the Challenge of Economic Development" in *The Challenge of Islam*, edited by Altaf Gauhar, 1978, pp. 339–49; and Abū'-l-'Ala' Mawdūdī's "Political Theory of Islam" in *Islam: Its Meaning and Message*, edited by Khurshid Ahmand, 1976, pp. 147–48, 158–61, 163–70.

The Islamic Foundation, Leicester, for Abū'-l-'Ala' Mawdūdī's "Nationalism and Islam," *Nationalism and India*, 1947, pp. 10–12, 24–28, 30–34; and M. 'Umar Chapra's "Islamic Welfare State and Its Role in the

Economy" from *Islamic Perspectives*, edited by Khurshid Ahmad, 1979, pp. 208–17.

Islamic Research Institute, Islamabad, for Fazlur Rahmān's "Implementation of the Islamic Concept of State in the Pakistani Milieu," *Islamic Studies* 6(1967), pp. 205–24.

Institute of Islamic Culture, Lahore, for Khalīfa 'Abd al-Hakīm's *Islam and Communism*, 1951, pp. 176–84, 187, 191–92.

François Maspero for 'Abdallāh Laroui's *L'idéologie arabe contemporaine*, 1967, pp. 15, 19–28.

Meenakshi Prakashan Publ., New Delhi, for *The Aligarh Movement: Basic Documents 1864–1898*, Vol. III, edited by Shan Muhammad, 1978, pp. 1069–72.

Movement for a New Society for Abūl Hasan Banī-Sadr's "Islamic Economics: Ownership and Tawhīd" from *Tell the American People*, 1980, pp. 157–63.

The Population Council for "Fatwā: Family Planning in Islam" in *Muslim Attitudes Toward Family Planning*, 1967, pp. 3–5.

Praeger Publ. for K.H. Karpat's *Political and Social Thought in the Contemporary Middle East*, © 1968 by Frederick A. Praeger, Inc., pp. 118–22, 123–26, 126–32.

University of California Press for S. Haim's *Arab Nationalism*, 1962, pp. 147–53, 172–76, 178–88; and N. Keddie's *An Islamic Response to Imperialism*, 1968, pp. 56, 87, 102–7.

D. Van Nostrand Co. for Robert G. Landen's *The Emergence of the Modern Middle East*, 1970, pp. 105–10.

CONTENTS

ISLAM IN TRANSITION

ISLAM IN TRANSITION: MUSLIM PERSPECTIVES

The history of humankind has seen the rise and decline of vast empires and civilizations. Perhaps no rise has been more astonishing than that of Islamic civilization, both for the speed and breadth of its geographic expansion as well as for the development of its rich cultural heritage.

Islamic civilization provided a remarkably coherent system, a worldview and a way of life that gave meaning and direction to the lives of Muslims for some twelve centuries. However, in the modern period (late nineteenth and twentieth centuries) the Islamic tradition has encountered its greatest challenges, both political and ideological. The central question has been: "Can Islam meet the political, social, and economic demands of modernity?"

This volume is designed to enable the reader to better appreciate and understand the varied ways in which Muslims have grappled with the problems of change during the modern period—from the late nineteenth century to the present. This will be accomplished by exploring the viewpoints of Muslims—those for whom the question of tradition and change is not simply an academic inquiry but an important existential concern. Although modern Muslim authors have addressed themselves to these problems, their writings are often inaccessible owing to lack of adequate translation and/or ready availability of their writings.

In response to this lacuna, this volume seeks 1) to provide direct access to modern Muslim thinkers as they grapple with the question of Islam and socio-political change; and 2) to do this in a way that reflects the diversity of Muslim thought and so avoids the all-too-common tendency to present Islam as a monolithic structure.

Because the Islamic tradition has been central to Muslim identity and self-understanding, some knowledge of this tradition is necessary to appreciate both the crisis of modernity and the heritage that influences Muslim responses to this crisis.[1]

Seventh-century Arabia saw the advent of a movement that in time would sweep across the Middle East, Europe, Asia, and Africa and which today includes over 750 million adherents. The central fact and inspiration of this movement is the one, true God (Allah) and his revelations to the Prophet Muhammad, which were recorded in the Qur'ān, the final, complete and perfect revelation of God's will for all of humanity. Islam means "submission" to this divine will. A Muslim, then, is one who submits to the will of God as revealed in the Qur'ān. However, this submission is not understood in a passive sense, since the Qur'ān declares that the Muslim's vocation is to strive (jihād) to realize God's will in history. This universal mission to spread the realm of Islam (dār al-islām) throughout the world was the driving force behind Muhammad and the early Muslims who established a religio-political community (umma) in Medina. After a protracted struggle, Mecca, the commercial and religious center of Arabia, was conquered and the tribes of the Arabian Peninsula were consolidated within an Islamic state. Within a hundred years of the prophet Muhammad's death, successive conquests, including the Byzantine and Persian (Sasanid) Empires, produced an empire, stretching from North Africa to South Asia, that was greater than any the world had known.

Muslim self-understanding is based upon the Qur'ān and this early glorious history. For succeeding generations of Muslims, the time of the Prophet and his immediate successors has constituted the ideal period—the embodiment and epitome of the Islamic way of life. As a result, basic to Muslim identity was the belief that the divinely mandated vocation to realize God's will in history was communal as well as individual. There was an organic holistic approach toward life in which religion was intimately intertwined with politics, law, and society. The traditional Islamic structure of state and society that had developed provided the paradigm or ideal to be emulated for centuries to come. The Islamic state was to be a community of believers whose common religious bond replaced individual tribal allegiance, which had been based on blood kinship. Allah was the sovereign of the state; Muhammad, his messenger on earth, served as prophet and leader of the community. Upon Muhammad's death, his successors (Caliphs), as leaders of the community, were to ensure the faithful following of the divine will as expressed in the sacred revealed law (Sharī'a) of Islam.[2] Thus, both ruler and ruled, according to Islamic politi-

---

1. For a better appreciation of the history of Islamic civilization in primary sources see William H. McNeill and Marilyn R. Waldman, eds., The Islamic World (Oxford University Press, 1977).
2. Sharī'a: road or path, the divinely ordained law (straight path) which is to govern all aspects of Muslim life and society.

cal theory, were subject to the *Sharīʿa*. Law, then, provided the blueprint for Islamic society. Based upon the Qurʾān and the example (Sunna) of the prophet,[3] a comprehensive law was formulated which served as a guide for every aspect of life—duties to God (worship, fast, pilgrimage, etc.) as well as duties to one's fellow Muslims. The latter category included prescriptions that fall within the domains of commercial, penal, and family law. Questions of contract, banking, marriage, and divorce were all part of the *Sharīʿa*. But who was to interpret and apply the *Sharīʿa*? This was the province of a class of scholars (*ʿulamāʾ*, "learned ones") of the *Sharīʿa* whose task it was to interpret the law and to advise the ruler. These scholars, where necessary, might also act as a curb on the government when and if a ruler's policies were un-Islamic. While this relationship between the ruler and the *ʿulamāʾ* might be mutually supportive, it has often been tension-filled. Given the comprehensive scope of the *Sharīʿa*, the *ʿulamāʾ*, who serve as legitimizers of political rulers and their policies (political, social and economic), have the power to declare a government's policies, or even the government itself, to be un-Islamic as demonstrated recently by the role of the *ʿulamāʾ* in toppling the ruling government in Pakistan and Iran.

For Muslims, then, the traditional Islamic socio-political system was rooted in revelation; its truth was validated by Islamic history, which attested to Allah's divine guidance of the community. Indeed, Muslims could look back to the glorious past—the vast expansion of the first Islamic centuries and the flourishing of a rich culture whose springs fed the Christian West. Despite the gradual breakdown of the Islamic Empire (*c.* 1000) and its destruction with the fall of the ʿAbbāsid Empire (1258) to the Mongols, Muslims could nevertheless witness Allah's continued guidance in the subsequent conversion of their conquerors and the eventual reemergence and rule of three Muslim empires: the Ottoman (Middle East), Safavid (Persia), and Mughal (Indian subcontinent) which extended down to the modern period (late nineteenth and early twentieth centuries).

However, from the seventeenth century onwards a long process of Western intervention and presence began which was to result in the most serious challenge ever encountered by the Islamic world. Gradual colonial economic control gave way to political and military dominance in the nineteenth century. Thus, for the first time in Islamic history, Muslims found themselves subjugated and ruled by the Christian West—foreign unbelievers who were their colonial masters and whose missionaries often claimed that their success was due to the superiority of Western Christian civilization. This challenge raised profound questions of identity for Mus-

---

3. *Sunna*: the exemplary behavior of the Prophet Muhammad (what he said, did, or permitted), became normative for the Muslim community. Therefore narrative traditions (*ḥadīth*) regarding his activities were preserved and written down and eventually brought together in vast collections.

lims. What had gone wrong in Islam? Where was the divine guidance that had assured past success? How could Muslims realize the divine imperative to spread the realm of Islam (*dār al-islām*)? Could one be a good Muslim in a non-Muslim state which was ruled by unbelievers and whose laws were not *Sharī'a* laws? Was there any contradiction between revelation and reason, science and technology? Was the Islamic way of life capable of meeting the demands of modernity? The beginnings of Muslim modernist thought resulted from this soul-searching inquiry and from the attempts of the "Fathers of Muslim Modernism," Jamāl al-Dīn al-Afghānī, Muhammad 'Abduh (Egypt), and Sir Sayyid Ahmād Khān (India), to provide a response and thus revive and renew their people.

Gradually in the twentieth century, Muslim political fortunes began to change with the rise of independence movements, the shedding of colonialist rule, and the founding of separate independent nation states throughout the Muslim world. Islam (Islamic religious leaders, parties, and symbols) often played an important role in liberation movements. With the establishment of modern Muslim nations, questions of Islamic identity, *viz.* the role of religion in the state (its constitution, laws and institutions), reemerged. While varying accommodations occurred, Islam seemed to recede from the public sphere as most states followed a more Western, secular path of modernization. Deep-seated questions regarding Islamic identity remained unresolved. This state of affairs has been reflected in constitutional debates regarding the status of Islam as the state religion, its role in national ideologies (Arab nationalism and Islamic socialism), the place of the *Sharī'a* in the state's legal system, the question of separate (secular and religious) judicial and educational systems, and especially the change in the status of women and the family through the reform of Muslim family law. Recently, these unresolved tensions regarding Islamic identity have been reflected in the political upheavals in Iran and Pakistan, and, more generally, in the calls for a more Islamic state and way of life which have been heard throughout the Muslim world. Such movements are often characterized popularly by such terms as the "Islamic resurgence," "Islamic renaissance" and "Islamic fundamentalism."

As we have seen in this brief introduction, for almost thirteen centuries Islam provided a divinely sanctioned political and social order, a coherent worldview, which gave direction and meaning to Muslims both as individuals and as a community. Through changing political fortunes, this ideal framework of state, society, and law assured a general stability and sense of identity. With the breakup of Muslim empires, the intervention of the West, and the establishment of modern Muslim nation states, these traditional societies have been subjected to all the pressures (intellectual, political, and social) associated with the process of modernization or development.

As we survey Muslim responses to the challenge of modernity, a number of considerations should be kept in mind. Muslim nations that have emerged from centuries of colonial rule have had but several decades as independent states to make a transition that in the West took several centuries. Out of this period, new Islamic responses and perhaps fresh syntheses are emerging. The formative period of Islam can serve as an inspiration, as Muslims look to their early history and the sources of Islam. For once again the Islamic community faces the challenge of a creative interpretation (*ijtihād*) and reapplication of Islamic values to met the needs of changing Muslim societies.

We hope that the selections included in this sourcebook will provide our readers with some insight into the complexity of the problems that characterize this period of transition and the broad spectrum of responses that have issued from the Muslim world.

I

EARLY RESPONSES: CRISIS AND THE SEARCH FOR IDENTITY

The selection of texts presented here takes us through a century of Muslim contact with the West and Muslims' reflections on their own plight. Rifā'a Badawī Rāfi' al-Tahtāwī first went to Paris in 1826 and began to recount what he saw and what Egyptians should do to be "civilized." He was concerned mainly with explaining the new world to the old and removing hesitations born of isolation. Political and economic organization, patriotism and civic concern, and science appeared to be the keys to European power and progress—and they were there for the borrowing. It all seemed so easy.

By the end of the century, the climate had changed. Jamāl al-Dīn al-Afghānī marked the turning point, as he roamed from India to Egypt arousing Muslims to resist the incursions of imperialism by galvanizing their forces as individual nations or as the Muslim "nation" (depending on his audience) to regain lost power and glory. He was an occasional critic of religion, an unhesitating advocate of science and philosophy, and also a proponent of a return to Islam, which touched traditional sensibilities.

Afghānī was the catalyst; Muhammed 'Abduh was the synthesizer. With considerable erudition and dedication, he reread Islamic history to discover, hidden under the silt of ages, that very rationality that the West was vaunting. In fact, the admirable traits of the West derived from its contact with Islam. Thus, there was no problem being modern and Muslim.

A disciple of 'Abduh's, 'Ali 'Abd al-Rāziq, pushed this rereading of Muslim history a bit further in 1926, trying to disprove the Muslim axiom that "Islam is both religion and state." He went beyond the tolerated limits and was retired to obscurity. Islam may be all that Europe was,

9

potentially, at least, but for the guardians of Islamic tradition Islam was much more, and that more was different from the West. This sense of being different is always present in some form or other in the texts, but rarely is it defined clearly. This, of course, is the problem of identity.

The search for identity among the Muslims of South Asia was characterized by a somewhat different process. A Muslim minority had ruled the Hindu majority of the Indian subcontinent for centuries. From the eighteenth century onwards, British colonial presence had meant increased military, economic, and political controls. As a result of the so-called Sepoy Mutiny of 1857 (which many South Asian historians prefer to call the First War of Independence) *de facto* British control gave way to British rule with British removal of the Mughal emperor.

Surveying the heavy price of Muslim political and cultural resistance to British rule and the inner weakness of the community, Sir Sayyid Ahmad Khān determined that the revival (indeed, survival) of the Muslim community was dependent upon Muslim acceptance of and accommodation with British rule and, most importantly, an inner renewal through religious, social, and educational reforms. Ahmad Khān maintained that Islam was the religion of reason and nature and, like Afghānī and 'Abduh, argued that there was no inherent conflict between Islam and modern thought.

Chirāgh 'Alī followed Khan's reformist path. He argued that the Qur'ān was not wedded to a single social system and that, therefore, Islam possessed the capacity to adapt to the changing political, social, and legal demands of modernity.

Muhammad 'Alī and the Khilāfat [Caliphate] Movement (1919–1924) mirrored the complex identity problems of Indian Muslims under British rule. This post–World War I movement saw extended political action by Indian Muslims against the dismemberment of the Ottoman Empire by Britain and her Western allies, since such a move threatened the autonomy of two important Islamic symbols: the Ottoman caliph and the sacred cities of Mecca and Medina. If Ahmad Khān argued that Indian Muslims could and should be loyal British subjects, Muhammad 'Alī in a speech delivered in London on behalf of the Indian Khilāfat Delegation maintained that this was possible only if their religion and its duties were respected.

He studied at al-Azhar University and was appointed imām of
the first large student mission sent by Muhammad ʿAlī to Paris.
His five years in France left a lasting impression, and his account
of his impressions circulated widely. He learned French, read
avidly, and translated some twenty books into Arabic. He
headed the new school of languages, and was editor of the first
official gazette.

Fatherland and Patriotism

The wisdom of the Almighty King has seen it fit that the sons of the
fatherland[1] be united always by their language, by their allegiance to one
king and by their obedience to one divine law and political administration.
These are some of the indications that God disposed men to work together
for the improvement of their fatherland and willed that they relate to one
another as members of one family. God willed that the fatherland would,
so to speak, take the place of father and mother and tutor and would be
the locus of the happiness shared by men. Thus, it is not fitting that one
nation be divided into numerous parties on the basis of different opinions,
because partisanship begets contradictory pressures, envy, and rancour
with consequent lack of security in the fatherland. This is especially so
because the holy law and the political administration which put all men on
an equal footing require that they be of one heart and consider no one
their enemy save him who sows discord among them by his treachery.
They must beware of such people, lest their sovereignty be flawed and
order disrupted. The obvious enemy is he who does not want the people to
be faithful to their fatherland or to enjoy fully their freedom.

The son of the fatherland—whether he be native born or a refugee who
has been naturalized—has a relation to the fatherland, which is expressed
in various ways. Sometimes he is referred to in terms of the fatherland
itself, for example he may be called "Egyptian," or in terms of his people,

---

1. The concepts of fatherland (*watan*) and patriotism (*wataniyyah*) were new to Muslim
thought. Tahtāwī appears to have been the first to introduce them into Arabic. See M.
ʾAmārah, ed., vol. I, p. 123. [Ed.]

From *Kitāb al-Murshid al-amīn lil-banāt waʾl-banīn* [The faithful guide for girls and boys],
(Beirut: Arab Foundation, 1973), pp. 433–35, 469–71, 480–81.

then he is called by an adjective derived from their name, or he may be described in terms of the idea of fatherland and be called a "patriot." This means that he enjoys the rights of his country, the greatest of which is complete freedom in that human society. The patriot, though, can be described in terms of freedom only if he is obedient to the law of the fatherland and aids its execution so that his subservience to the principles of his country necessarily entails that the fatherland will guarantee him the enjoyment of civil rights and municipal privileges. In this sense he is a patriot and a native, signifying that he is counted a member of the city and ranks as a member of its body. This is considered the greatest privilege in civilized nations. The people of the majority of nations had been deprived of this privilege, which is one of the greatest characteristics (of civilization.) This was so in those times when governors commanded according to their whims and acted as they wished. The people at that time had no channel by which they could oppose their rulers and no protection provided by the rules of the holy law. They were not able to inform their king that they considered certain things inappropriate nor could they write about his policies or administration. They could not express their opinion on any matter. Consequently, they were like foreigners with regard to the affairs of government, and they were not appointed to any functions or posts other than those which were below their merits. Now ideas have changed, and these dangers have been removed from the sons of the fatherland. Now the heart of a true patriot can be filled with love for his fatherland because he has become one of its members. . . .

The quality of patroitism demands not only that a man seek his due rights from the fatherland, but also that he fulfill his obligations to it. If one of the sons of the fatherland does not fulfill his obligations to it, then he loses the civil rights to which he had title.

The Romans in olden times demanded that a patriot who reached twenty years of age swear an oath that he would defend his fatherland and his government, and they bound him by covenant to this. The formula of the oath was: I take God as my witness that I will freely and willingly bear the weapon of honor for my fatherland and its people whenever there is occasion for me to aid them. And I call God to witness that I will fight, alone or with the army, to protect fatherland and religion. . . .

From this it can be understood how tenaciously the nation of the Romans loved their fatherland and why they came to rule over all the countries of the world. When this quality of patriotism declined, failure took hold of the members of this nation, and their situation deteriorated. Their organization was unravelled by the countless differences among princes and by the multiplicity of governors. After having been ruled by one Caesar, they split into East and West with two Caesars: Caesar of Rome and Caesar of Constantinople. From one great power they became two weak powers. They met defeat in all their wars and finally, after having reached the pinnacle, they dissolved into nothingness. Such is the case of a nation with divided government and a nation without organization.

Civilization, Islam, and Reason

The civilization of the fatherland consists in the acquisition by the people of the inhabited area of the instruments necessary to better their conditions sensibly and spiritually. It is an expression of their superiority in ameliorating their morals and customs and education, and an indication of their capacity to acquire praiseworthy qualities, attain the perfections of civilization, and make progress in refined living. This is what civilization is with respect to the nation which resides in the fatherland, but the individuals of this civilized nation differ one from another in the degree of progress and betterment each attains. Thus civilization is applied both to nations and to individuals in an equivocal sense. . . .

The opposite of civilization is crudity; it is a lack of refinement in the level of life. There is no doubt that the mission of God's messengers bringing holy laws is at the root of the true civilization, which is the norm and pole of attraction for all civilizations. The civilization which Islam brought with its principles and rules civilized the countries of the world without exception and diffused the light of guidance to all horizons. The Messenger of God said: "I have brought you the pure holy law which no prophet before me has brought, not even my brother Moses, and the other prophets in my time try only to follow my holy law."

Anyone who has devoted himself to the science of the principles of jurisprudence and has an understanding of the restraints and rules it contains, will judge that all the rational deductions arrived at by the intellects of the other civilized nations, which they have made the basis for drawing up the laws and rules of their civilization, rarely go beyond these principles on which the branches of jurisprudence are built and around which human relations turn. Consequently, what we call the science of the principles of jurisprudence, they call natural laws or the laws of instinct. These consist in rational rules, good and bad, and on them they base their civil laws. What we call the branches of jurisprudence, they call civil laws or regulations. What we call justice and good works, they call freedom and equality. The love of religion and the passion to protect it, which the people of Islam hold so tenaciously and which give them an advantage over other nations in power and force, they call love of fatherland. However, among us, the people of Islam, love of the fatherland is just one branch of the faith, and the defense of religion is its capstone. Every Islamic kingdom is a fatherland for all those in it who belong to Islam; it combines religion and patriotism. Its defense is a duty on its sons by reason of these two aspects.

However, it was customary to confine oneself to religion because it is so important a force, along with the will of the fatherland. The zeal for a specific fatherland may be incited by mere nationality and family, one can talk of sentiment, which is Qaysi, Yamani, Misri and Shami. However, in the fatherland all humans are put on the same level, so you will find two parties who differ from one another but unite against a foreigner in defense of their fatherland or their religion or their species.

The benefits of civilization are many and around them pivot all the sciences of harmonious living and of mutual enmity. For this reason some have said: whenever the orbit of civilization of the kingdoms of the earth widens, wars lessen, attacks decrease, conquests become more humane, reversals and triumphs more rare, until they finally cease altogether. Lawless tyranny and enslavement are wiped out, and poverty and wretchedness are removed. . . .

The Natural Law and the Sharī'a[2]

Man's actions must be in accord with these causes mentioned above; he must observe them, otherwise he will receive divine punishment for going contrary to the creator of these causes. For example, if a man wants to see in the pitch darkness of night and makes every effort to do so, or if he goes contrary to what the temporal seasons require, thinking that it is simple to obtain what only the seasons can produce, or if he contradicts the intrinsic nature of the elements, for instance, wishing to live permanently in water or to touch fire without being burned or to drink poison without dying, then he will be punished for his actions in this life to the degree that he contravenes the customary causes. He will drown or be burned, will choke or die. On the contrary, if he observed these causes and their intrinsic nature as much as possible, then he will protect himself to the same degree, since they are drawn up by the divine wisdom to guard and protect, to aid and help.

The regulations of the *Sharī'a* do not go contrary to most of these natural laws. They represent the innate character which God created along with man and made obligatory for him in existence. They are like a mold formed according to his likeness and fashioned to fit him. It is as if they were written on the tablet of his heart by divine inspiration without any intermediary. Then, later, there came the holy laws of the prophets

2. *Sharī'a:* The *Sharī'a* or path is the general term given to the corpus of rules and precepts governing all aspects of a Muslim's personal and social life. The rules are derived from the Qur'ān, the Sunna (practice) of the Prophet, from analogical reasoning, and consensus. The *Sharī'a* is considered to be divinely revealed. Also, the Qur'ān indicates that each people was given its *Sharī'a* by God. [Ed.]

through intermediaries and books which did not render these laws void in any way, for they preceded the legislation of holy laws among the peoples and nations. In former times the laws of the first sages and leaders of nations were based on these natural laws. From them they garnered guidance for mapping out the way of life in time past. On the basis of these laws, the ancients of Egypt, Iraq, Persia, and Greece arrived at a type of organization for human society. This can be attributed to God's kindness toward mankind, guiding them in their manner of living through the appearance of sages in their midst who legislated civil laws, especially those which are necessary like the protection of property, life and offspring, etc. . . .

SAYYID JAMĀL AL-DĪN AL-AFGHĀNĪ
1838–1897

Philosopher, writer, orator, journalist, and political activist, he traveled widely from India and Afghanistan to Istanbul, Cairo, Paris, and London, stirring in Muslims the consciousness of their potential strength in the face of colonialism. He is the father of modern Muslim nationalism, proponent of pan-Islam, and the main inspiration for the reform movement in Islam. He expresses almost all the attitudes and themes that are commonplaces in Muslim apologetics from 1900 to the present.

An Islamic Response to Imperialism

In the human world the bonds that have been extensive . . . have been two. One is this same unity of language of which nationality and national unity consist, and the other is religion. There is no doubt that the unity of language is more durable for survival and permanence in this world than unity of religion since it does not change in a short time in contrast to the latter. We see that a single people with one language in the course of a thousand years changes its religion two or three times without its nationality, which consists of unity of language, being destroyed. One may say that the ties and the unity that arise from the unity of language have more influence than religious ties in most affairs of the world. . . .

Religion and Progress

All religions are intolerant, each one in its way. The Christian religion, I mean the society that follows its inspirations and its teachings and is formed in its image, has emerged from the first period to which I have just alluded; thenceforth free and independent, it seems to advance rapidly on the road of progress and science, whereas Muslim society has not yet freed itself from the tutelage of religion. Realizing, however, that the Christian religion preceded the Muslim religion in the world by many centuries, I cannot keep from hoping that Muhammadan society will succeed someday in breaking its bonds and marching resolutely in the path of civilization

From *An Islamic Response to Imperialism: Political and Religious Writings of Sayyid Jamāl al-Dīn al-Afghānī,* trans. and ed. Nikki R. Keddie (Berkeley: University of California Press, 1968), pp. 56, 87, 102–7.

after the manner of Western society. . . . In truth, the Muslim religion has tried to stifle science and stop its progress. . . .

Science and Progress

The Europeans have now put their hands on every part of the world. The English have reached Afghanistan; the French have seized Tunisia. In reality this usurpation, aggression, and conquest have not come from the French or the English. Rather it is science that everywhere manifests its greatness and power. Ignorance had no alternative to prostrating itself humbly before science and acknowledging its submission.

In reality, sovereignty has never left the abode of science. However, this true ruler, which is science, is continually changing capitals. Sometimes it has moved from East to West, and other times from West to East. More than this, if we study the riches of the world we learn that wealth is the result of commerce, industry, and agriculture. Agriculture is achieved only with agricultural science, botannical chemistry, and geometry. Industry is produced only with physics, chemistry, mechanics, geometry, and mathematics; and commerce is based on agriculture and industry.

Thus it is evident that all wealth and riches are the result of science. There are no riches in the world without science, and there is no wealth in the world other than science. In sum, the whole world of humanity is an industrial world, meaning that the world is a world of science. If science were removed from the human sphere, no man would continue to remain in the world. . . .

The science that has the position of a comprehensive soul and the rank of a preserving force is the science of *falsafa* or philosophy, because its subject is universal. It is philosophy that shows man human prerequisites. It shows the sciences what is necessary. It employs each of the sciences in its proper place.

If a community did not have philosophy, and all the individuals of that community were learned in the sciences with particular subjects, those sciences could not last in that community for a century, that is, a hundred years. That community without the spirit of philosophy could not deduce conclusions from these sciences.

The Ottoman Government and the Khedivate of Egypt have been opening schools for the teaching of the new sciences for a period of sixty years, and until now they have not received any benefit from those sciences. The reason is that teaching the philosophical sciences was impossible in those schools, and because of the nonexistence of philosophy, no fruit was obtained from those sciences that are like limbs. Undoubtedly, if the spirit of philosophy had been in those schools, during this period of sixty years they themselves, independent of the European countries, would have striven to reform their kingdoms in accord with science. Also, they would not send their sons each year to European countries for education, and they would not invite teachers from there to their schools. I may say that if the spirit of philosophy were found in a community, even if that community did not have one of those sciences whose subject is particular, undoubtedly their philosophic spirit would call for the acquisition of all the sciences.

The first Muslims had no science, but, thanks to the Islamic religion, a philosophic spirit arose among them, and owing to that philosophic spirit they began to discuss the general affairs of the world and human necessities. This was why they acquired in a short time all the sciences with particular subjects that they translated from the Syriac, Persian, and Greek into the Arabic language. . . .

Jurisprudence among the Muslims includes all domestic, municipal, and state laws. Thus a person who has studied jurisprudence profoundly is worthy of being prime minister of the realm or chief ambassador of the state, whereas we see our jurisconsults after studying this science unable to manage their own households, although they are proud of their own foolishness.

The science of principles consists of the philosophy of the *Shari'a,* or *philosophy of law.* In it are explained the truth regarding right and wrong, benefit and loss, and the causes for the promulgation of laws. Certainly, a person who studies this science should be capable of establishing laws and enforcing civilization. However, we see that those who study this science among the Muslims are deprived of understanding of the benefits of laws, the rules of civilization, and the reform of the world.

Since the state of the *'ulamā'* has been demonstrated, we can say that our *'ulamā'* at this time are like a very narrow wick on top of which is a very small flame that neither lights its surroundings nor gives light to others. A scholar is a true light if he is a scholar. Thus, if a scholar is a scholar he must shed light on the whole world, and if his light does not reach the whole world, at least it should light up his region, his city, his village, or his home. What kind of scholar is it who does not enlighten even his own home?

The strangest thing of all is that our *'ulamā'* these days have divided science into two parts. One they call Muslim science, and one European science. Because of this they forbid others to teach some of the useful sciences. They have not understood that science is that noble thing that has no connection with any nation, and is not distinguished by anything but itself. Rather, everything that is known is known by science, and every nation that becomes renowned becomes renowned through science. Men must be related to science, not science to men.

How very strange it is that the Muslims study those sciences that are ascribed to Aristotle with the greatest delight, as if Aristotle were one of the pillars of the Muslims. However, if the discussion relates to Galileo, Newton, and Kepler, they consider them infidels. The father and mother of science is proof, and proof is neither Aristotle nor Galileo. The truth is where there is proof, and those who forbid science and knowledge in the belief that they are safeguarding the Islamic religion are really the enemies of that religion. The Islamic religion is the closest of religions to science and knowledge, and there is no incompatibility between science and knowledge and the foundation of the Islamic faith. . . .

SAYYID JAMĀL AL-DĪN AL-AFGHĀNĪ.

Islamic Solidarity

A study of the particular identity which characterizes some nations and an examination of their beliefs prove to anyone blessed with a clear and accurate sense of observation that in most nations there is a spirit of ethnic solidarity which in turn produces a sense of pride. Those whom this spirit animates are proud of the glorious deeds of their ethnic brothers. They become angry with any misfortune which touches them to the point where, in order to combat it, they kill without thinking about the reasons or the causes of the sentiment which pushes them to act. This is why many who are seeking for truth have come to the conclusion that a strong feeling of ethnic identity must be counted as integral to human nature. Yet their opinion is not correct, as we can ascertain by the behavior of a child who, born in one country subsequently is taken before he reaches the age of conscious thinking into the territories of another nation; if he grows up and reaches the age of reason in that place, he will not mention his birthplace or display any natural partiality for it. He will have no idea about his birthplace. Indeed, perhaps he will be more attached to the place where he grew up. Yet, that which is truly natural does not change.

Therefore, we do not think that such a feeling is natural to man, but rather that is is composed of a number of accidental attributes which necessity stamps upon the feelings. Actually, wherever he is, the human being has many wants. Individuals have a tendency to set themselves apart and to seek profit for themselves when they have not been properly taught. Also, they have a tendency to have numerous selfish desires which, when united with power, gives them an aggressive character. That is why some men find themselves struggling against the aggression of others. After fighting troubles for long years they were constrained to band together according to their parentage and in various ways until they formed ethnic units. That is how they became divided into nations such as the Indians, the Russians, the Turkomans, etc. Each of these groups, thanks to the combined strength of its members, was able to preserve its interests and to safeguard its rights from any encroachment by another group. Moreover, they have gone even farther than necessary as is common in the evolution of man: they have reached the point where each group is bitter if it falls under the rule of another. It believes that domination will be oppressive even if it is just. . . .

However, if necessity has created this sort of individualistic racial soli-

From *The Emergence of the Modern Middle East: Selected Readings*, trans. and ed. Robert G. Landen, (New York: Van Nostrand Reinhold Company, 1970), pp. 105–10.

darity, there is no doubt that such solidarity can disappear just as it can arise. Such can take place when an arbiter is accepted and the contending forces are brought together. . . . This arbiter is the Prince of all things, the Conqueror of heaven and earth. . . . When men recognize the existence of the Supreme Judge . . . they will leave it entirely to the possessor of sacred power to safeguard good and repel evil. No longer will they have any need for an ethnic sentiment which has lost its purpose and whose memory has been erased from their souls; judgment belongs to Allah, the Sublime, the Magnificent.

That is the secret of the aversion which Muslims have for manifestations of ethnic origin in every country where they live. That is why they reject all clan loyalty with the exception of Islamic sentiment and religious solidarity. The believers in Islam are preoccupied neither with their ethnic origins nor with the people of which they are a part because they are loyal to their faith; they have given up a narrow bond in favor of a universal bond: the bond of faith.

Actually, the principles of the Islamic religion are not restricted to calling man to the truth or to considering the soul only in a spiritual context which is concerned with the relationship between this world and the one to come. . . . There is more besides: Islamic principles are concerned with relationships among the believers, they explain the law in general and in detail, they define the executive power which administers the law, they determine sentences and limit their conditions; also, they are concerned with the unique goal that the holder of power ought to be the most submissive of men to the rules regulating that power which he gains neither by heritage, nor inheritance, nor by virtue of his race, tribe, material strength, or wealth. On the contrary, he acquires it only if he submits to the stipulations of the sacred law, if he has the strength to apply it, and if he judges with the concurrence of the community. Thus, in truth, the ruler of the Muslims will be their religious, holy, and divine law which makes no distinction among peoples. This will also be the summary of the ideas of the nation. A Muslim ruler has no other privilege than that of being the most ardent of all in safeguarding the sacred law and defending it.

In safeguarding the rights and the protection of people, of property, and of reputations, the lawgiver has not taken any account of lineage, nor of ancestral privilege. Moreover, any bond, with the exception of the bond of Islamic law, was disapproved by Him. Whoever relies upon such bonds is subject to blame and whoever advocates them deserves criticism. The Prophet said, in this matter: "Tribal solidarity should not exist among us; it does not exist among those of us who are bound by religion; it does not exist among those of us who die believers." The *hadīths* (tradition) of the Prophet all agree upon this point. In summary, whoever surpasses all men in piety, that is to say, in the practice of Islamic law, will be distinguished by the respect and veneration accorded to him: *The noblest among you in the eyes of God, is the most pious* (Qur'ān 49: 13). It has followed, down through many ages, and in spite of the differences in generations, that power has been wielded by men who are not noble in their race, nor especially privileged in their tribe; who do not hold sovereignty because of hereditary royalty, or do not claim it by virtue of their noble descent or highborn antecedents; they are raised to power only because of their obedience to the law and to the intense zeal they display in observing it.

The amount of power given to Muslim rulers is a product of their observance of divine regulations, of the way in which they follow the good directions which these prescribe, and of the absence of all personal ambition in them. Each time a ruler tries to distinguish himself by surpassing all others in luxury or the magnificence of his mode of life, or each time that he tries to assume a greater dignity than his people, then the people return to their tribal loyalties, differences arise, and the ruler's power declines.

Such is the lesson which one can learn from the history of the Muslims from the day their religion was revealed up to our own time. They set little value on either ethnic ties or racial sentiment but take only religious ties into consideration. That is why one can say that an Arab has no aversion to domination by Turks, why the Persian accepts the sovereignty of the Arab, and why the Indian obeys the laws of the Afghan without any bitterness or hesitancy among them. That is why one also can assert that the Muslim does not revolt or protest against either the regimes which impose themselves over him or against the transfer of power from one tribe to another so long as the possessor of authority maintains religious law and follows it precepts. But if these regimes stray in their conduct and unjustly deviate from the laws' teachings and attempt to execute that which is not right, then the hearts of the Muslims are detached from them and they become the object of disaffection, and even if they are a Muslim people's own blood brothers, they will appear more odious than foreigners in the people's eyes.

One can also say that Muslims are different from the adherents to other religions because of the emotion and regret they feel if one piece of Muslim territory is cut off from an Islamic government, whatever may be the ethnic origin of the inhabitants of this territory or the group which has taken it over.

If among the Muslims one found a minor ruler of whatever racial origin, who followed the divine commandments, was zealous in applying them, compelled the people to apply the punishments which they ordain, obeyed the law himself like his subjects, and gave up trying to distinguish himself through vain pomp, it would be possible for this ruler to enjoy widespread power and great influence. He could assume great authority in Muslim-inhabitated countries. He would not encounter great difficulty in doing this, for he would not have to spend money, or build up his army, or conclude alliances with the great powers, or seek the assistance of partisans of civilization and freedom. . . . He could accomplish all this by following the example of the orthodox caliphs [the early caliphs of Islam in the seventh century A.D., Ed.] and by returning to the original sources of Islamic religious law. His conduct would bring a revival of strength and a renewal of the prerequisites of power.

Let me repeat for you, reader, one more time, that unlike other religions, Islam is concerned not only with the life to come. Islam is more: it is concerned with its believers' interests in the world here below and with allowing them to realize success in this life as well as peace in the next life. It seeks "good fortune in two worlds." In its teachings it decrees equality among different peoples and nations.

The times have been so cruel and life so hard and confusing that some Muslims—they are rare—have lost patience and assert with difficulty that Islamic principles are their oppressors and they give up using religious principles of justice in their actions. They resort, even, to the protection of a foreign power but are filled with regret at the things that result from that course of action. . . . Actually, the schisms and divisions which have occurred in Muslim states originate only from the failure of rulers who deviate from the solid principles upon which the Islamic faith is built and stray from the road followed by their early ancestors. Certainly, opposition to solidly based precepts and wandering away from customary ways are the very actions that are most damaging to power. When those who rule Islam return to the rules of their law and model their conduct upon that practiced by early generations of Muslims, it will not be long before God gives them extensive power and bestows strength upon them comparable to that wielded by the orthodox caliphs, who were leaders of the faith. God give us the will to act with justice and lead us upon the road to integrity.

SHAYKH MUHAMMAD 'ABDUH
1849–1905

He received a traditional religious education but was transformed by his contact with Jamāl al-Dīn al-Afghānī. Exiled by the British, he spent time in Beirut and Tripoli, then in Paris where he edited a review with Afghānī for a brief time. He returned to hold high religious posts, including that of Mufti of Egypt. His desire to reform Islam and put it in harmony with modern times by a return to primitve purity pushed him to theological reflection and writing which make him the founder of the modernist school in Islam.

Islam, Reason, and Civilization

At all events, religion must not be made into a barrier, separating men's spirits from God-given abilities in the knowledge of the truths of the contingent world as far as in them lies. Rather, religion must promote this very search, demanding respect for evidence and enjoining the utmost possible devotion and endeavour through all the worlds of knowledge— and all within the true proportions of the goal, holding fast the while to sound itself. Any who assert the contrary do not know what religion is and do despite to it which the Lord of the worlds will not forgive. . . .

How then can reason be denied its right, being, as it is, the scrutineer of evidences so as to reach the truth within them and know that it is Divinely given? Having, however, once recognised the mission of a prophet, reason is obliged to acknowledge all that he brings, even though unable to attain the essential meaning within it or penetrate its full truth. Yet this obligation does not involve reason in accepting rational impossibilities such as two incompatibles or opposites together at the same time and point. For prophecies are immune from bringing such follies. But if there comes something which appears contradictory, reason must believe that the apparent is not the intended sense. It is then free to seek the true sense by reference to the rest of the prophet's message in whom the ambiguity occurred, or to fall back upon God and His omniscience. There have been those among our forebears who have chosen to do either one or the other. . . .

From *The Theology of Unity,* trans. Ishaq Musa'ad and Kenneth Cragg (London: George Allen & Unwin, 1966), pp. 103–4, 107–8, 133–35, 145–46, 148–50.

When religions first began, men understood their well-being, whether general or particular, only in a most rudimentary way, rather like infants lately born, who know only what comes within their senses and distinguish only with difficulty between the present and the past. . . . The religions took men and gave them straight commands and firm restraints, to which they required obedience to the utmost possible degree. Though the meaning and purpose were there to be known, obedience was irrespective of actual comprehension and intelligent knowledge. Religions came with astonishing and impressive miracles and laid upon men the forms of worship consonant with their condition.

At length, human society reached a point at which man came to his full stature, helped by the moral of the earlier vicissitudes. Islam supervened, to present its case to reason, to call on mind and intelligence for action, to take emotion and feeling into partnership for man's guidance to both earthly and heavenly blessedness. It clarified the things that provoked human discords and demonstrated that religion with God was one in all generations, that there was a single Divine purpose for their reform without and their cleansing within. Islam taught that the sole aim of outward forms of worship was to renew the inward recollection of God and that God looks not on the form but on the heart. It required the devotee to care as well for his body as for the soul, enjoining outward as well as inward integrity, both of which it made mandatory. Sincerity was made the very heart of worship and rites were only laid down in so far as they conduced to the hallowing of moral character. "Verily prayer preserves men from foul and evil things." (Qur'ān 29:45.) "Man is created restless. When evil befalls him he despairs, but touched with good fortune he becomes niggardly—though not those who pray." (Qur'ān 79:19–22.) The rich man who remembers to be grateful is raised by Islam to the same level as the poor man who endures patiently. Perhaps Islam even esteems him higher. Islam deals with man in its exhortations as a wise and sober counsellor would deal with a mature person summoning him to the full harnessing of his powers, both outward and inward, and affirmed this quite unequivocally to be the way of pleasing God and showing thankfulness for His grace. This world is the seedplot of the world to come. Men will not come by ultimate good save as they endeavour a present well-doing.

Islam removed all racial distinctions within humanity, in the common dignity of relationship with God, of participation in human-kind, in race group and particular setting, as well as the dignity of being in the way of the highest attainments prepared by God for men. This universal dignity contrasts sharply with the exclusive claims of those who pretend to privileged status denied to others and consign allegedly inferior mortals to permanent subjection, thus strangling the very spirit of the peoples, or most of them, and reducing them to walking shadows. . . .

Now the nations had what they were looking for—a religion with a mind to think. Now they had a faith which gave justice its due place. The main factor which deterred a massive and spontaneous accession to Islam to enjoy these things long-desired lay in the system of class privilege under which the nations laboured. By this some classes lorded it over others, without right. Rulers wrecked nothing of the interests of the common people if the desires of the higher classes conflicted with them. Here was a religion which regulated human rights and gave equal respect to persons of all classes, their beliefs, their dignity and their property. It gave, for example, to a poor non-Muslim woman the perfect right to refuse to sell her small dwelling, at any price, to some great amīr, ruling absolutely over a large territory, who wanted it, not for private purposes, but in order to enlarge a mosque. When, in this particular case, he doubled the price and took forcible steps to acquire it and she raised a complaint to the Caliph, he issued an order to ensure her possession and reproached the amīr for his action. Islamic justice permitted a Jew to take up a case before the judge against no less a person than 'Alī ibn Abī Tālib, who was made to stand with the plaintiff in the court-process until judgement was given.

The foregoing makes clear how the message and relationships Islam brought endeared even its enemies to it, and so revolutionized their outlook as to make them its allies and protégés. . . .

Islam Civilizes Its Conquerors

The light of Islam shone in the lands where its devotees went, and the only factor at work in their relation with the local people was the Word of God heard and apprehended. At times the Muslims were pre-occupied with their own affairs and fell away from the right path. Then Islam halted like a commander whose allies have disappointed him and is about to give ground. "God brings about what He intends." (Qur'ān 65:3.) The Islamic lands were invaded by the Tartar peoples, led by Jenghiz Khan, pagans who despoiled the Muslims and were bent on total conquest, plunder and rapine. But it was not long before their successors adopted Islam as their religion and propagated it among their kin with the same consequences as elsewhere. They came to conquer the Muslims and they stayed to do them good.

The West made a sustained attack against the East, involving all the kings and peoples, and continuing more than two hundred years, during which time the West engendered a quite unprecedented zeal and fervour for religion. With military forces and preparations to the utmost of their capacity, they advanced towards the Muslim heart-lands, fired by religious devotion. They overran many countries of Islamic allegiance. Yet in the end these violent wars closed with their evacuation.

Why did they come and why did they return? The religious leaders of the West successfully aroused their peoples to make havoc of the eastern world and to seize the sovereignty over those nations on what they believed to be their prescriptive right to tyrannize over masses of men. They came in great numbers of all sorts of men, estimated in millions, many settling in Muslim territory as residents. There were periods of truce in which the angry fires abated and quieter tempers prevailed, when there was even time to take a look at the surrounding culture, pick up something from the medley of ideas and react to what was to be seen and heard. It became clear that the exaggerations of their idle dreams which had shaped into such grievous efforts had no vestige of truth. And, furthermore, they found freedom in a religion where knowledge, law and art could be possessed with entire certitude. They discovered that liberty of thought and breadth of knowledge were means to faith and not its foes. By God's will they acquired some experience of refined culture and went off to their own territories thrilled with what they had gained from their wars—not to mention the great gains the travellers gathered in the lands of Andalusia by intercourse with its learned and polished society, whence they returned to their own peoples to taste the sweet fruits they had reaped. From that time on, there began to be much more traffic in ideas. In the West the desire for knowledge intensified and concern grew to break the entail of obscurantism. A strong resolve was generated to curb the authority of religious leaders and keep them from exceeding the proper precepts of religion and corrupting its valid meanings. It was not long after that a party made its appearance in the west calling for reform and a return to the simplicities of the faith—a reformation which included elements by no means unlike Islam. Indeed, some of the reforming groups brought their doctrines to a point closely in line with the dogma of Islam, with the exception of belief in the prophetic mission of Muhammad. Their religion was in all but name the religion of Muhammad; it differed only in the shape of worship, not in meaning or anything else.

Then it was that the nations of Europe began to throw off their bondage and reform their condition, re-ordering the affairs of their life in a manner akin to the message of Islam, though oblivious of who their real guide and leader was. So were enunciated the fundamental principles of modern civilization in which subsequent generations as compared with the peoples of earlier days have found their pride and glory.

All this was like a copious dew falling on the welcoming earth, which stirs and brings forth a glad growth of every kind. Those who had come for strife, stayed to benefit and returned to benefit others in turn. Their rulers thought that in stirring up their peoples they would find an outlet for their rancour and secure their own power. Instead they were shown up for what they were and their authority foundered. What we have shown about the nature of Islam, well enough known to every thoughtful student, is acknowledged by many scholars in western countries and they know its validity and confess that Islam has been the greatest of their mentors in attaining their present position. "God's is the final issue of all things." (Qur'ān 22:41.)

'ALĪ 'ABD AL-RĀZIQ
1888–1966

A disciple of 'Abduh, he studied at al-Azhar and later at Oxford University. In the debate that followed the abolition of the caliphate in 1924, he offered a contribution entitled *Islam and the Bases of Power* which led to his condemnation by a council of *'ulamā'* of al-Azhar University. He was forbidden from holding any public office, so he devoted his efforts to the Academy of Arabic Language in Cairo.

The Caliphate and the Bases of Power

Apostleship and Governance

We hope that the reader will not be alarmed by this study, which aims at discovering whether or not the Prophet was a king. One should not think that research like this is dangerous for religion or harmful to faith for those who undertake it. Reflection reveals that the matter is not so serious as to push a believer beyond the bounds of faith or to upset anyone's piety.

What makes the question seem grave is its connection with the dignity and rank of the Prophet. Nonetheless, it does not in any way touch the essence of religion or the foundations of Islam.

This research is probably new in Islam. Muslims have never faced the question frankly, and their *'ulamā'* have no clear and well-formed doctrine on the matter. Consequently, if, after study, one concludes either that the Prophet was a king as well as an apostle or that he was an apostle only, it can hardly be branded heresy or heterodoxy with regard to the opinions professed by Muslims. The study falls outside the area of those beliefs which the *'ulamā'* have treated and on which they profess well-established opinions. It belongs more to the area of scientific research than to that of religion. Let the reader follow us without fear and with a tranquil soul.

It is well known that prophecy is something other than royalty: there is no intrinsic connection between the two notions. Prophecy is one sort of dignity, royalty another. How many kings there are who were neither prophets nor apostles. How many prophets God raised up without making them kings. In fact, the majority of known prophets were prophets only.

From "L'Islam et Les Bases Du Pouvoir" [Islam and the bases of power], trans. from Arabic by L. Bercher in *Revue Ðes Etudes Islamiques*, VIII (1934), pp. 171–73, 185–87, 190–91, 200–208, 211–13, 218–22.

Jesus, son of Mary, was the apostle of Christianity and head of the Christians, and yet he preached submission to Caesar and accepted his authority. It was Jesus who addressed those profound words to his followers: "Render unto Caesar the things that are Caesar's and unto God those that are God's.". . . .

In the history of the prophets we find only rare examples of persons whom God permitted to accumulate the dignity of prophet along with that of king. Was Muhammad one of these, or was he prophet only and not king?

To our knowledge, not one of the 'ulamā' has expressed a clear opinion on this question: in fact, none has spoken about it. But by way of induction we can affirm this: Muslims in general tend to believe that the Prophet was both prophet and king and that he established with Islam a political government of which he was king and head. This is the opinion that best corresponds to the dominant taste of Muslims and the position to which they most easily relate. No doubt this is also the opinion of the majority of the 'ulamā' in Islam. When it comes to treating certain points which touch on the question, these people are inclined to consider Islam as a political unity and as a government founded by the Prophet. . . .

Prophetic Primacy

Thus we have seen the almost insurmountable difficulties facing those who wish to side with the opinion that the Prophet was both apostle of God, political sovereign and founder of a political government. . . .

There remains only one opinion for the reader to adopt. . . . This opinion holds that Muhammad was solely an apostle. He dedicated himself to purely religious propaganda without any tendency whatsoever towards temporal sovereignty, since he made no appeal in favor of a government. This same opinion maintains that the Prophet had neither temporal sovereignty nor government, that he established no kingdom in the political sense of the word nor anything synonomous with it, that he was a prophet only, like his brother prophets who preceded him, and that he was neither a king nor the founder of a state, nor did he make any appeal for a temporal empire.

This is not a very common opinion. In fact, it is so singular that it may clash with Muslim understanding. However, it is perfectly worthy of consideration and rests on solid reasons.

Before setting forth these reasons, we should put the reader on his guard against an error which anyone lacking sufficient wisdom and caution could easily commit. Actually, the prophetic mission itself demands that the Prophet have a sort of primacy in his nation, a form of authority over his people. But this has nothing in common with the primacy of temporal sovereigns,

nor with their authority over their subjects. Therefore, we should not confuse prophetic primacy with that of temporal sovereignty. We must remember that major differences set them apart one from the other. . . .

An effective religious appeal implies that the one making it have a certain perfection which is first of all physical—he should not bear any physical defect, and his senses should be perfectly sound. There should be
nothing about his physical person which would alienate and since he is
chief, he should inspire in all a reverential fear and manifest a sympathy
which attracts men and women. For the same reasons and because of his
constant relations with the other world, he should also possess spiritual
perfection.

The prophetic state demands that the prophet have a clearly privileged
social rank in his nation. There is an *hadīth* which says: God never raises
up a prophet who is not honored by his people and who is not powerful in
his family.

The prophetic state demands, moreover, that the prophet possess a
power which permits him to see that his injunctions are executed and his
preaching followed, for God does not consider the prophetic mission a
vain thing. He does not raise up a prophet as carrier of the truth without
having decided that his preaching will be effective, that its fundamentals
will be engraved on the tables of eternity and that it will be incorporated
intimately into the truths of this life. "We sent no messenger save that he
should be obeyed by God's leave." (Qur'ān 4:64). . . .

The prophet may have a role similar to that of monarchs in the political
direction of the nation. But he has a role which is proper to him and which
he shares with no one, namely it is his role to touch the soul which
inhabits the body and to pull back the veils covering hearts in order to
know them. He has the right or rather the duty to open the hearts of his
followers and touch the sources of love and hate, of good and evil, and to
know the intimate thoughts, the folds wherein temptation hides, the
sources of man's designs and the matrix within which their character is
formed. He has an obvious role in governing the masses, but he also
accomplishes a hidden work which regulates the relations among associates and allies, masters and slaves, parents and children. . . . He has the
right to scrutinize the internal as well as the external aspects of life. It is his
business to direct the affairs of the body and of the soul, our temporal and
our spiritual relations: his is the governance of this world and all that is
concerned with the next world. . . .

Muhammad's Authority

We wish also to draw the reader's attention to another point, for we come
across words which are sometimes used as synonyms and at other times

are given different meanings. Often this is a cause for debate, divergence and incoherent judgements. These words include "king," "sultan," "chief," "prince," "caliph," "state," "kingdom," "government," "caliphate," etc.

By asking ourselves if the Prophet was or was not a king, we are trying to discover if he had a quality other than that of apostle which would lead us to believe that he effectively founded or at least initiated the foundation of a political unit. . . .

We do not doubt that Islam forms a religious unit; that Muslims as such form a unique community; that the Prophet preached unity and that he realized it before his death; that he was at the head of this religious unit as the unique guide, unrivaled director, and master whose orders were never contested and whose instructions were never transgressed. We know that to make Islamic unity triumph, the Prophet fought with word and sword, that he obtained divine aid and victory, that the angels and the power of God aided him so effectively that he brought his apostolate to term, accomplished the task confided to him and exercised an authority over his nation such as no king before or since has ever wielded. . . .

If we want to call this religious unit a "state," give that unlimited power which was the Prophet's the name of kingdom or the dignity of caliphate, and give the Prophet himself the title of king, caliph, sultan, etc., we are free to do so. These are only words, and we should not stop at words. The important thing, as we have said, is the meaning, and we have defined that meaning for the reader.

What is important for us to know is whether the preeminence of the Prophet in his nation was that of an apostle or that of a king: if the manifestations of authority which we notice at times in the life of the Prophet were the manifestations of a political government or those of religious primacy, and whether this unit of which the Prophet was head was a unity of government and a state or a purely religious unity which was not political. In sum, we want to know if the Prophet was prophet only, or both king and prophet.

The Qur'ān clearly confirms the opinion that the Prophet had no connection with political royalty. The verses of the Holy Book reinforce one another in affirming that the heavenly work of the Prophet did not surpass the limits of the message which was completely foreign to the notion of temporal power. "He who obeys the Prophet obeys God. As for those who turn away, we have not sent you to be their guardian." (Qur'ān 4:80) "Your people have denied it, though it is the truth. Say, 'I am not in charge of you.' For every announcement there is a term, and you will come to know." (Qur'ān 6:66–7). . . .

Thus it is seen that it is not the Qur'ān alone that forbids us to believe that the Prophet, besides his religious preaching, engaged in propaganda with a view to constituting a political government. Nor is it the Sunna alone which prohibits a similar belief. It is reason and the true signifance and nature of the prophetic mission which join with the Qur'ān and the Sunna to reject this opinion.

The authority of Muhammad over the believers was the authority of apostleship; it had nothing in common with temporal power.

No, there was neither government, nor state, nor any type of political aspiration, nor any of these ambitions proper to kings and princes.

Perhaps the reader has now succeeded in finding the answer to the question he posed touching the absence of every manifestation of temporal authority and of established government in the time of the Prophet. No doubt he will have understood why there was no governmental organization, no governors, no judges, no ministers. . . .

A Universal Religious Message, Not an Arab State

Islam, as we have seen, is a sublime appeal enunciated by God for the good of the entire world, East and West, Arab and non-Arab, man and woman, rich and poor, learned and ignorant. It is a religious unity by which God wished to unite humanity and which he willed to extend to all the countries of the earth. . . .

Arabia, as is known, contained Arab groupings belonging to different tribes and peoples, speaking different dialects, living in different regions and tied to various political groupings. . . .

These nations, divided though they were, all rallied to the call of Islam in the time of the Prophet and gathered under his standard. These peoples, by God's grace, became brothers, joined together by the sole bond of religious feeling, held in check by one factor only: the primacy of the Prophet and his goodness and mercy. They became one nation with but one chief: the Prophet.

This unity which existed from the time of the Prophet was in no respect a political unity. It had none of the aspects of a state or a government. It was never anything other than a religious unity free from any admixture of politics. It was based on a unity of faith and religious dogma, not on a unity of state or a system of temporal authority.

What proves this is the conduct of the Prophet. We have no knowledge indicating that he sought to interfere in the political direction of the various nations, or that he changed anything in their mode of government or in the administrative or judicial regime of their tribes. Nor did he try to change the social and economic relations existing among the peoples or between them and other nations. We never hear that he deprived a governor of office, named a judge, organized a police force for these peoples, or regulated their commerce, agriculture or industry. On the contrary, the

Prophet left to them concern for all these interests, saying: "You know better than anyone." Thus, all these nations with the civil and political unity which they respectively enjoyed, with the anarchy or the order found among them were joined together only by the tie to which we referred, namely, the unity of Islam, its precepts and its morals.

The following objection, however, could be raised: these fundamental precepts, these moral rules, these laws which the Prophet brought to both Arab and non-Arab nations were very numerous and had considerable effect on most aspects of life in these nations. . . .

However, if we reflect attentively, we note that all the rules prescribed by Islam, all the obligations imposed by the Prophet on Muslims, all these rules, precepts and moral injunctions had nothing in common with the methods of political government or the civil organization of the state. All these taken together do not form even a feeble part of the political principles and legislation indispensible for a civil government. All that Islam brought in the areas of dogma juridical relations, customs, and penal law belongs to the religious domain; its intention is God alone and the service of the religious interests of humanity, nothing more. . . .

The Arabs, though reunited by the law of Islam, remained divided both politically and in their civil, social, and economic life. That is to say, the Arabs were formed into many different states, if we may be allowed to call the manner of life of the Arabs at that time by terms such as "state" or "government."

Such was the situation of the Arabs at the death of the Prophet. They formed a general religious unity embracing, with rare exceptions, completely different states. This is an indisputable truth. . . .

The Prophet went to his celestial repose without having named anyone to succeed him and without having indicated who might take his place in the nation.

There is no doubt about this. During all his life the Prophet made no allusion to anything which could be called an "Islamic State" or an "Arab state." It would be blasphemy to think otherwise. The Prophet did not leave this earth until he had entirely accomplished the mission given him by God and had explained to his nation the precepts of religion in their entirety without leaving anything vague or equivocal. How, then, if his work comprised the creation of a state, could he have left the Muslims without any precise directions concerning that state, especially since it was fated that after his death they would slip back into their old contentions and start killing one another? How could he have failed to concern himself with the question of succession to power when this has always been the primary concern of those who have founded governments? How could he have left the Muslims with nothing to guide them in this domain, abandoning them to incertitude? How could he leave them to grope in the darkness and to massacre one another while the body of the Prophet was still in their midst and his funeral had scarcely been held? . . .

The Prophet went to his celestial repose only after the religion had been completed, when grace had reached its fullness and the preaching of Islam had become a solid reality. On that day only did he die. His mission was accomplished, and that sublime union which in his august person joined heaven and earth came to an end.

The Confusion Between Prophetic Primacy and Caliphal Rule

The primacy of the Prophet was, as we have said, a religious primacy attributable solely to his prophetic mission. The prophetic mission finished with the death of the Prophet and, at the same time, the primacy ceased. It was not given to any person to succeed him in that primacy nor in his prophetic mission.

If it was absolutely necessary that one of the followers of the Prophet take a position of preeminence after his death, then that preeminence would have to be entirely new and different from that which we recognized in the Prophet. . . .

The Muslims knew then that they were instituting a civil or temporal government and nothing more. This is why they allowed themselves the liberty to revolt against this government and oppose it. They knew full well that their lack of accord centered on a question of the temporal order only and that their disagreement touched a question of political interest which did not affect their religion nor upset their faith. . . .

We do not hesitate for an instant to affirm categorically that the major part of what is called the "war of apostasy" in the first days of the caliphate of Abū-Bakr was not a war of religion but a purely political war. The masses believed it was a religious struggle, but, in fact, its goals were not entirely religious. . . .

There were circumstances particular to Abū-Bakr which aided the masses to fall into the error of attributing a religious character to the leadership of Abū-Bakr. For instance, there was the fact that Abū-Bakr enjoyed an elevated and privileged rank alongside the Prophet. He had a reputation for religious proselytism and was highly esteemed by the Muslims. . . .

Thanks to these explanations, the reader can understand that this title of "Caliph of the Prophet of God" given to Abū-Bakr was one of the sources of the error which spread among the mass of Muslims, leading them to believe that the institution of the caliphate was a religious dignity and that he who was charged with the direction of Muslims' affairs held the place occupied by the Prophet.

Thus it is that since the first days of Islam the opinion has been propagated that the institution of the caliphate is a religious office occupied by a successor to the Prophet, author of the law.

It was in the interest of monarchs to give credence to this error in public so that they could use religion as a shield protecting their thrones against the attacks of rebels. They maintained this policy in diverse ways, and anyone who looks into the matter will find how numerous were the means they employed. They let it be understood publicly that obedience to the imāms was part of obedience to God and a revolt against them was rebellion against God. That was not all. The caliphs were not the sort of men who would rest content with that nor would they be satisfied with what satisfied Abū-Bakr. That appellation which provoked his anger would not upset them; they went further and made the sovereign "the successor of God on earth and his shadow over his servants." But the "glory of God is too high to be affected by that which they wanted to associate with Him." (Qur'ān 9:31). . . .

And so the question of the office of caliph was added to religious studies and came to be integrated into the dogmas of theology. Muslims studied it along with the attributes of God and the prophets; the theory of the caliphate became as much a part of dogma as the profession of Muslim faith: "There is no God but God and Muhammad is the Prophet of God."

Such was the crime that kings in their tyranny committed against Muslims. They concealed aspects of the truth from them and made them swerve from the right path. In the name of religion they barred their way from the paths of light, treated them arbitrarily, humiliated them and prohibited them from studying political science. Also, in the name of religion they betrayed them and snuffed out their intelligence in such a way that they could find no recourse other than religion even in questions of simple administration and pure politics. . . .

The final result of all this was the death of the spirit of scientific research and intellectual activity among Muslims. They were stricken with paralysis in the area of political thought, incapable of examining anything connected with the institution of the caliphate or the caliphs.

The truth is that the Muslim religion is innocent of this institution of the caliphate such as it is commonly understood by Muslims. It is innocent of all the apparel of seduction and intimidation, and the pomp of force and power with which they surrounded the institution of the caliphate. This institution has nothing in common with religious functions, no more than the judiciary and the other essential functions and machinery of power and state. All these functions are purely political; they have nothing to do with religion. Religion neither admits nor denies them. It neither orders nor forbids them. It simply leaves them to our free choice so that we will have recourse to rational judgement in their regard and base our judgement on the experience of the nations and the rules of politics. . . .

There is nothing in religion which prohibits Muslims from rivaling other nations in all the political and social sciences. Muslims are free to demolish this worn-out system (of the caliphate) before which they have debased and humiliated themselves. They are free to establish the bases of their kingdom and the organization of their state according to more recent conceptions of the human spirit and according to the principles of government whose excellence and firmness have been consecrated by the experience of the nations. . . .

SIR SAYYID AHMAD KHĀN
1817–1898

He was for several decades a member of India's civil service and during the Mutiny of 1857 remained loyal to the British. In addition to his own prolific reformist writings, he founded a translation society for the introduction of modern Western texts (1864) and the Anglo-Muhammadan Oriental College at 'Aligarh (1874), modeled on the British university system. In 1886 he established the Muhammadan Anglo-Oriental Educational Conference, which promoted Western education, the translation of Western scientific works, and women's education.

India and English Government

A great calamity over India, the Mutiny of 1857, had passed. We attributed it to want of education in India, and to the fact that the Indians did not understand what right the Government, whose subjects we are, had upon us, and what was our duty towards it. Combined with these was the want of intercourse between the rulers and the ruled for want of education. By this time universities were established in India with the object of imparting high education. Most of the statesmen approved of high education and considered it the duty of Government, while a few of them were against it. No one, however, thought for a moment that simultaneously with education a proper training was essential, inasmuch as a men could not become a man (civilised) through mere education, nor could his moral character be improved, but would rather become like a restive horse which does not remain within its rider's control. . . .

In our opinion, if the children of respectable Muhammadan families received, alongwith high education, a proper training and were at the same time given moral discipline, formed into a good society which is most essential for moral development, then, of course, they would, on attaining high education, be not a burden but a boon to the community. At all events the education imparted at this time to the Hindu Bengalis, the Parsis of Bombay, and the Brahmins and Mahrattas of Bombay and Poona, and which is termed high education, has not borne good fruit for India. First of all they considered themselves as highly educated and as eminent states-

From Shan Muhammad, ed., *The Aligarh Movement: Basic Documents 1864–1898* (New Delhi: Prakashan, 1978), Vol. III, pp. 1069–72.

men. Then they argued that the English Goverment should govern India in the same way as it governs in Europe, and make no distinction between the conquerors and the conquered. Again, they learnt the word "liberty" and understood it to mean that they might say what came on their tongue or what passed in their mind; whether it was right or wrong, suited to the occasion or otherwise, whether there were sufficient reasons in support of it or not; they have fully to speak and print and publish throughout India. Then they came across the word "agitation" and said "Look at the people of Ireland, how much agitation they make on the Government measures, establish clubs and societies for fomenting agitation, and say what they please on the platform and in the press." Then it came into their head that the English Government is a Government that is afraid of general agitation, and that nothing could be obtained from the Government without spreading agitation. And again it occurred to them that unless an agitation is widespread and the general public or all the people of a country agree on agitating, there could be no agitation, proper and advantageous. So they tried to make agitation widespread.

So long as the acts of a Government, right or wrong, proper or improper, are not spread widely among the masses, no agitation can be got up against Government, and on this theory the National Congress came into existence. The Congress did all it could to have the sins of the Government made generally known throughout India. . . .

We do not believe for a moment that this party of agitators mean to rebel, or to incite the people to rebel, against the Government; but what they have done, and are still doing is enculated [sic] to spread general discontent against the Government, and what is to be regretted the more is that discontent is mostly or rather generally improper and unjustified, and is in itself calculated to create rebellious thoughts among the people. The advocates of this movement, no doubt, call themselves well-wishers of the Government. It may probably be true. But what they do creates general discontent and antagonism against the Government. . . .

Musalmans, with a few exceptions, have not up to this time joined the National Congress and its agitation, and those that have thrown in their lot do not understand what harm is thereby being, and will in future be, done both to their community and the country. Those who are against the agitation are styled by the agitators flatterers of the Government. They may say what they please, but the oppositionists believe with certainty that if the Government accedes to the wishes of the agitators (which is, however, quite impossible) there would be a great danger to the administration and peace of India. This belief, and not flattery of the Government, has impelled them to oppose the movement.

Although the Musalmans do not take any part in the agitation of the National Congress, still their newspapers which are in the hands of Muslim editors have with a few exceptions, imitated other papers and gone out of their way, and in writing articles have not restrained their pens, a fact which is much to be regretted. But they must understand that supposing all the Hindus and Muhammadans of India join the National Congress in its agitation, and all papers, Hindu and Muhammadan, agree on publishing articles distorting the facts and opposed to the Government, still no harm can be done to the Government. The Government will of course be compelled to curtail the sphere of liberty which is now allowed, and to frame a law for taking away the liberty of the press. The Government will not have to be blamed for this course; whatever it will do will be a punishment for actions of the Indians themselves.

Who can say that the Government is to be blamed for having, after the Mutiny of 1857, taken away arms from the people of India and prohibited their possession without a license? It was a punishment to the Indians for the misdeeds they committed during the Mutiny of 1857. Every fair-minded person will admit the Indians had in their evil deeds gone so far that the Government was compelled to pass the Arms Act. . . .

The well-being of the people of India, and especially of the Musalmans, lies in leading a quiet life under the benign rule of the English Government. They must understand that the religion of Islam enjoins us to remain faithful to those under who we live as their subjects and enjoy peace, and to dispel from our minds any idea of disloyalty, and to keep aloof from such persons as entertain such notions, and to consider them our worthy king, and our Creator as the king of kings and our real Lord. . . .

SIR SAYYID AHMAD KHĀN
Islam: The Religion
of Reason and Nature

You know well that in our time a new wisdom and philosophy have spread. Their tenets are entirely different from those of the former wisdom and philosophy [of the Greeks]. They are as much in disagreement with the tenets of ordinary present-day Islam as the tenets of Greek wisdom and philosophy were with the tenets of customary Islam during their time. . . . Yet the Muslim scholars of that time accepted them like religious tenets, . . . and this has made things even more difficult.

[Former science and modern science.] My friends! Another problem is the big difference between critical research today [and its results] and the tenets of Greek wisdom of old, because the tenets of former wisdom were based on rational and analogical arguments and not upon experience and observation. It was very easy for our forbears whilst sitting in the rooms of mosques and khānqahs,[1] to disprove teachings arrived at by analogous reasoning and to refute rational teachings by rational demonstrations, and not to accept them. But today a new situation has arisen which is quite different from that [brought about] by the investigations of former philosophy and wisdom. Today doctrines are established by natural experiments [i.e. experiments in natural science] and they are demonstrated before our eyes. These are not problems of the kind that could be solved by analogical arguments or which can be contested by assertions and principles which the 'ulamā' of former times have established. . . . One highly necessary subject has been neglected by the 'ulamā'. They did much to confront Greek wisdom and philosophy, but nothing or very little to satisfy the heart of the denier or doubter of Islam, by the way they would present to them the religion of Islam. It is neither sufficient for the firm believer, nor does it satisfy the mind of the doubter, to say simply that in Islam this has been taught in this way and has to be accepted.

[Need for a new theology] In the same way there are many other reasons for which in our time Muslims need to adopt new methods in controversy. The person who considers Islam to be true and believes firmly in it, his heart will testify that Islam alone is true—whatever changes may occur in logic, philosophy and natural science, and however much the doctrines of Islam seem to be in contradiction with them. This attitude is sufficient for

1. khānqah: a monastery of the Sūfī orders.

From "Lecture on Islam," *Sir Sayyid Ahmad Khān: A Reinterpretation of Muslim Theology*, tr. Christian W. Troll (Atlantic Highlands, N.J.: Humanities Press, Inc., 1978), pp. 311–19.

those who believe with a true and uncomplicated mind in Islam, but not for those who reject or doubt it. Furthermore, it is by no means a work of proper protection to confess just by the tongue that Islam is true, and to do nothing to strengthen it in its confrontation with the modern propositions of wisdom and philosophy. Today we need, as in former days, a modern theology ['ilm al-kalām] by which we either render futile the tenets of modern sciences or [show them to be] doubtful, or bring them into harmony with the doctrines of Islam. . . .

I happen to believe that there is nobody who is well acquainted with modern philosophy and modern and natural science as they exist in the English language, and who at the same time believes in all the doctrines which are considered doctrines of Islam in present-day understanding. . . . I am certain that as these sciences spread—and their spreading is inevitable and I myself after all, too, help and contribute towards spreading them— there will arise in the hearts of people an uneasiness and carelessness and even a positive disaffection towards Islam as it has been shaped in our time. At the same time, I believe firmly that this is not because of a defect in the original religion but rather because of those errors which have been made, willfully or not, to stain the face of Islam. . . . The person that states Islam to be true must also state how he can prove the truth of Islam. . . . in order to arrive at the truth it is necessary that we discover a criterion and establish a touchstone which is related to all religions in the same manner and by which we can prove our religion or belief to be true. . . .

By this criterion I shall justify without any wavering what I acknowledge to be the original religion of Islam which God and the Messenger have disclosed, not that religion which the 'ulamā' and preachers have fashioned. I shall prove this religion to be true and this will be the decisive difference between us and the followers of other religions. . . . the only criterion for the truth of the religions which are present before us is whether the religion [in question] is in correspondence with the natural disposition of man, or with nature. If yes, then it is true, and such correspondence is a clear sign that this religion has been sent by that person which has created man. But if this religion is against the nature of man and his natural constitution and against his forces and faculties, and if it hinders man from employing these profitably, then there can be no doubt that this religion is not sent by the person that created man, because everyone will agree that religion was made for man. You can turn this and state to the same effect that man was created for religion.

So I have determined the following principle for discerning the truth of the religion, and also for testing the truth of Islam, i.e. is the religion in question in correspondence with human nature or not, with the human nature that has been created into man or exists in man. And I have become certain that Islam is in correspondence with that nature. . . .

I hold for certain that God has created us and sent us his guidance. This guidance corresponds fully to our natural constitution, to our nature and this constitutes the proof for its truth. . . .

After determining this criterion I clarified that Islam is in full accordance with nature. So I formulated that "Islam is nature and nature is Islam." God is the Creator of all things, as He is the Creator of heaven and earth and what is in them, and of all creatures; so is He also the Creator of nature. What a tremendous slander is it, therefore, when my opponents state that I call nature Creator or—God forbid—nature God. What I declare to be created, they accuse me of calling Creator.

[This path is not entirely new in the history of Islam.] Can anybody say that the path I have outlined above is not apt to strengthen Islam? . . . No doubt it is a new path, and yet in it I have followed the ancient *'ulamā.'* As they developed a theology [*'ilm-al-kalām*] in a new fashion, so I, like them, have developed a new method to prove the same truth. We cannot exclude the possibility of a mistake. Yet future *'ulamā'* will render it fully correct and will help Islam. In my view Islam can be reaffirmed against doubters in this way and not in any other.

CHIRĀGH 'ALĪ
1844–1895

He was a protégé of Ahmad Khān. He undertook a comparative study of the Bible and the Qur'ān and, more importantly, critically reexamined the sources of Islamic law. As a result, he maintained that Islam was not tied to any particular social system. Thus, he advocated a thorough reinterpretation and reform of legal and political institutions in light of the Qur'ān.

Islam and Change

The ideas that Islam is essentially rigid and inaccessible to change, that its laws, religious, political and social, are based on a set of specific precepts which can neither be added to, nor taken from, nor modified to suit altered circumstances; that its political system is theocratic, and that in short the Islamitic code of law is unalterable and unchangeable, have taken a firm hold of the European mind, which is never at any trouble to be enlightened on the subject. The writers of Europe do not deeply search the foundations of Islam, in consequence of which their knowledge is not only superficial in the highest degree, but is often based on unreliable sources.

I have endeavoured to show in this book that Muhammadanism as taught by Muhammad, the Arabian Prophet, possesses sufficient elasticity to enable it to adapt itself to the social and political revolutions going on around it. The Muhammadan Common Law, or *Sharī'a,* if it can be called a Common Law, as it does not contain any Statute Law, is by no means unchangeable or unalterable. The only law of Muhammad or Islam is the Qur'ān, and only the Qur'ān. . . .

The Muhammadan States are not theocratic in their system of government, and the Muhammadan law being based on the principles of democracy is on this account a great check on Muslim tyrants. The first four or five caliphates were purely republican in all their features. The law, when originally framed, did not recognize the existence of a king, of a nobility, or even of a gentry in the sense in which the term was at first understood. The position of the early caliphs and their authority might be compared to that of the Dictators of the ancient Republic of Rome, each successor

From *The Proposed Political, Legal and Social Reforms Under Moslem Rule* (Bombay: Education Society's Press, 1883), pp. ii–vi, xll–xv, xvii–xxvii, xxlx–xxxvi, 10.

being chosen from amongst the people by common consent. The Government of Turkey does not and cannot claim or profess to be theocratic. . . .

There have been several churches, or schools of jurisprudence, developed in accordance with the social and political changes going on around the Muhammadan world, with a view of adapting the law still further to the progressive needs and altered circumstances of the Muslim. But none of these schools was final, all of them being decidedly progressive; they were merely halting stages in the march of Muhammadan legislation.

It might be supposed that as the growing needs of the Muslim Empire led to the formation of the several schools of jurisprudence, the various systems of interpretation of the Qur'ān, and the different methods of testing and accepting the authority of the oral traditions; so now the requirements of modern social and political life, as well as the change of circumstances, as is to be perceived in Turkey and India, might be met by a new system of analogical reasonings and strict adherence to the principles of the Qur'ān hitherto not regarded as the sole and all-sufficient guide. Legislation is a science experimental and inductive, not logical and deductive. The differences of climate, character, or history must be observed; the wants and wishes of men, their social and political circumstances must be taken into consideration, as it was done in the various stages of the first days of the growing Muslim Empire.

All the four *mujtahids,* or founders of the schools of Muhammadan jurisprudence now in force, and others whose schools have now become extinct, had adhered to the principles above referred to, which were moreover local in their applications, and hence could not be binding either on the Muhammadans of India or those of Turkey. . . .

The founders of the four schools of jurisprudence never claimed any authority for their system or legal decisions as being final. They could not dare do so. They were very far from imposing their analogical deductions or private judgments on their contemporaries, much less of making their system binding on the future generation of the wide-spreading Muslim Empire. In the second place none of the *mujtahids* . . . would accord such a high position to any of the four Imāms or doctors of jurisprudence.

This account of some of the important and main schools of jurisprudence will be sufficient to prove that none of the systems was imposed as finite [sic] or divine, and that neither the founders of these sundry systems intended them to be so, nor wished their own to bear precedence over others. Every system was progressive, incomplete, changeable and undergoing alterations and improvements. The logical deductions, analogical judgments and capricious speculations which were adhered to for want of information in the beginning were wholly done away with in after days, in the system of legislation. Every tendency was centred in legislating with regard to the wants and wishes of the people, and to the changes in the political and social circumstances of the new Empire. Every new school of jurisprudence made legislation experimental and inductive, while the former systems of speculative and deductive legislation were shelved into oblivion. . . .

The Qu'rān does not profess to teach a social and political law; all its precepts and preachings being aimed at a complete regeneration of the Arabian community. It was neither the object of the Qur'ān, the Muhammadan Revealed Law, to give particular and detailed instructions in the Civil Law, nor to lay down general principles of jurisprudence. Some points of civil and political law which were the most corrupt and abused have been noticed in it, such as Polygamy, Divorce, Concubinage, and Slavery. In these as well as other denunciations against immoral practices the Qur'ān has checked and removed the gross levity of the age. . . .

The more important civil and political institutions of the Muhammadan Common Law based on the Qur'ān are bare inferences and deductions from a single word of an isolated sentence. Slavish adherence to the letter and taking not the least notice of the spirit of the Qur'ān is the sad characteristic of the Qur'ānic interpretations and deductions of the Muhammadan doctors. . . .

In short the Qur'ān does not interfere in political questions, nor does it lay down specific rules of conduct in the Civil Law. What it teaches is a revelation of certain doctrines of religion and certain general rules of morality . . .

There is no doubt that the several codes of Muhammadan jurisprudence were well suited to the then existing state of life in each stage of its development, and even now where things have underwent no changes, they are sufficient enough for the purpose of good government and regulation of society. But there are certain points in which the Muhammadan Common Law is irreconcilable with the modern needs of Islam, whether in India or Turkey, and requires modifications. The several chapters of the Common Law, as those on Political Institutions, Slavery, Concubinage, Marriage, Divorce, and the Disabilities of non-Muslim fellow-subjects are to be remodelled and rewritten in accordance with the strict interpretations of the Qur'ān, as I have shown in the following pages. . . .

But now the question naturally comes up before us, who can effect the proposed reforms mentioned above? I reply at once, His Imperial Majesty the Sultan. He is competent enough to bring about any political legal or social reforms on the authority of the Qur'ān, just as the former Sultans introduced certain beneficial measures both in law and politics in direct contravention of the Hanafite school of the Common Law. He is the only legal authority on matters of innovation; being a successor to the successors of the Prophet (*Khalīfat Khulafā' Rasūl-allāh*). . . .

As a Caliph, the Sultan is not bound to maintain the Hanafi Law which is said to suit ill the conditions of modern life. . . .

I have shown here . . . that Islam as a religion is quite apart from inculcating a social system. The Muhammadan polity and social system have nothing to do with religion. Although Muhammadans in after days have tried to mix up their social system with the Qur'ān, just as the Jews and Christians have done in applying the precepts of the Bible to the institutions of their daily life, they are not so intermingled that, "it is hard to see they can be disentangled without destroying both." In effecting the proposed reforms it is not necessary to modify the theory of Inspiration.

In short, the Qur'ān or the teachings of Muhammad are neither barriers to spiritual development or free-thinking on the part of Muhammadans, nor an obstacle to innovation in any sphere of life, whether political, social, intellectual, or moral. All efforts at spiritual and social development are encouraged as meritorious and hinted at in several verses of the Qur'ān. . . .

There is a tradition related by the Imām Muslim to the effect that Muhammad the Prophet while coming to Medina saw certain persons fecundating datetrees. He advised them from doing so. They acted accordingly, and the yield was meagre that year. It being reported to him, he said, "He was merely a man. What he instructed them in their religion they must take, but when he ventured his opinion in other matters he was only a man."

This shows that Muhammad never set up his own acts and words as an infallible or unchangeable rule of conduct in civil and political affairs, or, in other words, he never combined the Church and State into one. The Arab proverb, "State and Religion are twins—is a mere saying of the common people, and not a Muslim religious maxim. It is incorrect to suppose that the acts and sayings of the Prophet cover all law, whether political, civil, social, or moral. . . .

Islam is capable of progress, and possesses sufficient elasticity to enable it to adapt itself to the social and political changes going on around it. The Islam, by which I mean the pure Islam as taught by Muhammad in the Qur'ān, and not that Islam as taught by the Muhammadan Common Law, was itself a progress and a change for the better. It has the vital principles of rapid development, of progress, of rationalism, and of adaptability to new circumstances. . . .

MUHAMMAD 'ALĪ
1878–1931

He was educated in India and at Oxford and pursued a career first in the civil service and then in journalism as editor of the *Comrade* (English) and later *Hamdard* (Urdu). However, he is best remembered as leader of the Khilāfat (Caliphate) movement and as one of the organizers of the Muslim League. After the abolition of the Caliphate (1924), Muhammad 'Alī continued his political activism, advocating both Indian independence and Muslim separatism.

Justice to Islam and Turkey

The resolution that I have the honour to place before you this evening is:

> That this meeting urges upon the Government the necessity for taking into serious consideration, in the Turkish settlement, the religious obligations of the Muslims (who in India alone number some 70 million citizens of the British Empire) and the national sentiment of United India. . . .

Now, what is our case? We are told in the *Times* and other newspapers that the Muslims of India must not dictate the foreign policy of the British Government. Well, ladies and gentlemen, in our wildest dreams it certainly did not occur to us to dictate the foreign policy of the British Government. . . .

If you, ladies and gentlemen, who are of British birth and Christian faith, do not like your policy to be dictated to you by black heathens of the East, then I say we also do not want the foreign policy of *our* Empire to be dictated to us by a tiny fraction of forty-five millions of people of British birth and Christian faith. . . .

When the Queen of England, in the days of my grandfather, took into her hands the reins of office of India, and began to rule over the territories of the East India Company, a trading company which had become a sovereign power entirely against its will, after passing numerous self-denying ordinances—when the reins of Government in these territories passed into the hands of the Queen, a proclamation was issued that did

From Afzal Iqbal, ed., *Selected Speeches and Statements of Maulana Mohamed Ali* (Lahore, 1963), II, 33–45.

her credit and did your people credit. It was a noble one and we have always believed in it. The most important thing that that document contained was that no matter what changes should take place, one thing would remain unchanged—our religious obligations would be respected. Ladies and gentlemen, we have given you whatever you needed, we were certainly not "picy" and never stinted money. In fact we have been spendthrifts perhaps, and squandered what wealth was left to us after having squandered away an Empire; but whatever we may or may not have thrown away, one thing was dear to us and that was faith—and it was understood that it was to be in all circumstances respected by the British. . . .

We, who number three hundred and fifteen millions in an Empire of four hundred and fifteen millions, should, I say, have some kind of voice, if not the prepondering voice, in the making of peace, though we had none in the making of a war which, nevertheless, we were called upon to wage.

It may have been that we were too powerless at the time to have stopped you from exercising religious tyranny over the country, you with your powerful guns, ships and weapons of destruction: it may have been that we would have been entirely powerless to stop you even if you had chosen not to respect our faith; but whatever the situation, it is a fact that in the name of Great Britain the Queen gave us the charter of our religous liberties, and gave us the pledge that our religious obligations would be entirely respected. That was the price of our allegiance to the Queen of Great Britain. Today, when the Muslims are called upon to disregard their religous obligations, it is clearly because of that charter that Indians have a right to say "this shall not be." They will have to go, not only to His Majesty, the successor of Queen Victoria, not only to 10 Downing Street, where Mr. Lloyd George now lives, and hopes to live for ever and ever, they will have to go to every British man and woman who has drawn the least benefit from British rule over India, and tell them that they cannot possibly ask them to disregard their religious obligations without the most palpable breach of faith with more than three hundred millions of people.

If the religious claims of the Indian Muslims, which were to them solemn obligations, were now to be ignored, the pledge contained in the noble Proclamation of 1858 would be broken. You may, if you choose, question our claims and examine whether the preservation of the Khilāfat [Caliphate], with adequate temporal power for the defense of the faith, and the maintenance of exclusive Muslim control over Syria, Palestine and Mesopotamia, are duties imposed by Islam on every Muslim or not. But once they are acknowledged to be so, as they must be, then you cannot thereafter say we must dismember the Khilāfat and demand a mandate in Mesopotamia and still expect from us the same loyal allegiance. This cannot and shall not be.

In the House of Commons the hero of Paisley, fresh from his triumph, in the very first debate that he could start on the subject after his election, talked of the connection of the Khilāfat and Constantinople as being a fairly modern matter, and maintained that the Sultan as Khalīfa [Caliph] has not been there more than four hundred years. Well, that is still 300 years longer than the rule of English kings and queens in India, but I will come to that by and by. Well, Mr. Asquith wanted to "Vaticanise" the Khalīfa. But the Khalīfa, as even Mr. Lloyd George could now tell him, was not the Pope, and the moment he would consent to be "Vaticanised," he would cease to be the Khalīfa. He was the Commander of the Faithful, the President of our Theocratic Commonwealth, the Leader of all Muslims in peace and war, though he could neither claim to be infallible like the Pope, nor could he in all circumstances exercise unquestioned authority, for Allah was the only Sovereign, and in case of dispute Muslims were bound to refer back to the Holy Qur'ān and to the Traditions of the Prophet whose successor the Khalīfa is.

But whatever he could or could not do, the Khalīfa was certainly not a pious old gentleman, whose only function in life was to mumble his prayers and repeat his beads as Mr. Asquith clearly seems to think. If such is the ignorance of Mr. Asquith with regard to such fundamental doctrines of Islam, even after having been enlightened by our Delegation, then is it not a shame and a disgrace to one who has once been, and apparently still dreams of being once more, the Prime Minister of the Imperial Government of Great Britain?

Having claimed to shape the destinies of three or four hundred million Indians, including over 70 million Muslims, if this is the extent of their knowledge, then I say it is a shame and a disgrace. Mr. Asquith said, no doubt humorously, that in these days even if a Khalīfa goes to war he cannot hope to go to war with limited liabilities. Well, I will say this to him, that even in this twentieth century we are a very backward people in India, and if you will go to war with the Khalīfa in order to oust him from the seat of the Khilāfat, if you go to war with him in order to dismember his Empire, and if you go to war with him in order to step into the sanctuaries of our faith, because there is oil in Mosul, if you go to war with him because the sanctity of the Holy Land of Islam must be violated by exploiters demanding a mandate in Mesopotamia, no doubt in the Sacred name of the Self-Determination spelt with three letters, O—I—L— then even in these days you will have to go to war, I am afraid, with very limited assets indeed.

It is sometimes said, "The Turks waged war against us; we fought them and we have defeated them, now we are going to treat them as a defeated people. We have beaten the Turks and must deal with them as we wish." This argument is all very fine, but who is "We"? Who fought, and who won the war? Who went to war in Mesopotamia? Who went to war in the Holy Land? India won Baghdad, and India and Muslims won the Holy Land. According to Mr. Lloyd George, the Allies are not dealing with the Turks differently from other defeated people. We are told there is nothing of the Christian and the Crusading spirit in this matter. And yet, when proposing a gratuity for Lord Allenby he said: "The name of General Allenby will be ever renowned as that of the brilliant Commander who fought and won the last and most triumphant of the Crusades. It was his good fortune by his skill to bring to a glorious end an enterprise which absorbed the chivalry of Europe for centuries. We forget now that the military strength of Europe was concentrated for generations upon this purpose in vain, and a British Army under the command of General Allenby achieved it finally." So there was after all something of the crusading spirit somewhere when General Allenby, in the words of Mr. Lloyd George himself, "won the last and most triumphant of the crusades." However, at the very time Lord Allenby was saying that two-thirds of his army in this crusade was composed of Muslims, a wonderful crusade, in which the Crescent was fighting the battle of the Cross. But, anyhow, were not the co-religionists and compatriots of these strange Crusaders who repudiated the Cross and yet fought the Crescent, entitled to demand that the religious obligations of the Muslims and the overwhelming national sentiment of India should be considered in the Turkish settlement?

Whatever the Indian soldiers have done, this I will say about them—I have seen them; we had always avoided contact with them in deference to official susceptibilities—but when we came out of gaol these people have rushed to us like the rest of their countrymen; they have kissed our hands, embraced us, shown to us in an unmistakable manner that if you demanded from them, conscripted soldiers as they almost were, that they should go against their own religious obligations, they have unmistakably shown to us that that day you will be using a weapon which will break in your hands.

Therefore, although I do not threaten, although we have not come here to threaten you, it ought to be made clear to you that the situation is now different. Today it is not only the Muslims who feel like this, but the Hindus, and even the Sikhs—after Amritsar. India today is one and united. That is why in our resolution we have asked the Government to show respect not only for Muslim obligations, but also for the national sentiment of United India. How is this sentiment expressing itself? On the 17th October last the Muslims observed the Khilāfat Day, a day on which the Muslims suspended business and fasted and prayed, and many Hindus joined them. Now on the 19th March, precisely the day that we were being received in 10 Downing Street by Mr. Lloyd George, from one end of India to another there was a total suspension of business, in which not

only Muslims and Hindus and Sikhs, but Parsees and others also participated. In order to realise what this suspension of business means, I will ask
you not to think of a railway strike, nor even of a general strike in England
or Germany; you have got to think of the total suspension of business
throughout the Continent of Europe. Yet, primitive as some of our people
are, very impulsive as they seem to be, in spite of this universal demonstration, there was no violence. . . .

We are being led by a man who believes in Soul-force. If thoughout the
world today there is anyone who tries to live up to the Sermon on the
Mount—that sermon which is often overrated but at the same time always forgotten in the shaping of your foreign policy—if any man tries to
live up to that sermon it is Mahatma Gandhi. He is not a Muslim. He is a
Hindu of Hindus. . . . He has at last himself drawn up a manifesto, which
we have brought with us as the mandate of the Indian Delegation. The
claim put forward is a simple claim. It says that it is one of the fundamental doctrines of Islam, absolutely unalterable, that there should always be a
Khalīfa, and that the Khalīfa should have temporal power at all times
adequate for the defence of the Faith, and that is the measure of the
irreducible minimum of temporal power. . . .

The second claim is that the local centre of our Faith, the land known as
the Island of Arabia, should be free from non-Islamic control in any shape
or form. Arabia to the European geographer is a peninsula bounded only
on three sides by water; but to the Islamic religion it has always been an
island. You will understand this when I tell you that it is surrounded on
one side by the Mediterranean and the Red Sea, on another side by the
Indian Ocean, on the third side by the Persian Gulf, and on the fourth by
the waters of the Euphrates and the Tigris; and on his death-bed our
Prophet gave an injunction, binding on all sections of Muslims, that in that
region no kind of non-Muslim control should be allowed.

But even if you disregard our religious requirements, what about your
own political principles? We have heard a great deal of the principle of
self-determination, and now that we have seen some applications of this
principle, we find that it has about as many interpretations as love or
religion. There is one interpretation when the principle is applied to Ireland; on this you are all well informed, and I shall not waste your time.
There is another interpretation of self-determination for Montenegro,
when it is assured it is not good to be a cock's head when you can be a
bull's tail. In spite of Montenegro's desire for independence, she is assured
that it is better in her own interest to be part of a larger unit. When we ask
that the Arabs should not be forced to get out of the larger unit we are
told by Mr. Lloyd George: "Is the sacred principle of self-determination
not to be applied to an Arab simply because he is a Muslim?" But surely
the last interpretation of self-determination is the best of all. We never

knew that that large mouthful of a word, self-determination, could be spelt with three letters: O—I—L. This is the latest interpretation of self-determination. But whatever Mr. Lloyd George may say, the people of Mesopotamia, as well as those of Syria and Palestine, have clearly determined that they will have no mandates and no protectorates.

Then we come to Constantinople, which has been very generously spared to the Khalīfa, out of deference to Muslim wishes or to French wishes, I cannot tell which.

But did not Mr. Lloyd George, Mr. Bonar Law, and Sir Edward Carson tell us that this had to be since there was no other alternative, and the late lamented and always lamentable Tsarist autocracy was no more? And is it not because Mr. Lloyd George desires to keep the head of the Khalīfa in chancery? The Khalīfa is to remain a hostage in the hands of the Powers, and we are to express our gratitude for it. This is an outrage which Islam will never tolerate. The Straits are to be taken out of Turkish control, and British guns are always to be trained on the Khalīfa's palace. Whether it is oil, whether it is Bolshevism, that suggests this policy—whatever it is, the Muslims cannot permit that their Khalifa is to remain as a hostage. They claim that it is part of their Faith that the Khilāfat should exist as an independent sovereignty, and its Empire should not be dismembered any further after the very great spoliation that had already taken place after the Balkan War. After that large spoliation, the Khalīfa's Empire has really been reduced to such small proportions that they cannot allow the least little bit of the Khilāfat territory to be taken away from the Khalīfa, and they must insist that in the Holy Lands, even in spite of oil, they would not have a British Protectorate, or French or American mandate . . . If you will use force to compel us to submit to a peace that contravenes Islamic religious requirements, and blood is shed for blood, then the guilt of blood will be yours, because you are prepared to use force, but you are not prepated to do justice to the Muslims.

This is what we have come to ask. I tell you this, we have not come to threaten, and we do not threaten you. My friend Mr. Wedgwood, in the House of Commons, said, "you can get more out of English people by persuasion than by threats," and I believe him. But he says, "what can you threaten us with?" Well, that is the worst part of the whole business. There is nothing at all after less than a hundred years of British rule that we can threaten you with. It is true, as Colonel Wedgwood asked, what can we threaten you with? though the measure of our impotence, in spite of our righteous wrath today, is also the measure of success of your crushing rule achieved in no more than a century. But having reduced us to this state of impotence, I ask you to consider this. If we want to threaten you we obviously cannot threaten you with Howitzers and Dreadnoughts and Aeroplanes and Tanks; but we possess a thing that is unconquerable;

our determination to die true to our Faith. Money is being poured into the Fund for the Khilāfat. But every Muslim who pays is told that this is not money; it is only a draft on the life of every subscriber. We do not threaten you with our undying determination to die kings of our consciences and masters of our souls.

11

ISLAM AND THE MODERN STATE

ISLAM AND NATIONALISM

The concern of the first modern reformers in the Middle East was directed toward adopting European political systems and toward restating Islam as a religion in perfect harmony with modernity. But the solutions which appeared so facile engendered much more serious questions about the basis of political organization and the function of religion in society. In the section which follows, the writings of Rashīd Ridā and Shakīb Arslān slip easily from national identity to Muslim nationalism, as if they were conditioned by their allegiance to the Ottoman Empire, the last of the Muslim Empires. Sāti' al-Husrī addresses the problem clearly: any new union raises the question of political organization and for the Arabs, common language, history and geography, not religion, are the only solid bases for political union. The Arabism advocated by al-Husrī found less of a response in Egypt than in other Arab countries, as the selections from Ahmad Lutfi al-Sayyid and Tāhā Husayn demonstrate. The latter dismisses the problem of East/West as inapplicable to Egypt, but his countryman Hasan al-Bannā' shows that Tāhā Husayn's judgments had not filtered down to the masses. It was impossible to dismiss Islam, and so we find 'Abd al-Rahmān al-Bazzāz adroitly showing how Arabism and Islam are completely in harmony. This marks the attempt at a new synthesis of Islam and Arab nationalism. But note that the references to Islam in Bazzāz are basically historical. Islam, as such, is not seen as the basis of political organization.

Questions of independence and national identity went through two important phases in South Asia during the first half of the twentieth century. Initially, Hindus and Muslims of the Indian National Congress and the

55

Muslim League had worked together in the independence movement. Yet, progressively, many Muslims came to fear for the rights of a Muslim minority in a Hindu-dominated secular state. Thus, for example, Muhammad 'Alī, once president of the Indian National Congress and a founder of the Muslim League, quit the Congress in 1930. Muhammad Iqbāl, regarded by many as the spiritual father of Pakistan, articulated this Muslim communal concern in his presidential address before the All-India Muslim League (December 19, 1930) in which he called for a separate state for Muslims within India.

However, there were those in India who argued that any form of nationalism (whether Indian nationalism or Muslim nationalism) was antithetical to Islam, since the Islamic community or state (*umma*) is one that transcends all ethnic, tribal, regional, and racial divisions. We see this line of argument in the writings of Mawlānā Abū-l-'Alā' Mawdūdī. Mawdūdī sharply contrasts the ideals and values of Islam vis-à-vis nationalism—the one sustained by a divinely revealed law and the other by force.

RASHĪD RIDĀ
1865–1935

He studied at the Ottoman government school and at Shaykh
Husayn Jisr's school, both in Tripoli, Lebanon. Here he made
his first contact with Muhammad 'Abduh, and later, in 1897,
when he took refuge in Egypt, he became 'Abduh's faithful disciple and guardian of his ideas. In 1898, Ridā founded the periodical *al-Manār,* which was the most important voice of Islamic
reform in the Arab world. The following selection is a *fatwā*
(legal opinion) given by Ridā in response to an inquiry from an
Indonesian Muslim.

Patriotism, Nationalism, and Group Spirit in Islam

To the Excellent and Learned Shaykh Rashīd Ridā,
may God give you long life.

Greetings and peace. In my country, Indonesia, at present there is a strong
movement for independence involving a continual struggle against the colonialists. Unfortunately, in the midst of this holy war a group of *'ulamā'*[1]
have risen up forbidding patriotism and making war on patroits in the
name of the Islamic religion and its doctrines. They claim the patroits have
deviated and are inciting enmity among the masses and their leaders. As a
result the patriots are caught between two fires, that of the colonialists and
that of the *'ulamā'.*

I am aware of the development of the national movement in Egypt and I
know that religious men were in the avant garde of the combatants carrying
the banner of nationalism. . . . Yes, I refer to the men, the students, and the
'ulamā' of al-Azhar[2] who led demonstration after demonstration and fell in
the squares and in the streets. Because of this I turn to you to ask for
clarification on these matters, especially the following questions. An answer
will help Indonesia and point out the way of truth and guidance.

1. *'ulamā':* religious scholars. [Ed.]
2. al-Azhar University: Center of Islamic learning in Cairo. [Ed.]

From *Fatwās,* trans. from *al-Manār,* vol. 33 (1933), pp. 191–92.

57

1. Is it correct that there are *hadīths* forbidding the notion of patriotism and nationalism?
2. Are his (Muhammad) sayings "There is no group feeling in Islam" and "There is no one among us who invokes the invocation of the *jāhiliyya*"[3] two clear *hadīths* forbidding patriotism?
3. Is there a distinction between group feeling and patriotism? Is patriotism included in the notion of group feeling? What was group feeling among the Arabs?
4. What is the view of Islam concerning the idea of patriotism and does this idea run counter to Islamic unity? What is intended by Islamic unity?
5. It is known that Shaykh Muhammad 'Abduh, the great philosopher, was the father of patriotism and of patriots. In his house in Halwan, Sa'd (Zaghlul) grew up and there the men of Egypt met. What do you, his disciple and biographer, judge in this matter?
6. What kind of patriotism should Muslim youth have?

Answer of *al-Manār:*

These questions on the subject can be reduced to one problem with subdivisions. . . . Consequently, we will answer them with a single comprehensive yet brief answer. . . . "Group feeling" among the Arabs is related to "the group," i.e. a man's people who take sides with him; that is, they protect and defend him and aid him whenever he needs help or is wronged. The word "group" originally signifies the relatives of a man who are his heirs; then it becomes used in a wider sense. The word derives from *'isb,* an ivy plant which winds itself around a tree or the like.

It is well known that one of the imperatives of Islam is its prohibition of partisanship in wrong for the sake of relatives, people, or fatherland. It prohibits enmity and divisions among Muslims arising from the partisanship of any group, country, or region against their brothers in religion and against others except those against whom war should be waged.

The Prophet made this clear in his words: "Group spirit is a man's supporting his people in wrong." The Imām Ahmad[4] related this.

It is also well known that another imperative of Islam obliges its people to attack and combat the foreigners who attack them. All the jurisprudents have declared that holy war is a duty incumbent on all individuals when an enemy commits aggression against Muslims or occupies any of their lands. This is warding off wrong, so it is shameful ignorance to prohibit it and to deduce the prohibition from the group feeling of the Jāhiliyya, such

---

3. Jāhiliyya: the period of "ignorance" before Islam. [Ed.]
4. Ahmad ibn Hanbal: founder of one of the four main legal schools. [Ed.]

as that which existed between the 'Aws and the Khazraj[5] among the Ansār,[6] which was prohibited by some *hadīths*.[7]

This is the summary answer to the first three questions.

The contemporary notion of patriotism expresses the unity of the people of different religions in their homeland, and their cooperation in defending the homeland they share. They cooperate to preserve its independence, to win it back if it was lost, and to develop it. In the islands of Indonesia this does not appear as it does in Egypt.

Islam's view of this is that Muslims are obligated to defend the non-Muslim who enters under their rule and to treat him as an equal according to the just rules of the *Sharī'a*.[8] Consequently, how could it not be allowed to join with them in defending the country, preserving its independence and developing it? The Companions of the Prophet exempted the *dhimmī*[9] who joined them in war from the head tax during the Caliphate of 'Umar, as we have demonstrated from evidence in the tenth volume of the *Manār Commentary*.[10]

The type of patriotism that should adorn Muslim youth is that he be a good example for the people of the homeland, no matter what their religious affiliation, cooperating with them in every legitimate action for independence, for developing science, virtue, force, and resources on the basis of the Islamic law of preferring the closest relations in rights and duties. In his service of his homeland and his people he must not, however, neglect Islam which has honored him and raised him up by making him a brother to hundreds of millions of Muslims in the world. He is a member of a body greater than his people, and his personal homeland is part of the homeland of his religious community. He must be intent on making the progress of the part a means for the progress of the whole.

5. 'Aws and Khazraj: tribal groupings at Medina. [Ed.]
6. the Ansār: "helpers" of Muhammad at Medina. [Ed.]
7. *Hadīths:* traditions of the Prophet Muhammad; narratives of what the Prophet said, did, or permitted. [Ed.]
8. *Sharī'a:* Islamic law. [Ed.]
9. *dhimmī:* the protected people in a Muslim country, i.e. the Jews and Christians. They paid a head tax for this protection. [Ed.]
10. *Manār Commentary:* a commentary on the Qur'ān begun by Muhammad 'Abduh and continued by Ridā, published in the periodical *al-Manār*. [Ed.]

AMĪR SHAKĪB-ARSLĀN
1869–1946

A member of a leading Lebanese Druze family, he studied at the American school in Shwayfat, then at al-Hikmah school in Beirut. In 1889 a trip to Egypt brought him into contact with 'Abduh and his circle. He was elected to the Ottoman parliament in 1913, but after the First World War he spent much of his time in Europe. He was a link between Middle Eastern and North African Islam, and a proponent of Arab causes at the League of Nations. He published a periodical *La Nation Arabe*. His writings emphasize the Islamic nature of Arab Nationalism.

Our Decline and Its Causes

It may be said without exaggeration about the Muslims that their condition, spiritual as well as material, is deplorably unsatisfactory. With very few exceptions, in all countries where Muslims and non-Muslims live side by side, the Muslims lag far behind in almost everything. . . .

It cannot, however, be gainsaid that throughout the Islamic world, there has been a great stir, a powerful convulsion and an awakening in matters spiritual and temporal which is indeed phenomenal. The Europeans are carefully observing these revolutionary manifestations and are studying their directions and tendencies. That some of them are indeed apprehensive and suspicious of this awakening and stir, is vouched for by the articles and books they have published. But it can easily be seen that this forward movement of the Muslims has not advanced so far as to enable them to come anywhere near the nations of Europe, America, or Japan.

This, then, is the general condition of the modern Muslims. What are the causes that led to the general degradation of Muslims? Was it not the Muslims who were credited wtih leadership in the East as well as in the West, for about eight or nine centuries, and acquired name and fame all over the world? Let us, therefore, first of all examine the factors that contributed to their greatness and advancement, before investigating the causes that led to their decline and fall.

The causes of the advancement of the Muslims were, briefly, those origi-

From *Our Decline and Its Causes: A Diagnosis of the Symptoms of the Downfall of Muslims,* trans. M.A. Shakoor (Lahore, 1944; reprint ed., 1968), pp. 1–4, 6–8, 10–13, 15, 29, 39–40, 44–45, 48, 68–71, 73–75, 83–86, 96–97, 99, 132, 134.

nating in Islam, which made its advent in the Arabian Peninsula. Its birth gathered together and consolidated the scattered races and tribes of Arabia, brought them out of barbarism into civilization, replaced their hardheadedness with mutual love and sympathy, eradicated idolatry and restored the worship of the one God. . . . Renovated and inspired by this dynamic force they made themselves masters of half the world in the short span of half a century. But for the internecine strife which lifted its head once again among them, towards the close of 'Uthmān's Caliphate and during the Caliphate of 'Alī,[1] no power on earth could have prevented them from conquering the whole world. . . .

As we scrutinize the matter minutely, it will be found that the greater part of the inspiring force that accounted for their victories and achievements has disappeared, although vestiges of it are visible here and there like the fading lines on a tattooed hand. Were it only for the bearing of the designation of "Muslims" without ever performing the duties of a Muslim, that God had promised the reward of greatness, glory and honor for the Believers, we could have, with justice, asked, "Where is the honor for the Muslims?" as according to the Qur'ānic verse, "Honor belongs to God and to His Apostle and to the Believers."

> And it was due from Us
> To aid those who believed (Qur'ān 30:47)

Do these words of God mean that they are only to proclaim themselves Muslims but never need encounter the tribulations of life in the field of action? If it be so, one cannot but wonder at the decline and degradation of the Muslims. But the Qur'ānic verses do not mean this; nor does God break His promises; and the Qur'ān has remained the same as it then was. Not a syllable has been changed in its text. The change has occurred in the Muslims themselves:

> Verily, never will God change the condition
> of a people until they change it themselves (Qur'ān 13:11)

How can you expect that God will help a nation that shuns the field of action, and that He will shower upon them the magnificent rewards once bestowed on their glorious and heroic ancestors, although they have none of the valour, vitality and stout-heartedness of the latter? . . . How absurd it would be for the present-day Muslims to desire that they should get for the five per cent work they do, the same reward as their illustrious forbears who performed their one hundred per cent work. . . .

Today that zeal of our ancestors, their fervor and their ennobling devotion to their faith, has disappeared from among the Muslims. This spirit is

---

1. 'Uthmān and 'Alī: the third and fourth Caliphs or leaders of the Muslim community after the death of Muhammad. [Ed.]

found transfused in the enemies of Islam, though they received no such inspiration from the scriptures of their religions. . . .

Can anyone point out a single Muslim nation of modern times which has sacrificed men and money as unstintingly and unhesitatingly for their country and their nation as these Christian nations of Europe have done for theirs (during World War I). . . .

If, therefore, the Islamic nations, following in the footsteps of their illustrious ancestors, act as they have been commanded, or at least, like the Europeans, sacrifice their persons and properties for defending their honor and heritage and for resisting aggressors, they will certainly be entitled to the same blessings as others have enjoyed by dint of their sufferings and sacrifices, and will find themselves in safety and security by the grace of God.

But without sufferings and sacrifices, without the spirit of self-abnegation and readiness to court death, without spending their wealth and properties, without the burning zeal for pursuing the right path prescribed by God, the Muslims instead hope to defend their dignity, honor and independence, by merely praying to God for help! . . .

But Islam is, on the contrary, not confined to prayer, fasting, meditation or supplication. Is God to accept the prayers of those who, while they are capable of positive work and sacrifices in person and material, choose to live a negative life of idleness and apathy to action? . . .

If the foreign intruders in Muslim countries are enraged at those Muslims who refuse to betray their own brethren in pursuance of foreign behests, it is because most Muslims offer help to these foreigners betraying their own brethren and enthusiastically assist them with advice against their own nation and faithfully cooperate with these foreigners from greed and perfidy. But for the assistance obtained by the foreigners through the treachery of one section of the Muslims and the zeal with which the latter rendered them help against their own countrymen and brethren, these foreigners would have neither usurped their sovereignty and established their rule over them nor acted in such a manner as to contravene and supercede their religious laws and undermine the foundations of those social codes and conventions which are the offsprings of those laws, nor would they have dragged down the Muslims into the valley of the shadow of death and laid them to a disgraceful death. . . .

These Muslims would hardly deserve any recompense from God even if they had not engaged in conspiracies against their own religion, or placed themselves at the beck and call of the covetous foreigners for undermining their own nation, or lent their shoulders to be used as a ladder for the foreigner to climb on to power and wealth. They believe they have performed their religious duty when they have said their prayers, uttered the formulas, chanted a few verses, sung their hymns and spent their time in supplications. This is all Islam means to them. If this were all that was needed to be a Muslim and to be victorious in this world as well as in the next, then the Qur'ān would never have been so full of counsels, commands, and inspiring words calling upon the Muslims to serve Islam with their minds, bodies, and material wealth, to make the greatest sacrifices, to be steadfast in honesty and patience, to work for the benefit of their fellow believers, to maintain justice and equity and to acquire all noble qualities. . . .

There are people who ask why degradation has overtaken the Muslims and why they are not able to keep pace with others. Anyone who realizes how they differ from others in the degree of awakening, devotion, and sense of duty and self-respect, will easily find the answer to these questions. . . .

Another important cause of the decline of Muslims is the blind obstinacy with which they insist upon the maintenance of hackneyed conventions. Serious are the dangers to a nation from men who condemn everything old as absurd and worthless, without giving thought to their intrinsic value, simply because they are "old"; no less serious are the dangers that arise from the conservative school, which insists that no change can be permissible in anything. . . . Thus these sophisticated "ultra-moderns" and the conservative conventionalists are ruining Islam between themselves. . . .

The best examples in this matter are the Europeans. Study them as closely as we may; we shall not find even a single nation among them that desires to lose its identity in another. The English would remain but English. The French want to remain French, etc. . . . To the extent the European civilization is sufficient for the Europeans, to the same extent is Japanese civilization sufficient for the Japanese. In other words, the civilizations of both are confined within the bounds of their nationalities, languages, customs, religions, their conceptions of freedom, ethical peculiarities, modes of thought, etc. . . .

Every nation adheres rigorously to its religion and clings steadfastly to its religious heritage, traditions, and national characteristics and peculiarities. They never speak of these things with contempt or ridicule. The Muslims alone seem not to understand their value. If anyone tells them that they should hold fast to the Qur'ān, their faith, their religious traditions, and their natural characteristics, or that they should not abandon the Arabic language, or that they should preserve their oriental mode of life and conduct and etiquette, they would yell like lunatics: "Down with your traditionalism . . . in these civilized days how can you progress like others with your outworn traditions and customs of the Middle Ages?" . . .

As for the conservative Muslims . . . they have made the Muslims helpless victims of poverty and indigence by reducing Islam to a religion of mere other-worldly preoccupations. . . . It is these conservatives who declared war on natural science, mathematics, and all creative arts, condemned them as the practices of infidels and thereby deprived Muslims of the fruits of science. . . .

The quintessence of Islamic teaching is that man should make proper use of his intellect which God has given him as a guiding light to help him think for himself, and that having done everything in his power, he should resign himself to the Will of God, for the happy fructification of his labor. . . .

Islam is by its very nature and genius a revolt against all degenerate tradition. It dug the grave for the abominable and debased traditions and usages of old and cut off all relationship with what was false and untrue. How can it then be called a religion of static inaction and conservatism. . . .

In order that Muslims may awake, arise and ascend the highest pinnacle of advancement and progress, like any other modern nation, it is their sacred duty to embark on a *jihād*[2] by sacrificing their life and wealth in consonance with the oft repeated commandments of the Qur'ān. It is this kind of *jihād* that is known in modern parlance as "sacrifice." No nation has achieved victory but by sacrifice. . . .

If Muslims will resolve and strive, taking their inspiration from the Qur'ān, they can attain the rank of the Europeans, the Americans and the Japanese in learning and science and making progress. Yet withal they can preserve their own faith, just as others have done. Nay more, if we derive our inspiration from the Qur'ān, we would be better qualified for progress than others.

---

2. *jihād:* "to strive, struggle" to realize God's Will. The term applies to moral (spiritual perfection), intellectual (the reasoning or interpretation of *ijtihād*), and military (holy war) efforts or struggles. [Ed.]

SĀTI' AL-HUSRĪ
1880–1964

Born in North Yemen of Syrian parents, he was educated as an official in the Ottoman Empire. After the Arab Revolt, he was Minister of Education for Faysal's brief reign in Syria. The leading proponent of Arab unity and Arabism between the two world wars, he became Director General of Cultural Affairs for the Arab League, and then Dean of the Institute of Higher Arab Studies in Cairo.

Muslim Unity and Arab Unity

I have read and heard many opinions and observations concerning Muslim unity and Arab unity, and which is to be preferred. I have been receiving for some time now various questions concerning this matter: Why, it is asked, are you interested in Arab unity, and why do you neglect Muslim unity? Do you not see that the goal of Muslim unity is higher than the goal of Arab unity, and that the power generated by Muslim union would be greater than that generated by Arab union? Do you not agree that religious feeling in the East is much stronger than national feeling? Why, then, do you want us to neglect the exploitation of this powerful feeling and to spend our energies in order to strengthen a weak feeling? Do you believe that the variety of languages will prevent the union of the Muslims? Do you not notice that the principles of communism, socialism, Freemasonry, and other systems unite people of different languages, races, countries, and climates; that none of these differences have prevented them from coming to understanding, from drawing nearer to another, and from agreeing on one plan and one creed? Do you not know that every Muslim in Syria, Egypt, or Iraq believes that the Indian Muslim, the Japanese Muslim, or the European Muslim is as much his brother as the Muslim with whom he lives side by side? Whence, then, the impossibility of realizing Muslim union? Some say that Muslim unity is more powerful than any other and that its realization is easier than the realization of any other. What do you say to this? Some pretend, mistakenly, that the idea of Arab union is a plot the aim of which is to prevent the spread of the idea of Muslim union, in

From Sylvia G. Haim, ed., *Arab Nationalism* (Berkeley: University of California Press, 1962), pp. 147–53.

order to isolate some of the countries of the Muslim world and facilitate their continued subjugation. What is your opinion of this allegation? . . .

I think that the essential point which has to be studied and solved when deciding which to prefer, Muslim unity or Arab unity, may be summarized as follows: Is Muslim unity a reasonable hope capable of realization? Or is it a utopian dream incapable of realization? And assuming the first alternative, is its realization easier or more difficult than the realization of Arab unity? Does one of these two schemes exclude the other? And is there a way of realizing Muslim unity without realizing Arab unity? When we think about such questions and analyze them, we have, in the first place, to define clearly what we mean by Muslim unity and by Arab unity and to delimit without any ambiguity the use of the two expressions.

It goes without saying that Arab unity requires the creation of a political union of the different Arab countries the inhabitants of which speak Arabic. As for Muslim unity, that naturally requires the creation of a political union of the different Muslim countries, the inhabitants of which profess the Muslim religion, regardless of the variety of their languages and races. It is also well known that the Muslim world includes the Arab countries, Turkey, Iran, Afghanistan, Turkestan, parts of India, the East Indies, the Caucasus, North Africa, as well as parts of Central Africa, without considering a few scattered units in Europe and Asia, as in Albania, Yugoslavia, Poland, China, and Japan. Further, there is no need to show that the Arab countries occupy the central portion of this far-flung world.

Whoever will examine these evident facts and picture the map of the Muslim world, noticing the position of the Arab world within it, will have to concede that Arab unity is much easier to bring about than Muslim unity, and that this latter is not capable of realization, assuming that it can be realized, except through Arab unity. It is not possible for any sane person to imagine union among Cairo, Baghdad, Tehran, Kabul, Haiderabad, and Bukhara, or Kashgar, Persia, and Timbuctoo, without there being a union among Cairo, Baghdad, Damascus, Mecca, and Tunis. It is not possible for any sane person to conceive the possibility of union among Turks, Arabs, Persians, Malayans, and Negroes, while denying unity to the Arabs themselves. If, contrary to fact, the Arab world were more extensive and wider than the Muslim world, it would have been possible to imagine a Muslim union without Arab union, and it would have been permissible to say that Muslim union is easier to realize than Arab union. But as the position is the exact opposite, there is no logical scope whatever for such statements and speculations. We must not forget this truth when we think and speak concerning Muslim unity and Arab unity. The idea of Muslim unity is, it is true, wider and more inclusive than the concept of Arab unity, but it is not possible to advocate Muslim unity without advocating Arab unity. We have, therefore, the right to assert that whoever opposes

Arab unity also opposes Muslim unity. As for him who opposes Arab unity, in the name of Muslim unity or for the sake of Muslim unity, he contradicts the simplest necessities of reason and logic.

Having established this truth, to disagree with which is not logically possible, we ought to notice another truth which is no less important. We must not forget that the expression "unity," in this context, means political unity; and we must constantly remember that the concept of Islamic unity greatly differs from that of Muslim brotherhood. Unity is one thing and affection another, political unity is one thing and agreement on a certain principle another. To advocate Muslim unity, therefore, is different from advocating the improvement of conditions in Islam and different also from advocating an increase in understanding, in affection, and in cooperation among Muslims. We can therefore say that he who talks about the principle of Muslim brotherhood, and discusses the benefits of understanding among the Muslims, does not prove that Muslim unity is possible. Contrariwise, he who denies the possibility of realizing Muslim unity does not deny the principle of Muslim brotherhood or oppose the efforts toward the awakening of the Muslims and understanding among them. What may be said concerning the ideal of brotherhood is not sufficient proof of the possibility of realizing Muslim unity. Further, it is not intelligent or logical to prove the possibility of realizing Muslim unity by quoting the example of Freemasonry or socialism or communism, because the Freemasons do not constitute a political unity and the socialist parties in the different European countries have not combined to form a new state. Even communism itself has not formed a new state, but has taken the place of the Czarist Russian state. We have, therefore, to distinguish quite clearly between the question of Muslim brotherhood and that of Muslim unity, and we must consider directly whether or not it is possible to realize Muslim unity in the political sense.

If we cast a general glance at history and review the influence of religions over the formation of political units, we find that the world religions have not been able to unify peoples speaking different languages, except in the Middle Ages, and that only in limited areas and for a short time. The political unity which the Christian Church sought to bring about did not at any time merge the Orthodox world with the Catholic. Neither did the political unity which the papacy tried to bring about in the Catholic world last for any length of time. So it was also in the Muslim world; the political unity which existed at the beginning of its life was not able to withstand the changes of circumstance for any length of time. Even the 'Abbāsid caliphate, at the height of its power and glory, could not unite all the Muslims under its political banner. Similarly, the lands ruled by this caliphate did not effectively preserve their political unity for very long. Nor was it long after the founding of the caliphate that its control over some of the provinces became symbolic rather than real; it could not prevent the secession of these provinces and their transformation into independent political units. It deserves to be mentioned in this connection that the spread of the Muslim religion in some areas took place after the Muslim caliphate lost effective unity and real power, so much so that in some countries Islam spread in a manner independent of the political authority, at the hands of missionary tradesmen, holy men, and dervishes. In short, the Muslim world, within its present extensive limits, never at any time formed a political unity. If, then, political unity could not be realized in past centuries, when social life was simple and political relations were primitive, when religious customs controlled every aspect of behavior and thought, it will not be possible to realize it in this century, when social life has become complicated, political problems have become intractable, and science and technology have liberated themselves from the control of tradition and religious beliefs.

I know that what I have stated here will displease many doctors of Islam; I know that the indications of history which I have set out above will have no influence over the beliefs of a great many of the men of religion, because they have been accustomed to discuss these matters without paying heed to historical facts or to the geographical picture; nor are they used to distinguishing between the meaning of religious brotherhood and the meaning of political ties. They have been accustomed to confuse the principles of Islamic brotherhood, in its moral sense, and the idea of Islamic unity, in its political sense. I think it useless to try to persuade these people of the falsity of their beliefs, but I think it necessary to ask them to remember what reason and logic require in this respect. Let them maintain their belief in the possibility of realizing Islamic unity, but let them at the same time agree to the necessity of furthering Arab unity, at least as one stage toward the realization of the Islamic unity in which they believe. In any event, let them not oppose the efforts which are being made to bring about Arab unity, on the pretext of serving the Islamic unity which they desire. I repeat here what I have written above: whoever opposes Arab unity, on the pretext of Muslim unity, contradicts the simplest requirements of reason and logic, and I unhesitatingly say that to contradict logic to this extent can be the result only of deceit or of deception. The deceit is that of some separatists who dislike the awakening of the Arab nation and try to arouse religious feeling against the idea of Arab unity, and the deception is that of the simple-minded, who incline to believe whatever is said to them in the name of religion, without realizing what hidden purposes might lurk behind the speeches. I therefore regard it as my duty to draw the attention of all the Muslim Arabs to this important matter and I ask them not to be deceived by the myths of the separatists on this chapter.

Perhaps the strangest and most misleading views that have been expressed regarding Arab unity and Islamic unity are the views of those who say that the idea of Arab unity was created to combat Islamic unity in order to isolate some Islamic countries, the better to exercise continuous power over them. I cannot imagine a view further removed from the realities of history and politics or more contradictory to the laws of reason and logic. The details I have mentioned above concerning the relation of Muslim unity to Arab unity are sufficient, basically, to refute such allegations. Yet I think it advisable to add to these details some observations for further proof and clarity. It cannot be denied that the British, more than any other state, have humored and indulged the Arab movement. This is only because they are more practiced in politics and quicker to understand the psychology of nations and the realities of social life. Before anybody else they realized the hidden powers lying in the Arab idea, and thought it wise, therefore, to humor it somewhat, instead of directly opposing it. This was in order to preserve themselves against the harm they might sustain through it and to make it more advantageous to their interests.

We must understand that British policy is a practical policy, changing with circumstances and always making use of opportunities. We must not forget that it was Great Britain who, many times, saved the Ottoman state, then the depository of the Islamic caliphate, from Russian domination. She it was who halted Egyptian armies in the heart of Anatolia to save the seat of the Muslim caliphate from these victorious troops, and she it was who opposed the union of Egypt with Syria at the time of Muhammad 'Alī. Whoever, then, charges that the idea of Arab unity is a foreign plot utters a greater falsehood than any that has ever been uttered, and he is the victim of the greatest of deceptions. We must know full well that the idea of Arab unity is a natural idea. It has not been artificially started. It is a natural consequence of the existence of the Arab nation itself. It is a social force drawing its vitality from the life of the Arabic language, from the history of the Arab nation, and from the connectedness of the Arab countries. No one can logically pretend that it is the British who created the idea of Arab unity, unless he can prove that it is the British who have created the Arabic language, originating the history of the Arab nation and putting together the geography of the Arab countries. The idea of Arab unity is a natural concept springing from the depths of social nature and not from the artificial views which can be invented by individuals or by states. It remained latent, like many natural and social forces, for many centuries, as a result of many historical factors which cannot be analyzed here. But everything indicates that this period is now at an end, that the movement has come into the open and will manifest itself with ever-increasing power. It will, without any doubt, spread all over the Arab countries, to whom it will bring back their ancient glory and primeval youth; it will indeed bring back what is most fertile, most powerful, and highest in these countries. This ought to be the faith of the enlightened among the speakers of the *dad* [Arabic].

AHMĀD LUTFĪ AL-SAYYID
1872–1963

A disciple of 'Abduh, he studied law and entered government service. He read European authors widely and gave much time to literary and cultural pursuits as editor of *al-Jaridah*. He dabbled in politics for a time as founder of the People's Party but later withdrew. He was director of the National Library and aided the founding of the new Egyptian University, where he was professor of philosophy and later Rector.

Egyptianness

One of our respected scholars was asked, "What is an Egyptian?" His answer, as I was told, was this: An Egyptian is one who recognizes no fatherland other than Egypt. A man who has two fatherlands in the sense that he resides in Egypt and chooses another fatherland to be on the safe side is far from being an Egyptian in the true sense of the word.

Among our forefathers were those who maintained that the land of Islam is the fatherland of all Muslims. However, that is a colonialist formula used to advantage by every colonizing nation that seeks to expand its possessions and to extend its influence daily over neighboring countries. It is a formula quite compatible with that power which conquers lands in the name of religion and wants its individual members to enjoy full national rights in any conquered region. In this way it can unite the various elements in diverse countries in such a way that no one of the conquered nations will violate its covenant, chafe under the supreme power, or aspire to independence and self-rule.

Now, however, the regions of the East have become the object of Western colonialism, and any hope these Eastern nations might have had of colonizing has been thwarted. Their ambitions have been limited to defense; attack is out of the question. Their only wish is to preserve the peace and security of every nation within its territory, for fear that its nationality may be obliterated and its very existence terminated. The greatest desire of every Eastern nation is independence.

In the present situation, the [traditional Islamic] formula has no *raison d'être* because it fits neither the present state of affairs in Islamic nations nor their aspirations. One option remains, to replace this formula by the

From *Ta'ammulāt* (Cairo: Dār al-Ma'ārif, n.d.), pp. 68–71.

only doctrine that is in accord with the aspirations of every Eastern nation which possesses a clearly defined sense of fatherland. That doctrine is nationalism.

Taking this point of view, we are forced to acknowledge that Egyptians comprise both the original people of this Egyptian region and every Ottoman who resides in it and has chosen it as his fatherland in preference to other Ottoman lands. This is not a new doctrine, it has been part of Egyptian law for a long time.

These Egyptians, first and foremost, have the right to benefit from Egypt and, similarly, they are subject to those national obligations prescribed by law and imposed by custom. Their love for Egypt must be free from all conflicting associations, and their self-sacrifice in its service must take precedence over every other consideration. Their words and deeds must demonstrate that they have no home other than Egypt and no tribe except the Egyptians. These are the Egyptians, not those who think that Egypt is a field they can exploit while there is opportunity, taking its spoils while avoiding its liabilities. Neither are those who picture the fatherland in commercial terms without any trace of national sentiment to be considered true Egyptians. It is difficult for Egypt to take such people as its sons and place its present concerns and future aspirations on their shoulders.

Let no one think that we are calling for any division among the various elements which form the bloc of the Egyptian population. On the contrary, we are calling for an Egyptian community of interests just as we have done previously. We appeal to those who are dissatisfied with an Egyptian nationality acquired by residence in Egypt, not to abandon their affiliation with this noble nationality. They reside bodily in Egypt, yet their minds and hearts often long for another fatherland which shaped their accent but begrudged them its bounty. We appeal to them that, as long as they remain Egyptians, they suppress their propensity for anything other than Egypt because patriotism, which is love of fatherland, does not permit such ties and because the progress of Egypt requires their superior intellects and strong arms.

They will say that there is nothing new in what we relate but that we are restating national priorities which we should have finished with long ago. Yes, we agree, but these national priorities, sad to say, have not been acted on. We have some well-known examples in mind, which indicate in a general way the faulty understanding of Egyptian patriotism and the decadence of Egyptian aspirations.

There are many among us who should examine themselves, gaze deep into their consciences, and think over what they say in their sessions and what they actually do; then they would see that they cherish their affiliation to Syria, or Turkey, or some Arab country more than their tie to Egypt. Who can label this propensity and its repercussions allegiance to

Egypt? And without stretching toleration, who can call those who love other than Egypt Egyptians?

Our Egyptian-ness demands that our fatherland be our *qibla*[1] and that we not turn our face to any other. We are happy that this truth is well known by most Egyptians and that it is about to become general among all Egyptians without exception.

1. *qibla:* the direction which one turns in prayer, i.e. Mecca for Muslims. [Ed.]

TĀHĀ HUSAYN
1889–1973

A childhood accident rendered him totally blind, but he persisted in studies, going on to al-Azhar and attending lectures at the new Egyptian University in Cairo. He became a member of the circle which formed around Lutfi al-Sayyid and the newspaper *al-Jarīdah*. In 1915 he went to France for studies for four years and returned to front stage in the literary and academic life in Egypt. He was a university administrator and later Minister of Education. His ideas were precocious for Egypt of the early twentieth century: in 1926 his book rejecting pre-Islamic poetry as forgery caused a scandal and was taken off the book stands, and in 1938 his *Future of Culture in Egypt* was equally provocative.

The Future of Culture in Egypt

I do not like illusions. I am persuaded that it is only God who can create something from nothing. I therefore believe that the new Egypt will not come into being except from the ancient, eternal Egypt. I believe further that the new Egypt will have to be built on the great old one, and that the future of culture in Egypt will be an extension, a superior version, of the humble, exhausted, and feeble present. For this reason we should think of the future of culture in Egypt in the light of its remote past and near present. We do not wish, nor are we able, to break the link between ourselves and our forefathers. To the degree that we establish our future life upon our past and present we shall avoid most of the dangers caused by excesses and miscalculations deriving from illusions and dreams.

At the outset we must answer this fundamental question: is Egypt of the East or of the West? Naturally, I mean East or West in the cultural, not the geographical sense. It seems to me that there are two distinctly different and bitterly antagonistic cultures on the earth. Both have existed since time immemorial, the one in Europe, the other in the Far East.

We may paraphrase the question as follows: Is the Egyptian mind Eastern or Western in its imagination, perception, comprehension and judgment? . . .

The meaning of all this is very clear: the Egyptian mind had no serious

From *The Future of Culture in Egypt,* trans. S. Glazer (Washington, D.C.: American Council of Learned Societies, 1954), sections 2–5, 7, 10.

contact with the Far Eastern mind; nor did it live harmoniously with the Persian mind. The Egyptian mind has had regular, peaceful, and mutually beneficial relations only with the Near East and Greece. In short, it has been influenced from earliest times by the Mediterranean Sea and the various peoples living around it. . . . I clearly, indeed intuitively, understand our consciousness of the positive relationships existing between us and the Near East not only because of identity of language and religion, but also because of geographical propinquity as well as similarity of origin and historical evolution. When we go beyond the Near East, however, these factors no longer obtain, except for religion and temporary considerations of a political or economic nature.

History shows that religious and linguistic unity do not necessarily go hand in hand with political unity, nor are they the props on which states rely. The Muslims realized this a long time ago. They established their states on the basis of practical interests, abandoning religion, language, and race as exclusively determining factors before the end of the second century A. H. (eighth century of the Christian Era). . . .

Egypt was one of the earliest among the Islamic states to recover her ancient, unforgotten personality. History tells us that she violently opposed the Persians and Macedonians, the latter being eventually absorbed into the local population. Egypt yielded to the Western and Eastern Roman rulers only under duress and had to be kept under continuous martial law. History further relates that she acquiesced most reluctantly even to Arab domination. The spirit of resistance and rebelliousness that followed the conquest did not subside until she regained her independent personality under Ibn Ṭūlūn and the dynasties that followed him.

From earliest times Muslims have been well aware of the now universally acknowledged principle that a political system and a religion are different things, that a constitution and a state rest, above everything else, on practical foundations. . . . Islam arose and spread over the world. Egypt was receptive and hastened at top speed to adopt it as her religion and to make the Arabic of Islam her language. Did that obliterate her original mentality? Did that make her an Eastern nation in the present meaning of the term? Not at all! Europe did not become Eastern nor did the nature of the European mind change because Christianity, which originated in the East, flooded Europe and absorbed the other religions. If modern European philosophers and thinkers deem Christianity to be an element of the European mind, they must explain what distinguishes Christianity from Islam; for both were born in the geographical East, both issued from one noble source and were inspired by the one God in whom Easterners and Westerners alike believe. . . .

The essence and source of Islam are the essence and source of Christianity. The connection of Islam with Greek philosophy is identical to that of

Christianity. Whence, then, comes the difference in the effect of these two faiths on the creation of the mind that mankind inherited from the people of the Near East and Greece? . . .

No, there are no intellectual or cultural differences to be found among the peoples who grew up around the Mediterranean and were influenced by it. Purely political and economic circumstances made the inhabitants of one shore prevail against those of the other. The same factors led them to treat each other now with friendliness, now with enmity.

The development of modern communications has served to link Egypt closely to Europe, as indeed they linked all parts of the world. Although the renaissance of Egypt, which began early in the nineteenth century, is still unclear in some respects, its modern orientation is unmistakable. As far as the materialistic side of life, particularly among the upper classes, is concerned, it is purely European. The other classes more or less resemble their European counterparts, depending only on the capabilities and wealth of the various individuals and groups. We adopted and still retain the European attitude toward the external manifestations and embellishments of existence. Whether we did so consciously and deliberately or not, I do not know, but the fact remains that there is no power on earth capable of preventing us from enjoying life the way they do.

Like the Europeans, we have built railroads, telegraph lines, and telephones. We learned from Europe to sit at the table and eat with a knife and fork. We wear the same kind of clothes. All this we did without discrimination, without examination to know what is actually bad and what is unsuitable for us. So far has the European ideal become our ideal that we now measure the material progress of all individuals and groups by the amount of borrowing from Europe. Moreover, even the intangible aspects of life, surface differences notwithstanding, show the same influence. We did not hesitate, for example, to adopt the European system of government; and if we criticize ourselves for something, this is simply that we have been slow in following European administrative and political practices. Our political life in recent times has been in a state of confusion between absolute government and limited government, for which we have no precedent in our Middle Ages. I mean that our modern absolute government was affected by the European absolutism prevalent before the rise of democracy; in similar fashion our form of limited government was shaped by the systems of limited government also existing in Europe.

Those who sought to impose arbitrary rule on modern Egypt patterned themselves upon Louis XIV rather than 'Abd al-Hamīd. Proponents of a form of limited government based on justice but without the people's participation accepted curbs to their power that were European not Eastern. They set up national courts and enacted civil laws in conformity with European rather than Islamic codes. Their administrative, fiscal, and eco-

nomic statutes were almost wholly Western. They sought no guidance
from the procedures of the medieval Muslim kings and caliphs. The cabinet, governmental ministries, and the several administrative agencies connected with them are European in origin, spirit, and form. Until the modern era the Muslims had never heard of them.

Certain old Islamic institutions, to be sure, have survived because of
their more or less close association with religion, but even these have
changed greatly, at least in form, under the strong influence of their European counterparts. Take the *Sharī'a* courts, for example; there is no doubt
that if a Muslim judge were to be resurrected today he would find many of
the legal procedures unfamiliar. Although we have kept the institution of
the *waqf* (endowed foundation), we set up without delay a special ministry
to administer it in a way that I believe the ancients would neither recognize
nor approve if they were returned to life. Most of us, however, feel that
this ministry is still too backward for the times. Some would like to abolish or change the institution of *waqf* itself in conformity with modern
economic requirements.

We have also retained al-Azhar University, which has been in a serious
condition since before the time of Ismā'īl. The crisis, in my opinion, will
not end soon, but will continue until the struggle between the old and the
new reaches a state of balance. The available evidence indicates, however,
that the institution is proceeding very rapidly in the direction of the new.
Indeed, if God were to resurrect the Azhar scholars who lived at the
beginning of the modern era, they would beg Him in all sincerity to return
them to their graves so that they would not have to look upon the great
innovations that have already been introduced into the university.

The dominant and undeniable fact of our times is that day by day we are
drawing closer to Europe and becoming an integral part of her, literally
and figuratively. This process would be much more difficult than it is if the
Egyptian mind were basically different from the European.

This is not all. Since the world war we have taken such decisive steps
forward that any attempt to retrace them or abrogate the rights won
would, I am certain, be violently resisted by many Egyptians. Which one of
us is willing to see Egypt retreat from the progress she had made toward
democracy, or who would go back to a system that did not center about a
constitutional representative government? This form of government, although adopted from Europe, became almost immediately a vital and
inseparable part of our being. Anyone urging Egyptians to return to the
way of life characteristic of Pharaonic, Greco-Roman, or early Islamic
times would be ridiculed by the people, including the arch-conservatives
and those who loathe any tampering whatsoever with our ancient heritage.
We must also realize, too, that our signatures on the treaties by which we
gained our independence and rid ourselves of the capitulations have clearly

obliged us to follow the Europeans in government, administration, and legislation.

Our educational system is also based on exclusively European methods, which are applied through our primary, secondary, and higher schools. If for the sake of argument we suppose that the mentality of our fathers and grandfathers may have been Eastern and essentially antithetic to the Europeans, we must see that our children are quite different. We have been putting into their heads modes of thought and ideas that are almost completely European. I cannot conceive of anyone seriously advocating abandonment of the European system in our schools and revival of techniques used by our ancestors. As a matter of fact, the Europeans borrowed the methods that prevailed in the Islamic world during the Middle Ages. They did then just what we are doing now. It is essentially a matter of time. They began their new life in the fifteenth century, while we were delayed by the Ottoman Turks until the nineteenth century. If God has preserved us from the Ottoman conquest, we should have remained in unbroken touch with Europe and shared in her renaissance. This would certainly have fashioned a different kind of civilization from the one in which we are now living.

However, God has bestowed on us a boon to compensate for our misfortune and calamities. The world has struggled for hundreds of years to attain the present stage of progress. It is within our power to reach it in a short time. Woe to us if we do not seize the opportunity! . . . Obviously then I am pleading for a selective approach to European culture, not wholesale and indiscriminate borrowing. . . .

HASAN AL-BANNĀ'
1906–1949

After studies at a teachers' training college, he went to Dār al-'Ulūm in Cairo. He was fired with religious zeal as a student, and once he began his career as a teacher, he was not long in founding the Muslim Brotherhood (1928), which soon became one of the best organized and largest of the political groups in Egypt. He preached a return to the sources of Islam and a rejection of currents from abroad. The military arm of the Muslim Brothers was implicated in some political assassinations; this led to Hasan al-Bannā' 's assassination in 1949. The Muslim Brothers are still a strong force throughout the Arab world.

The New Renaissance

When we observe the evolution in the political, social, and moral spheres of the lives of nations and peoples, we note that the Islamic world—and, naturally, in the forefront, the Arab world—gives to its rebirth an Islamic flavor. This trend is ever-increasing. Until recently, writers, intellectuals, scholars, and governments glorified the principles of European civilization, gave themselves a Western tint, and adopted a European style and manner; today, on the contrary, the wind has changed, and reserve and distrust have taken their place. Voices are raised proclaiming the necessity for a return to the principles, teachings, and ways of Islam, and, taking into account the situation, for initiating the reconciliation of modern life with these principles, as a prelude to a final "Islamization."

Causes

This development worries a good number of governments and Arab powers, which, having lived during the past generations in a state of mind that had retained from Islam only lessons of fanaticism and inertia, regarded the Muslims only as weak drudges or as nations easily exploitable by colonialism. In trying to understand the new movement [the Brotherhood], these governments have produced all sorts of possible interpretations: "It is the result," said some, "of the growth of extremist organiza-

From Kemal H. Karpat, ed., *Political and Social Thought in the Contemporary Middle East* (New York: Praeger, 1968), pp. 118–22.

tions and fanatical groups." Others explained that it was a reaction to present-day political and economic pressures, of which the Islamic nations had become aware. Finally, others said, "It is only a means whereby those seeking government or other honors may achieve renown and position."

Now all these reasons are, in our opinion, as far as possible from the truth; for this new movement can only be the result of the following three factors, which we will now examine.

The Failure of the West

The first of the three is the failure of the social principles on which the civilization of the Western nations has been built. The Western way of life—bounded in effect on practical and technical knowledge, discovery, invention, and the flooding of world markets with mechanical products—has remained incapable of offering to men's minds a flicker of light, a ray of hope, a grain of faith, or of providing anxious persons the smallest path toward rest and tranquillity. Man is not simply an instrument among others. Naturally, he has become tired of purely materialistic conditions and desires some spiritual comfort. But the materialistic life of the West could only offer him as reassurance a new materialism of sin, passion, drink, women, noisy gatherings, and showy attractions which he had come to enjoy. Man's hunger grows from day to day: he wants to free his spirit, to destroy this materialistic prison and find space to breathe the air of faith and consolation.

Perfection of Islam

The second factor—the decisive factor in the circumstances—is the discovery by Islamic thinkers of the noble, honorable, moral, and perfect content of the principles and rules of this religion, which is infinitely more accomplished, more pure, more glorious, more complete, and more beautiful than all that has been discovered up till now by social theorists and reformers. For a long time, Muslims neglected all this, but once God had enlightened their thinkers and they had compared the social rules of their religion with what they had been told by the greatest sociologists and the cleverest leading theorists, they noted the wide gap and the great distance between a heritage of immense value on one side and the conditions experienced on the other. Then, Muslims could not but do justice to the spirit and the history of their people, proclaiming the value of this heritage and inviting all peoples—nonpracticing Muslims or non-Muslims—to follow the sacred path that God had traced for them and to hold to a straight course.

Type of Development

The third factor is the development of social conditions between the two murderous world wars (which involved all the world powers and monopolized the minds of regimes, nations, and individuals) which resulted in a set of principles of reform and social organization that certain powers, in deciding to put them into practice, have taken as an instructional basis. These principles have become the prey of change and transformation, in fact subject to disappearance and ruin. Muslim thinkers looked on, observed, and returned to what they already possessed in their own right—the great Book of God, the brilliant manifest example of their Prophet and their glorious history. There was nothing of value they could accredit to any existing regime that could not be already found inspiring their thought and conduct and already inscribed in Islamic social organization. There was no blemish against which the social organization of a watchful Islam could not guard [its people] by showing them its fearful consequences.

The world has long been ruled by democratic systems, and man has everywhere glorified and honored the conquests of democracy: freedom of the individual, freedom of nations, justice and freedom of thought, justice for the human soul with freedom of action and will, justice for the peoples who became the source of power. Victory at the end of World War I reinforced these thoughts, but men were not slow to realize that their collective liberty had not come intact out of the chaos, that their individual liberty was not safe from anarchy, and that the government of the people had not in many cases freed society from camouflaged dictatorship that destroyed responsibility without limiting jurisdiction. Quite the contrary, vice and violence led to the breaking loose of nations and peoples, to the overthrow of collective organization and family structure, and to the setting up of dictatorial regimes.

Thus, German Nazism and Italian Fascism rose to the fore; Mussolini and Hitler led their two peoples to unity, order, recovery, power, and glory. In record time, they ensured internal order at home and, through force, made themselves feared abroad. Their regimes gave real hope, and also gave rise to thoughts of steadfastness and perseverance and the reuniting of different, divided men around the words "chief" and "order." In their resolutions and speeches, the Führer and the Duce began to frighten the world and to upset their epoch.

What happened then? It became evident that in a powerful and well-knit regime, where the wishes of the individual were based on those of their chiefs, the mistakes of the chiefs became those of the regime, which shared also in their acts of violence, their decline, and their fall; then, everything was at an end, all had been cut down as in a single day, but not until the world had lost in a second war thousands of men, the flower of her youth, and masses of wealth and material.

The star of socialism and Communism, symbol of success and victory, shone with an increasing brilliance; Soviet Russia was at the head of the collectivist camp. She launched her message and, in the eyes of the world, demonstrated a system which had been modified several times in thirty years. The democratic powers—or, to use a more precise expression, the colonialist powers, the old ones worn out, the new ones full of greed—took up a position to stem the current. The struggle intensified, in some places openly, in others under cover, and nations and peoples, perplexed, hesitated at the crossroads, not knowing which way was best; among them were the nations of Islam and the peoples of the Qur'ān; the future, whatever the circumstances, is in the hands of God, the decision with history, and immortality with the most worthy.

This social evolution and violent, hard struggle stirred the minds of Muslim thinkers; the parallels and the prescribed comparisons led to a healthy conclusion: to free themselves from the existing state of affairs, to allow the necessary return of the nations and peoples to Islam.

The Three Regimes and Prayer

In a whimsical moment, I happened to say to my audience at a meeting—which, thanks to God, was a complete success—that this Islamic prayer which we perform five times a day is nothing but a daily training in practical social organization uniting the features of the Communist regime with those of the dictatorial and democratic regimes. Astonished, my questioners demanded an explanation. "The greatest value of the Communist regime," I said, "is the reinforcement of the notion of equality, the condemnation of class distinction, and the struggle against the claim to property, source of these differences." Now this lesson is present in the mind of the Muslim; he is perfectly conscious of it and his spririt is filled with it the moment he enters the mosque; yes, the moment he enters, he realizes that the mosque belongs to God and not to anyone of his creatures; he knows himself to be the equal of all those who are there, whoever they may be; here there are no great, no small, no high, no low, no more groups or classes. And when the muezzin calls, "Now is the hour of prayer," they form an equal mass, a compact block, behind the *imām*.[1] None bows unless the *imām* bows, none prostrates himself unless the *imām* prostrates himself; none moves or remains motionless unless following the *imām's* example. That is the principal merit of the dictatorial regime: unity and order in the will under the appear-

---

1. The *imām* referred to here is a leader of prayer, and should not be confused with the Shī'īte *Imām,* who is the supreme head of the community.

ance of equality. The *imām* himself is in any case limited by the teachings and rules of the prayer, and if he stumbles or makes a mistake in his reading or in his actions, all those behind him—young boys, old men, or women at prayer—have the imperative duty to tell him of his error in order to put him back on the right road during the prayer, and the *imām* himself is bound absolutely to accept this good advice and, forsaking his error, return to reason and truth. That is what is most appealing in democracy.

How, therefore, can these regimes be superior to Islam, which astonishingly unites all their merits and avoids all their sins? "If this message came from some other than God, many contradictions would be found in it" (Qur'ān).

No Incentive for Trouble

As I have said, [the people of] the West—and with them those who are blind—are worried by this development, which they consider serious, since they see themselves forced to combat it by every means, being less accustomed to finding themselves facing such a situation than to seeing the success of their reactionary principles on the less developed nations, in contempt of all the rules of civilization followed by cultivated and orderly peoples; judgment steeped in error and the flagrant suppression of rights can be seen as clearly as daylight. Here, our intention is to demonstrate to the West two points:

1. Demonstration of the excellence of Islamic principles of collective organization, and their superiority over everything known to man until now, these principles being:

   a. Brotherly love: condemnation of hatred and fanaticism.
   b. Peace: Error is committed by the misguided thinking on the legitimacy of the Holy War.
   c. Liberty: Error is committed by those who suspect Islam of tolerating slavery and interfering with liberty.
   d. Social justice: obvious character of the Islamic theory of power and class structure.
   e. Happiness: manifest error in the appreciation of the reality of abstinence.
   f. Family: matters concerning the rights of women, number of wives, and repudiation.
   g. Work and profit: matters concerning the different kinds of profit, and error in the appreciation of the fact of relying on God.
   h. Knowledge: Error is committed by those who accuse Islam of encouraging ignorance and apathy.

    i. Organization and determination of duties: Error is committed by those who see in the nature of Islam a source of imperfection and indolence.

    j. Piety: the reality of faith, and the merit and reward attached to it.

2. Demonstration of the following facts:

    a. For the good of man in general, Muslims must move toward a return to their religion.

    b. Islam will find in this return her principal strength on earth.

    c. Far from receiving impetus from a blind fanaticism, this movement will be inspired by a strong regard for the values of Islam which correspond fully to what modern thought has discovered as most noble, sound, and tested in society. It is God who says what is true and who shows the way.

'ABD AL-RAHMĀN AL-BAZZĀZ
1913–197?

Lawyer, historian, and man of politics, he was Dean of the Law
School at Baghdad in 1955, and in 1965 became Prime Minister.
After the Ba'th coup in 1968, he fell out of favor, spent a few
years in prison and died in exile. His speeches and writings
emphasize the accord between Arabism and Islam

Islam and Arab Nationalism

Before I begin, I had better explain the significance of the title of this talk
and limit its scope somewhat. . . . All I aim at this evening is to define the
relation of Arab nationalism, insofar as it is a 'belief and a movement," to
the Islamic Sharī'a,[1] insofar as it is "a religion, a civilization, and a philosophy of life". . . . The question is: Is it possible for one of us to be a
loyal nationalist and a sincere Muslim, at one and the same time? Is there
a fundamental contradiction between Arab nationalism, in its precise scientific sense, and true Muslim feeling? And does the acceptance of the one
entail the rejection of the other?

I think the apparent contradiction between Islam and Arab nationalism
which is still present in the minds of many people is, in the first place, due
to misunderstanding, misrepresentation, and misinterpretation, involving
both Islam and Arab nationalism.

The misunderstanding of Islam is due to the wrong significance attributed to the word "religion." We are influenced here—as a result of the
intellectual imperialism under which a group of us still labor—by the
Western concepts which restrict religion within narrow limits not extend-
ing beyond worship, ritual, and the spiritual beliefs, which govern a man
in his behavior, in relation to his God and to his brother man, in his
capacity of an individual independent of society. Islam does not admit this
narrow view of religion, but opposes it and the purpose it serves to the
utmost. Many people still believe that Islam is similar to Christianity or
Buddhism, and consists in devotional beliefs and exercises, ethical rules
and no more. But, in fact, Islam, in its precise sense, is a social order, a
philosophy of life, a system of economic principles, a rule of government,

1. Sharī'a: Islamic law. [Ed.]

From Sylvia G. Haim, ed., *Arab Nationalism* (Berkeley: University of California Press, 1962),
pp. 172–76, 178–88.

in addition to its being a religious creed in the narrow Western sense. Some of the Western thinkers have come to realize the wide difference between the comprehensive nature of Islam and the limited nature of Christianity; Christianity pays more attention to the individual, as such, and to his spiritual purity, than to the individual as part of a whole and to his relation to this whole. This was inevitable because of the difference in the nature of the two religions, their circumstances, and the periods in which they were revealed. Christ was a member of the Israelite society which, under the authority of the Roman state, was devoid of any active share in the existing political organization. But the Prophet—Peace be on Him—was a leader and a statesman, as much as he was a social reformer and a religious teacher. . . . Because Islam is a political religion . . . it does not therefore necessarily contradict Arab nationalism, unless their political aims differ. But this is unthinkable, as we shall see later.

Just as Islam has been misunderstood, so has Arab nationalism. The reason for this may be that some think that nationalism can be built only upon racial appeal or racial chauvinism, and that it would therefore be contrary to the universal nature of Islam. The exaggeration of some nationalists has undoubtedly been one of the important reasons for this misunderstanding; and no doubt what some Umayyad governors, princes, and walis have done in their enthusiastic tribal chauvinism and their racial propaganda was contrary to the nature of Islam. But the Arab nationalism in which we believe, and for which we call, is based, on our national pact stipulates, not on racial appeal but on linguistic, historical, cultural, and spiritual ties, and on fundamental vital interests. In this respect, too, there is no contradiction between Arab nationalism and Islam. Many young people have greatly misunderstood Arab nationalism. They know something of the history of the West, of its national revivals, and have found there obvious signs of contradiction between Christianity and these national movements; this is, of course, natural in Western societies. The Church, which used to claim great spiritual power over all the Christians, looked askance on all political movements which aimed at shaking off ecclesiastical authority. In other words, European society gave allegiance to two fundamental authorities, the spiritual authority of the Pope and the temporal authority of the Emperor.

This dualism, although it has come to us in some stages of our slow social evolution, is not known in true Islam, where it is not admitted. On the contrary, the unity of creed has led to the unity of life, and the unity of life has made the caliph of the Muslims the leader in prayer, the leader of the army, and the political head at the same time. The opposition of German or Italian nationalism to Christiantiy, for instance, does not therefore necessarily mean that Arab nationalism should be opposed to Islam. It befits us to remember here the great difference between the relation of

Christianity to the West, and the relation of Islam to the Arabs. Christianity is a religion introduced to the West. It arose out of the spirituality of the East, and is in complete opposition to the nature of the Teutonic tribes in Germany and the Celtic in France; that is why the German or the French nationalist finds great difficulty in reconciling it with the elements of the nationality which he cherishes, and realizes that Christianity has not found it possible to penetrate to the roots of Germanic and Celtic life. The opposite is true of Islam and its influence over Arab society and the Arab nation, as we shall explain in some measure. . . .

The correct scientific explanation of the emergence of the Arabs in the first period of Islam is that it was one of the waves out of the Arabian Peninsula, although it was the most venerable of these waves and the most illustrious in the history of the Arabs themselves and in the history of the whole of mankind. There is no contradiction at all between our sincere Muslim feeling and our holding precious the ancient Arab civilizations. . . . Islam abandoned only what was bad in our customs and what was false in our laws and traditions. Islam holds, as the noble *hadīth* has it, that men are metals like gold and silver, those among them who were the best in the *jāhilyya* remain the best in Islam. It would not have been possible for the Arabs to achieve such a revival and accomplish such tremendous actions, in war, politics, legislation, literature, art, sociology, and the other aspects of life, in such a short time, if their metal had not been pure and their abilities latent in them from long ago, their nature creative and their spirit strong and true. There could not shine among the Arabs, in one or two generations, men like Abū-Bakr, 'Umar, 'Alī, Ibn Ubayda, Sa'd, Khālid, Ibn 'Abbās, Abū-Dharr, and Ibn Mas'ūd, or women like Khadīja, Fātima, 'Ā' isha, Asma', al-Khansa, and many other men and women of genius of that age, had the Arabs not inherited an ancient and continuous civilization and had they not been prepared by their instinct to create and build and renovate. The fact that the Prophet Muhammad was Arab was not a matter of chance; a genius, he belonged to a nation of great abilities and qualities. . . .

It is clear form all this that the Arabs are the backbone of Islam. They were the first to be addressed in the verses of Revelation; they were the *Muhājirīn* and the *Ansār;* their swords conquered countries and lands, and on the whole they are as "Umar has described them in a saying of his: "Do not attack the Arabs and humiliate them for they are the essence of Islam."

After this clear exposition of the intellectual problems and the factors that contribute to the mistaken belief that there is a contradiction between the principles of Islam and Arab nationalism, it befits us to define the meaning of nationalism, more particularly of Arab nationalism and of its assumptions, and to look into these assumptions in order to see which are accepted by Islam and which, if any, are rejected.

Nationalism is a political and social idea which aims, in the first place, to unify each group of mankind and to make it obey one political order. The factors and the assumptions of nationalism are varied, and we do not intend to analyze them in this lecture. But we can assert that modern nationalism is based on language, history, literature, customs, and qualities. On the whole, the ties that bind individuals together and make them into a nation are both intellectual and material. If we examine these assumptions carefully and inquire into the position of Islam toward each of them, we find a great similarity, and sometimes complete agreement, between what Arab nationalism teaches and what is affirmed by Islam. Language, then, is the primary tenet of our national creed; it is the soul of our Arab nation and the primary aspect of its life. The nation that loses its language is destined to disappear and perish. It is the good fortune of the Arabs that their language is not only a national duty but also a religous one, and the influence of Islam on its propagation and preservation is very great. . . . Moreover, as we have explained above, the Arabs had a glorious history before Islam, and their history is even more glorious and of greater moment after Islam; the Muslim Arab, when he exalts his heroes, partakes of two emotions, that of the pious Muslim and that of the proud nationalist.

In fact, the most glorious pages of Muslim history are the pages of Arab Muslim history, as the Western historians themselves admit. . . .

As for Arabic literature which is the result of Arab feeling and emotion all through the ages, its greatest and most venerable parts came from Islam, and indeed, the Qur'ān itself, in addition to being a book of direction, is the most awesome example of the elevated prose which the Arab, irrespective of his religion, exalts. How I wish the youth especially would read a small original book, *Descriptive Technique in the Qur'ān,* by Sayyid Qutb to see the artistic beauty of the style of the Qur'ān. Who can belittle the influence of the Qur'ān on Arabic literature? As for pre-Islamic poetry, and especially descriptive and wisdom verse, there is in most of it nothing which contradicts the spirit of Islam.

The fourth element in Arab nationalism consists of "the good Arab customs and qualities." Here, undoubtedly, there is similarity, not to say complete identity, between the ethical ideal of Arab nationalism and that prescribed by Islam. . . . We do not pretend to say that all the pre-Islamic customs of the Arabs were good, but we maintain that Islam has confirmed all that was best in Arab character. In our national call for exalting the Arab character, we mean those polished virtues which elevate man and make of him a being worthy of the description "polite."

Let us leave the Arab factors aside and examine nationalism as a political movement working to unite the Arabs and to give them self-government. The national movement is "democratic," "socialist," "popular," and "coöperative." Islam, although it did not lay down in detail the organization of government, requires consultation, and does, without any doubt, accept completely democratic organization. Its financial legislation and juristic principles are, in essence, socialist; Sayyid Qutb has succeeded in explaining this in his book *Social Justice in Islam*. It is enough to remember something of the life of the Prophet and of the caliphs, to realize the extent of the coöperative and the popular spirit of Islam. The position being such, the government for which we call does not in any way contradict Islam.

But to say this is not to imply a call for Pan-Islamism. To say that Islam does not contradict the Arab national spirit is one thing, and to make propaganda for Pan-Islamism is another. Pan-Islamism, in its precise and true meaning, aims to form a comprehensive political organization which all the Muslims must obey. This organization, although it may be desired by all the pious Muslims, is not possible in practice, for many reasons— geographical, political, social—or, at least, it is not possible under the present conditions, even if we agreed to limit this union to the parts of the Muslim homeland which are contiguous. And even if we assumed that these parts could be united, then the unification of the parts which speak the same language, inherit the same literature, and have the same history, is more urgently needed and more worthy of consideration; it is not natural to expect the union of Iraq with Iran or Afghanistan, for instance, before Syria and Jordan are united. A view contrary to this is nonsense and deserves no answer. It follows, therefore, that the call to unite the Arabs— and this is the clearest and most important objective of Arab nationalism—is the practical step which must precede the call for Pan-Islamism. It is strange, however, to find that some of those who call themselves supporters of Pan-Islamism in the Arab countries are the most violent opponents of Pan-Arabism. If they would understand things as they are and would appreciate matters properly, if they did not follow mere emotion, they would admit that their call is misplaced, until the first aim of the Arab nationalists is fulfilled, namely the erection of a collective organization for the Arabs in Asia and Africa.

The conclusion is that no fundamental contradiction or clear opposition exists between Arab nationalism and Islam. The nearest analogy for the relation between them is that of the general to the particular. If we wanted to represent that relationship geometrically, we can imagine Islam and Arabism as two circles overlapping in the greater part of their surface, and in what remains outside the area that is common to the two circles the two are not in fundamental opposition to each other. This is a truth which we must realize, and it befits the Arabs to rejoice in this great good fortune, that their nationalism does not contradict their religion; the Muslim Turk, for instance, who wants to glory in his nationalism, finds an insoluble difficulty in reconciling this sentiment with his sincere religious feeling. His national feeling requires him to be proud of his language and to purify it of other foreign languages; this may drive him to belittle Arabic, which is the flowing source from which Turkish language and literature drew from the earliest days. And if he wants to exalt the glorious actions and the heroes of the past, this will drive him, in most cases, to feel that the Muslim Arabs were strangers to him and that they were, in spite of external appearances, his real colonizers, mentally, spiritually, and culturally; the nationalist Muslim Arab will not often encounter this kind of difficulty.

I do not know whether it is necessary for me to say that our call for Arab nationalism and for a comprehensive Arab being does not, under any circumstances, make us antagonistic to the non-Arab Muslims; for, as our national pact defines it, we consider the group of the Islamic peoples the nearest of all other groups to us; we see in this group a great force which we cherish, and we work to strengthen the ties with it and to coöperate with it. Our relation to the non-Arab Muslims who inhabit the Arab homeland is a brotherly one, for they are the brothers of the Arabs and have all the rights and all the duties of the Arabs. There is not in our nationalism a call to persecute any of the human races; on the contrary, there is no empty national arrogance nor blind racial chauvinism in it. When we take pride in our great actions and cherish our nationality, we want to inspire our nation to reach the place which it deserves among the peoples and the nations of the earth. This is a natural right, accepted by all religions, and recognized by the principles of justice. there is in it no feeling of superiority over others and no desire to oppress other races.

It also befits us to make it clear that there is nothing in this national call of ours which need exercise the non-Muslims among the Arabs or diminish their rights as good compatriots. Chauvinism, in all its aspects and forms, is incompatible with the nature of the Arabs; the non-Muslim Arabs used to enjoy all their rights under the shadow of the Arab state, from the earliest times, and the scope open to them was wide. The loyal nationalists among the Arab Christians realize this and know that Islam and the civilization which accompanied it are an indivisible part of our national heritage, and they must, as nationalists, cherish it as their brother Muslims cherish it.

I realize indeed that this talk of mine and tens of other better ones on this subject will not be enough to dispel all the common myths and mistakes about the meaning of Arab nationalism and Islam, and will not succeed in removing all the illusions which assume the existence of contradictions between the two. What those harmful pictures and wrong explanations, what past centuries have left, cannot be erased or effaced if we do not realize the three following matters:

First. We must free ourselves from the intellectual power of the West and its imported concepts, and we must think independently and with originality about our problems, affairs, and history. We must abandon false standards in intellectual and social matters, because the difference of the borrowed concepts and the variation in the factors and conditions will lead us to mistaken results and false judgments. We must become intellectually independent and consider things objectively; we must not borrow from the West, or when we do we must borrow and reject after a careful examination and a full and complete comparison.

Second. We must work earnestly and sincerely to present anew our nation's past and to write our history in a correct scientific manner, in order to eradicate these distorted pictures and to put a stop to these iniquitous judgments, to tear out those black pages which the pens of prejudiced intriguers have drawn. . . .

Third. Last but not least, we must look to Islam, which we cherish so much and which we believe to be the reflection of the Arab soul and its spiritual source which does not exhaust itself. We must look at it as a whole, devoid of its communal and sectarian character, the Book of God and his Sunna flowing out of its clear and original sources, as our ancient ancestors used to understand it before some backward Muslims burdened it with what there remained in their subconsious of the influence of Zoroastrianism, of Buddhism, of the Israelite traditions, of Roman and Greek sophistry. We must receive it straight from its clear Arab environment, not mixed in an imaginary international environment, and not weighed down by the chains of symbolic Sufism or burdened by the dead hand of a petrified clergy.

MUHAMMAD IQBĀL
1875–1938

No other single person has captured the minds and imaginations of Muslims in India-Pakistan as has Iqbāl. After an early classical Islamic education, he studied at Cambridge and Munich, earning a doctorate in philosophy as well as a law degree. Conversant with Western philosophical and scientific thought, Iqbāl advocated a fundamental rethinking of Islamic thought as reflected in his *The Reconstruction of Religious Thought* in Islam. A prolific author, his poetry and prose touched every area of Muslim life—religion, politics, and society.

A Separate Muslim State
in the Subcontinent

What, then, is the problem and its implications? Is religion a private affair? Would you like to see Islam, as a moral and political idea, meeting the same fate in the world of Islam as Christianity has already met in Europe? Is it possible to retain Islam as an ethical ideal and to reject it as a polity in favour of national polities in which religious attitude is not permitted to play any part? This question becomes of special importance in India where the Muslims happen to be in minority. The proposition that religion is a private individual experience is not surprising on the lips of a European. In Europe the conception of Christianity as a monastic order, renouncing the world of matter and fixing its gaze entirely on the world of spirit, led by a logical process of thought to the view embodied in this proposition. The nature of the Prophet's religious experience, as disclosed in the Qur'ān, however, is wholly different. It is not mere experience in the sense of a purely biological event, happening inside the experient and necessitating no reactions on its social environment. It is individual experience creative of a social order. Its immediate outcome is the fundamentals of a polity with implicit legal concepts whose civic significance cannot be belittled merely because their origin is revelational. The religious ideal of Islam, therefore, is organically related to the social order which it has created. The rejection of the one will eventually involve the rejection of the other. Therefore, the construction of a polity on national lines, if it means a

From *Struggle for Independence: 1857–1947* (Karachi, 1958), App. IV, pp. 14–18.

displacement of the Islamic principle of solidarity, is simply unthinkable to a Muslim. This is a matter which at the present moment directly concerns the Muslims of India.

. . . It is, however, painful to observe that our attempts to discover such a principle of internal harmony have so far failed. Why have they failed? Perhaps we suspect each other's intentions, and inwardly aim at dominating each other. Perhaps in the higher interests of mutual co-operation, we cannot afford to part with the monopolies which circumstances have placed in our hands, and conceal our egoism under the cloak of a nationalism, outwardly simulating a large-hearted patriotism, but inwardly as narrow-minded as a caste or a tribe. Perhaps we are unwilling to recognise that each group has a right to free development according to its own cultural traditions. But whatever may be the causes of our failure, I still feel hopeful. Events seem to be tending in the direction of some sort of internal harmony. And as far as I have been able to read the Muslim mind, I have no hesitation in declaring that if the principle that the Indian Muslim is entitled to full and free development on the lines of his own culture and tradition in his own Indian homelands is recognized as the basis of a permanent communal settlement, he will be ready to stake his all for the freedom of India. The principle that each group is entitled to free development on its own lines is not inspired by any feeling of narrow communalism. There are communalisms and communalisms. A community which is inspired by feeling of ill-will towards other communities is low and ignoble. I entertain the highest respect for the customs, laws, religious and social institutions of other communities. Nay, it is my duty, according to the teaching of the Qur'ān, even to defend their places of worship if need be. Yet I love the communal group which is the source of my life and behaviour; and which has formed me what I am by giving me its religion, its literature, its thought, its culture, and thereby recreating its whole past, as a living operative factor, in my present consciousness.

Communalism, in its higher aspect, then, is indispensable to the formation of a harmonious whole in a country like India. The units of Indian society are not territorial as in European countries. India is a continent of human groups belonging to different races, speaking different languages and professing different religions. Their behaviour is not at all determined by a common race-consciousness. Even the Hindus do not form a homogeneous group. The principle of European democracy cannot be applied to India without recognising the fact of communal groups. The Muslim demand for the creation of a Muslim India within India is, therefore, perfectly justified. The resolution of the All-Parties Muslim Conference at Delhi is, to my mind, wholly inspired by this noble ideal of a harmonious whole which, instead of stifling the respective individualites of its component wholes, affords them chances of fully working out the possibilities that may be latent in them. And I have no doubt that this house will emphatically endorse the Muslim demands embodied in this resolution. Personally I would go further than the demands embodied in it. I would like to see the Punjab, North-West Frontier, Sind and Baluchistan amalgamated into a single state. Self-government within the British Empire, or without the British Empire, and the formation of a consolidated North-West Indian Muslim state appears to me to be the final destiny of the Muslims, at least of North-West India.

The idea need not alarm the Hindus or the British. India is the greatest Muslim country in the world. The life of Islam as a cultural force in this country very largely depends on its centralisation in a specified territory. This centralisation of the most living portion of the Muslims of India whose military and police service has, notwithstanding unfair treatment from the British, made the British rule possible in this country, will eventually solve the problem of India as well as of Asia. It will intensify their sense of responsibility and deepen their patriotic feeling. Thus, possessing full opportunity of development within the body-politic of India, the North-West Indian Muslims will prove the best defenders of India against a foreign invasion, be that invasion one of ideas or of bayonets. . . .

. . . the Muslim demand . . . is actuated by a genuine desire for free development which is practically impossible under the type of unitary government contemplated by the nationalist Hindu politicians with a view to secure permanent communal dominance in the whole of India.

Nor should the Hindus fear that the creation of autonomous Muslim states will mean the introduction of a kind of religious rule in such states. I have already indicated to you the meaning of the word 'religion,' as applied to Islam. The truth is that Islam is not a church. It is a state, conceived as a contractual organism long before Rousseau ever thought of such a thing, and animated by an ethical ideal which regards man not as an earth-rooted creature, defined by this or that portion of the earth, but as a spiritual being understood in terms of a social mechanism, and possessing rights and duties as a living factor in that mechanism. . . . I, therefore, demand the formation of a consolidated Muslim state in the best interests of India and Islam. For India it means security and peace resulting from an internal balance of power; for Islam an opportunity to rid itself of the stamp that Arabian Imperialism was forced to give it, to mobilize its law, its education, its culture, and to bring them into closer contact with its own original spirit and with the spirit of modern times.

Mawlānā Mawdūdī received an early traditional religious education, which was supplemented by his self-taught knowledge of Western thought. He pursued a career in journalism and in 1933 assumed editorship ot *Tarjuman al-Qur'ān* [Exegesis of the Qur'ān], which throughout the years served as a vehicle of his thought. He has been perhaps the most systematic modern Muslim writer, and his many writings have been translated into English and Arabic and circulated throughout the Muslim world. In 1941 Mawdūdī established the Jamā'at-i-Islāmī [The Islamic Association], an extremely well organized association committed to the reestablishment of an Islamic world order or society (politically, legally, and socially). Although originally against any form of nationalism and thus opposed to the establishment of Pakistan, Mawdūdī nevertheless migrated to Pakistan, after the partitioning, where the Jamā'at-i-Islāmī has been very active in politics.

Nationalism and Islam

Even a cursory glance at the meaning and essence of nationalism would convince a person that in their spirit and in their aims Islam and nationalism are diametrically opposed to each other. Islam deals with man as man. It presents to all mankind a social system of justice and piety based on creed and morality and invites all towards it. And then it admits him in its circle, with equal rights, whosoever accepts this system. Be it in the sphere of economics or politics or civics or legal rights and duties or anything else, those who accept the principles of Islam are not divided by any distinction of nationality or race or class or country. The ultimate goal of Islam is a world-state in which the chains of racial and national prejudices would be dismantled and all mankind incorporated in a cultural and political system, with equal rights and equal opportunities for all, and in which hostile competition would give way to friendly co-operation between peoples so that they might mutually assist and contribute to the material and moral good of one another. Whatever the principle of human good Islam defines, and whatever the scheme of life it prescribes, it would

From *Nationalism and India* (Lahore: Maktaba-e-Jama'at-e-Islami; new edition, 1947), 10–12, 24–28, 30–34.

appeal to mankind in general only when they would free themselves of all ignorant prejudices and dissociate themselves altogether from their national traditions, with their sentiments of racial pride, and with their love of sanguinary and material affinities, and be prepared, as mere human beings, to enquire what is truth, where lies righteousness, justice and honesty, and what is the path that leads to the well-being of, not a class or a nation or a country, but of humanity as a whole. . . .

As opposed to this, nationalism divides man from man on the basis of nationality. Nationalism simply means that the nationalist should give preference to his nationality over all other nationalities. Even if he were not an aggressive nationalist, nationalism, at least, demands that culturally, economically, politically and legally he should differentiate between national and non-national; secure the maximum of advantages for his nation; build up barriers of economic preferences for national profit; protect with tenacity the historical traditions and the traditional prejudices which have come down to wake his nationality, and breed in him the sentiments of national pride. He would not admit with him members of other nationalities in any walk of life on an equal basis. Whenever there is a chance of his nation obtaining more advantages, as against the other, his heart would be sealed against all sentiments of justice and propriety. His ultimate goal would be a nation-state *rather* than a world-state, nevertheless if he upholds any world ideology, that ideology would necessarily take the form of imperialism or world domination, because members of other nationalities cannot participate in his state as equals, they may do so only as "slaves" or subjects. . . .

The Fundamental Difference between Nationalism and Islam

. . . The law of God (the *Sharī'a*) has always aimed at bringing together mankind into one moral and spiritual frame-work and make them mutually assistant to one another on a universal scale. But nationalism at once demolishes this frame-work with the noxious instruments of racial and national distinction, and by creating bitterness and hatred between nations makes them fight and exterminate rather than help one another.

The *Sharī'as* of God provide the highest opportunities of free contact between man and man because on this very contact depends the progress of human civilisation and culture. But nationalism comes in the way of these contacts with a thousand hindrances; it makes the mere existence of foreign nationals in a country impossible.

The *Sharī'as* of God want that every individual, every nation, every race should obtain full opportunities of developing its natural characteristics and its inherent potentialities so that it may be able to subscribe its due share to the collective progress of mankind. But nationalism urges upon every race, every nation, that it should secure power and degrade and disgrace and belittle other races and nations and bring them under servility, and deny them any chance of developing their natural talents and resources, and deprive them even of the primary right of mere existence.

The fundamental principle of the *Sharī'as* of God is that the rights of man are based on moral code and not on force. That is, if the moral law sanctions a right to a weak individual or weak people, the powerful individual or the powerful people must honour this right. But in contrast to this nationalism establishes the principle that "might is right" and that the weak has no right because he has no might. . . .

Again an essential feature of this nationalism is that it makes man opportunist. The *Sharī'as* of God are given to man to make him live by principles and relate his behaviour to permanent laws which would not alter with individual or national interests. But, unlike it, nationalism makes man unprincipled. A nationalist has no principles in the world except that he wishes the good of his nation. If the laws of ethics, injunctions of religion, and principles of culture serve his purpose he would put his faith in them gladly, but if they interfered with his interest he would set them aside and invent and adopt some other principles and theories.

But a more direct conflict between nationalism and the *Sharī'as* of God occurs in yet another way. It is obvious that whatever messenger is sent by God, he must take birth in some nation and in some country. Again, the Book of Laws which he would be given must necessarily be in the language of the country to which he has been deputed. Moreover, the sacred and holy places associated with the mission of that Rasūl [messenger, prophet] must be situated mostly in that particular country. But in spite of these limitations the truth and that divine teaching which a Rasūl brings from God, is not confined to one nation or country, it is intended for humanity at large. The entire human race is called upon to believe in that Rasūl and his teachings, and whether that Rasūl has a limited mission, as Noah and Moses and many other Rasūls had, or a universal mission, as Abraham and Muhammad had, in either case all mankind are ordered to respect and believe in every Rasūl and when the mission of a Rasūl is universal, it is natural that the Book of Laws given to him by God must acquire an international status; the cultural influence of the language he speaks must be international; the sacred places associated with his mission, in spite of their being situated in one country must become centres of international importance. And not only that Rasūl but also his companions and the prominent persons taking part in his movement at its inception, in spite of their being connected with one nation would become the heroes of all nations. All this falls contrary to the taste, temperament, sentiments and thoughts of a nationalist. The national self-consciousness of a nationalist can never brook it that he should take as his heroes persons who do not belong to his nationality; accept the central importance and sanctity of such places as are not situated within his country; admit the cultural influence of a language which may not be his own; secure inspiration from traditions which may have been imported from outside. He would regard all these things not only as foreign but would look upon them with that displeasure and hatred with which everything of foreign invader is received, and would endeavour his best to eliminate and cast out all these external influences from the life of his nation. It is the natural demand of his nationalistic sentiment that he should associate his sentiments of sacredness and sanctity with his own homeland, that he should sing hymns to rivers and mountains of his own country, that he should revive his ancient national historical traditions (traditions which this foreign religion describes as the relics of the age of ignorance) and pride in them, that he should relate his present with his own past and link his national culture with that of his ancestors in a chronicle sequence, that he should take as his heroes, historical or legendary, persons from his own nation and take inspiration only from their deeds, imaginary or real. In short, it is in the nature and constitution of nationalism that it should condemn everything that comes from outside and praise all those things which are the products of its own home. The ultimate goal to which this path leads is that even the religion which has been imported must be completely abandoned, and those religious traditions which may have come down to a nationalist from the "age of ignorance" of his own national history be praised and glorified. Many nationalists might not have reached this ultimate goal and might be lingering somewhere midway, but the path they are traversing only leads to this goal.

ISLAM AND SOCIALISM

In the wake of World War II, attitudes in the Muslim world began to change radically. The West's creation of Israel in 1948 spelled the demise of the liberal nationalist current of political thought in most of the Arab world. A series of military coups d'état brought to power regimes that were disillusioned with the liberal West and attracted by the progress of socialism in Russia and Eastern Europe. For the new generation of leaders, independence meant positive neutrality and a concern for authentic Arab identity. Arab socialism became the shibboleth that separated the "progressives" from the "reactionaries." Nāsirism and the ideology of the Ba'th Party became the two major forces in the area. Egypt's Jamāl 'Abd al-Nāsir espoused socialism, and Shaykh Mahmūd Shaltūt, the leading religious figure in Egypt (Shaykh al-Azhar), gives assurance that Arab socialism fits perfectly with Islam. After Nāsir's death in 1970 it has not been easy to say exactly what Nāsirism is, but one version is given in the selection from Libyan leader Mu'ammar al-Qadhdhāfī, a fervent disciple of Nāsir.

Arab specificity is also the preoccupation of the Ba'th Party and selections from one of the founding fathers Michel Aflāq, a Christian, present a rather original attempt at weaving Islam into the pattern of Arab revolutionary thought.

Both Nāsirism and Ba'thism represent new forms of nationalist thought. But they did not have the political stage entirely to themselves; there were also universalist currents present trying to establish a popular base. At one pole was Marxism, never too popular, represented here by Sadiq al-'Azm, and at the opposite pole was Islamic socialism, represented here by Mustafā al-Sibā'ī and Sayyid Qutb, spokesman for the Muslim Brotherhood.

South Asia has witnessed similar concerns to relate Islam to socio-economic reform and to do so in the name of Islamic socialism. During the 1950's, Khalīfa 'Abd al-Hakīm sought to show how Islam avoided the pitfalls of both capitalism and communism and provided the essentials for a just social order.

Finally, A.K. Brohi reflects the position of many Muslims who believe that Islam provides its own blueprint for a socially just society and who object to the association of Islam with the term "socialism."

SHAYKH MAHMŪD SHALTŪT
1892–1963

Born in Minya, Mahmud Shaltut studied and then taught in
Alexandria. In 1927 he joined the faculty of al-Azhar University
and was among those who proposed the reform of al-Azhar. He
was dismissed from his post in the 1930s because of his reformist views. However, he later returned and in 1958 became the
Rector of al-Azhar (Shaykh al-Azhar).

Socialism and Islam

Islam and Society

Islam is not only a spiritual religion, as some wrongly imagine, thinking
that it limits itself to establishing relations between the servant and his
Lord, without being concerned with organizing the affairs of the community and establishing its rules of conduct. On the contrary, Islam is universal in character. Not only does it determine the relations between man and
his Lord, but it also lays down the rules that regulate human relations and
public affairs, with the aim of ensuring the welfare of society. . . .

Mutual Social Aid Among Muslims

Members of human society cannot be considered independent of one
another. On the contrary, as a result of their existence in this world and
the very conditions of their lives, they render each other mutual service
and cooperate to satisfy their needs. . . .

This bond is, in Islam, the "religious brotherhood" among Muslims. It is
in the "brotherhood" that rights and social duties are expressed in the
most sincere fashion. It is this that constitutes the most powerful factor
leading toward clemency, sympathy, and cooperation; and giving a sense
of the idea, it leads society toward good and banishes evil.

Islam has established this "brotherhood" among Muslims. "The believers are a band of brothers" (Qur'ān. 49:10), and the Prophet said,
"Muslim is brother to Muslim." Moreover, Islam has raised the religious
brotherhood over and above the blood relationship.

From Kemal H. Karpat, ed. *Political and Social Thought in the Contemporary Middle East*
(New York: Praeger, 1968), pp. 126–32.

Muslims have attained social solidarity to a unique degree in their Islamic society, which God has immortalized in His Book, which says, "Prize them above themselves, though they are in want" (59:9). . . .

Social Solidarity Among Muslims

Social solidarity among Muslims is of two kinds—the moral and the material. Moral solidarity derives from two factors. The first is recognizing good and virtue and inviting one's neighbor to conform to it with sincerity and fidelity. "You are the noblest nation that has ever been raised up for mankind. You enjoin justice and forbid evil. You believe in Allah" (Qur'ān 3:106).

The second allows one to hear the Word of God and receive it with gratitude and acknowledgment. "Give good news to My servants, who listen to My precepts and follow what is best in them. These are they whom Allah has guided. These are they who are endued with understanding" (Qur'ān 39:19–20).

The interaction of these two forces makes cooperation between members of a Muslim society more sound.

Material solidarity consists of meeting the needs of society, of consoling the unfortunate, of helping to achieve what is in the general interest, i.e., whatever increases the standard of living and serves all individuals in a beneficial manner.

It is not to be doubted that all those foundations on which life rests, such as perfection, happiness, and grandeur, matters of science, health, greatness, dignity, civilization, power, and strength, cannot be attained without wealth.

In its attitude toward allowing man to assure his needs. Islam considers wealth realistically. Islam has made wealth an "ornament" of this life (Qur'ān 18:44). It also qualified it as the "support of man." Wealth is not an end in itself. It is only one of the means of rendering mutual service and procuring what one needs. Used thus, it is a good thing, both for the one who possesses it and for society. Considered as an end in itself, and with the sole aim of being enjoyed, wealth becomes for its owner the cause of great harm, and at the same time sows corruption among men. . . .

That is why the Qur'ān regards wealth as a good thing, on condition that it is acquired legally and spent for the good of others, and that it remains not an end in itself but simply a means.

Agriculture, industry, and commerce, on which the material life of society depends, are the sources of wealth. Society needs agriculture for the foodstuffs that are produced by the soil. It also needs the various industries that are necessary to man. Clothing, housing, agriculture, machinery, roads, waterways, and railways are also necessary for the protection and defense of the state. All these can be acquired only through industry.

Agriculture, industry, and commerce must therefore be developed as much as possible. That is why the men of Islamic religious learning ['ulamā'] teach that it is a collective obligation to learn to make all that one cannot do without, and that if this obligation is not fulfilled the sin that falls back on the whole nation can be effaced only if a part of the nation discharges the obligation.

There is no doubt that this obligation consists in working for the achievement of the principle that Islam imposes on its followers, i.e., the autarky [or establishment of self-sufficiency] that allows the Muslim community itself to meet all its needs. . . .

Muslim jurists are unanimous in recognizing the right of authorities to expropriate [land] in order to enlarge the place of prayer [i.e., the jurisdiction of Islam] until the whole world becomes a mosque. They also have the right to act likewise to enlarge a street or any other public service, in the interests of both individuals and the community. . . .

Worldly possessions are the possessions of God, given by Him to His servants for the benefit of the universe. God sometimes claims possession of these goods: "Allah gives without measure to whom he wills" (Qur'ān 24:38). At other times, He attributes them to their previous owners: "Do not give to the feeble-minded the property with which Allah has entrusted you for their support" (Qur'ān 4:4).

God has clearly established that the possessors of goods, who are the holders after Him, must preserve, increase, and spend them in a manner laid down by Him: "Give in alms of that which He has made your inheritance" (Qur'ān 57:7). God also has put his wealth at the disposal of all men equally: "Allah created the heavens and the earth to reveal the truth and to reward each soul according to its deeds. None shall be wronged" (Qur'ān 45:12).

If worldly possessions are the possessions of God, if all men are the servants of God, and if the life in which they toil and do honor to the possessions of God belongs to God, then wealth, although it may be attributed to a private person, should also belong to all the servants of God, should be placed in the safekeeping of all, and all should profit from it. "Men, serve your Lord, who has created you and those who have gone before you, so that you may guard yourselves against evil; who has made the earth a bed for you and the sky a dome, and has sent down water from heaven to bring forth fruits for your sustenance" (Qur'ān 2:19–21).

Thus, to be rich is a social function whose aim is to ensure the happiness of society and satisfy its needs and interests.

So that all men may profit from worldly goods and their souls be free from all greed in this regard, Islam has opposed all who hoard and jealously watch over their wealth. . . . "Proclaim a woeful punishment to those who hoard up gold and silver and do not spend it in Allah's cause. The day will surely come when their treasures shall be heated in the fire of Hell, and their foreheads, sides, and backs branded with them. Their tormentors will say to them: 'These are the riches which you hoarded. Taste then the punishment which is your due' " (Qur'ān 9:36).

Similarly, Islam has fought the stupidity that leads to the squandering of goods uselessly: "The wasteful are Satan's brothers" (Qur'ān 17:29).

Islam has fought luxury, which has created hatred among the social classes, which menaces a peaceful and stable life, not to mention corruption and anarchy. . . .

Islam has traced the straight path of the ideal society; it is a path of solidarity by which the nation lives and which ensures the strength of society. With this end in view, Islam has abolished from the minds of owners [of property] and capitalists such vices as meanness, the taste for squandering the luxury. It has employed all means to encourage men to give generously and to be afraid of appearing miserly and of neglecting the right of the people and of society, to such a point that it has raised liberality to the rank of faith. . . .

"The true servants of the Merciful are those who walk humbly on the earth and say 'Peace!' to the ignorant who accost them; . . . who are neither extravagant nor niggardly but keep the golden mean; who invoke no other God besides Allah . . . " (Qur'ān 25:64–66).

For Islam, avarice similarly is one of the traits that condemn the infidel: " 'What has brought you into Hell?' They will reply: 'We never prayed or fed the hungry . . . ' " (Qur'ān 74:43–44).

Islam has maintained this view for so long that it considers it a denial of the Judgment not to encourage giving to the needy: "Have you thought of him that denies the Last Judgement? It is he who turns away the orphan and does not urge others to feed the poor" (Qur'ān 107).

Briefly summarized, such is the doctrine of Islam regarding the relations among men from the point of view of the solidarity of members of society. It contains in detail all the solid foundations necessary to make our nation a magnificent stronghold, a haven of happiness for those who shelter there.

The doctrine also contains a clear statement of what the socialism of Islam is, for adoption by those who wish to adopt it. Can man find a more perfect, more complete, more useful, and more profound socialism than that decreed by Islam? It is founded on the basis of faith and belief, and all that is decreed on that basis participates in the perpetuation of life and doctrine.

MU 'AMMAR AL-QADHDHĀFĪ
1942–

He studied history at Benghazi University while training at the Military Academy. In 1969 he was one of the leaders of the Libyan revolution and emerged as chairman of the Revolutionary Council and President of the country. A devoted admirer of Jamāl 'Abd al-Nāsir, he has developed his own Islamic ideology, which he labels the "Third Way."

The Third Way

We will fasten our tie to the past and reconsider our present in order to cut our way through to the future, generation after generation. This is no simple task. The advance began in the East and went West. Now . . . here we are speaking in the Libyan Arab Republic, on the subject of the third theory which, as we said, is not new. It exists, and it was the first and will be the last . . . in our theory we focus on the Qur'ān, since the Qur'ān is the perfect book which contains nothing false whatever, is from God Almighty, may He be praised, who created man and created the rules (*sunan*) which govern the universe.

We must take the Qur'ān as the focal point of our journey in life because the Qur'ān is perfect; it is light, and in it are solutions to the problems of man . . . from personal status . . . to international problems.

Both the East and the West want to corrupt us from within, obliterate every distinguishing mark of our personality and snuff out the light which guides us. Both have focused their sights on the Qur'ān in a menacing way and have zeroed in on religion . . . in order to tie religion to reactionism and to associate it with superstitions. As a result we began returning to the pagan society which existed at the time Islam first appeared. When the heavenly messages were revealed, the pagans used to charge that the revealed books were fables, or poetry, or the saying of some seer or crazy man. Have we returned to that pagan society in which one speaks those same words the pagans spoke when the heavenly messages appeared . . . an appeal to morality is called reactionism . . . religion is labeled fables. . . . Any personal action on our part springing from our personality or from our values is cast into doubt, and we ourselves have begun to doubt. That precisely is how colonialism has affected us. And this is what I

From *Fīl-Nazariyyah al-Thālithah* [The third way], (n.p.:n.d.), pp. 65–71.

want to repeat: I say that we must be awake and alert. We must reconsider so that we will know . . . what word we will speak? What are the needs in which we believe? . . . We want to reconsider our situation because we were in darkness. We were prey, but now . . . the prey is standing on its own two feet and desires to resist its predators and wants to live on an equal footing with them. . . . The prey must re-examine itself . . . treat its wounds and regain strength of movement.

With our theory or our creed we have no need of communism nor capitalism; we did not need East or West in our creation, nor do we need them in our resurrection. This does not mean that we have no need of East or West in our human and international relations. No, we interact with the world; we affect it and are affected by it in turn. We are part of mankind, whether men be communist or capitalist. What we want to say is that we have no need for anyone to reconstruct us brick by brick, to restructure our personality and dicate the positions we should take. We must have the possibility to profit from the experience of mankind, but we too have an experience which others should respect and profit from. In this way we interact with the world that it may benefit from us as we benefit from it. But if someone thinks he can come and rebuild us from zero and mold us into new forms according to his lights, we will resist stubbornly. We will not allow ourselves to be molded into slaves of some new creator. We are slaves to no one but God, God it is who created us.

The details of the theory, its component parts and its elucidation, are not my specialization. They are the specialization of every cultured and learned person, every thinker, every *mujtahid* [one capable of interpretation], every researcher. This is their task . . . to refute the calumnies leveled against us; to expose the economic, military, legal, social and political aspects of the Qur'ān; to demonstrate how the foundations of present civilization were established by the Arabs. The Arabs, deformed by colonialism, were beginning to doubt themselves. It was becoming impossible for them to believe that the foundations of contemporary civilization were laid by Arabs and Muslims because a comparison of the present flourishing civilization with the backward state of the Arabs was embarrassing. It meant that this backwardness was the artisan of this progress and anyone lacking literary courage would be embarrassed to say that the Arabs and Muslims were the architects of the present civilization.

In fact, there is a certain justification for this embarrassment because the backwardness in which we live makes us too embarrassed to attribute anything progressive to ourselves. Courage is needed to speak these words. Anyone who looks at the books of astronomy we have today will find all the names of the stars are Arabic . . . this means that the Arabs or the Muslims created the science of astronomy. The sciences of chemistry, accounting, algebra, medicine, all have authors who are known by name. . . .

The time has come to manifest the truth of Islam as a force to move mankind, to make progress, and to change the course of history as we changed it formerly.

We must establish the fact that religion is the effective motive in the life of man and that the world in its long history was moved by religion which, along with nationalism, played the basic role. That is, nationalism and religion are the two forces that have moved history and have set the tempo for the march of all humanity. A disavowal of the role of religion and nationalism in the movement of history is obstructionism born of disbelieving despair; it has no pretext except the desire to dominate by force.

As for capitalism, we must oppose it forcefully in order to demonstrate the corruption of wealth, the corruption of exploiting capital. If capital is amassed, it is transformed into evil; we must demonstrate this from the Qur'ān. The Qur'ān is replete with sayings about those living in luxury, those who squander, and those who are prodigal. There are verses from the Qur'ān which we can take as titles for the volumes we will compose by our practice because the Qur'ān does not give details for everything. The Qur'ān is verses which explain a very large part of life. When the Qur'ān says "Nay, but verily man is rebellious, that he thinketh himself independent" (96:6–7), this verse is an encyclopedia in itself, it says clearly that if a man sees he is rich and has wealth and power, it is inevitable that he will be conceited and tyrannical; and tyranny begets corruption and absolutism, it enslaves people and debases life. Sowing corruption on earth . . . the meaning of "that he thinketh himself independent" is that if he sees himself rich he will be tyrannical. So the problem is that riches or wealth, power or possessions by themselves push man to tyranny. Thus, wealth is a problem which must be treated and solved. Restraints must be part of it. And as long as wealth is sometimes an evil, we must search out other things and other states in which wealth will not be evil. We must search for justice in this subject. . . .

We must search out the causes of corruption to discover what it is that makes man sow corruption on earth in order to eliminate these causes so that man may be just and society may be just. We will establish the ideal society.

The world, East and West, is incapable of arriving at a true solution, and attempts to solve the problem by extremist solutions have failed. . . . One sets wealth at liberty and allows all things to follow their inclinations arbitrarily until they arrive at some result which society must adapt to in a spontaneous way . . . the other maintains: there is no way except for us to interfere violently, uproot everything and then reshape it all even though it be contrary to the nature of man such as is done in communism. . . . Thus, the world is not led to the true path. We have the true path . . . it was present before communism and before capitalism. America is only a century old, whereas these words have been present with us for more than a thousand years. The rights of man existed among us before the American society was formed. When we articulated the rights of man, the American continent was devoid of human life. Now they have been present for 100 years and have started bragging that they are the ones who have fashioned the rights of man . . . also the communist revolution of 1917 is of very recent vintage.

We are a people with authentic roots set deep in history, and the truths about which we speak were present before the formation of American society which leads capitalism, and present before Marxist philosophy, the philosophy of the communists who lead communist society. These truths were present before they were, and we call these truths the first theory and the last theory. Because of this, we call it "the third theory" in the sense that we have here a third thing which may be the first, in fact, is the first, and also the last.

But in the vast struggle between the other two systems, this authentic system marking out the middle way was lost sight of. We see that all civilizations have ended in doubt. The offspring of non-Islamic civilizations brought man to the world of doubt; all of them ended in doubt. Islamic civilization is the only one that brought man to certainty and faith. This subject is extremely important, if only the perplexed generations in the East and West today would come to recognize this. . . . Here is a civilization that leads to faith and to certainty, quite the contrary of the civilizations which led man to doubt. Decidedly man by nature does not want to live in doubt; it is inevitable that he search for the path that will lead him to faith and certainty. Islamic civilization is the one which leads to this result. All other civilizations lead to doubt.

MICHEL AFLĀQ
1910–

After obtaining a licentiate in history at the Sorbonne, he taught
in Damascus. In 1940 he joined with Salāh al-Dīn Bitār to form
the Ba'th (Resurrection) Party. He was Minister of Education in
1949 and in 1956 fused his party with the Socialist party of
Akram Hourani to form the Arab Ba'th Socialist party, now
ruling Syria and Iraq. He was expelled from the party in Syria in
1966 but remains in favor with the Iraqi branch.

The Arab Personality
Between Past and Present

We are faced with the fact that our glorious past has been cut off from or
rather is in contradiction to our shameful present. The Arab personality
was a unified whole. There was no difference between its spirit and
thought, its words and action, its specific and general morality. . . .

Now is the time for us to remove this contradiction and to restore unity
to our Arab personality and wholeness to our Arab life. . . .

Our affiliation with our heroic forebears has been mere formalism, nothing more, and our modern history has had no organic relation with our
glorious past but has fed on it like a parasite. Today we must resurrect our
specific characteristics and act in a manner which will justify our official
lineage and demonstrate our legitimacy. In as far as we are able we must
root out stagnation and decline so that our glorious, authentic blood will
flow back into our veins. . . .

The movement of Islam represented in the life of the Prophet was no
mere historical event for the Arab. True, it can be described by time and
place, cause and effect; but because of its profundity, its ardor and its
breadth, it was directly tied to the life of the Arabs. It gives a true picture
and stands as complete eternal symbol of the nature of the Arab soul with
all its rich possibilities and its authentic bent. Accordingly, we are correct
in considering that it is continually capable of renewal in spirit, not in
form or letter. Islam is the vibrant convulsion which shook the forces
latent in the Arab *umma* and mobilized them in a surge of life which

From *Dhikrā-l-Rasūl al-'Arabī* [In remembrance of the Arab prophet] (Beirut: Arab Foundation 1972), pp. 5–24.

rocked the barriers of tradition and the bonds of convention to reestablish its connection with the profound sense of being. The *umma* was gripped by fervor and a sense of wonder which it expressed in new syllables and in magnificent works. It was no longer capable of keeping within its bounds; its thoughts and actions flowed out to other nations, and thus it became all-enveloping. The Arabs, then, by means of this crucial moral experience know how to rebel against their own reality and to divide in order to go beyond themselves to a stage in which a higher unity is achieved. In it they tested their souls in order to uncover their potential and strengthen their virtues. Whatever fruit Islam later bore in conquests and civilization was already present seminally in the first twenty years of its mission (*ba'tha*). Before the Arabs conquered the earth, they conquered themselves; they sounded their depths and tested their inner self. Before they ruled nations, they ruled themselves; they dominated their passions and mastered their will. The sciences they developed, the arts they created, the civilization (*'umrān*) they raised up were nothing, but the partial, material, limited realization of the powerful, all-embracing dream they lived in those years with all its strength—nothing but a faint echo of that heavenly voice they heard, a pale shadow of that enchanting vision they saw the day that the angels fought in their ranks and paradise flashed off their swords.

This experience is not an historical event remembered with pride for the moral it holds, rather it is a permanent predisposition of the Arab *umma*—if Islam is correctly understood. This *umma* arises every time matter dominates spirit and outward forms weight on its essence. Then it divides within itself to reach a higher unity and a sound harmony. . . .

The life of the prophet mirrors the Arab soul in its absolute reality, but this reality cannot be grasped by the mind; it is known only by living experience. . . .

Until now we have been looking at the life of the Prophet from the outside, as a marvelous picture held up for our admiration and reverence. We must begin to look at it from within in order to give it life. Every Arab at the present time can enliven the life of the Arab Prophet. . . . as long as he is affiliated with the *umma* which mobilized all its forces to give birth to Muhammad, or more exactly, as long as this man is an individual of this *umma* which Muhammad mobilized all his forces to bring forth. In a past time the life of a whole *umma* was epitomized in one man; today the life of this *umma* in its new renaissance must become a detailed exposition of the life of its greatest man. Muhammad was all the Arabs, so let all the Arabs today be Muhammad.

The dazzling truth, which only the stubborn would deny, is that the Arabs were chosen to bring the message of Islam because of their basic characteristics and virtues, and the choice of the era for the appearance of Islam was due to the fact that the Arabs had matured and were in a perfect state for receiving a message like this and carrying it to mankind. The triumph of Islam was postponed for all those years so that the Arabs could arrive at the truth by their own proper effort. This truth would be the result of their experience of themselves and the world, tempered by hardship and sorrow, despair and hope, failure and victory. In other words, in order that faith would spring from the depths of their souls, thus true faith would be blended with experience and be rooted in the marrow of life. Islam, then, was an Arab movement. Its meaning was the renewal and perfection of Arabism. The language in which it was revealed was Arabic, its comprehension of things was filtered through the Arab intellect. The virtues it strengthened were Arab virtues, explicit or latent. The faults it fought against were Arab faults already on the way to extinction. The Muslim at that time was nothing but an Arab, but he was a new Arab, evolved and perfected. Today we label many individuals of the *umma* "patriot" or "nationalist"—though all the *umma* should be "nationalist." We use this term to characterize the group who believe in their country because they possess the qualities and virtues necessary to make them conscious of their deep affiliation to their *umma* and ready to bear the consequent responsibilty. The Muslim was the Arab who believed in the new religion because he had the qualities and virtues necessary to understand that this religion represented the leap of Arabism to unity, power, and progress.

But does this mean that Islam should be limited to the Arabs? To say this would be to stray from the truth and contradict reality. Every great nation, with profound ties to the eternal sense of being, is oriented from its inception to all-embracing immortal values. Islam is the most eloquent expression of the orientation of the Arab *umma* to immortality and comprehensiveness. In its reality it is Arabic and in its ideal goals it is human. The message of Islam is the creation of Arab humanity.

The Arabs are singled out from other nations by this characteristic: their national consciousness is joined to a religious message; or more precisely this message is an eloquent expression of that national consciousness. They did not expand for the purpose of expansion nor did they conquer countries and rule for merely economic motives, for reasons of race or for the desire of dominating and subjugating . . . but to fulfill a religious duty which was truth, guidance, mercy, justice, and sacrifice. They shed their blood for this and counted their sacrifice trivial as they went forward rejoicing in the face of God. As long as the tie between Arabism and Islam remains strong and as long as we see in Arabism a body whose soul is Islam, there is no reason to fear that the Arabs will go to extremes in their nationalism. It will never attain the fanaticism of injustice and colonialism. . . .

Naturally, the Arabs cannot fulfill this duty unless they are a strong, active nation because Islam can be personified only in an Arab nation with its authentic virtues, morals and talents. Accordingly the first duty imposed by the humanism of Islam is that the Arabs be strong and sovereign in their lands.

Islam is universal and immortal, but its universality does not mean that it expands once for all to embrace various concepts and currents. Rather, in every critical period of history and at every decisive stage of development, it expresses one of the infinite concepts concealed within it since the beginning. Its immortality does not mean that it is frozen so that no change or transformation overtakes it or that life passes over it leaving it untouched. Rather, it means that despite its continuous changing—it discards garments which wear thin and sloughs off old skins—its roots remain one and the same, and its ability to grow, generate, and create is one and the same. It is never deficient; it is never ephemeral. It relates to specific times and places with absolute meaning and action, within the limits of this time and this place.

Do these zealots who want to make Islam a knapsack which includes everything, a factory producing various vehicles and medicines, do they understand that instead of proving its force and guarding its basic charism from every extraneous change, they annihilate its spirit and its personality and make it lose its vital, independent characteristics? And from another angle, they smooth the way for propagandists of injustice and masters of despotic rule. In their attempt to arm themselves with Islam, they discredit the very matter of Islam, that is, the Arab nation.

Therefore, the meaning that Islam expresses in this critical period of history and at this decisive stage of development is that all efforts should be directed to strengthening and resuscitating the Arabs and that these efforts should be confined to the frame of Arab nationalism.

The Arabs' connection with the West is commonly traced back to Bonaparte's campaign against Egypt and symbolized by his act of hanging up verses from the Qur'ān beside a text of the "rights of man." Since that time, the Arabs (or the leaders spuriously converted to Arabism) have been pushing their new renaissance in this distorted direction. They contort themselves and warp the texts of their history and the Qur'ān to show that not only is there no difference between the principles of their civilization and creed and those of Western civilization, but they, in fact, preceded the Westerners in their declaration and application of the same. This means only one thing: they stand as accused before the West, affirming the soundness and superiority of Western values. . . . Before long they pushed this logic to its conclusion by admitting that with European civilization they had no need of their own. The ruse of European colonialism was not that it led the Arab mind to acknowledge immortal principles and concepts; it had acknowledged them and adopted them as its base from the beginning. The ruse was in seizing on the inertia and creative incapacity of the Arabs to force them to adopt the peculiar European content of these concepts. We have no argument with the Europeans about the principle of freedom, but we contest their assumption that they alone are the purveyors of true freedom.

Europe today, as in the past, fears Islam, but it knows now that the force of Islam (which formerly expressed the force of the Arabs) has revived and appears in a new form which is Arab nationalism. For this reason Europe turns all its weapons against this new force while it befriends and aids the old form of Islam. International Islam, which is limited to superficial worship and pale general themes, is about to be Europeanized. The day will come when the nationalists will find themselves the sole defenders of Islam, and they will be forced to breathe into its proper meaning if they want the Arab nation to remain the sound basis for survival.

The modern Arab mind has been infiltrated by two European notions of nationalism and humanism which are false and present a grave danger. The notion of abstract nationalism in the West is logical; Westerners decided to separate nationalism from religion, since religion having entered Europe from without was foreign to its nature and its history. Religion was a distillation of the creed and morals of the hereafter; it was not revealed in their national languages, it did not express the needs of their milieu, nor was it woven into their history. Whereas Islam, in relation to the Arabs, is not merely a creed of the hereafter nor is it mere morals, it is of this world, expressing their universal feelings and their view of life; it is the strongest expression of the unity of their personality.... Over and above that, it is the image of their language and literature and the most weighty part of their national history. We cannot sing of any one of our immortal heroes merely as Arab while neglecting or avoiding his quality as a Muslim. The relation of Islam to Arabism is not like the relation of a religion to any nationalism. The Christian Arabs will know, once their nationalism has fully awakened within them and their authentic nature has returned, that Islam is their national culture. They must fill themselves with it until they understand it and love it. Then they will guard Islam as they guard the most precious thing in their Arabism. Since reality remains far from this aspiration, the new generation of Arab Christians has the task of realizing it with daring and freedom, sacrificing its pride and advantages, since nothing is equal to Arabism and the honor of being affiliated to it.

The second danger is the European notion of abstract humanity; it leads in the last analysis to considering peoples as blocs of static, homogeneous humanity with no roots in the earth, unaffected by time. Consequently, it is possible to apply to any one of these groups the reforms and alternatives which developed to meet the needs and dispositions of another....

It is not enough that theories and reforms be intelligible in themselves; they must spring in a vital way from the general spirit which was their source and origin. Today some think that bringing various reforms into the Arab milieu will suffice to revivify the nation. We think this attitude is another indication of our decline because it is content to mirror others and puts the branch in place of the root and the effect in place of the cause. The fact is that these reforms are branches which must spring from a root as blossoms flower on trees, and this root is above all psychological. It is the nation's faith in its mission and the faith of its sons in it.

From the preceding, it is clear why we attach all our concern to profound and alert national feelings. They are the root because they alone guarantee that social reforms will be vibrant, effective and courageous and in harmony with the spirit and the needs of the people, who will accomplish them because they want them.

We celebrate the memory of the hero of Arabism and Islam. What is Islam if not the offspring of pains, the pains of Arabism. These pains have returned to the land of the Arabs to a degree more excruciating and deeper than the Arabs of the *jāhiliyya* (pre-Islamic period) ever knew. How appropriate it would be if there welled up in us today a purifying formative revolution like that whose banner was borne by Islam. It is only the new Arab generation that can assume the revolution; they appreciate its necessity because the pains of the present have prepared them to carry its standard. Their love of their land and their history have led them to know the spirit of revolution and the direction it must take.

We, the new Arab generation, have a mission not a policy; we have faith and creed not theories and words. That band of Shuʻūbīyya[1] supported by foreign weapons, moved by racial envy against Arabism, do not frighten us because God and the nature of history are with us. . . . No one understands us except those who believe in God. We may not be seen praying with those who pray or fasting with those who fast, but we believe in God because we have a pressing need for him. Our burden is heavy, our road is rough and our goal is distant. We arrived at this faith, we did not begin with it. . . . I do not reckon that an Arab youth who is conscious of the corruption deeply embeded in his nation and who appreciates the dangers surrounding the future of Arabism . . . can dispense with faith in God. That is, faith in the right, the inevitable victory of right and the necessity of striving so that right may be victorious.

---

1. *Shuʻūbīyya:* the *Shuʻūbīyya* were the anti-Arab Muslims, or Persianizers, of the eighth and ninth centuries who vaunted Persian values and belittled Arab culture.

SADIQ AL-'AZM
1936–

The descendent of a prominent Syrian political family and
graduate of American University of Beirut, he holds a Ph.D. in
philosophy from Yale University. His Marxist criticism of religious thought published in 1970 caused a scandal. He was
brought to trial in Beirut in the same year on charges of provok-
ing religious troubles, but was acquitted.

A Criticism of Religious Thought

Even before the defeat of 1967, the Arab liberation movement knew that
Arab reactionaries and their international allies were using religious thought
as an ideological weapon, and yet no great importance was attached to this
fact. Apparently no one saw the necessity of disarming the reactionaries by
exposing their thought to a critical, scientific analysis to reveal the forgeries
they employ to exploit the Arab man. In fact, the political and intellectual
leaders of the Arab liberation movement espoused a negative attitude which
abetted the conservative position inasmuch as they refrained from any criticism of the Arab intellectual and social heritage and refused to seek out
ways of effecting change at the higher levels corresponding to the changes
which had occurred in the composition of the society's infrastructure. The
Arab liberation movement considered the cultural superstructure worthy of
respect and veneration. It surrounded retarded mental habits, bedouin and
feudal values, backward human relations, and obscurantist, quietistic world
views with an aura of sacredness which put them outside the pale of scientific criticism and historical analysis. . . .
   The fact is that the Arab liberation movement changed some of the
economic and social conditions of the Arab man but, at the same time,
placed all sorts of obstacles on the path leading to parallel changes in the
intellect and conscience of the Arab man, which would aid his "view of
himself, of life and the world to evolve". . . . To put it another way, the
Arab liberation movement stood "on its head rather than on its feet" . . .
in the sense that it wanted to put the revolutionary economic and social
changes it introduced and its use of modern science and technology at the
service of existing social relations and class divisions. . . . This posture

From *Naqd al-Fikr al-Dīnī* [A criticism of religious thought] (Beirut:Dār al-Talī'ah, 1970),
pp. 10–13, 20–25, 26–31, 40–43, 45–51, 57–58, 60–62, 64–69, 76–78.

113

found expression in the cultural policies of the Arab liberation movement such as its superficial but conservative preoccupation with the religious heritage, traditions, values, and thought, which, of course, impeded the hoped for changes in the Arab man. . . . Under the cover of protecting the people's traditions, values, art, religion, and morals, the cultural effort of the Arab liberation movement was used to protect the backward institutions and the medieval culture and thought of obscurantist ideology. . . .

In our view, the old religious position, full of serenity and optimism, is collapsing completely. We are passing through a stage of real renaissance marked by a complete scientific and cultural upheaval and a radical industrial and socialist transformation. We have been affected by the two most important books of the last two centuries: *Capitalism* and *The Origin of the Species.* The corpse of traditional feudal society has been shredded by the machine, and its bones have crumbled under the weight of modern economic and social organization, and with it has passed the fateful, positive attitude toward relition and its problems.

In this frantic atmosphere two problems loom large, the first is of a general cultural and ideological nature—the problem of the struggle between science and religion (Islam, for us). The second is a special problem, which is the concern of everyone radically affected by the scientific culture, which has begun to flood his society and milieu and forces him to face up to a basic question: "Can I accept in all honesty and sincerity the religious tenets my father and grandfathers accepted without betraying the principle of intellectual integrity?". . . .

There is a widely accepted opinion claiming that the struggle between science and religion is only apparent and that the difference between scientific knowledge of religious creeds is merely superficial. The propagandists of this opinion also claim that the spirit of Islam, for example, cannot conflict with science and that apparent conflicts are between science and the extraneous silt of the ages which has buried the true spirit. I would like to expand a bit to clarify this opinion, criticize it and explain the opposite viewpoint, to show that religion as it enters the core of our life and affects our intellectual and psychological makeup is in opposition to science and scientific knowledge—heart and soul, literally and figuratively.

First, we should not forget that more than two-and-a-half centuries passed in Europe before science was decisively victorious in its long war against the religious mentality which was dominant on that continent and before it established itself definitively in its cultural heritage. Science is still fighting a similar war in developing countries, including the Arab homeland, even though the battle is hidden and its lineaments are only occasionally apparent to all.

Second, the Islamic religion comprises opinions and tenets on the growth, composition, and nature of the universe, on the origin, history, and life of

man through the ages which form an inseparable part of the religion. It is
not necessary to emphasize that these opinions and tenets are clearly in
opposition to our scientific information on these subjects. But contradictions between religion and science concerning their convictions on a limited
subject is not very important. The conflict and struggle go much deeper than
that when they touch the problem of the methodology which must be
adopted to arrive at our convictions and knowledge in the subjects mentioned. It is a question of the way we must follow to be certain of the truth
or falsehood of these convictions. Islam and science in this matter are on
contradictory paths. For the Islamic religion (as for other religions) the
correct methodology for arriving at knowledge and conviction is to return
to specified texts considered as sacred or revealed, or to go back to the
writings of the sages and the learned who studied and explained these texts.
That is, the justification of the whole operation is reduced to faith and blind
trust in the wisdom at the source of these texts and their freedom from
error. It goes without saying that the scientific path to arrive at knowledge
and conviction concerning the growth and nature of the universe and man
and his history is completely incompatible with this subservient methodology which dominates religion because scientific methodology rests on observation and deduction and because the unique justification for the soundness
of the results arrived at by this methodology is the degree of its internal
logical harmony and its conformity with reality.

Third, among the essential things that the Islamic religion insists on is
that all basic truths that touch the core of man's life and all knowledge
connected with his destiny in this life and the next were uncovered at one
specific and decisive moment in history (the revelation of the Qur'ān and
perhaps the other books before it). For this reason we find the gaze of
believers always directed backwards to that time in which they believe
these truths and this knowledge were uncovered by God through angels
and messengers. The result is that the function of the believer, sage, philosopher, and learned man is not to discover new essential truths or gain
important knowledge not known previously but only to work for a more
profound view and more comprehensive grasp of the revealed texts. The
scientific spirit is far removed from the logic of this religious view because
science does not acknowledge the existence of texts which are impervious
to objective criticism and serious study and because the most outstanding
characteristic of scientific thought is discovery. . . . But religion from the
nature of its firm, stable, and limited beliefs lives in eternal verities and
looks backwards seeking inspiration from its infancy. For this reason religion has always formed a metaphysical obscurantist justification for the
social, economic, and political status quo. It has always been and is still a
strong fortress against those who exert effort for a revolutionary change of
these conditions. . . .

There is a resemblance between religion and science in that both attempt to explain events and define causes. Religion is an imaginative substitute for science. But the problem arises when religion claims for itself and its beliefs a type of veracity which no imaginative substitute is capable of claiming. The attempt to efface the features of the struggle between religion and science is nothing but a hopeless effort to defend religion. It is resorted to every time religion is forced to concede a traditional position and every time it is forced to withdraw from a center it formerly held. . . .

Now we turn to what we called our particular problem. The question around which our study will center can be summarized as follows: what should be the position of a man who has been exposed to scientific culture and has been radically affected by it vis-à-vis traditional religious beliefs and the institutions in which they are embodied? Can this man continue to believe in Adam and Eve, hell and heaven, that Moses divided the Red Sea and turned his rod into a serpent? What can be the position of a man who had a religious upbringing and accepted it lock, stock, and barrel vis-à-vis the natural scientific view of life, the universe, and man? It is difficult to find among us a person enjoying a bit of sensitivity and even a modest share of intelligence and scientific education who does not feel at some stage of his life and development the anxiety which surrounds this question and the worry it provokes. The intellectual and psychological state which this question expresses has become a basic part of our makeup; sometimes it floats on the surface of consciousness and we feel its existence strongly; at other times it is buried deep within us where it affects our conduct and thought in hidden ways. In any case it is always active. . . .

Various explanations concerning science and religion

The First Solution: Concordism. Among the sayings repeated by "concordist" speakers to confirm their claim that there is no conflict between religion and science is the Prophetic Tradition saying, "Seek science even if it is in China," and numerous well-known Qur'ānic verses which encourage man to think and meditate on things and to seek science and knowledge, etc. They attempt to demonstrate that Islam's concern for science and intellect extends back to its beginning. Naturally these thinkers attribute an absolute sense to these Islamic phrases. They speak as if these phrases belong to no time or place and can be separated from the historical context and the circumstances which gave them meaning and import at the time. It is clear to us that the science which Islam encourages one to seek is essentially religious and legal science and what is associated with it, and not physics and chemistry, for example. The intellect which Islam encourages man to use seeks knowledge of God by meditating on what he has created as did Hayy ibn Yaqzān in the story of Ibn Tufayl. The aim is not the formation of the dialectical theory of matter or the theory of Durkheim on religious customs and worship, or a theory of a convex universe. Islam is not at fault for that. At that time religious sciences were regarded as the most lofty and weighty, the extreme limit sought by anyone seeking science.

In this regard it should be remarked that the vast majority of these "concordists" know only very little about modern science, its methods of research, and what we may call the "scientific soul" or the "scientific spirit." However, they stand perplexed and breathless before the achievements of science and its practical applications. They are forced to respond to its effects in their everyday life and for this reason find that they can do nothing but announce perfect harmony and complete concord between their Islam and this great force. Therefore, Islam and modern science are harmonious and concordant in everything! No wonder then that they fall into strange contradictions. . . .

This type of thought declaring concord between Islam and contemporary life is concerned with justifying the social and political conditions which exist, no matter what they may be, on the basis of their complete harmony with the pure religion, its doctrines and law. The religious men of Islam supervise this operation defending the *status quo* and its personalities and policies. They put all their effort into laying a veneer of Islamic law over the political and social order, no matter what it may be, with which they are associated.

We find that every Arab system of government, no matter what its color, is not lacking esteemed Islamic institutions ready to issue *fatwās*[1] declaring that its policy is in complete harmony with Islam and contradicts it in nothing. There is no need to point out that the Islamic institutions in each state amass Qur'ānic verses, prophetic traditions, and legal opinions to demonstrate that the position of the given state is truth itself. . . .

Also, this methodology of concord between Islam and modern science is epitomized in the derivation of all modern sciences, theories and methodologies from verses of the Qur'ān. It is an arbitrary and ridiculous exercise of cramming every bit of modern science, great and small, into verses of the Qur'ān, then claiming that the Qur'ān contained all science from the beginning. In other words, the proponents of this current lie in wait for every new scientific theory and every scientific discovery, then exert themselves to find a verse in the Qur'ān claiming that it contained the theory and the discovery for fourteen centuries if not forever. . . .

The Second Solution: the complete rejection of scientific theory and all the ideas and opinions it contains, and complete enclosure within the religious view to defend it unto death. In fact it is very difficult to take this

---

1. *fatwā:* a formal legal opinion given by a jurist (*muftī*) on a legal problem submitted to him either by an individual or a judge.

view either individually or as a group because in its most extreme form it is a kind of intellectual suicide, and in its moderate form it leads to a progressive cleavage between man and the world around him. It is a type of escape that saves man from the effort of facing up to truths that do not harmonize with his own emotional, intellectual, and religious makeup. If he cannot bear this contradiction between his inner world and the world which surrounds him, then he will manifest the symptoms of the disease: complete nervous collapse or a type of general paralysis preventing any productive or frutiful work. He is hypersensitive to the burden which the religious heritage and the culture of the past place on him, and he is unable to adapt to the new conditions surrounding him. . . .

The Third Solution: distinguishing between the temporal and the eternal or spiritual dimensions of religion by saying that all that we find in religion concerning nature and history, etc., is included under the temporal dimension, which can be ceded completely to science. The spiritual dimension, however, has absolutely no connection with science; it is the area of eternal truths, hidden things, faith, and mystical experience. The proponents of this current say that scientific method and knowledge do not go beyond the scope of nature and for that reason it is not easy for them to investigate religious beliefs which are supported by pure faith not by intellectual argument nor by science and its proofs. In other words the propagandists for this opinion say that religious knowledge differs specifically from scientific and intellectual knowledge. For this reason we always fail when we try to apply logic to religious knowledge. It always appears to contradict logic and to be incompatible with the scientific mentality because this special kind of knowledge is the result of mystical experience or of the leap of pure faith or something similar.

The question which confronts me is this: Is it possible for me, a son of this century and a stepson of its civilization and science, to believe with the faith of miracles what appears to me with certainty to be in clear contradiction with science, knowing that my faith, or lack of it, will never change the pitch of this contradiction or diminish it? If I accept this clear contradiction, what prevents me from accepting all other contradictions which I find in all religions and fables and stories? This claim for naive acceptance of matters which appear contradictory to the intellect opens wide the door to things that modern science has struggled for long years to eradicate from the intellect of man. Every attempt to reinstate them ruins scientific values and confounds objective methodology and its application for the solution of the great and difficult problems of man. . . .

The Fourth and Final Solution. Now we will proceed to the solution which William James presented in the article. . . . "The Will to Believe." In that article James establishes a general principle for verifying the opinions and judgments presented to us. It is this: we cannot accept or reject any opinion as long as sufficient indications and testimonies to its truth or falsehood are not present. As long as these conditions are not met, we must suspend judgment. Likewise, the force with which we defend any given opinion we hold should be proportionate to the strength of the arguments supporting it and the number of signs indicating its correctness. There is no doubt that this principle enunciates a noble ideal which man can realize only to a certain degree, no matter how intelligent or how free he may be from fanaticism and passion in forming his studied opinions on the various subjects of life. . . . James asks if there are various cases in which a man is right in affirming a matter despite the clear lack of indications and confirmation of its truth or falsehood. He answers that religious belief or faith in the existence of God is one of these cases. According to James the person who faces the difficult choice between belief in the existence of God or lack of belief will never find any intellectual confirmation or scientific demonstration proving God's existence or non-existence. Here James confirms the right of this man to believe in the existence of God relying on what his emotional nature indicates about this subject. . . . But the question which comes to our mind is, why do we give the question of religion this preference and privilege to the point of excepting it from the comprehensive moral principle which governs the operation and content of certainty?. . . . Harmonizing our opinions with our emotional nature cannot form acceptable justification for our belief in these opinions, not if we wish to have studied opinions rather than merely inherited views. . . .

This does not mean that I want to invalidate religious feelings in man's experience of existence, but I think it is necessary to distinguish religion from religious feeling. Those feelings ground down by the burden of petrified traditional religious beliefs and the weight of frozen rites and rituals must be freed from their prison so that they may flower and express themselves by ways and means appropriate to our conditions of life in twentieth century civilization. For this reason we must renounce the traditional notion stating that existence is a special religious truth, and we must direct our concern towards religious feelings liberated from these weights and burdens. Likewise it seems to me that it is not necessary to attach religious feelings to hidden beings, concealed existences and strange forces as was always done. These feelings constitute a property which can shape all our other feelings, thoughts and goals. We can look to these feelings to bring order, harmony and assurance to our view towards the changing events of life. In this sense, religious feelings may be represented in the artist's view of beauty, or in the scientist's search for truth, or in the militant's conception of the goals he works to achieve, or in the view of the common man towards fulfilling the daily duties of life.

MUSTAFĀ SIBĀ'Ī
1915–1964

He was head of the Syrian branch of the Muslim Brothers and editor of their publications, *al-Manār* (Damascus) and *al-Muslimīn*. He studied at al-Azhar University, later taught at Damascus University where he became dean of the Sharī'a College. In 1949 he was elected to the Syrian parliament.

Islamic Socialism

Islamic socialism rests on five fundamental rights that must be guaranteed to all its citizens:

1. The right to live and, as its corollary, the safeguarding and protection of health and illness.
2. The right to liberty in all its forms, and particularly to political liberty.
3. The right to knowledge: This right extends to all the knowledge the nation needs, both spiritual and material.
4. The right to dignity, in all its aspects.
5. The right to property, subject to certain conditions.

I have also mentioned in my book the most important principles on which property is based in Islam:

1. Work—the most important way of acquiring property. All work leads to possession; it is legal if it involves neither fraud nor injustice.
2. Private property is an indefeasible right. The state guarantees it and punishes those who interfere with it.
3. Property is a social function; the state forbids its utilization as a means of oppression and exploitation.
4. Wealth involves social duties: legitimate charity, pensions for relatives, mutual social aid.
5. Inheritance is a legitimate right protected by the state.

Nationalization can be applied to goods and articles necessary to society only if their possession by one or several individuals involves the exploitation of society, on condition also that economic experts agree that it is in the obvious interest of the nation.

From Kemal H. Karpat, ed. *Political and Social Thought in the Contemporary Middle East* (New York: Praeger, 1968), pp. 123–26.

Henceforth, when the state has recourse to nationalization in cases of social or economic necessity, it is obliged to afford adequate compensation to the dispossessed proprietors.

The principles of Islam, our social situation, and the obligation placed upon us by our religion to wipe out oppression and give human dignity to the peasants—all this renders the limitation of landed property legal in the eyes of the law and makes it one of the duties of the state. Nevertheless, it must be applied in all fairness and in conformity to the general interest, and not merley to satisfy rancor and vengeance.

Moreover, the seizure of private goods should be carried out only under certain conditions, especially in cases of extreme danger, invasion, public disaster, famine, flood, or earthquake. Only if the state treasury and the funds held by the authorities are inadequate to guard against any danger is it lawful to deduct from people's wealth what is strictly necessary to meet such necessity, as proclaimed by the '*ulamā*' of Islam, such as al-Nawāwī, al-Ghazzālī, etc.

I have then cited the rules of mutual social aid. Numering twenty-nine, they guarantee the fulfillment by the state of this obligation vis-à-vis its subjects, thus assuring them as well as their children a decent life in case of incapacity, illness, or unemployment.

Briefly summarized, such is the conception of Islamic socialism that I have set out in my book. I have then compared it with the socialism of the extreme left.

1. In recognizing the lawful character of private property, Islamic socialism allows those with talent to participate in constructive competition, an essential condition for the expansion of civilization and the development of production.
2. This socialism encourages and leads to cooperation and friendship, not to class struggle.
3. It is a moral socialism based on sound morals, of which it makes a foundation in its doctrine.
4. All that concerns man comes under the care of this socialism: religion, morals, education, clothing, food, and not only the material aspects of life.
5. It is an integral part of the credo of the Muslim, who can but apply it. It constitutes a more rapid and more effectual method than any other socialism for the reform of our society.

As for the socialism of extreme left, this is what I wrote: "Its roots are not in the depths of the human soul; it is not based upon religion or human nature or conviction. It cannot therefore be applied except by force and in an atmosphere of terror".

Such are the aspects and characteristics of socialism in Islam. Without doubt, it is totally different from the type of socialism that attaches no importance to religious values, relies on the class struggle in society, seizes private property without good reason, nationalizes industry and economic concerns that contribute to the national economic prosperity, paralyzes initiative and competition in the individual as well as the community, impoverishes the rich without enriching the poor, originates from hate and not from love, claims to work for the people while it terrorizes them, impoverishes them, and humiliates them. A socialism of this kind is as far removed as possible from Islam and has nothing in common with it. Moreover, Islam foresees in it the inevitable ruin of any society where it reigns and exercises influence.

Finally, since our revolutionary order [the Syrian revolution] and our government have agreed on socialism as a social regime, and since they have published a detailed program which is in no way contrary to Islam, it is good—and I say this in all sincerity and frankness—that the cause of Islamic socialism should be encouraged, because of its profound influence on the minds of the masses and its facility for building a worth-while society, unique and advanced in its economy and its social relations. It is also desirable that this socialism should be embraced by every zealous defender of our nation who is anxious to avert the danger of extreme left-wing socialism.

In fact, Islamic socialism conforms to human nature. It satisfies the dignity of all citizens as well as their interests. To the workers, it grants a decent standard of living and an assured future; to the holder of capital, it opens up wide horizons as regards production under state control. Finally, it applies to all citizens without discrimination, and is not the prerogative of the followers of one religion to the exclusion of those of another.

SAYYID QUTB
1906–1966

Son of a landowner, he completed secondary and college studies
in Cairo, obtaining a licentiate in Arabic language and literature
from Dār al-'Ulūm. After a brief tenure as an inspector in the
Ministry of Education he left to devote himself to writing. In
1939 he turned to more religious writing. In 1948 he published
Social Justice in Islam, then spent two years in the United States
studying educational organization. On his return to Egypt he
joined the Muslim Brothers. He spent ten years in prison under
Nāsir, was freed in 1964, only to be imprisoned again and executed in 1966 on suspicion of plotting against the government.

Social Justice in Islam

Islam grew up in an independent country owing allegiance to no empire
and to no king, in a form of society never again achieved. It had to
embody this society in itself, had to order, encourage, and promote it. It
had to order and regulate this society, adopting from the beginning its
principles and its spirit along with its methods of life and work. It had to
join together the world and the faith by its exhortations and laws. So Islam
chose to unite earth and Heaven in one spiritual organization, and one
that recognized no difference between worldly zeal and religious coercion.
Essentially Islam never infringes that unity even when its outward forms
and customs change. . . . One of the characteristic marks of this faith is the
fact that it is essentially a unity. It is at once worship and work, religious
law and exhortation. Its theological beliefs are not divorced in nature or in
objective from secular life and customs. . . . However we approach the
question, there can be no shadow of doubt that the theory of society is
obviously reflected in the beliefs and the customs of this religion, and that
these latter represent the basic, powerful, and universal theory of all social
life. So if in any age we find a desire to over-emphasize the pietistic aspect
of this faith and to divorce it from the social aspect, or to divorce the
social aspect from it, it will be the fault of that age rather than that of
Islam. . . .

We have, then, not a single reason to make any separation between

From *Social Justice in Islam*, trans. John B. Hardie (Washington, D.C.: American Council of
Learned Societies, 1953/Octagon Books reprint, 1970), pp. 7–9, 13–16, 24–28.

Islam and society, either from the point of view of the essential nature of Islam, or from that of its historical course; such reasons as there are attach only to European Christianity. And yet the world has grown away from religion; to it the world has left only the education of the conscience and the perfecting of piety, while to the temporal and secular laws has been committed the ordering of society and the organizing of human life.

Similarly we have no good grounds for any hostility between Islam and the thought of social justice, such as the hostility that persists between Christianity and Communism. For Islam prescribes the basic principles of social justice, and establishes the claim of the poor to the wealth of the rich; it lays down a just principle for power and for money, and therefore has no need to drug the minds of men, and summon them to neglect their earthly rights in favor of their expectations in Heaven. On the contrary, it warns those who abdicate their natural rights that they will be severely punished in the next world, and it calls them "self-oppressors." "Surely the angels said to those who died when they were oppressing themselves, 'In what circumstances were you?' They answered, 'We were poor in the earth.' The angels said, 'Was not Allah's earth wide enough for you to migrate?' 'The abode of such is Hell—an evil place to go.' " Thus Islam urges men to fight for their rights; "and he who fights without injustice, the same is a martyr." So while Europe is compelled to put religion apart from the common life, we are not compelled to tread the same path; and while communism is compelled to oppose religion in order to safeguard the rights of the workers, we have no need of any such hostility to religion.

But can we be certain that this "two-in-one" social order which was established by Islam in one specific period of history will continue to have the potential for growth and renewal? Can we be sure that it is suitable for application to other periods of history whose circumstances differ to a greater or lesser degree from those which obtained in the age which gave birth to Islam?

This is a fundamental question. It is not possible to give an exhaustive answer to it here, as it will be answered in detail in what is to follow; first, we must examine this social order itself, define its sources and roots, and scrutinize its applications in every-day life. Suffice it here—for we are still in the stage of general discussion—to say that Islam has already experienced such an historical process, and the social, economic, and intellectual developments connected with it.

This process Islam has survived by laying down the general, universal rules and principles, and leaving their application in detail to be determined by the processes of time and by the emergence of individual problems. But Islam itself does not deal with the incidental related issues of the principle, except insofar as such are expressions of an unchanging principle whose impact is felt universally. This is the limit of the authority which can be claimed by an religion, in order that it may guarantee its flexibility and ensure the possibility of its own growth and expansion over a period of time. . . .

The conclusion from this is that we should not put away the social aspect of our faith on the shelf; we should not go to French legislation to derive our laws, or to communist ideals to derive our social order, without first examining what can be supplied from our Islamic legislation which was the foundation of our first form of society. But there is a wide ignorance of the nature of our faith; there is a spiritual and intellectual laziness which is opposed to a return to our former resources; there is a ridiculous servility to the European fashion of divorcing religion from life—a separation necessitated by the nature of their religion, but not by the nature of Islam. For with them there still exists that gulf between religion on the one hand and learning and the State on the other, the product of historical reasons which have no parallel in the history of Islam.

This does not mean that our summons is to an intellectual, spiritual, and social avoidance of the ways of the rest of the world; the spirit of Islam rejects such an avoidance, for Islam reckons itself to be a gospel for the whole world. Rather our summons is to return to our own stored-up resources, to become familiar with their ideas, and to proclaim their value and permanent worth, before we have recourse to an untimely servility which will deprive us of the historical background of our life, and through which our individuality will be lost to the point that we will become merely the hangers-on to the progress of mankind. Whereas our religion demands that we should be ever in the forefront: "You are the best nation which I have produced among men; you encourage what is approved of God, and you forbid what is disapproved." . . .

While we are examining this universal theory which takes its rise from the nature of Islamic thought about the world and life and humanity, we may study also the fundamental outlines of social justice in Islam. Above all other things it is a comprehensive human justice, and not merely an economic justice; that is to say, it embraces all sides of life and all aspects of freedom. It is concerned alike with the mind and the body, with the heart and the conscience. The values with which this justice deals are not only economic values, nor are they merely material values in general; rather they are a mixture of moral and spiritual values together. Christianity looks at man only from the stand-point of his spiritual desires and seeks to crush down the human instincts in order to encourage those desires. On the other hand Communism looks at man only from the stand-point of his material needs; it looks not only at human nature, but also at the world and at life from a purely material point of view. But Islam looks at man as forming a unity whose spiritual desires cannot be separated from his bodily appetites, and whose moral needs cannot be divorced from his material needs. It looks at the world and at life with this all-embracing view which permits of no separation or division. In this fact lies the main divergence between Communism, Christianity, and Islam.

Thus, in the Islamic view, life consists of mercy, love, help, and a mutual responsibility between Muslims in particular, and between all human beings in general. Whereas in the Communist view, life is a continual strife and struggle between the classes, a struggle which must end in one class overcoming the other; at which point the Communist dream is realized. Hence it is patent that Islam is the undying goodness of humanity, embodied in a living faith, working in the world; while communism is the evil of human nature, limited to a single nation.

There are, then, these two great facts: the absolute, just, and coherent unity of existence, and the general, mutual responsibility of individuals and societies. On these two facts Islam bases its definition of social justice, having regard to the basic elements of the nature of man, yet not unmindful of human abilities. . . .

Accordingly, when Islam comes to lay down its rules and laws, its counsels and controls, that natural "love of gain" is not overlooked, nor is that deep natural avarice forgotten; selfishness is rebuked, avarice is dealt with by regulations and laws, and the duty laid on man is that of liberality. At the same time, Islam does not overlook the needs and the welfare of society, nor does it it forget the great achievements of individuals in life and society in every age and among different nations, which is inconsistent with justice, when the greed and cupidity of the individual prey upon society; or that same oppression may also take the form of society preying upon the nature and ability of the individual. Such oppression is a sin, not against one individual alone, but against the whole principle of the community. It is an encroachment upon the freedom of the individual whose natural rights are infringed; but its evil effects do not touch merely the welfare and rights of that one individual; they go beyond him to touch the welfare of the whole community, because it cannot profit to the full from his abilities. So the regulations lay down the rights of the community over the powers and abilities of the individual; they also establish limiting boundaries to the freedom, the desires, and the wants of the individual, but they must also be ever mindful of the rights of the individual, to give him freedom in his desires and inclinations; and over all there must be the limits which the community must not overstep, and which the individual on his side must not transgress. Nor must there be interference with great individual achievements; for life is a matter of mutual help and mutual responsibility according to Islam, and not a constant warfare, to be lived in a spirit of struggle and hostility. Thus there must be freedom for individual and general abilities, rather than repression and a restrictive constraint. Everything that is not legally forbidden is perfectly permissible;

and everything that is not useless is of value. So the individual is to be encouraged by having every freedom in a life which reflects the Divine nature and which gives promise of the highest achievement.

This breadth of vision in the Islamic view of life, together with the fact that it goes beyond merely economic values to those other values on which life depends—these things make the Islamic faith the more powerful to provide equity and justice in society, and to establish justice in the whole of the human sphere. It also frees Islam from the narrow interpretation of justice as understood by Communism. For justice to the Communist is an equality of wages, in order to prevent economic discrimination; but within recent days when theory has come into opposition with practice, Communism has found itself unable to achieve this equality. Justice in Islam is a human equality, envisaging the adjustment of all values, of which the economic is but one.

In the Islamic view values are so very composite that justice must include all of them; therefore Islam does not demand a compulsory economic equality in the narrow literal sense of the term. This is against nature, and conflicts with the essential fact, which is that of the differing native endowments of individuals. It arrests the development of outstanding ability, and makes it equal to lesser ability; it prevents those who have great gifts from using their gifts to their own advantage and to that of the community, and it discourages the community and the individual from producing such gifts. . . .

Islam does, of course, acknowledge a fundamental equality of all men, and a fundamental justice among all, but over and above that it leaves the door open for achievement of preeminence through hard work, just as it lays in the balance values other than the economic. "Verily the noblest among you in Allah's eyes is the most pious." "Allah will raise up in degrees of honor those of you who believe, and to whom knowledge has been brought." "Wealth and children are an ornament to life in the world, but the things which endure, the works of righteousness are better in thy Lord's eyes—better for reward and better for hope." From this it is apparent that there are values other than the merely economic; with these values Islam reckons, and these it brings into relation with the idea of justice in society, since different individuals have different methods of gaining their livelihood. Islam admits the reasonable causes of these differences, as being differences in strength and in endowment. It does not admit differences that depend on rank and station; such it absolutely denies. . . .

Islam, then, does not demand a literal equality of wealth, because the distribution of wealth depends on men's endowments, which are not uniform. Hence absolute justice demands that men's rewards be similarly different, and that some have more than others—so long as human justice is upheld by the provision of equal opportunity for all. Thus rank or upbringing, origin or class should not stand in the way of any individual, nor should anyone be fettered by the chains that shackle enterprise. Justice must be upheld also by the inclusion of all kinds of values in the reckoning, and by the freeing of the human mind completely from the tyranny of the purely economic values, and by the relegation of these to their true and reasonable place. Economic values must not be given an intrinsically high standing, such as they enjoy in those human societies which lack a certainty of true values, or which give to them too slight an importance; in such conditions money alone becomes the supreme and fundamental value.

In Islam money is not given this value; Islam refuses to admit that life can be reckoned in terms of a mouthful of bread, the appetites of the body, or a handful of money. Yet at the same time it demands a competence for every individual, and at times more than a competence, in order to remove the fear of destitution. On the other side it forbids that unbridled luxury in possessions and desires, which produces social divisions and classes. It prescribes the claims of the poor upon the wealth of the rich, according to their needs, and according to the best interests of society, so that social life may be full, just, and productive. Thus it is not unmindful of any one of the various aspects of life, material, intellectual, religious and worldly; but it organizes them all, that they may be related together and thus furnish an all-embracing unity in which it will be difficult to neglect any one of their various integral parts. So these departments of life become an organized unity, similar to the great oneness of the universe, and to that of life, of the nation, and of all mankind.

THE NATIONAL CHARTER OF THE ALGERIAN POPULAR DEMOCRATIC REPUBLIC, 1976

The Algerian Charter, published July 5, 1976, as the highest source for national policy and state law, was drawn up by the Front for National Liberation, the sole political party in the country.

Islam and the Socialist Revolution

The Algerian people is a Muslim people.

Islam is the state religion.

As an integral part of our historic personality, Islam is one of our strongest defenses against all attempts at depersonalization. In the worst hours of colonial domination, the Algerian people, driven by a sense of justice and equality, entrenched themselves in a militant, austere Islam and drew from it that moral energy and that spiritual sense that preserved them from despair and allowed them to overcome.

The decline of the Muslim world cannot be explained by moral causes alone. Other factors of a material, economic, and social nature such as foreign invasions, internal struggles, the rise of despotism, the spread of feudal oppression and the disappearance of certain world trade routes played a determining role in this. Also, the rise of superstitions and the general preoccupation with the past should not be considered as causes but as effects. To concentrate attacks on aberrant practices while neglecting social conditioning is to fall into inefficacious moralism. As a matter of fact, the Muslim world has only one way out of its predicament to regeneration: it must go beyond reformism and commit itself to the path of social revolution.

Revolution fits easily into the historical perspective of Islam. Islam, if its spirit is correctly understood, is not tied to any particular interests, to no specific clergy, to no temporal power. Neither feudalism nor capitalism can claim it as their own. Islam brought to the world a lofty notion of human dignity which condemns racism, chauvinism, and the exploitation of man by man. Its fundamental egalitarianism can find an expression adapted to every epoch.

From *Charte Nationale* (République Algérienne, 1976), pp. 21–22.

It behooves the Muslim people, whose destiny today is mingled with that of the Third World, to become aware of the positive aspects of their spiritual and cultural patrimony and to reassimilate them in the light of contemporary values and mutations. That is to say that every undertaking which aims at a reconstruction of Muslim thought today if it wishes to be credible, must necessarily refer to a much vaster undertaking: the total refashioning of society.

In our period of decisive social transformation, the Muslim peoples are called to shake off the anachronistic yoke of feudalism, despotism, and every form of obscurantism.

The Muslim peoples are coming to realize more fully that it is in reinforcing their struggle against imperialism and in adopting resolutely the path of socialism that they respond best to the imperatives of their faith and make their action accord with its principles.

After obtaining his doctorate in Germany, he spent many years
as a professor and later dean at Osmania University. In 1951,
he became director of the Institute of Islamic Culture in Lahore. A Muslim modernist writer, he sought to situate Islamic
socialism between a laissez-faire capitalism and totalitarian
Marxism. His two major works are *Islamic Ideology* and *Islam
and Communism*.

Islamic Socialism

In dealing with Islam it will make for clarity if we deal with the ideal
teachings and trends of Islam separately from the experiment it made with
the actual economic and social conditions at its advent; we must also
beware of confusing the whole issue by wrongly identifying Islam with the
laws and customs prevailing at the present time in various Muslim countries. Ideals are never completely actualised in the life of an individual or
epoch. Actual circumstances always impose certain limitations, and consequently the realisation is never equal to the aspiration. But the genuineness
and practicability of an ideology has to be tested by the earnestness of the
efforts made and the success achieved though in a more or less compro-
mised or modified form.

In distinction from many other older religions, Islam aimed at not only a
total change of outlook but a total revolution in social, political and
economic life of the people who profess it. We will study its chief features
in a broad outline and then leave it to the reader to judge whether society
as intended to be moulded by Islam would be called socialist and if so, in
what way it resembles in some of its traits other socialistic experiments
carried on elsewhere and in what respect it possesses some distinctive
characteristics.

Socialism is generally considered to be a remedy for removing the inequality of opportunities created by an unjust accumulation and unfair
distribution of wealth. When reformists with a zeal for social justice see
that society has been split up into the over-nourished and the under-
nourished, with superfluous wealth extravagantly squandered on the one

From *Islam and Communism* (Lahore: Institute of Islamic Culture, 1951), pp. 176–84, 187,
191–92.

hand and abject poverty and insecurity on the other, their first cry is for equality. They say that men are born equal and hence they have equal rights to the goods of life. In their enthusiasm men cease to distinguish between natural and man-made inequalities. One must state, at the outset, quite frankly that Islam does not believe in any utopian, unrealistic equality between individuals of all types. Human beings are born with varying gifts. As they differ in their bodies and their features so that no two individuals even among countless millions are ever completely alike, so they differ in their mental and other inborn traits. And after having been born, they will encounter different environments and circumstances which would materially affect their conduct and character. This is what is called *taqdīr* or destiny of man which for him is the data of life or the raw material which he has to mould as best as he can. It is only the broad features of the human shape and human nature which may be called the common inheritance of all humanity. If this is the equality meant by those who say that men are born equal, Islam has no quarrel with this idea. But within the framework of these broad uniformities, there are infinite diversities due to differences in natural endowments. The Qur'ān says explicitly that some men are more gifted than others.

See how We have made some of them to excel others (17:21). . . .

The relation between the relative influences of heredity and environment can never be satisfactorily established or demonstrated. Similarly, the roles of destiny and freewill remain wrapped in mystery. Islam teaches only this, that both are indubitable facts of life; however logic may fall short of grasping it. Numerous verses of the Qur'ān give both aspects almost in the same verse. So the Islamic doctrine is that men are equal or similar in some respects and unequal or dissimilar in other respects. Nature in general is a system of uniformities and diversities and a set of phenomena are uniform and diverse at the same time. According to the Islamic teaching, any system of society that would try to create a dead level of equality among human individuals would fail because it would contravene fundamental laws of Nature. But these natural inequalities must not be reinforced and fortified by artificial inequalities. Gifts are not meant to be hardened into privileges. Individual inequalities are real, but no classes should be allowed to be formed on the basis of distinctive rights with special laws governing different classes. Society must not be divided into classes of the rulers and the ruled, the privileged and the unprivileged.

Let us take one by one the measures that Islam adopted to abolish artificial privileges which always went hand in hand with economic exploitation.

The greatest economic exploiter is the monarchy. A monarch considered himself the master of his realm and lord of his subjects. The entire revenues of his kingdom collected justly or unjustly formed his private purse.

In spending these revenues he was not responsible to anyone. He bestowed as much as he liked on those who gained his favours and took away as much as he chose from those who earned his wrath. The first step in socialism must necessarily be the abolition of this institution. One might say that a limited constitutional monarchy may go well together with a good measure of socialism, but Islam in its purity recognises no type of hereditary monarchy. The original polity of Islam was republican democracy where the head of the State must be chosen by the consensus of citizens. He must be the first servant of the State and have no special privileges. He must be subject to all the civil and criminal laws of the State. He is entitled to claim from the State only the essentials of a decent livelihood. The Prophet himself, the first head of a State, claimed even less than this and led the life of a poor man who was not always sure of his daily bread. The Caliphs that followed him immediately tried to follow his example. The second Caliph 'Umar said: "The head of the State is like the guardian of orphans; if he has means of his own he should avoid getting any remuneration for his guardianship, but if he is himself in want, he may take only bare sustenance and no more." As he would have no court or courtiers, society would be rid of thousands of parasites.

Having repudiated the institution of monarchy, Islam turned its attention to another set of exploiters: the feudal lords who form a class of aristocracy or nobility. Islam arose in a country of large nomadic and a small agricultural population with a sprinkling of traders in its few towns. . . .

But even if large tracts of land had been granted to the early Muslims, feudalism and large-scale land-lordism could not have developed. The Islamic law of inheritance would have split up these large estates within a generation or two into small peasant-proprietorships. Feudalism and holding of large estates is possible only with the law of primogeniture according to which only the eldest son inherits the entire estate to the total exclusion of other heirs, who have to shift for themselves.

The spirit of the Qur'ānic teaching is that land is like the other free gifts of God; it is created for the benefit of all humanity. Any system of ownership which prevents the maximum utilisation of land for productive purposes would be against the injunctions and the spirit of Islam. Land is not like other commodities owned by an individual. A person may possess some articles of furniture or dress which he never uses and no law would take it away from him, but land which is not being properly used can be lawfully taken away from the owner. This means that, according to Islam, the owner of land is a kind of trustee for the community. If the community comes to the conclusion that owing to a particular system of use or abuse the land is not yielding as much as it should or could, the State has a right to step in. The Prophet had granted Bilāl a large tract of land which he was later on found to be unable to cultivate. 'Umar forced him to give it up. For all kinds of socialism the ownership of land is a vital problem. Islam has definite injunctions against landlordism or retention of large estates intact.

As under the Islamic system land would necessarily be partitioned after the death of an owner, big landlordism would find no place. On the other hand, after partition through inheritance, males as well as females having a prescribed share, there would crop up danger of the fragmentation of holdings. This can be prevented by legislation prescribing the size of a minimum holding, one person or one family owning a minimum holding by paying off the other heirs in convenient instalments. Egypt has already passed such legislation, and other Muslim countries are bound to follow her during the course of agrarian reforms that are being rapidly effected in all Muslim lands. Muslim peasant-proprietors may be encouraged by the State in the interests of increased production to adopt a system of co-operative farming. The Russian method of forced collectivisation by total expropriation entailed untold misery and caused a terrible famine, with large-scale destruction of livestock. After doing great violence to human nature, Russia has now guaranteed a kind of collective ownership to the families working on a collective farm. They shall now have a right to continue as partners in the same collective farm along with the concession of holding a strip of land and some livestock in absolute private ownership.

Another revolutionary step in the process of establishing a classless society was the abolition of priesthood as a caste and a privileged class. This class, having been recognised as the monopolist of spirituality and salvation, acquired economic advantages at the same time. Churches, temples and monasteries became centres of wealth, and a large horde of priests which took no part in economic production lived comfortably and parasitically on the labours of the working classes. The priests became allies of ruling groups, and both classes established a co-dominion. A very large portion of land in Europe belonged to the Church and fees of a great variety were levied upon the people. . . . Places of worship may be built where people should gather to pray to God in a congregation without any professional priest working as intermediary. . . .

Another great source of economic exploitation and tyranny was usury. The usurers everywhere were callous, blood-suckers, fattening themselves on the life-blood of the poor and the needy. Large portions of population were enslaved by them: anyone who could not pay his debts with exorbitant, compound interest sold himself as a slave to the creditor. Sometime this kind of bondage was passed on to his descendants who could not be free until all the debt was paid. The moral sense of prophets and philosophers had always revolted against this tyranny, but there is no example in history in which the prophet of a great religion and a great State fought more systematically and more successfully against this evil than the Prophet of Islam. Prohibition of usury by Islam was so categorical that no loophole was left to practise it in disguised forms. . . . The usurer said that interest was like trade. Islam said: No, the two are radically different. Then they said interest increases wealth. Islam said that, looked at closely, its tendencies are not productive but destructive.

> Those who swallow down usury cannot rise as one whom the devil has prostrated by his touch does rise. That is because they say, Trading is only like usury; and Allah has allowed trading and forbidden usury (Qur'ān 2:275),
> Allah does not bless usury, but causes charity to prosper (2:276).

The Qur'ān says that he who insists on usury wages war against God and His Prophet which meant undermining the social fabric and sabotaging the State:

> O you who believe! be careful of (your duty to) Allah and relinquish what remains due from usury if you are believers. But if you do it not, then be apprised of war from Allah and His Apostle (2:278). . . .

Now we pass on from the problem of interest to another important tenet of Islam, called *zakāt*, which is a tax on capital of various types which has accumulated as a surplus at the end of every year. Islam inculcates industry and deprecates extravagance which means that an able-bodied worker, trader, or industrialist will have some surpluses in gold or silver or money or goods of various kinds, which have remained over after satisfying all natural needs. These surpluses, as a right belong to the individuals whose fruits of effort they represent. But here again this right to ownership is not absolute; out of this a percentage must be handed over to the State to be utilised mainly for the benefits of the needy who have, somehow been handicapped in the race of life. In society which allows private property and individual initiative in all the walks of life, differences in acquisitions are bound to occur, but Islam says that these differences must not be allowed to create classes of the rich and the poor with an unpassable social gulf between them. Efforts must be made to level up and level down by methods which the people should believe to be moral and spiritual. Out of the funds secured by tax or surpluses the needy shall be rehabilitated by gifts and interest-free loans. Lest anyone feel proud and self-righteous in bestowing charity, the Qur'ān says (51:19) that the needy have a right on the wealth of the rich:

> And in their wealth
> Is the right of him,
> Who asks, and him
> Who is needy.

And to illustrate this the Prophet is reported to have said that, after all, the wealth and comforts of the rich are the products of the labours of the poor.

It is a principle laid down in the Qur'ān that economic life should be so organised that wealth does not circulate only among the rich:

> Whatever Allah has restored to His Apostle from the people of the town, it is for Allah and for the Apostle and for the near of the kin and the orphans and needy and the wayfarer, so that it may not be a thing taken by turns among the rich of you only (59:7).

National wealth is like blood in an organism; it should not create plethora in one part and atrophy in another part. Islam desired to mould the economic life of society in such a manner that antagonistic class-divisions of millionaires and paupers should not come into existence. The Prophet did not approve of private dispensation of charity, and he envisaged a state of affairs in which a person would walk through the land with charity to offer but would find none who would receive it. All his efforts were directed towards the creation of a classless society; at first with the gradual emancipation of slaves and the elimination of pauperism. All surpluses should come to the State in prescribed proportions and administered by the State; so that no individual should feel any shame in being obliged to receive charity at private hands. He considered it as the duty of the State that if it possesses enough resources, no citizen should be deprived of the fundamental needs of life. . . .

A. K. BROHI
1915–

A leading lawyer and statesman, A.K. Brohi has over the years
held numerous posts in Pakistan's government, among them
Minister of Law and Religious Affairs. He is currently oversee-
ing the establishment of the Sharī'a College in Islamabad.

The Concept of Islamic Socialism

One of the terms which nowdays so frequently appears in the daily Press,
or is heard *ad nauseam* within the so-called intellectual circles, is that of
Islamic Socialism. It is claimed that "Islamic Socialism" if we could only
realise it as a practical possibility is a panacea for all our ills. Speaking for
myself, I find much difficulty in understanding precisely what is meant by
the concept of Islamic Socialism. The term "socialism" one can understand; and, to some extent, I suppose I understand what "Islam" is. But it
is, if I am permitted to so put it, the spurious concoction of these two
concepts which creates complications for the rational mind. The dilemma
posed to normal human intelligence by this hybrid expression "Islamic
Socialism" can be presented as follows: If "Socialism" is precisely what
Islam enjoins us to accept, then Socialism by itself should be acceptable to
us as our national ideology. If, however, it is not the conventional type of
Socialism that Islam enjoins upon us to accept, then in what essential
particulars, one may ask, has Islam modified this concept so that it must
be designated as *Islamic Socialism* to distinguish it from its non-Islamic
varieties. Why is the word "Islam," which is substantive, being degraded
into becoming an adjective of "socialism" is a question that no one that I
know of in this country can, consistently with logic, honestly answer. On
the one hand we say (do we not?) that Islam provides a comprehensive
code of life bearing upon questions related to the economic, political and
social organisations of mankind; yet, on the other hand, we are called
upon to say that there is an ideology called "Socialism" which is what we
need provided we could somewhat modify it: thus it is said, not Islam
simply, but Islamic Socialism will redeem us and will help us to organise
our lives much more meaningfully than we are able to do so at present.

If Islam is a universal religion, that is to say, a way of life which is valid

From *Islam in the Modern World* (Lahore: Publishers United Ltd.), pp. 93–98.

for all time, for all people, and for all geographical habitats, then why does it not also have an adequate answer to those specific economico-political problems with which we are confronted in Pakistan—so that we are forced to borrow our "model" from an alien culture and civilization? If Socialism may be defined as a theory or a policy of social organisation which advocates the ownership and control of the means of production, capital, land, property etc., by the community as a whole and their administration or distribution in the interests of all, it is clear that Islam cannot have much to say in the matter. If you think that is the only way to secure justice, you may subscribe to the theory or the policy of Socialism; but on the other hand, if you think that it will not advance the cause of justice but frustrate it, you may not subscribe to its doctrine. But what has that got to do with Islam, anyway! This strategy of Socialism may be of some importance today to realise the ideal of justice but tomorrow it may not—it is no use, therefore, implicating Islam in this manoeuvre.

By "Socialism" one ordinarily understands an economic philosophy which enjoins upon its votaries the necessity of regarding the instruments of production and the questions relating to the distribution of wealth to be matters exclusively for state's ownership and concern. In the context of the Marxian philosophy, which necessarily is a part and parcel of the materialistic interpretation of history, we are asked to believe in the primacy of economic categories. Contrary to this view, within the framework of a Muslim view of life, this avowedly materialistic approach must be rejected, since it is in conflict with the contention of the Qur'ān, that it is the moral and spiritual categories which are primary and fundamental.

There is, accordingly, no place in Islam for the materialistic interpretation of history so that you might, with some justification, be able to argue for the primacy of the economic factor. Therefore socialism, as an offspring of materialistic interpretation of history, cannot be acceptable to a Muslim. Hence, no wonder, efforts are afoot to suggest that "socialism" can be spiritualised—and this is sought to be achieved by the simple device of labelling it as "Islamic."

I suspect that the word "Islam" is in Pakistan constantly being utilised as a cloak for importing alien stuff—be these ideologies or institutions. By this device, ideologies and cognate principles of social organisation which have been sanctioned by the growth of atheistic, nihilistic, and materialistic philosophies of the West in our time are given an air of plausibility, an appearance of respectability. I have often heard it said: if you add God to Communism the product becomes equal to Islam. Although I am a philosopher by training, I confess, I do not know much about this "dialectical arithmetic" and I will not therefore venture to say anything about it. But what I can say with some authority is this: that God is too all-comprehensive to be added to anything, and Communism which is assuredly based on the cult of Godlessness cannot survive for you to accept it, if you are to be a believer in God. You cannot have both together: you have to make up your mind as to what you want and then you have some choice in the matter. "Theistic Communism" is absurd—as is "Islamic Socialism" or "Islamic Capitalism."

To the age-old question: "What is the state to do for the individual where the individual is not able to provide for himself those bare necessities of life which he is to have if he is to survive?" Islam has its own answer to return. It is the responsibility of the State to provide conditions upon which not only the mind and character of its citizens must develop but also the conditions upon which its citizens are to win by their own efforts all that is necessary to full civic efficiency. It is not for the State to feed, house or clothe them. It is for the State to take care that the economic conditions are such that the normal man, who is not defective in mind or body or will can, by useful labour, feed, house, and clothe himself and his family. The "right to work" and "the right to a living wage" are just as valid as the rights of persons or property—that is to say, they are integral conditions of a good social order. This was the concept of social order upon which "liberalism" of the nineteenth-century European politics was based. Man's pre-occupation with the task of founding a just society is as old as the hills. This was long before Socialism—or, as a matter of fact, long before any "ism" was born. What could you say of the economic and political system of Abū-Bakr, or 'Umar or 'Uthmān or of 'Alī? Were they socialists? The instruments of production were not owned by the state of their day nor had they the type of control which a socialist state claims to have on the means of distribution of wealth. And yet they were, I suppose, consistently with conditions that obtained in their times, practising the Gospel of Islam by founding society on justice.

ISLAM IN THE CONTEMPORARY SECULAR STATE

This section presents a more contemporary treatment of the problem of Islam and the modern state. A new generation building on the efforts of their predecessors feels more free to criticize as well as to explicate what was implicit in much of the preceding argumentation. We have included the section from 'Abdallāh Laroui's *Contemporary Arab Ideology* because it brings out so well the three basic mentalities (cleric, politician, and technocrat)—caricatures perhaps, but nonetheless instructive, indicating how the basic confrontation has been skirted. Hichem Djait and Muhammad Nuwayhi, however, do not skirt the issue; they attack it head on and call for a radical change in mentality. But lest the reader take away the impression that these selections represent the dominant thought of today, we have included a selection from the very popular Egyptian writer Mustafā Mahmūd. The other authors wrestle with the roots of the problem and address intellectuals; Mustafā Mahmūd focuses on showing how one can be modern and still be a tradition-oriented Muslim. He treats the problem at a popular level for a much broader audience. Note that in practically all the selections there is a desire to maintain a specific identity free of the West in its capitalist and Marxist forms.

The Muslims of India, the fourth largest Muslim population in the world, have faced a unique situation. As a result of the partitioning in 1947, those that did not migrate to Pakistan became a minority in India, a land they had once ruled. Moreover, whereas historically the Islamic community had always been understood to be a religio-political state or empire, Indian Muslims were now living in a secular state, a community in which religion and the state were separate, a situation which many saw as antithetical to the Islamic way of life.

S. 'Ābid Husain, an early leader among those who accepted India's secular path, addressed the ambivalent mood of many Muslims by underscoring the positive values of secularism and nationalism. Mushīr-ul-Haq, writing several decades after India's independence, distinguishes between Indian Muslims' acceptance of a secular state and the majority's rejection of secularism, which they see as a threat to their distinctive identity and traditions. Yet the importance of change ("fashioning a new social order") and the *'ulamā*'s role in legitimating it, continues to be the major challenge facing the Muslim community in a secular India.

'ABDALLĀH LAROUI
1933–

He is a historian and political theoretician, active in the Moroccan national movement. He studied in Paris and is now professor of history at Muhammad V University, Rabat.

Contemporary Arab Ideology

For three quarters of a century the Arabs have been asking themselves one and the same question: "who is the other and who am I?"

In February 1952 Salama Mūsa entitled one of his articles, "Why Are They powerful?" The "they" have no need to be defined; "they," "them" are the others who are always present beside us, in us. To think is, first of all, to think of the other. This proposition, whether true or false for the individual, is true at every instant for our life as a collectivity. This, then, is where we should begin.

Who is the other for the Arabs? For a long time the other was called Christianity and Europe; today it bears a name vague and precise at the same time, that of the West.

Three men, three definitions.

In contemporary Arab ideology it is possible to distinguish three principle ways of grasping the essential problem of Arab society: the first situates itself in religious faith, the second in political organization, and the last in scientific and technical activity.

1. The Cleric

The man of religion keeps the East-West opposition in the frame of an opposition between Christianity and Islam. He carries on a twelve-century-old tradition of the East and West of the Mediterranean basin. For a long time, victories and defeats alternated. This time, however, the war was rapid and the defeat durable: the enemy takes up his position and organizes himself according to his own norms. Nonetheless, the cleric can maintain the illusion that it is the old confrontation that continues. Besides, for this type of accident, he has a justification which is always ready: "When we

From *L'idéologie arabe contemporaine* [Contemporary Arab Ideology] (Paris: Maspero, 1967), pp. 15, 19–28.

want to make a city perish, we order the rich and they give themselves over to their villainy. The word against that city fulfills itself and we destroy it entirely," says the Qur'ān (17: 16). There is no need then to study the enemy; he is nothing but the instrument of evil. Everything finally resolves itself in the relations of society with its God. This position has an unlimited advantage because, in theory, it settles the problem definitively.

Whether the years of misery are numbered by tens or by hundreds, they are explained and justified once for all.

Why is it, then, that at a given moment this satisfaction wears off? Because of the dialogue which the other imposes.

A response, then, is called for, so the cleric, having guarded an inspired silence, begins a study which is condemned in advance: reducing everything to the letter of dogma, he tries to find there the secrets of strength and weakness, and naturally he finds nothing but words.

He hears it said: "the weakness of Islam derives from fanaticism and superstition." He takes up his texts, reads and re-reads them, and finds there nothing but tolerance and reasoned faith. Islam, he replies, is recognition of God according to the paths of reason; absolute monotheism, it abrogates all false divinities, human and inhuman, and thus guarantees the most absolute liberty to the individual; a religion clear and without mystery, it has more chance than any other religion to unite reasonable men around the one God.

He also hears it said: "the strength of the West is based on reason and liberty." While trying to get an idea of that liberty in history, he comes across anti-clerical writers, not by chance, and is horrified to hear that Galileo was imprisoned, Descartes was calumniated, Rousseau persecuted, and Giordano Bruno perished at the stake because he dared to defend the rights of reason against the state. His thoughts turn to Abraham in the Qur'ān, hero of personal investigation, and he asks himself: How can Christians dare to speak of tolerance after so many crimes? Of course, he does not think for a moment about the persectuion of the Mu'tazilites by the Caliph Mutawakkil[1], nor about the auto-da-fés of the Almoravids.[2] In the history of Islam he sees nothing but the translators of Ma'mūn[3] hunched over their Greek and Syriac books, and the rare manuscripts of Hakam[4] which the Spanish barbarians, it is said, grabbed up after the fall of Cordova[5] to use for making cheap bridges.

1. Caliph Mutawakkil in the ninth century stamped out the somewhat rationalist theological school of the Mu'tazilites. [Ed.]
2. Almoravids: Muslim dynasty controlling North Africa and Spain (1049–1145). [Ed.]
3. Ma'mūn: Caliph in the ninth century, predecessor of Mutawakkil who encouraged the Mu'tazilites and also the translation of Greek science and philosophy. [Ed.]
4. Hakam II: most famous of Umayyad Caliphs of Spain. Under him in the tenth century Cordova became an intellectual capital. [Ed.]
5. Fall of Cordova from Muslim control in second quarter of thirteenth century. [Ed.]

However, it is not long before a complication arises which risks putting the whole system of polemic in jeopardy. If reason is truly on the side of Islam and fanaticism on the side of Christianity, how explain the blossoming of the one and the decadence of the other? Muhammad 'Abduh wrote: If we can validly judge a religion according to the actual state of those who practice it, we can affirm that there is no tie between Christianity and modern civilization.

Then the cleric recalls certain facts: the solitude of the philosophers Fārābi (d. 950) and Rāzi (d. 1209), the duplicity of Averroes (d. 1198), the anonymity of the "Brothers of Purity"[6] who, in the fourth century A.H. wanted to amalgamate Islamic faith and Greek philosophy. Henceforth he wants to recall all the ruses which reason had to use to defend its right to life, and he answers: "The cause of our weakness? It is our infidelity to the divine message." The cleric then separates dogma from life. The first is kept pure and spotless while actual history is seen as nothing but a series of avatars of a revelation betrayed.

Previously, God, tired of being humiliated by his chosen people, took refuge among the Arabs, but later reason, hemmed-in by despotism and obscurantism, withdrew, in spite, to the Christians and gave them glory, power, and riches despite their religion. Andalusia[7] is no longer a land like others, conquered then lost. It becomes the symbol of reason which unloved and too often abandoned, abandoned us in turn. Fortunately, it is not vindictive; it can be tamed again if we decide to return to ourselves. Such are the thoughts of the modern cleric.

By that slight nudge everything is pushed back into order, and the promise God made to "his good servants" can be realized once more. This vision, still put forth by the man of religion, is not ephemeral. All through modern history it is found repeated by the pens of Arab publicists. It begins first by creating unanimity, then little by little loses its adepts, but remains in groups generally considered as backward. However, is it necessary to scratch very deeply to rediscover it, barely changed, among men who pretend to be open to objective truth?

2. The Politician
Little by little the West is better known. Western history is studied for itself and not in small pieces for polemic. In the end, one is persuaded that if reason is perhaps absent from Christianity, it is certainly not absent from Europe and, in any case, whether it came from Andalusia or elsewhere, it has found propitious soil in the West.

6. Brothers of Purity: anonymous authors of some fifty letters, mid-tenth century, representing Ismā'īlī doctrine. [Ed.]
7. Andalusia: for Muslims, includes practically all the Iberian peninsula, which was held by the Muslims for seven centuries. [Ed.]

To the extent that the cleric searches for polemical arguments against the Church everywhere and finds them especially in the writers of the century of enlightenment, to the same extent he opens the way for the domination that this century is going to exercise, little by little, over the Arab intelligence.

The eighteenth century still fascinates the Arabs. This century will always be loved for good and bad reasons because it supplies most of the arguments against the Church and its depravity and because it gives credibility to certain myths. What language is sweeter than that of Rousseau when he criticizes the duality of power in the Christian world and writes: "Muhammad had sound views; he tied his political system together in good fashion and as long as his form of government existed under his successors, the Caliphs, the government was one and good." A single law ruling over this world and the next, guaranteed by the infallible instinct which God put in the heart of every man, isn't this the very essence of the Muslim city described by Rousseau which he justifies without knowing its ultimate goal?

However, can one read Rousseau continually without drawing close to Montesquieu, can one use indefinitely the philosophy of light uniquely against the Church? The moment comes when the unity of the system appears, and the Arab reader no longer sees Europe as the domain of the Pope and bishops alone. He begins to notice the Emperor also and the feudal noble, especially if he comes from Egypt or Syria where he suffered from Turkish tyranny and hears it said that those ancient lands of civilization fell precisely because of the Turkish occupation. When Montesquieu dissects oriental despotism, the Middle Eastern reader feels hatred for the Turkish usurper rise in himself. Still, he recognizes willingly that the Caliph, even in the brilliant periods of Muslim empire, governed according to his own good pleasure; conquered people were persecuted; the state had no end other than the exploitation of subject populations. He recognizes that property was precarious, commerce was discouraged, taxes were unequal, administration was venal, and justice was subjective. Yes, he finishes by admitting it was a reign of violence, fear, the unlimited power of one, and the slavery of all. The Caliph, shadow of God on earth, respected neither the life nor property of his subjects, and his violence, punctuated by brief and bloody revolts, resembled that of all who ruled over the ancient land of Asia.

The new man, the politician who has taken the place of the cleric on front stage, thinks: our decadence certainly had secular slavery as its ultimate cause. All of a sudden, all the classical judgments, which he read formerly but did not assimilate, are going to regain force: that the slave could neither work well or fight, that agriculture, commerce, science, and philosophy can never flower in servitude. Like many others he reflects on the misadventures of Athens and Rome and lets himself be convinced that the fall of empires is always the victory of liberty over slavery.

Then Islam will be disassociated from decline, and the Turk will become the symbol of misery and failure. It will be said: as long as Islam was Arab it was free, tolerant, and victorious. Once it became Turkish it changed its nature and declined. Turkish Islam was victor as long as Europe was subservient and fatalistic, but as soon as it liberated itself at the time of the reformation, it conquered everywhere.

The new man, jurist and politician, is going to amalgamate Rousseau and Montesquieu and understand ideal democracy after the fashion of the English watchmaker.

Since the evil has been diagnosed, the remedy has been found. The Turkish regime was the power of a sole ruler; therefore, we should elect an assembly. The Turkish regime regulated all activities, therefore we should give free reins to private enterprise. The Turkish regime accommodated itself to ignorance, then we must sacrifice everything to spread instruction.

This jurist-politician is going to put himself to the task with quibbles and subtleties. The Prophet was wrong once concerning the technique of pollinating date palms and frankly admitted his error. From that the conclusion is abusively drawn that Islamic dogma does not impose a strict organization of public powers and that it can, consequently, accommodate itself to any regime whatever that Muslims choose.

Ijmā' (juridical consensus) becomes a veritable democratic charter, corroborated by the procedure which the Caliph 'Umar chose to designate his successor. Ignorant or forgetful of the lessons of ethnology, he claims that the Arab is by nature free and that he cannot independently found a regime which is not democratic—an argument which at base takes up the racist determinism of E.F. Gautier.

Thus dogma is saved a second time because every classical despotic organization is declared non-Muslim and with the same stroke the future is uncovered: let us organize a representative democracy and power will return to us again. Everyday floods of eloquence are going to be poured out at the feet of creative liberty, and this great hope, now visible after so many years, takes on the melancholy aspect of a youth betrayed by destiny. Tāhā Husayn after twenty-five years reflected on his dreams, contradicted by reality, and lamented: "Believe me, the good, all the good for a man of culture and courage is to escape with his heart, his spirit and his conscience far from these times. If he cannot go elsewhere, let him at least exile himself in one of the epochs of past history."

This liberal vision which carries in itself both diagnosis and therapy, is still found in all Arab countries. In certain countries like Egypt, discredited by its failures, it scarcely dares to make itself heard from time to time in the university or the parliament; in others like Morocco, it still has sufficient self-confidence to present itself openly.

3. The Technocrat

Political liberty and parliaments do not give power; daily experience was not long in demonstrating this. No one yet doubted the real representation of the deputy, but knew very well that his speeches were forgotten as soon as they were delivered in the temple of the nation. This deputy: lawyer, doctor, journalist, or professor, fought to occupy high positions, but when he arrived there he sensed correctly that everything, politics and administration, escaped him and that his presence was necessary only during official feasts. He consoled himself knowing that his chief had no more power than he. Sometimes the latter explained to him that the big boss himself is only the shadow of a shadow. For a long time he used an image: the people, an invincible force; now he mouths it with bitterness. Even the people, guided by their elected representatives, keep an obstinate silence. The politician asks: liberty we have, but power? Since he believes that power is his due, he turns against the people. For the first time, with necesary distance, he sees the people as they are: ignorant, squalid, drowsy. Then the residences of the great families are fortified, the clubs close, and the cars streak along the streets with shades drawn to protect oneself against sights which are too violent. The peasant becomes the expression of another world, another humanity, and the politican-jurist no longer rejects with indignation the insinuation of foreigners about the influence of climate, race, and sun. Exasperated and disillusioned, betrayed by events, the man of quibbles keeps silence.

A newcomer then takes the floor. He is neither lawyer, magistrate, nor doctor. Son of a shop-keeper, perhaps a peasant, occasionally from a minority, in short the one who up till now was marginal. During this period of silence, he has acquired a new image of the West shaped by various pressures, and this image will serve as the norm by which he judges the society and the work of his elders.

The West, he will say, is not defined either by a religion without superstitions nor by a state without despotism, but simply by a material force acquired by work and applied science. Henceforth he will laugh at the ideas of the West the cleric and the ploitican shaped for themselves. In the great amphitheatre of Cairo University, Salama Mūsa in 1930 will pose the following question to Egyptian youth: "Do the Westerners have the same religion? the same racial origin? the same institutions?" And he answered: "During the past quarter of a century a single truth has become clear to me, and it is this: the difference which separates us from civilized Europeans is industry and industry alone." The technocrat will cite often the example of

Japan: does a religion more foreign to reasoned monotheism exist, is there a history more bloody, a people more subservient than those we find in Japan of the Samurai? Nonetheless, in little time Japan conquered whites and yellows simply because it went straight to the secret of the West. Let us do likewise; let us not waste our time any longer in theological discussions and in lamentations over an unfinished destiny. Science is certainly very beautiful, but it must be subordinated to technique; culture is a noble goal, but it comes after a specialized trade. Salama Mūsa affirms: "Today civilization is industry; its culture is science. Whereas the culture of agrarian societies is literature, religion and philosophy."

The criticism of Islamic history which the liberal politician had timidly begun is now totally put aside. The technocrat feels no need to interpret dogma or to warp it from its traditional sense. He simply ignores it, since it does not determine the strength or weakness.

In excluding tradition from the discussion, he helps save it for the last time. The technocrat answers the argument of the preceding generation with: "Was it not under Cromwell that England laid the bases of its maritime hegemony? Was it not under the two Napoleons that France became an industrial power? Despotism hinders nothing; perhaps it is even a condition for the advancement of a people."

This man, worshiper of technology, is often sad and quiet, but intellectually he is a terrorist; he refuses to put himself in question, and he scorns disinterested science. For him, the West is no longer opaque as it was for the cleric. He feels at home there, speaks its language, follows its logic and slowly, the past and its problems grow dim in his mind. He no longer asks: "What was our greatness?", nor "Why, our decadence?" Insipid questions, he thinks, and goes off crying out: truth is for tomorrow, truth is technology. He believes he has gone beyond the cleric and the liberal politician; actually he has appropriated the West for himself by a short, effortless leap, having jettisoned his past a bit too easily. For all that, the West has not really become clearer to him; it is his history which has become more opaque.

While the liberal politician, betrayed by events, discredited himself more each day, the technocrat was preparing intellectually for the installation of the new state. When this day arrives, the technocrat will cry victory and will say as did Salama Mūsa in July 1952: "It is the most beautiful day of my life." But the new state will not be long in recognizing that this technocrat is most often not a technician; it will listen to him for a while, then turn away quickly.

The question will be asked:

What do these three men represent in reality? Were they picked at hazard? Are they the expurgated editions of actual writers? If so, why were they not presented under their true names?

These three men, in fact, represent three moments of the Arab conscience which has been trying since the end of the last century to understand itself and to understand the West. They were described abstractly
because they are found in diverse forms of literature (essays, newspaper
articles, plays), and they are not incarnated in the same man for all the
Arab countries.

No doubt there is already a presentiment that to judge these forms of
conscience several questions must be answered: Do they form an historical
sequence? Who has given them their general problematic? What relation is
there between each of them and the social forces active in Arab society or
in the West? However, it can be affirmed presently that the worst methodological error would be to deny the interdependence, already so evident,
between Arab ideology and Western ideology.

HICHEM DJAIT
1935–

He studied at Tunisia's Sadiqi College and went to Paris to
continue studies, first at the Ecole normale supérieure, then at
the Sorbonne. He is *agrégé* in history and now teaches at the
University of Tunis.

Islam, Reform, and the New Arab Man

How can we follow the wake of our glorious historical tradition, holding
to a course stable enough to avoid lurches into alienation and flexible
enough to adjust to the dynamics of change? Reformism and modernism
asked themselves this question and gave answers which were fragmentary
and biased, each in its own way. For the fundamentalism of 'Abduh, for
example, Islamic society and the modern world confront each other in the
context of our reality. The fundamentals of the first must be maintained,
the second must be absorbed as a foreign body. Moreover, it is the material manifestations (the signs of power) of the second that are sought more
than the spirit which gives them life. Imperialism and the plasticity of
eternal Islam! A *ruse de guerre* and a defensive tactic at one and the same
time despite appearances; the cart has been put before the horse. We do
not start with evidence of the perennial nature of Islamic society—such as
it has been defined up to now—in order to adapt the benefits of the
modern world to it; rather we set out from the necessity of implanting
modernity in our society without severing society from its Arab-Islamic
tradition. Or rather, we start by abandoning ourselves to the dynamism of
history, a history we will shape to fit our aspirations once we have defined
our hopes. In our view, Islam cannot be the unique positive foundation of
present-day society as the reformism of *al-Manār* would have it.[1] Nor, on
the contrary, can Islam be merely a condiment, an historic decoration:
playing a minor role in the great theatre of Arabism, as the diverse tendencies of Arab neo-modernism would have it. One cannot deny to the indi-

1. *al-Manār*—periodical published from 1897 to 1935 which served as principal vehicle for
   reformist thought of Muhammad 'Abduh and continued as such even after his death in
   1905 under his disciple Rashīd Ridā.

From *La personnalité et le devenir arabo-islamiques* [The future of the Arab-Islamic person-
ality] in *Collections Esprit—La Condition Humaine* (Paris:Editions du Seuil, 1974), pp. 126–
35.

vidual Arab, if and when he wishes, the possibility of interiorizing Islam as a religion, a source of moral inspiration and a metaphysic, without falling into a narrow materialism devoid of any consideration for the validity of religious action. No systematic de-Islamizing of conscience, then, but a de-Islamizing of the central and operative core of the society.

However, it is clear that an interiorized Islam and a society in the process of being rationalized will interpenetrate, or, to be more precise, religion will have to adapt itself to a different humanity. Up to the present, religion has been closely coupled to a certain form of society which it helped to shape and which in turn affected it; tomorrow it will be able to correlate differently.

Contemporary reflection has become mired in an impossible problem because it has not been able to separate Islam and society correctly—the confusion derives from the West's medieval apprehension of Islam as an antagonistic, monolithic religious form. But an Islam rethought, reformulated, and revitalized can respond to the modern, rationalized conscience to the extent that it associates itself with new dimensions of affectivity and reason. But how can we do this without disfiguring Islam, without depriving it of its historic asset of authority, the sacred part of its scriptural bases, and finally, that which is its major contribution, the perspective of going beyond the human which it contains within itself to the transcendence which it offers to every anxious soul? Have no doubts, this will be an intellectual and moral struggle cut to the measure of those who are inspired both by religious faith and faith in the future of modern man, and who live out that double affiliation in conflict. It is for them to redefine the essence of the Islamic design and to redirect the very structure of Islamic religious sensibility towards other paths. In any case, this may be a rearguard action, because humanity is well on the way to abandoning all religious structures of the classical type.

To contract Islam to its pure and positive religious content and to plumb its depths will mean, in a sense, to separate religion from society. The latter must be freed from the closely knit structures of "Islam-society" which still weigh heavily upon it from the very distant past. The state can act as the catalyst for this liberation, but action from above will not suffice if it is not accompanied by an interior movement which is both broad and deep, that is to say, by a resounding affirmation of new ideas and new ways of acting.

To tell the truth, the principal obstacle to such changes lies in the close solidarity of the elements under discussion, and this solidarity has not been explained clearly. Islam cannot abandon the positions it holds in the social fabric by title of ancient conquest unless it ceases to be on the defensive, and it will not lower its guard unless new spiritual perspectives are opened up for it. Furthermore, the collective mentality of society will not accommodate itself to new plans of action unless they are coherent and carry in themselves the germ of a better life, and to make this accommodation, the collective mentality must be rationalized, that is to say, secularized. This poses the problem in its full dialectical breadth.

The solution will come from the dynamism and creativity of the future which will jar the weight of the past. History must be set in motion once again to press out new strata and new traditions. *The Arab problem is one of a totality which seeks a vital, inner motive force.*

Once the voyage is begun, our authentic values must be reaffirmed as the guides of our human action; the reel of history must roll smoothly.

The motive force of which we spoke is a determination springing from the depths of our Arab being; it is the unleashing of latent potentiality and a reorientation of the spirit that animates society.

In this present phase of our history, because of human resources and a thousand and one other reasons . . . it is impossible to imagine Arab society becoming completely neutral vis-à-vis ideology, whether religious or secular. An Arab society sterilized and remade such that its actvity will be directed to the pure co-existence of all men who are motivated by material well-being—a well-being which is still hypothetical—is impossible today. What is more, the voice of Arab conscience rejects it.

But in a contrary sense, an Arab society dominated by a "lay ideology of progress" in the form of a specific Marxism is fully possible. History is contingent; it may or may not follow this direction. All we know for certain is that at the present time Arab Marxism is a minority current. In any case, we do not desire this solution. The reason is not that it would entail a loss of our historic personality: Soviet Marxism was adept in wedding itself to Russian nationalism and Chinese Marxism. Despite the universal horizons it projects for itself, it is, in fact, the new destiny of eternal China. No, our reason is that at the heart of the Arab dialectic the question is not merely one of finding a recipe for socio-economic development; nor is it one of making ourselves presentable to the outside world; rather it is much more a question of living in a society made of better human stuff and of participating in a civilization of quality.

Judging from models which exist, we fear that an Arab-Marxism would mean the modern perpetration and legitimation of the oriental totalitarianism which is still present in society's bias towards a medieval type of ethno-religious constraint and present also in the structure and function of Arab states. Man, society, and power must be liberated. Above all, we refuse to let this violent world lose its soul and shut itself up again in a drab, suffocating structure. We do not deny that Marxism represents a hope for humanity as a whole, but, in any case, some non-Arab countries have assumed responsibility for its continued existence and survival.

In short we want neither an ideologically neutral society like that of the post-industrial West, nor a society propelled by Marxist ideology—true Marxism can be grasped but not its pale substitutes which we think are stripped of value—nor, finally, and *a fortiori*, a society obsessed with static souvenirs which go back to the sources of medieval unanimity and is closed in on itself. Arab society should find the way for its own fulfillment and start searching for its own ideology.

This ideology should synthesize contradictory aspirations and exigencies: tradition and modernity, profound interior appeal (past and present) and necessary rapport with the outside world. If we reformulate the problems in another manner, we can move beyond certain false problems and allow the real, absorbing, and urgent questions to come into the full light of conscience. This is how the alternatives Islam-Marxism, Islam-westernization should be surmounted, and, *a fortiori*, that of tradition-modernism. For us the problem lies in reconciling an Arab personality, which, for the most part, we only tolerate even though we love it, with a future to be chosen. Tensions like this are common in periods of mutation—recall the inner divisions which rent France, or those which were the lot of the Church, in the process of incorporating the values of the modern world, even though these values issued from Western soil and matured slowly.

In the Arab and Islamic case, modernization has always been a deformed superimposition; it has appeared as an attack or the repercussion of a previous attack. Modernity has to be nationalized; it must be acclimatized and wedded to our deep personality. If we make modernity identical with either westernization or Marxization, we will falsify our personality in exchange for a borrowed future; this may be progress, but the price paid is alienation. The truth is that this modernity has sprung free from its country of origin and is now in universal orbit. To grasp it in its universal dimensions, to integrate it and make it ours, to add to it and express it in the language of our own particularity, this is our primary goal: it is the dialectic of perpetuity in renovation.

What is demanded of Arab humanity today is not to promote a model for universal revolution which will make the Arabs the avant garde of their time as they once were with Islam. This type of historical miracle does not repeat itself. Nor will the European renaissance, the French revolution, or the Russian revolution be repeated. Arab humanity is asked to totalize its experience and that of humanity, to remain itself while taking on a new body, and to make its identity a source of energy which penetrates the whole effort and enlivens it part by part.

Though open to criticism, the Arab renaissance of the nineteenth century did prepare the way for the present epoch. Like every renaissance it advocated a return to sources, straddling between a recent and burdensome tradition and a more ancient tradition seen as disfigured or betrayed. But, apart from the fact that this renaissance limited itself to its own cultural horizons, there is also the danger that such a movement if prolonged in the same sense risks focusing us on the past and its grandeur. As we already suggested, we have to break with the past in a certain sense. A second renaissance will not have the sense of progress unless its anxious search for the authentic and its intention to restore are put in proper perspective so that the essential thing stands out, namely, the unspoken things must come to full maturity and we must be ready to fecundate our reality and our being. In this way, the renaissance will rediscover its true function, that of giving new birth by means of the ancient. From this pro-classical illusion will arise the promise of a culture, not renewed, but new, expressing the universal in an original way. The radically new, the *jamais vu,* by projecting itself onto the nostalgia for the ancient, will mature—but the new will be formless and consequently ineffable.

A true renaissance is both a revival of certain privileged sectors of the past and a leap into the unknown. It is an affirmation of creative liberty and presupposes peeling away the scales of certain parts of our being. The Arab renaissance, if understood in a sense other than pure nostalgia or mere repetition, must recover its breadth culturally so that it can show us that we are as able as the ancients and as capable as our contemporaries. Then it will become a cultural birth, not merely a resurrection. But given the ambiguity of the term "renaissance," we prefer to speak in terms of an Arab future which will be a total, complex, and powerful dialectic. It will not be possible to stop at a cultural and religious superstructure and from there to preach renaissance and reform, allowing the political concept of revolution to fade out of focus. No, our aim must be a general, long-term action in which the confrontation with oneself will be completed by a confrontation with the other. The spark once struck penetrates and sets fire to the deepest social, political, and mental strata. The rhythm of the movement will be one of accompaniment, simultaneity, and solidarity; it will group all the elements present. This totalizing action, based on clear objectives, is our only way out of the vicious circle which hems us in. It is clear, for example, that our mentality will not evolve towards rationality unless there is an anterior material development. But one can also claim that the latter presupposes the former. In the same vein, the overthrow of present structures will yield only ephemeral and fictive results unless it is supported by the allegiance of vital social forces. Inversely, an action from on high will never be effective unless mature aims and ideals are developed. Adopting techniques and inventions will have no meaning if this adoption is separated from the tendencies and historic roots of popular identity.

There is more: The principal stake, to wit, the quality of civilization and the framework of life within which man can expand to the maximum. For this and for the rest, a fundamental revision of the values by which we live is necessary. We need a radical redefinition of our image of man, and we should start with the complex network of Arab humanity. Here the role of thought comes into play; it lays the foundations for action. Nothing of value will be accomplished among the Arabs unless three capital elements of their existence are revised: religion and its place in society; man himself and his personality; and the relations between state and society, or, if you wish, the model of development. Reform in the religious order, rationalization of the individual, mutation in society—this triptych is the *sine qua non* condition of this renewal, which we wish to be a leap forward and a pledge for the future. Coupled with the affirmation of the Arab personality, under its ideologies—cultural form or as political destiny—it constitutes, in our eyes, the praxis for the Arab universe, the surest preface to its emancipation.

MUSTAFĀ MAHMŪD
1921–

After primary and secondary education at Tanta, he entered the medical college of Cairo University and on graduation practiced medicine in Cairo from 1952 to 1966. In the mid-fifties he began writing on religion and modern problems and now has become a full-time writer and spiritual counselor.

Islam vs. Marxism and Capitalism

As developing nations we normally look at two pioneering experiences only: communism in the East and capitalism in the West. We can hardly imagine that there may be another solution, so if we discover that both the two experiences are not advantageous to us we begin to search for a solution midway between the two schools and we start to manufacture an appropriate composite.

If we were to look to Islam we would find a source of thought and truth which surpasses both systems in its progressiveness and contemporaneity. We would find that everything we reckon new in scientific socialism was old hat thirteen centuries ago in Islam. Islam came establishing, from the very beginning, the principle of equal opportunity, guaranteeing minimal needs to the individual and achieving a balance between the liberty of the individual to profit and the rights of society, the principle of private and public property(private and public sectors), the principle of state interference in the economy—this is what we call today a directed economy—the principle of confiscating the wealth of exploiters for the benefit of the poor and the oppressed.

Islam does not allow classes and forbids that wealth circulate among a limited group of rich.

"That it become not a commodity between the rich among you" (Qur'ān 59:7).

Rank in Islam is based on piety not riches.

"The noblest of you in the sight of God is the best in conduct" (Qur'ān 49:13).

"God does not look at your form or your wealth but only at your hearts and your actions" (Prophetic Tradition).

From *al-Marksiyyah wal-Islām* [Marxism and Islam] (Cairo: Dār al-Maʿārif, 1975), pp. 66–79.

"People are equal like the teeth of a comb; there is no preference for the Arab over the non-Arab except in piety" (Prophetic Tradition). . . .

Islam is against excessive disparity in resources. There is more than one verse against luxury and the luxurious. "The wrongdoers followed that by which they became opulent, and were guilty" (Qur'ān 11:116). "Till when we grasp their luxurious ones with the punishment, behold they suplicate" (Qur'ān 23:64). . . .

Despite this, Islam is not against the rich man if he is restrained.

"There is no objection against the rich man who is pious" (Prophetic Tradition). "Yes, just wealth for the just servant" (Prophetic Tradition). "In their wealth the beggar and the outcast had due share" (Qur'ān 51:19).

The minimum for life must be guaranteed to all. "People share in three things: water, pasture and fire" (Prophetic Tradition).

The wealth of the rich is illegal if there is one poor person in the society who cannot find food. "There is no one of us who goes to sleep full when his neighbor is hungry (Prophetic Tradition). "Let him who has surplus give to him who has not" (Prophetic Tradition).

We have seen examples of state interference in the economy under 'Umar ibn al-Khattāb[1]. . . .

'Umar refused to let Muslims take possession of land conquered in raids, considering it the property of the community, just as he refused to allow possession of beneficient trusts, mines, and underground resources, considering them under the rule of the public sector.

'Umar forbade the buying and consumption of meat two days in succession when meat was scarce, and anyone violating the prohibition he struck with an udder, saying: "Now your stomach will close up for two days."

'Umar bought monopolized products forcibly from the monopolists for a symbolic price and used to fix the price for certain items to prevent arbitrary pricing which might harm people. . . .

Abū-Dharr al-Ghiffārī[2] considered the wealth of the wealthy fair game for others as long as there was one poor man in the society who could not find sufficiency.

Private property is inviolable in Islam as is public property. "The blood, honor and wealth of every Muslim is inviolable" (Prophetic Tradition).

The one who violates private property has his hand cut off like the one who violates public property.

In Islam, formal logic is joined with dialectical logic. (Formal logic is

---

1. 'Umar b. al-Khattāb: second Caliph after death of Muhammad.
2. Abū-Dharr al-Ghiffārī: companion of the Prophet, known for his humility and asceticism. Because of his criticism of abuses of wealth he has been adopted recently as the first socialist.

Aristotelian and talks of the permanence of existing things, so what is a tree today will be a tree tomorrow. Dialectical logic is Hegelian dialectical logic and talks of the continual change of existing things, so every existing thing carries the seed of its own destruction.) These two are the logics of permanence and evolution. Islam joins adherence to permanent dogmatic principles with personal interpretation (*ijtihād*) in derived branches, details, and applications (this is what we call development). It says that derived rules change with changes in time and place. This is what jurisprudents call "difference of time and place," not difference in argument and proof. Hence the Prophetic Tradition: "differences among Imāms is a blessing," because they are differences in details necessitated by changing circumstances.

For this reason we say that economic policy in Islam is divine policy in what concerns principles but positive policy in what concerns application and detail.

The divine principles in the Islamic program are based on the notion of accommodation of the interests of the individual with those of the group. It does not crush the individual for the good of the group (as in communism) nor does it crush the group for the good of the individual (as in capitalism).

But if accommodation is impossible as in time of war or famine or plague, the Islamic application chooses the group interest and decrees that people divide food equally, though all may be only half full. . . .

However, in a normal situation the Islamic program is bound by divine principles which aim at a delicate balance between individual and community interest. . . .

For this reason anyone who thinks Islam is capitalistic is mistaken. Likewise anyone who thinks Islam is communistic is mistaken. And so too, the one who thinks Islam is a mathematical mean between the two systems or a concoction from both is mistaken. The truth is that Islam has a distinctive economic program which proceeds from basically different points of departure, although some point or other may be in accord with this or that system.

It proceeds from the notions of accomodation, interest, cooperation, and complementarity, not from the notion of class struggle and contradiction. It seeks a balance between the individual and the group, not the melting of individuals into the group (as in scientific socialism) nor the sacrifice of the group for the good of a minority of individual capitalists (as in capitalist throught). Accomodation and interest are always the starting point.

In capitalist economics we find that the freedom of the individual for gain is the principle and the interference of the state is the exception. In scientific socialism we find that the interference of the state and its isolated role in economic activity is the principle and the granting of some freedom to the individual is the exception. It is clear, then, that in Islam we are in the presence of something very different.

Individual freedom to profit is a principle in the Islamic system along with individual property, so too are state interference in the economy and public property principles. And when Islam established the zakāt[3] it legalized state interference and set up the first institution of social security. Islam makes interference a duty so that wealth will not remain among the rich as the monopoly of one class to the exclusion of the rest of the citizens. . . .

The freedom of the individual to gain is a principle, but Islam does not allow it to become an absolute. It puts fetters on it, so production of wine, usurious transactions, monopoly, amassing wealth and spending it foolishly or gathering it by graft, and infringement on the rights of others and over-pricing are not allowed.

The Islamic economic program is characterized by another thing not found in capitalism or in scientific socialism, namely its satisfaction of spiritual as well as material needs. Relations with God and acting to please him in expenditure and performance of good deeds is a principle. Our prophet says: "Alms fall into God's hand before they reach the hand of the deprived."

This gives the economic program a lofty goal and enables economic activity. The believer feels he is dealing directly with God.

Also, it provides the governor with a two-fold supervision over his actions in addition to the supervision of the commissioner of taxes, namely, the supervision of God and the supervision of his conscience.

This spiritual satisfaction protects the society from the psychological emptiness and malaise which occur in opulent European societies like Sweden or in socialist atheistic societies in the East where we find the highest proportion of insanity and suicide despite the abundant guarantees of life for all.

The reason is that the system does not satisfy spiritual needs and does not quench that holy thirst within man, the thirst for the true God, even though it satisfies his stomach and natural dispositions. They do not understand that man is not merely stomach and instincts. . . .

There is no separation in Islam between the spiritual and the material. . . . Sincere, upright action before God is both material and spiritual.

Wealth is not sought for itself in Islam but is sought as a means to piety and a way to upright, merciful, and loving action. This marks it as very different from the meaning of wealth in materialist capitalist economy and materialist socialist economy. These latter look at wealth as economic power and as a means for domination and conquest. Activity without a spiritual sense is dry and lifeless.

---

3. zakāt: obligatory tax on capital holdings enjoined by Muhammad.

We, however, say, "Seek, in what God gives you, this life and the next." This makes our use of wealth in construction and development something similar to prayer or obligatory devotions by which we seek the next life in pleasing the Creator. . . .

Were we to execute our economic plan with this religious, devotional spirit we would accomplish miracles in a few years and overtake the cavalcade of progress with the speed of a rocket. The Arab states complement on another economically and form a nation which could become richer and stronger than the American nation—a geographical area with petroleum, iron, coal, copper, magnesium, gold, and uranium in addition to abundant agricultural produce, unlimited animal and marine resources and a numerous work force. Imagine the possibilities were we to join the potential of Saudi Arabia, Kuwait, and the Gulf States with that of Egypt, Sudan, and North America; if only we did the necessary planning, brought them together and exploited our possibilities. . . .

Only by searching into the depths of Islam, the Qur'ān and the Sunna[4] for this Islamic economic plan and by searching for its limits and its specifications will we all be saved from stumbling around between capitalism and scientific socialism (which is not scientific as we saw). By this too we will be saved from patching up our great civilization with civilizations which are in fact either in old age and decline (like capitalism) or in a stage of trial and experiment (like scientific socialism). Both these civilizations are materialistic standing on hypothetical philosophies oriented to dry material interest without any trace of spirit or divine knowledge and lacking that certainty which is supported by heaven and sustained by God.

Islamic economics, as we saw, gives us the advantages which are found in scientific socialism plus spiritual satisfaction and dogmatic enthusiasm along with more progressive and contemporary points of view and more humanistic procedures. Moreover, it will help us to avoid the pitfalls, errors, and presumptions of materialistic thought and that strangeness which it has for us as imported thought which remains at the door of our hearts and does not enter no matter what propaganda or tyranny the ruler may use. We are a believing people. Faith for us is our pillar, our heart, and our backbone. In this valley [Nile] we came to know God and worshipped him during seven thousand years when these "civilizers" were barbarians who did not know how to talk. . . .

4. Sunna: the practice of the Prophet.

MUHAMMAD NUWAYHI
(1917–1980)

A literary critic, thinker, professor of Arabic literature, he studied at Cairo University, and then did doctoral studies at the school of Oriental and African Studies, London University, writing a thesis on early Arabic poetry. He taught at London and Khartoum Universities and from 1973 to his death was Director of Arabic Studies at the American University of Cairo.

A Revolution in Religious Thought

If we are serious about striving towards a "comprehensive Arab cultural revolution" we must begin by facing the fact, that the first obstacle along this path is religious, and that we will not arrive at the revolution we seek unless we overcome this obstacle and remove it from our path.

Religious objections are always the first to be raised against any new idea, whether the idea deals with problems of religion itself, or with ethics, politics, the system of government, economics, the system of production and distribution of wealth, the traditions, customs, and practices of society, science, philosophy, art, language and literature. For in our Arab countries, religious considerations continue to outweight all other considerations in the minds of the people. And it is still from the religious point of view that they first consider any new opinion that is announced to them, or any new school of thought which claims their support. They do not ask themselves: is this opinion right or wrong in itself, or is this school of thought useful or harmful in itself? Instead, they ask themselves: is it in conformity with religion or contrary to it?

This being their attitude, how are we to cope with it? Shall we be content, every time we announce a new opinion or support a new school of thought, to spend effort and time showing them that it is in agreement with religion rather than opposed to it? This has been the limit of our attempts at religious reform up to now. But this is no longer sufficient. If we really want to achieve a "comprehensive cultural revolution," and if we understand the word "revolution" in its true and complete sense, this "reform" is neither sufficient nor useful. We have no other alternative but to get to the root of this thorny question, in order to induce a radical

From "Nahwa-l-thawra fil-fikr al-dīnī" [Towards a revolution in religious thought], al-Ādāb 18 (1970), pp. 23–31, 98–107.

change in the people's concept of the nature of religion itself. We must bring about a complete transformation in the people's understanding of the role of [religion] in human society, in order to persuade them not to exaggerate the legitimate domain within which the authority of religion should be confined. [Once this has been done] their first concern will not be to ask whether this or that new opinion or approach is conformed to religion or not, but rather to study the new opinion or approach it itself in order to discover whether it is in fact sound and beneficial or erroneous and deleterious. In other words, they will have gone beyond the narrow religious stage of thinking to reach the stage of broad-minded secularism ['almāniyah] in all their earthly affairs. . . .

How can we persuade the people not to set up religion as a stumbling block in the way of every new opinion and every new ideology?. . . .

How can we spread among them that secularist outlook which we have mentioned above?. . . .

The astonishing thing about it is that most of the non-Muslim thinkers who have studied Islam acknowledge that, in the beginning, Islam was the greatest movement of liberation that human history has ever witnessed, and its striving towards liberation was not limited to the domain of spirit and thought, but went beyond these to the domain of the material and of earthly life. Some of them even characterize the Islamic movement of liberation as "revolutionary" and "modern". . . .

. . . If we reflect on this strange phenomenon, and ask ourselves how it was that a movement which at the beginning was revolutionary, progressive, and modern, could be turned into an agent of intellect petrification and social stagnation, our reflection will lead us to two factors which were not present in Islam originally, but which appeared together during the ages of the decline of Islamic civilization and became so firmly rooted that the people imagined them to be among the fundamental principles of the Islamic religion. The first (of the two factors) was the appearance of a caste [the 'ulamā'] which monopolized the explanation of religion, claiming that it alone (the caste) had the right to speak in the name of religion and to pass judgment as to which opinions and schools of thought were in agreement with religion and which were in conflict with it. In other words, it was a priestly caste, even though it was not explicitly named as such. The second factor was the conviction of this caste that any laws, decisions, and solutions found in earlier religious sources were binding doctrines whose observance was obligatory, and which could not be modified or changed in any respect, whether they dealt with matters of doctrine or touched on the affairs of daily life.

I have said that if we are to bring about the desired cultural revolution, it is necessary that we introduce a radical change in the people's understanding of the nature of religion, and of its function, and of the legitimate scope of its authority. Let me now add that we will not succeed in this unless we call into question the two factors (mentioned above) and demonstrate to what extent they are alien and extraneous to Islam. . . .

Many readers will be quick to say that although other religions established an official priestly caste, this does not apply to Islam, which neither established nor recognized such a caste. This is absolutely true, but what we are concerned with here is what happened in actual fact. It is true that Islam has the distinction acknowledged by many who do not believe in it—and envied by many believers of other religions—of being a religion without a priesthood. It has not erected a special class of men to preserve and protect religion and to monopolize the right to represent and explain and apply it— these being the "religious" men and the rest of the people being "civilians."

But what happened? What became of us? Did there not, as a matter of fact, grow up amongst us a group of people claiming for themselves this guardianship and this monopoly and this representativity? Yes, indeed, and they called themselves "men of religion" most of the time or allowed the writers to call them that without opposing or objecting to the title, in spite of its certainly being alien to Islam. In this connection, I have a large number of quotations from Arab newspaper and magazines. Also they (the men of religion) cling to a manner of dressing proper to them, which is called "The religious garb," and in this they imitate perfectly the clergy of the other religions.

The important thing in all this is that [the caste] had hardly come into existence—during the ages of decline and reaction which followed the collapse of 'Abbāsid culture—when it claimed for itself the right to draw the lines between faith, unbelief and deviation, and to pass judgment on every opinion, thus setting itself up as the foe of liberty of expression and liberty of discussion. . . .

It is true that the revolutionary government in Egypt has wrested from [the men of religion] the weapon whereby they used religion in support of feudalism, and capitalism, and embezzlement and monopoly. Moreover, it has got them to go along with its principal political and economic policies. We now hear them talking about "Socialism" and its agreement with religion. Let us hope they are sincere in what they say. In the other Arab regions, however, which are still subject to reactionary governments, they are still using the authority of religion as a support for political and economic reactionism. Furthermore, in all the Arab countries, in both those which are still under reactionary rule and those which have attained to revolutionary governments [the men of religion] continue to play the same role of strengthening intellectual reaction and resisting new thought, and opposing movements for social change. In other words, they continue to use religion as an instrument of immobilzation and petrification, not renewal and change. . . . Indeed, if we reflect on the present situation in

Egypt, for instance, we find that the aggressiveness of the "men of religion" in crushing and repressing new thought is greater today than it was during the first half of the century.

This is the strange and saddening fact which must be acknowledged and faced. A brief look at books written by al-Māzanī, al-'Aqqād and Tāhā Husayn written in the twenties and thirties of this century is enough to remind the reader of many daring opinions the likes of which our writers of today could not publish. It is as though our revolutionary government, in exchange for its success in bringing the "men of religion" in Egypt to go along with its principal political and economic policies, paid a heavy price in deferring to their opinions concerning other intellectual and social matters. It [the government] is increasingly sensitive about any issue which might give rise to religious controversy either directly or remotely.

Now that we have discussed the claim by "men of religion" and the 'ulamā' that they have the right to interdict opinions which they do not like, let us look at their claim that they possess in their religious books a perfect system which solves all problems and answers all questions, a system which is suitable to all places and all times with no need of change or addition, a system which encompasses everything great or small, not only in matters of belief, but also in the affairs of this world and the needs of daily life.

If we were to accept what they say, we would be making Islam a stagnant reactionary religion, in the strict sense of the word "reactionary." It would be a religion that does not look forward nor prompt man to look ahead, nor urge him to look forward to evolution and improvement and a closer approach to perfection in the future, and continued progress reaching from horizon to horizon of discovery and research. [We would be making of Islam a religion] that looks backward and believes that man reached the highest attainable degree of perfection in a past age, and that all he has to do is to return to that golden past and to attempt to restore it with all its practices and circumstances. And that is "reactionism" in the exact meaning of the word.

But is what they say true, and are we compelled to accept it? Those people whose enthusiasm so overpowers their reason that they claim that the Qur'ān and the Sunna and the ancient schools [of Islamic law] have anticipated all modern laws and codes and regulations in providing the answers to all questions and the solutions to all problems—those people manifest great ignorance on two scores.

The first is their ignorance of modern law and legislation, and of contemporary legal systems, with their great scope, voluminousness and complexity, and of the multiplicity of opinions, schools of thought and interpretations [of legal systems]. . . .

They display also their great ignorance of a second area, that of the history of Islamic legislation itself, and of the stages of change and growth which it has passed through, and the vitality, flexibility and broadmindedness it manifested in the age of its awakening.

Constant evolution actually took place in the early history of Islam. The life of the Muslims of Medina after the death of the Prophet of God was different from what it had been while he was alive. And in the time of the Orthodox Caliphs, there sprang up new problems that did not exist during the time [of the Prophet], peace be on him, and the Orthodox Caliphs and the learned people of their time made laws [concerning these problems]. Moreover, the life of the Muslims in Syria was different from that of both [Hijaz and Syria]. Likewise life was different in Persia and Egypt and the other conquered lands. And in each of these regions it continued to change with the passage of generations, with the evolution of customs and the variations of circumstances. As a result, Islamic jurisprudence, in its ages of vitality, grew and evolved and expanded and changed in keeping with this continual change. . . .

Every impartial student is convinced that the early legislators did not draw their laws from earlier Islamic legal sources, as is said by certain people among us who speak about the history of Islamic legislation. On the contrary, they used to adopt the laws and procedures of the conquered nations first, and then check them against the Book and the Sunna, looking for an argument and justification for the laws and systems they had adopted from the non-Arabs. [They did this] in exactly the same way as they adopted the philosophy and science of the Greeks, the culture and literature of the Persians, the wisdom and folk-tales of the Indians, the arts and industries of the Byzantines, and other foreign science, learning, industry and art. They did not say "these are non-Islamic cultures, and they will contaminate our Islam if we import them," nor did they say that the Qur'ān has everything that the human intellect needs, and that, thanks to the Qur'ān, [the Muslim] can do without the infidel cultures.

That is what happened and kept on happening during the first centuries of Islam when Islamic legislation still retained its vitality and dynamism, before Islamic civilization allowed itself to stand still and dry up, and then to stiffen and petrify, having locked the doors of *ijtihād*.[1]

Our question now is this; if life evolved and changed during the first century A.H., and if, during the second, third and fourth centuries A.H., life became greatly different from what it had been in the time of the Prophet and the Orthodox Caliphs, and if this led to such extensive growth and far-reaching evolution in Islamic legislation, [if all this is true] how can we believe that after all those ages human life suddenly froze and became ossified, its evolution at an end, and that it [life] settled down into

---

1. *Ijtihād:* personal interpretation. [Ed.]

a fixed pattern in which any problem could be treated by simply referring to the four rites or the other rites now extinct, there being no need for creativity in law-making or for conforming to varying circumstances and changing customs, or of profiting from the legislation of other nations with whom we continued to rub shoulders and whose customs, structures and procedures continued to influence us?. . . . Apart from fixing the principles of doctrine and the corresponding rites and worship; Islam has done two things: first it has set up the lofty ethical goals which Muslims must try to realize in every law they formulated, those undying goals which they must always strive to attain insofar as is humanly possible for them, and insofar as their conditions and circumstances allow them to approach ever closer to the hoped for perfection. But [Islam] allows them, and obliges them, to determine the means for themselves, and to devise the ways in which they will strive for these goals, and to vary [the means] according to the varying requirements of different milieux and the succession of the centuries. In acting thus, Islam gave evidence of its wisdom and internal coherence, and it gave evidence of its power of constant self-renewal and, therefore, of its worthiness to perdure. That is the only meaning for "the suitability [of Islam] for all times and places" that we can understand and accept, i.e. the capacity for self-renewal in order to conform to all times and places.

The second (of the two things Islam did) is that, in the time of the Prohpet, may peace be upon him, Islam, either through Revelation or in the Sunna of the Prophet[2] laid down the minimum of the civil legislation badly needed by the Muslims. But in doing this, it contented itself with what was absolutely necessary. The reason for this was clear: [Islam] actually preferred to leave it up to the people to create their own solutions by using their own reasoning and expending their knowledge, and exercising their ingenuity and skill, and profiting from their experience. Now the Arabs in the time of the Prophet, may peace be upon him, were in need of quick solutions to certain of the problems which arose out of the sudden sociological transformations accompanying the advent of Islam, the abolition of the *jāhilī* order,[3] and the establishment of the new state at Medina.

And so Islam, by means of the twin sources, the Book and the Sunna, provided them with that minimum [of legislation] which they needed in their epoch. . . . Isn't it one of the principles of Qur'ānic legislation itself that a gradual approach is to be adopted in imposing a law on the people, as, for example, was done in the steps leading to the prohibition of wine? Were there not in the Qur'ān itself rules which were revealed, and later adjusted, suspended, or abrogated? And what would have happened if the

2. Sunna: the practice of the Prophet [Ed]
3. jāhilī order: reign of ignorance before Islam. [Ed]

Prophet's life were long, and circumstances became increasingly different and many other new affairs arose? . . .

A certain amount of thought concerning this issue will convince us that the logic of the evolution of circumstances is one of the most important principles to which Qur'ānic legislation adheres, the significance of this logic is that it brings us face to face with a truth, namely that we have the right to perfect the Qur'ānic legislation in areas where it is incomplete, provided that we adhere to its lofty goals. This is the only condition imposed on this work of perfecting [the Qur'ānic legislation]. . . .

In fact, I believe that our religious thinking has now attained a degree of rationality which should allow us to declare frankly that the ruler, guided by the opinion of competent persons, has the right to prohibit some things which have been permitted, whenever he is persuaded that changing circumstances necessitate this prohibition in order to remedy an evil or prevent corruption. Such a right can also be applied to other problems which now require restrictions not imposed by the original legislation, for example, the husband's right to divorce and to multiple marriage. Let us add now that this right has been put into practice in the course of the history of Islamic legislation. The exposition of this truth brings us to a new stage of our discussion, and we ask: even with regard to the questions with which the Qur'ān did deal, are all the laws of the Qur'ān itself definitive binding texts of command or prohibitation?

Here we are going to spare ourselves long controversy by pointing once more to a fact that everyone is aware of . . . the way in which the Orthodox Caliph 'Umar ibn al-Khattāb[4]. . . . dared to issue laws which were, beyond all doubt, contrary to the letter of Qur'ānic law. But his understanding of the true spirit of Islam made him fearless in issuing [(these laws]) whenever he was convinced that they were urgently needed, and that changed circumstances and situations no longer allowed the literal application of the Qur'ānic law . . . (e.g.) his supression of the penalty for theft in certain circumstances, and his refusal to give money to those who had been reconciled with Muslims.

[In doing this] what was 'Umar doing but abrogating a Qur'ānic law whenever he judged that the changed circumstances no longer justified it? But do our *'ulamā'* and writers have the courage to face this evident fact? On the contrary, they resort to all sorts of explanations to escape from it. . . . We believe that ['Umar] was giving evidence of his correct understanding of the spirit of Islam, and of the living logic of Islam which evolves with the evolution of circumstances. It is the Muslims—ever since the time of their decline and their domination by political, economic and intellectual reactionism—it is they who have failed to adapt to this logic

---

4. 'Umar ibn al-Khattāb: second Caliph after death of Muhammad. [Ed]

and to persevere in applying it. Thus they ended up by immobilizing Islam, paralyzing its spirit and making of it, in fact, an instrument of ossification and reaction in the community.

There remains another fact which we want to mention . . . our great religious reformer the Imām Muhammad 'Abduh and his pupils and disciples in the school of al-Manār⁵ were aiming at [it]. They distinguished between the roots [usūl] of religion and its branches. . . . The former consist of two things: the creed with its accompanying rite and worship and the ethics or the lofty undying goals which have been set up by Islam. The branches include matters of procedures and social relations existing between people, for example, ownership, slavery, interest on bank deposits, and legacies . . . divorce and plurality of wives. The roots we may not change, but we have the right to introduce in the branches whatever changes are dictated by evolving circumstances. . . .

This radical change in understanding the substance of religion and in perceiving its mission and role is what our nation sorely needs. Limiting ourselves to partial, disordered reform no longer suffices and no longer dispenses us from a radical, revolutionary confrontation with religious thought. That partial reform puts the Islamic nation in serious danger, the danger of contradiction and fragmentation between its continued conviction concerning religion and its role and the laws and transactions which new conditions force it to adopt, even though the nation believes they violate its religion.

In truth, anyone who reflects on the present state of the Islamic nation finds it in great calamity. Practically, changing circumstances have forced it to adopt new laws taken directly from foreign codes for civil, commercial and penal matters. In the legislation of these laws, it never tried to derive them from Islamic juridical sources; on the contrary, it was forced to go against many regulations and curtail several things permitted by preceding sources of legislation. But in theory, the Islamic nation still believes it is bound by those regulations and permissions because its thinkers have not yet dared to confront the problem in the radical way of which we spoke. The Islamic nation harbors resentment against the new conditions which have forced it to arrest its ancient legislation and dreams of going back to it and to the past conditions which allowed its application. For example, in most regions, except the most backward, the punishment for stealing is not inflicted and the right of holding slaves no longer remains. In some regions the right of private property has been restrained, in others right of divorce has been limited and in others the right to a plurality of wives has been curtailed or completely abolished. But in all

---

5. *Al-Manār:* periodical published in Arabic in Cairo representing teachings of Muhammad 'Abduh. [Ed]

these different regions the nation is still not convinced that what it has done does not contradict religion. The nation is tormented and resentful, plagued by inner contradictions and fragmentation, its reality is contrary to its ideals and its comportment goes against its creed. What a horrible state for any nation to live in. . . .

When will we gather sufficient courage to admit to ourselves and proclaim to the nation that when we promulgate our new legislation, we are not bound to search for some justification for it in the sayings of an ancient jurisprudent of an old school, preferable or preferred, widespread or restricted, in vigor or defunct, in the Sunna or outside it. The only thing which obligates us is to make sure that the new legislation prevents harm and promotes benefits, and that as long as it does this it goes hand in hand with the spirit of religion and seeks to realize its goals. . . .

S. 'ĀBID HUSAIN
1896–1978

After earning his Ph.D. in Berlin, S. 'Ābid Husain enjoyed a long and distinguished career as professor of philosophy and literature at the Jamia Millia Islamia University (1925–56) and the Aligarh Muslim University (1957–60). He published more than forty volumes on Indian culture and Indian Nationalism and was a founder of the Islam and the Modern Age Society (New Delhi) as well as editor of its journal until his death.

Indian Muslims in a Secular State

Once the Indian Muslims have decided that they have to live in this country, not as a sullen, irritable, suspecting and suspected minority, but as a healthy, strong and vital part of the Indian nation and to play in new India and the new world a role which is worthy of them, they will have to remember that Indian national life itself is part of the modern world-culture, which free India has adopted as the foundation of its social and political life, and that to accept Indian nationhood is really to accept the general pattern of modern world-culture. This, as the greatest Indian leaders have understood, is made up of the secular and scientific attitude of mind, the democratic and socialistic way of life, the principles of nationalism and patriotism and the new pattern of international relationship. To do justice to their Indian nationhood, Muslims have to understand the nature of these fundamental constituents of modern culture and to assimilate them.

About the meaning of the secular outlook or secularism there is a serious misunderstanding among the people of our country and specially among the Muslims. The take it to mean an attitude of mind which completely rejects religion as one of the highest values in life. But as a matter of fact secularism is not necessarily opposed to or indifferent to religion. Many people who sincerely believe in the scientific and the political aspects of secularism, pay homage, all the same time, to religion as the supreme value. If we examine the evolution of secularism in Western countries, we see that as far as scientific secularism is concerned, the first step to separate its sphere from that of religious faith was taken by religious reformers

From *The Destiny of Indian Muslims* (New York: Asia Publishing House, 1965), pp. 170, 174–75, 195–202.

themselves and finally the partition took place with the mutual agreement of both science and religion and both were greatly benefited by it. On the other hand, in the case of political secularism, that is, in freeing the state from the domination of religion, the initiative was taken by the men of science, while the men of religion resisted it as long as they could. But later on in Protestant countries they accepted the secular state on the ground that it recognized religious and moral values as its guiding principles, though not on the basis of religious faith, at least, on that of reason and experience. Indian Muslims should consider the following facts:

    1. The secularism which India has adopted and incorporated in her national constitution, is not of the anti-religious kind which flourished in the days of the French revolution but the secularism which has taken shape in other countries of Western Europe, specially in Great Britain, through the cooperation of science and religion and embodies the quintessence of the political and cultural thoughts of many centuries and the moral spirit of Christianity and other religions. It was this secularism which saintly men like Ghandi and Vinoba and religious thinkers like Abūl Kalām Āzād and Radhakrishnan accepted as being in consonance with the universal religion of man.

    2. The secular constitution of India has given to the Muslims, as to the followers of other religions, complete freedom of religious faith and practice and of teaching and propagating it.

    3. This Constitution has recognized a number of Islamic values like the freedom of the human spirit and of conscience, the universal brotherhood of man wthout distinction of race or colour and legal, social and economic justice as fundamental rights and adopted them as the most important ideals of the Indian State.

Moreover, as it is the constitution of a democratic State, it gives to Muslims, as Indian citizens, the right and opportunity to try to change anything in the national constitution or national life which appears to them to be in conflict with Islamic values and to advocate the recognition and adoption of more Islamic values. But their effort in this direction can only be effective if they speak to the Indian nation not in religious, but in secular language and argue their case for the reforms which they think are necessary, not on the basis of religious authority and tradition, but on that of observation, experience and reason. Muslims firmly believe that Islamic teachings are in harmony with the fundamental urges of human nature and can stand the test of reason, observation and experience. They should, therefore, not find it difficult to express the need for the desired reforms in secular terms and to prove it by rational arguments.

Keeping these points in view, we can confidently say that both scientific and political secularism should be acceptable to Indian Muslims. To regard observation, experience and reason as the basis of exact knowledge or science is by no means against their religious faith. On the contrary, it is in perfect harmony with their religious and cultural traditions. Similarly, the pattern of political secularism, which those who formulated the national Constitution of India had in mind, though not fully in consonance with the Islamic political theory, has accepted a number of Islamic values as the highest human values and can accept others if they are proved to be reasonable and useful in theory and practice. So under the present circumstances in the world and specially in India, there can be no better political organization from the Muslim point of view than a secular state and they should, instead of merely tolerating it in a passive way, support it actively and zealously.

But it should be remembered that secularism is really based on the scientific attitude of mind and, until Indian Muslims thoroughly understand this attitude and seriously adopt it, their secularism would be merely superficial.

Nationalism, Patriotism and Internationalism

. . . So far Muslims throughout the world seem to have taken two extreme and opposite views of nationalism and patriotism, both of which are based on an imperfect understanding of the real import of these concepts. The popular meaning of nationalism and patriotism is, love of, and loyalty to, one's own people and country. But when they are used as sociological terms they come to mean absolute loyalty to nation and country. No Muslim can have the slightest doubt that nationalism and patriotism in the former and general sense are not only good but essential. But when they are used as technical terms, all Muslims have to ask themselves whether or not loyalty to the nation is prior to and more important than the loyalty which they owe to religion. One party, consisting of the Westernized classes in many Muslim countries, openly avers that in a conflict of loyalties it would unhesitatingly opt for loyalty to the nation and the country. The other party, with equal vehemence, refuses to regard the interests of the nation and the country as having priority over religious duty. Both have taken for granted that a conflict of loyalties is likely or at least possible.

In the Islamic world, as we have said before, for about six hundred years during the middle ages, the great majority of Muslims, in principle, regarded the religious State or *Khilāfat* [Caliphate] as the object of their undivided loyalty. But actually in the last centuries of the 'Abbāsid Khilāfat, separate Muslin States had been formed which obeyed the *Khilāfat* neither in political nor in religious matters; yet they expressed their loyalty to it to the extent that their rulers, after ascending the throne, generally obtained confirmation of their right to rule from the *Khalīfa*

[Caliph]. After the end of the ʿAbbāsid *Khilāfat* in the thirteenth century the sultans of the Ottoman Turkish dynasty claimed to be the inheritors of the *Khilāfat* and Muslims of some countries including India recognized them as Khalīfas. . . . This nominal loyalty automatically lapsed in 1924 when Mustafā Kamāl put an end to the *Khilāfat*. The unsuccessful attempts which were subsequently made to preserve the *Khilāfat* in one form or the other have already been mentioned. So as a matter of fact, historical forces had compelled Muslims in the greater part of the world to separate the spheres of their political and religious loyalties as soon as the disintegration of the ʿAbbāsid *Khilāfat* began. Their political loyalty was offered to their country and their king and a nominal loyalty to the *Khalīfa* of Baghdad and later to the Ottoman Turkish Sultan. After the end of the Ottoman *Khilāfat* democratic governments were set up in Turkey and several other Muslim countries. The people in each of these countries owe their allegiance to their nation and the state, and even the nominal religious loyalty to the Turkish *Khilāfat* has ceased to exist. But the real religious loyalty, which had in practice been offered for centuries not to any temporal ruler or organization, but only to God and the Prophet, or in other words to the Word of God and the Traditions of the Prophet, is still there. Some Muslims are not satisfied with this state of things and are dreaming of building a national or international religious State which should organize and direct not only their political and economic but also their religious and moral life. But so far, their efforts to realize this dream have proved unsuccessful and apparently there are no prospects of any success in future.

So far we have spoken of countries where the whole or the larger part of the population is Muslim. Now let us turn to India where Muslims form less than 11 per cent of the population. They had perforce to decide and have decided that while maintaining their religious loyalty to the Word of God and the Traditions of the Prophet, they shall owe their political allegiance to the national State of India. As this state is a secular and democratic one and the constitution which has been adopted guarantees their religious freedom, there should be no fear of its interfering with their religious life. As long as this situation continues there is no possibility of a conflict between their religious and political loyalties. The problem before them now is how far nationalism and patriotism which really are two names for a single concept, are necessary for fulfilling their pact of loyalty to this secular democratic State and how far they are in harmony with the religious spirit of Islam.

State is really an abstract idea which has no objective existence. The modern democratic state expresses itself in a code of fundamental principles known as its constitution according to which a country and its inhabitants are governed. The technical term for people living in one country under one state is a "nation" and the whole country is their homeland. Obviously, the life and stability of a state depend on the condition that those who live under it shoudl be so strongly attached to their homeland that they can work together for its security and prosperity and are prepared to suffer and sacrifice for it. The attachment and love of a people for their country is called patriotism and for their countrymen as a whole is called nationalism. After this explanation, hardly any sensible person would disagree that in a democratic state where there is no hereditary or permanent head, there can be no other tie except love of the nation and the country which binds people living under it to one another and thus strengthens the foundations of the State. Consequently loyalty to the State necessarily demands loyalty to the nation and the country. So the Indian Muslims who have accepted loyalty to the state as a fundamental principle, will have to accept nationalism and patriotism as its necessary corollaries.

We have already said that Indian Muslims, like all others, regard the love of the nation and the country, as a natural sentiment, good and necessary. But when nationalism and patriotism are used as political terms and mean giving loyalty to the nation and the country the highest place in social obligations, Indian Muslims will have to be careful in determining and defining their attitude to them because they mean different things to different people. They would naturally want them to be clearly enunciated and they would also ask the precise meaning of "the highest place in social obligations."

There is a fetishist school of nationalism and patriotism which prescribes some sort of religious devotion to the nation and the country and worships them like deities. Its followers are expected to adopt this new faith instead of, or along with, their traditional religious faith, and to regard it not only as a means of welfare in this world but also of salvation in the next. To this school belonged some revolutionaries in India and, to a certain extent, the Nazis in Germany. Of course no Muslim, as long as he is a Muslim, would subscribe to any such faith. He would be prepared to give his motherland the status of a real mother which is the highest and the most beautiful in social relations. But he cannot have a devotional feeling, which he regards above all worldly emotions, for any idea or any being except God. Similarly that brand of nationalism and patriotism which advocates a unitary national culture, a single language and a uniform pattern of living for the whole country, is as unacceptable to the Indian Muslims as to many other linguistic or regional communities in India. Generally, Muslims fully appreciate the need for a common national culture. They had, at one time actually taken the leading part in building a common Hindustani culture and they are fully prepared today to participate in evolving a new national culture, but on the condition that it should not displace regional and communal cultures but coexist with them and serve as a common sphere of life for all.

. . . Considering the political climate in which Indian Muslims have lived so far, it is possible that if the trend towards negative and agressive nationalism which exists in our country to some extent, increases and, rising above religious prejudices, tries to draw them to it, they may be easily attracted. But they will do well to remember that such a fanatical form of nationalism and patriotism is incompatible with the religious and moral spirit of Islam. As a matter of fact, it is these unhealthy forms of nationalism and patriotism which Iqbal, the poet of Islam, condemns and rejects. It is regrettable that Iqbal, the Indian Muslim politician, dragged even the healthy forms of nationalism and patriotism into the fire of his condemnation.

So from the point of view of Indian Muslims, the healthy concept of nationalism and patriotism demands that their political loyalty and affection should go entirely to their national State and its secular democratic constitution and they should be prepared to sacrifice everything, except their religion and culture, for its security, honour, dignity, progress and welfare. . . .

MUSHĪR UL-HAQ
1933–

After graduation ('Ālim) from Nadwat al-Ulema, Lucknow, Mushīr ul-Haq earned his B.A. (Jamia Millia Islamia, Delhi) and M.A. (Muslim University, Aligarh) in Islamic and Arabic Studies. In 1967, he received a Ph.D. in Islamic Studies from McGill University. He has been a member of the Institute of Advanced Studies in Simla and is presently chairman of the Department of Arabic Studies, Jamia Millia University.

Islam in Secular India

The Constitution of India designates the country a "Sovereign Democratic Republic" but makes no mention of "secularism." For the last two decades Indians have been talking of secularism, yet the term remains vague and ambiguous. One may, therefore, be justified in asking: what does secularism really mean—especially in the Indian context? . . .

It should be remembered that when India became independent the makers of the Indian Constitution had hardly any alternative to taking secularism as their guideline. The leaders of the Independence Movement were so committed to a noncommunal and non-religious policy that even after the partition of the country they could not retreat from their stand. The Muslim community of India also welcomed the idea of a secular state because they feared the alternative would be a "Hindu state." . . .

All through the freedom struggle hardly any national leader dared to question the importance of religion. The leaders of both the Hindu and the Muslim communities most of the times used a religous vocabulary in their speeches and writings to achieve political ends. In the case of the Hindu community one may say that religion did not mean a codified and systematized set of principles, rather it was understood in term of higher moral values. But this cannot be said about the Muslims. Religion to them was not just moral values: it was the *Sharī'a,* a system, an institution: Muslims were told this time and again. . . .

The *Sharī'a* (which means a "way") and is usually translated as "Islamic law") is believed by generality of the Muslims to be "the Islamic way of life, comprehending beliefs, ritual, practices, public and personal law, and

From *Islam in Secular India* (Simla: Indian Institute of Advanced Study, 1972), pp. 6, 8–9, 14–16, 19–21, 85–86.

being stretched even to include dress, personal appearance and rules of behaviour in social intercourse . . .

The Indian Muslims generally hold "Islam" as "faith" and "*Sharī'a*" or "the practical exhibition of the faith" to be inseparable. Faith must show in action. And action has to be strictly in line with the rules and regulations formulated by the *fuqahā'* ("jurists") in the golden days of Islam, chiefly on the basis of the Qur'ān and the Prophetic traditions. Therefore no part of life is regarded to be outside of the purview of the *Sharī'a*, and its violation is considered "crime" as well as "sin."

Thus secularism and secular state are to be accepted or rejected on the basis of the *Sharī'a*. The secular state, as we have seen, has a precedent in Islamic history and is, therefore, acceptable, but secularism as a doctrine is believed to be incompatible with Islam. since no serious effort has so far been made to explain to the Indian Muslims—as it has been done in the case of Turkey—that "secularism" is a foreign word, and in Islamic society it can be interpreted quite differently from what it is understood in a Christian society, naturally we find the Indian Muslims still groping after the meaning of secularism. . . .

On the question of secularism, however, Indian Muslims appear broadly divided into two sections. The first group, in a minority and rather contemptuously called "secularist" includes mostly modern educated Muslims who hold that religion, as a faith, can co-exist with secularism. The second group, led by the *'ulamā*,' stands by the view that religion is not only faith but *Sharī'a* also. Faith may co-exist with secularism, but *Sharī'a* cannot. . . .

There are then two groups of Indian Muslims—the "secularists" and the "nationalist" *'ulamā'*—who are are suspect in the eyes of many Muslims, but there is little hope of their joining hands. These two are quite different from each other. They have practically nothing in common in their education, or mental make-up, or in their approach to this world and the next, in short, in anything. The only point common to them is that both are frowned upon by the generality of the Muslims, of course, for different reasons altogether.

In short it can be said that the Indian Muslims are in a dilemma: so far as the secular state is concerned, it is acceptable, for one thing, no alternative is available and, for the other, a secular state guarantees religious freedom. Buth the philosophy of secularism is considered to be a poison for religious life. . . .

Conclusion

The key to understanding the Muslims' lack of response to the demand for secularization appears to lie in two words: innovation and tradition. If secularism places worldly life outside the control of religion, this is an innovation without precedent in Islamic history: hence, to the faithful, unacceptable. But if secularism denotes only that the state does not favour any particular community in matters of religion, it is believed to be in accord with Islamic tradition which gives religious freedom to every citizen. This concept of secularism is not alien to a Muslim and therefore he sees no conflict between his religion, Islam, and secularism.

However, secularism becomes anti-religion when it demands a share in what belongs to God. At this point a devout Muslim hesitates to accept secularism as a way of life because it is not the life of this world which he lives for; it is the "next" for which he is supposed to live and work. It is true that in the past Muslims have quite often allowed Caesar to take what he wished and to leave for God what he pleased: British rule in India is a recent example of the fact. Thus, one may say, it would not have been very difficult for the Muslims to let the tradition continue. But it is often forgotten that the Muslims' participation in the struggle for freedom was mostly inspired by the promises from their religious leadership, the 'ulamā,' that after the departure of the British from India they would have an opportunity to live a life according to their religion. The partition blighted the Muslim hope of religious revival in India: yet the prospect of living in a secular state which is supposed to guarantee freedom of religious belief and practice to all its citizens without any distinction restored their confidence in their religious future.

Had religion meant to the Muslims only a personal relation between man and God, they might have surrendered unconditionally to the forces of secularization. But they are constantly told by their religious leaders, the 'ulamā,' that Islam is not just a philosophy; it is man's total and unconditional submission to God: its demands from the adherents are much more than those of a state. This makes the Muslims hesitate to cooperate in building up a completely secular society.

Some people may not like to be told that the Muslim community, by and large, is still religious in the sense that it invariably seeks a religious sanction for every innovation, but we have seen how strongly they believe in the institutionalized procedures for seeking this sanction. To be fully accepted an innovation has to transform itself into a tradition. It appears, therefore, that until secularism is "blessed" by the 'ulamā,' it will not make much headway in the Muslim community. . . .

III
ISLAM AND SOCIAL CHANGE

THE MODERNIZATION OF ISLAMIC LAW

Under the impact of the West, modern change in Islamic law first occurred in the nineteenth century in the Ottoman Middle East and in the Indian subcontinent. This was accomplished through the enactment of commercial and penal codes, which, both in form and substance, were derived from European models. In addition, secular (*nizāmiyya*) courts were established to handle civil and criminal cases and thus the religious (*Sharī'a*) courts' jurisdiction was limited to the area of family law. At the same time, the first attempts at codification of civil law took place, resulting in, for example, the Ottoman *Mejelle* of 1877. Thus, from the latter part of the nineteenth century, Islamic law in much of the Muslim world was restricted to the domain of family law.

The twentieth century saw the continuation of the trend toward modernization through the adoption of Western secular codes. In some Muslim countries the functions of the *Sharī'a* courts were absorbed by the civil court system, thus ending the dual court system (religious and secular) which had been created during the nineteenth century. In addition, as will be discussed following p. 200, for the first time changes were introduced in Muslim family law. However, the methodology employed was one of reinterpretation and reform of the *Sharī'a* rather than its displacement by secular codes.

Although Turkey decided to follow a path of complete secularization and adopted the Swiss Civil Code (1928), even in the area of family law, she was a unique exception. Most Muslim countries have continued to acknowledge the *Sharī'a* as "a source" if not "the source" of their nation's law. In effect, these Muslim nations have developed modern legal systems in which the *Sharī'a* has been primarily restricted to family law.

In the contemporary Islamic world there have been renewed demands for a return to a more Islamic way of life. This reemergence of Islam in the political sphere has been accompanied by demands for a more Islamic legal system by those who maintain that it is the *Sharī'a* that determines the Islamic character of a state and its people.

The first two selections exemplify two quite divergent approaches to the problem of Islamic legal reform. Subhī Mahmasānī advocates the need to reinterpret and adapt Islamic law to the modern world. However, Āsaf A.A. Fyzee espouses a secular path and thus argues the need for modern Islam to separate religion from politics and law.

In addition to legal reform, another way in which law has been relevant to the process of modernizaton is the use of *fatwās (fatwā,* pl. *fatāwa)*— formal legal opinions or interpretations given by a *muftī* (a legal specialist). *Fatwās* have been used to legitimate social changes from birth control to land reform.

SUBHĪ MAHMASĀNĪ
1911–

An LL.B. and *Docteur en Droit* (University of Lyons), he has
served as magistrate, president of the Appeals Court (1944–46),
member of Parliament and minister of Economy (1966). He has
taught at a number of universities, including the American University of Beirut and the Lebanese University.

Adaptation of Islamic Jurisprudence
to Modern Social Needs

Closing the Door of Ijtihād and Neglect of Education

Islamic Jurisprudence dealt with questions of religion and acts of worship,
and with legal transactions, along with all provisions, rules, and particulars derived from them. That is why jurists in Islam were at once men of
religion and jurisprudence. They were called "scholars" (*'ulamā'*) because
their field of study included all departments of ancient knowledge. As a
result, Islamic jurisprudence played such a significant role in the history of
Islamic thought as well as in all aspects of Muslim life.

It is known that Islamic jurisprudence is based on various sources; some
religious, the Qur'ān and the Sunna, and some secondary accepted by the
majority of the jurists; *ijmā'* (consensus of opinion) and *qiyās* (analogy).
There are other sources acknowledged by some schools but refuted by
others. These are based on necessity, custom and equity; such as *istihsān*
(appropriateness) in the Hanafī school, *al-masālih al-mursalat* (excepted
interests) in the Mālikī school, and the like.

The jurists took up all these sources, known as evidence (*adillat*) of law,
in a special branch of knowledge called *'ilm al-usūl* (science of basic
sources). They began to work at discovering legal solutions from such
sources and evidences. This sort of activity was referred to as *ijtihād*
(endeavor or interpretation). It was a cause for expanding legal provisions
to comprise new cases, as well as a strong factor in the development of
Islamic law according to the needs of different countries and the conditions of changing times. Thus, *ijtihād* had led to the flourishing of Islamic
jurisprudence, especially at the early stage of the 'Abbāsid period.

From: "Muslims: Decadence and Renaissance" in *Muslim World* 44 (1954), pp. 186–91,
196–97, 199–201.

181

When Baghdad fell in the middle of the seventh century A.H., intellectual activities diminished, and Arab civilization began to decline. This took place after the Sunni jurists unanimously agreed to close the door of *ijtihād* and to be contented with the four known Sunnite schools: the Hanafite, the Mālikite, the Shāfi'ite, and the Hanbalite. The result was that Islamic thought met a dead end, and imitation and stagnation in jurisprudence and other Arabic and Islamic learning became predominant.

In fact, the closure of *ijtihād* violates the provisions and concepts of Islamic jurisprudence and condemns all Muslims to permanent stagnation and exclusion from the application of the laws of evolution. It imposes upon them to maintain the same conditions prevailing at the time of ancient jurists, and to follow the pattern they had set for themselves and for the Muslims of their days and the days that will follow until eternity.

No doubt, the remedy lies in opening what the ancients had closed or attempted to close. The door of *ijtihād* should be thrown wide open for anyone juristically qualified. The error, all the error, lies in blind imitation and restraint of thought. What is right is to allow freedom of interpretation of Islamic jurisprudence, and to liberate thought and make it capable of true scientific creativeness. . . .

Adherence to Doubtful Texts

What brought about disagreement in law is the fact that the Prophet did not order the writing of the *Sunna* as he did regarding the Qur'ān. On the contrary, he prohibited such an action by saying: "Don't write down from me, and whoever wrote down from me other than the Qur'ān should have it destroyed. There is no harm in relating from me." (*Sahīh Muslim*, Vol. 8, pp. 229). This made 'Umar ibn al-Khattāb refuse to compile the traditions. He was afraid lest the people would take them up and leave the Qur'ān.

However, despite such discouragement, traditions were forged in great number during certain periods of Islamic history. This was done to serve and support certain policies or factions, or to popularize storytelling or to achieve other purposes. Consequently, the traditions became impossibly numerous. Many unreliable and absurd traditions could not possibly stand in logic and reason.

Faced with this situation, Muslim jurists began to study and examine them. They laid down a set of scientific rules by which to judge and determine their authenticity. These rules came to constitute a special science called the Science of Traditional Method (*Mustalah al-Hadīth*). In addition, many were prompted to write, warning their readers of false traditions. As a result, there was agreement among jurists regarding some traditions and disagreement regarding others. As an example of fabricated traditions, one may cite the following: "The sea is of hell." "The mouse is Jewish." "Eggplant is the cure of all sickness."

Modernist jurists, such as Ibn Taimiyyat and Muhammad 'Abduh, also revolted against this deplorable situation. They began to examine traditions in the light of the principles of jurisprudence and reason . . .

The remedy of this evil is obvious and within reach. All forged traditions without exception should be discarded. Nothing should remain except those authentic traditions on which agreement by jurists of the known schools had been unanimous.

In compliance with this warning, Muslim reformists should liberate themselves from the remnants of error, forgery, falsehood and fabrication. They must discard made-up traditions which are incompatible with legal texts and principles, or with the rules laid down by the Science of the Sources of Law (*Usūl al-Fiqh*), or by logic and reason, on which all provisions of Islamic jurisprudence are based.

Adherence to Formalism and Particulars

The provisions of Islamic jurisprudence are based less on the texts than on interpretations of the jurists. The texts form the bases of the principles and universal rules; whereas most details and particulars are based on the interpretation of jurists by way of unanimity, (*ijmā'*) analogy (*qiyās*), or other legal sources. These details and particulars fill huge volumes of legal work, so that research regarding them requires a long time and considerable effort.

Furthermore, this great body of particulars often dominated the general principles, and, with repeated imitation, took a rigid and formalistic taint alien to the original substance. Some jurists of late adhered to them and through blind imitation transmitted them as basic obligatory provisions, without any discrimination or examination in the light of the original principles and texts and without the criterion of reason and thought. Thus, details dominated the basis and the form overshadowed the substance. Such a state of things was one of the causes which led to the decline and stagnation of Islamic culture. . . .

Sectarian Differences

. . . In general, disagreements among schools were not on the whole disagreements on basic principles and doctrines, but rather on details as a result of diversity of interpretations and differences of views in applying principles to practical cases.

The existence of diversity of opinions was a reason for flexibility in Islamic jurisprudence, as well as a cause of relief to the people. Thus it was said: "Disagreement among jurists is the nation's bliss." This is supported by the fact that the Ottoman Empire which adopted the Hanafite School in law and religion borrowed from other schools many legal provisions, particularly in its Family Code. . . .

However, alongside those advantages of diversity of schools there were disadvantages too, most important of which was sectarianism, with all its outcome of discord, animosity and hatred. Followers of each school were often so by inheritance and tradition rather than by reason and conviction. They displayed strong fanaticism towards their own school and its leaders and attacked other schools and leaders with flagrant bitterness. There were days when strife became intense between the Shī'ītes and the Sunnites as well as among the different schools and sects within these two groups. Such a strife was one of the causes leading to disunity and backwardness among Muslims.

The Sources of Law and Modern Legal Reform

To cure this evil, struggle must be waged against sectarian partisanship. Efforts must be made to reconcile all hearts and unite the various schools. This, in my opinion, can be achieved by a return to the same and only original sources of law. Such a return should take into consideration the following bases:

I. To adopt the provisions of the Qur'ān as the first basis for Islamic teachings and jurisprudence; to distinguish in this respect between compulsory and voluntary or directive provisions on the lines already attempted by interpreters of the Qur'ān and scholars of the Science of Legal Sources; and then to apply these provisions in accordance with their respective significance.

II. To adopt the Sunna in all obligatory religious provisions, provided that this Sunna is authentic and acceptable in the various Muslim schools and that it is not inconsistent with the text of the Qur'ān.

III. To adopt the rest of the Sunna, that is to say the traditional teachings and precepts whose authenticity had been disputed by reliable leaders of the schools, provided they are consistent with reason and acceptable to jurists and scholars of the Science of Legal Sources ('Ilm al-Usūl) on the basis of the principle mentioned above, namely that the truly traditional is always consistent with the truly rational.

IV. To choose from the legal rules based on interpretations of jurists those which are most suitable to the needs of modern society, public interest and principles of justice and equity.

Such are the practical fundamental lines which will lead to the unification of Muslim schools—a unification that has become at the present time an urgent necessity. . . .

Moreover, the idea of unifying the various schools is consistent with the spirit of Islamic jurisprudence and its teachings.

"Those who are discordant in their religion and separated into parties, do not belong to you." (Qur'ān 4:159).

If Islam prohibits religious fanaticism and demands brotherhood and tolerance between Muslims and the rest of the world, for better reason it does not allow sectarianism among Muslims themselves. . . .

Muslim jurists, as we have already mentioned, studied Islam as being a religion, a law and a social system. This is why Islamic jurisprudence contained provisions pertaining to acts of worship as well as to legal transactions.

As a consequence, there has been in inter-action between the teachings of religion and ethics on the one hand, and the provisions of law on the other hand. Thus we find justice and charity, coupled by the Qur'ān in one single verse: "God enjoins justice and charity," so that it has become a rule of justice not to do harm to one another, and a duty in legal transactions to abide by the principles of honesty and tolerance. All of this, no doubt, has been a source of benefit for the Muslims. It has made Islamic jurisprudence human and just.

Accordingly, earlier Muslim jurists made a differentiation in certain cases between the legal and the religious rulings, a differentiation similar to that made today between civil and natural obligations. They were, for instance, of the opinion that if a man had the right to repudiate his wife in law, his repudiation in order to be valid in religion must be based on justifiable grounds. Otherwise it would be proof of rashness and ingratitude towards the blessings of marriage which is based on love and mercy.

However, some jurists were influenced by dominant pre-Islamic customs and therefore did not go beyond this imperfect step. They declined to apply in such cases the ruling imposed by the teachings of religion. If they had done so, giving religious and ethical principles more consideration, along with as much implementation in law as had been possible, their attitude would have been closer to the spirit of Islamic jurisprudence and teachings.

In addition, we find that some jurists, especially during the period of imitation and decline, had, despite their differentiation between legal and religious rulings, discarded such differentiation with regard to other matters. They mixed religion with the daily ways of life and studied Islam as comprising both categories in similar degree. They were, thus, unmindful of the fact that the basis in Islam is the religion and its teachings and that the world and its affairs are only the accessories. Indeed, their excess in this respect was such that incidental worldly matters were placed on the same level with the original, essential and immortal provisions of religion.

As a result, stagnation in Islamic thought and culture was bound to take place. Muslims of earlier days adhered to trivialities, so much so that they condemned as a prohibited innovation anything unknown during the time of the Prophet or their time. Thus, for instance, they advocated the prohibition of the study of foreign languages, eating with the fork, wearing the hat, and other worldly trivial matters.

But if we refer to the essence of Islamic jurisprudence, we find that the teachings of the Prophet do not bind the Muslims except in cases pertaining to religion and ethics, along with their accessories. Traditions which refer to secondary matters of daily living and which the Prophet had mentioned as a matter of opinion, are not mandatory. In support of this statement, we may cite the tradition included by Muslim in his collection of traditions (Vol. 7, p. 95), namely that the Prophet once passed by some people who were fecundating-palm trees and he asked: "What are these people doing?" The answer was that they were fecundating palm trees. To this the Prophet said: "If they would not do that (the trees) would be prolific." When they were told of his words they stopped that pollination. But the fruits did not ripen. Upon learning about this, the Prophet said: "I am only a human being; If I order you to do something regarding your religion you must comply. But if I order you to do something on the basis of my opinion, well I am just a human being. You know better in matters concerning your worldly affairs."

Therefore, no relation whatever exists between Islam and matters of daily living, unless these are concerned with a principle of religion. By religion, here, is meant the provisions of the faith, the unity of God, acts of worship, along with the principles of ethics and the fundamental rules of legal transactions. Outside these, the above-mentioned tradition leaves to the Muslims freedom in secondary matters relating to their daily life. It is because they know more about such matters, and because such matters are subject to changes in accordance with their needs and interests.

Muslims must comprehend this rule, and thereby separate provisions of religion from matters of daily life in the manner explained. They ought to adhere to their religion and ethical code, and manage their ways of life according to the spirit of Islam and requirements of science and civilization. It is by so doing that they will be able to put an end to their backwardness in this respect and to rise towards happiness and prosperity.

To sum up, the most important factor in the decline of Muslims is their neglect of the duties of Islam. Improvement of their condition can be brought about by their return to the true principles of Islam, their understanding of the effective causes of legal rules, and their giving what belongs to religion to religion and what belongs to the world to the world, along with their determination to destroy the walls of ignorance and imitation, to reject unauthentic texts, formalistic technicalities, particulars, and details, together with sectarian partisanship—all of which have distorted the real essence of Islam.

Muslims have to choose between two courses: the course of ignorant imitators, thereby accepting darkness and ignorance and oblivion; or the course of the pious predecessors which leads to light and knowledge and life. . . .

ĀSAF A.A. FYZEE
1899–

He is a distinguished jurist, professor of law, and former Vice-
Chancellor of the University of Jammu and Kashmir as well as a
former visiting professor at Cambridge University and U.C.L.A.
Among his more important works are *Outlines of Muhammadan Law* and *A Modern Approach to Islam*.

The Reinterpretation of Islam

In Islam law is not distinct from religion. The two streams flow in a single
channel and are indistinguishable. They are known as *Sharī'a* (Pers., Tur.,
Urdu,—*Sharī'a*) and *fiqh*, the two aspects of the religious law of Islam.
Sharī'a is the wider circle, it embraces in its orbit all human actions; *fiqh*
is the narrower one, and deals with what are commonly understood as
legal acts. *Sharī'a* always reminds us of revelation, that *'ilm* (knowledge)
which we could never have possessed by for the Qu'rān or *hadīth*; in *fiqh*,
the power of reasoning is stressed, and deductions based upon *'ilm* are
continuously cited with approval. The path of *Sharī'a* is laid down by God
and His Prophet; the edifice of *fiqh* is erected by human endeavour.

It must, however, be candidly confessed that the line of distinction is by
no means clearly drawn, and very often the Muslim doctors themselves use
the terms synonymously: for, the criterion of all human action, whether in
the *Sharī'a* or in the *fiqh*, is the same—seeking the approval of Allah by
conforming to an ideally perfect code. . . . The faith of Islam teaches the
belief in one God and His Messengers; but it cannot and ought not to lay
down how it can enforce such obedience. By "enforce" is meant (*a*) order
the doing of a thing and (*b*) punish its disobedience. How can a matter of
faith be a matter of enforcement by an outside agency? A teacher may
teach me; he can inspire me by his example; he can fire my enthusiasm.
But how can he make me believe? Thus there is a clear difference between
a rule of law which can be enforced by the state, and a rule of conscience
which is entirely a man's own affair.

Today in Islam this is the greatest difficulty. *Sharī'a* embraces both law
and religion. Religion is based upon spiritual experience; law is based
upon the will of the community as expressed by its legislature, or any
other law-making authority. Religion is unchangeable in its innermost

From: *A Modern Approach to Islam* (Bombay: Asia Publ. House, 1962), pp. 85–96, 98–108.

kernel—the love of God for His own sake is sung by *sūfīs* and mystics throughout the world. If *sharī'a* is the name given to this duality, then one of the forces constantly pulls in the other direction. The cognition of God is a mystery, and man is forever pursuing it. In this pursuit, all men of faith regardless of their particular religion are equal. But laws differ from country to country, from time to time. They must ever seek to conform to the changing pattern of society. The laws of the Arabs cannot be applied to the Eskimos; and the laws of the bushmen of Australia are unsuitable for the fertile basin of Uttar Pradesh. Laws are like metals in the crucible of time and circumstance; they melt, they gradually solidify into different shapes; they re-melt and assume diverse forms. This process of evolution is coterminous with human society. Nothing is static except that which is dead and lifeless. Laws can never be static. India is changing with the rest of the world before our own eyes. These changes are the result of our powers over nature, our views on life, and our desire to improve the social conditions of men. Our legislature pours out a stream of statutory law, and this legislative activity attempts to regulate our dealings in society.

But the mind and conscience of man is free. He must be permitted to believe what he will in respect of the ultimate things in the universe, and he cannot be fettered in his faith and imagination. There is thus an internal strife in Islam. First, the ageless concepts of the religious law come into conflict with modern civil law, e.g. insurance or the loans which Government raises. Insurance and the giving or taking of interest is forbidden by the *Sharī'a;* while it is not only permitted but encouraged by the modern state.

Secondly, in order to do away with the rigours of the older law, principles of a newer system are engrafted upon the ancient law of Islam; or a new set of laws replaced the *Sharī'a.* An illustration of the former is the Muhammadan law of Gifts in India, where the principles of English equity are grafted upon the *fiqh* (Islamic law, proper). An illustration of the latter is the Evidence Act in India, which completely replaces the Islamic law of Evidence. Everywhere in Islamic countries this dual process is at work— *qānūn,* the secular law, is eating into and replacing the laws of the *Sharī'a.* In North Africa, French jurisprudence; in Central Asia, the Soviet laws; in India, the English common law; in Indonesia, the Dutch law and above all, International law, are profoundly influencing not only the body of law but the meaning of justice as it affects the Muslims.

We have seen that the *Sharī'a* is both law and religion. Law is by its very nature subject to change. The heart of religion, on the other hand, is unchangeable, or at any rate, the belief in God is an unalterable ideal, a perennial quest. If two such divergent forces are made to live together, there will be a clash. . . . My solution is (*a*) to define religion and law in terms of twentieth century thought, (*b*) to distinguish between religion and law in Islam, and (c) to interpret Islam on this basis and give a fresh meaning to the faith of Islam. If by this analysis some elements that we have regarded as part of the essence of Islam have to be modified, or given up altogether, then we have to face the consequences. If, on the other hand, belief in the innermost core can be preserved and strengthened, the operation although painful will produce health and vigour in an anaemic body which is languishing without a fresh ideal to guide it. . . .

General Principles of Reinterpretation

Historical Approach. The message of Islam was sent to the world fourteen centuries ago. Does it need reinterpretation? Is it not meant for the whole world and for all time? The answer to both questions is in the affirmative. Even if a message is true, and, in a sense eternal, it is by the very premises essential to understand it in accordance with the science, philosophy, psychology, metaphysics and theology of the modern world; nay, the sum-total of the world's thinking and its blazing light should be brought to bear upon it. . . . No language remains static. The evocative power of words and phrases increases and decreases; it is not a constant factor, it is one of the known variables. . . . I wish to *understand* the Qu'rān as it was understood by the Arabs of the time of the Prophet only to *reinterpret* it and apply it to my conditions of life and to believe in it, so far as it appeals to me as a twentieth-century man. I cannot be called upon to live in the desert, to traverse it on camel back, to eat locusts, to indulge in vendetta, to wear a beard and a cloak, and to cultivate a pseudo-Arab mentality. I must distinguish between poetic truth and factual truth. I must distinguish between the husk and the kernel of religion, between law and legend. I am bound to understand and accept the message of Islam as a modern man, and not as one who lived centuries ago. I respect authority, but cannot accept it "without how" (*bilā kayfa*) in the matter of conscience.

Islam is based upon the Qu'rān, and the Qur'ān is to be interpreted in its historical setting and on chronological principles. We must first study the main principles of Judaism and Christianity before approaching Islam. . . .

Specific Rules of Interpretation

Fundamental Principles The six principles which are proposed for a modern reinterpretaton of Islam are as follows:

i. Study of History of Religions.
ii. Comparative Religion of the Semitic Races.
iii. Study of Semitic languages and philology.
iv. Separation of Law and Religion.
v. Re-examination of *Sharī'a* and *kalām*.
vi. Reinterpretation of cosmology and scientific facts . . .

Separation of Law from Religion. The separation of *civil* law from the *moral* or *religious* law can now no longer be delayed in Islam. We must in the first instance distinguish between the universal moral rule, such as, truthfulness, marital purity, honesty, etc., and the particular moral rules, such as the prohibition of ham and of wine. The former are enjoined by all religions; the latter are not. A difference of emphasis is clearly indicated in such cases.

And then we must deal with the law. The first task is to separate logically the dogmas and doctrines of religion from the principles and rules of law. The essential faith of man is something different from the outward observance of rules; moral rules apply to the conscience, but legal rules can be enforced only by the state. Ethical norms are subjective, legal rules are objective. The inner life of the spirit, the "Idea of the Holy," must be separated to some extent from the outward forms of social behaviour. The separation is not simple; it will even be considered un-Islamic. But the attempt at a rethinking of the *Sharī'a* can only begin with the acceptance of this principle. . . .

Such a liberal interpretation would affect the constitution of an Islamic country. According to Islam, God is the owner of everything; He is the true sovereign in a state. Such a theory would be impractical in the modern world, and the only workable principle is as laid down by numerous modern democratic constitutions, namely, that the people of a country are sovereign within their own domain. If religion is gradually freed from the shackles of civil law, and law (*qānūn*) is allowed to grow and develop freely, Muslim society is bound to progress rapidly. . . .

Re-examination of Sharī'a and Kalām (Theology).
The theology of Islam must be re-examined in all its aspects, and modern philosophy, metaphysics, ethics, psychology and logic should be applied to formulate and restate its essential dogmas. The scholastic theology of Islam (*'ilm al-kalām*) in its various aspects has not been substantially reformed since the days of Ghazālī. The current stream of European thought; the great advances made by Protestant thinkers from Luther downwards, and by the scholastics from St. Thomas Aquinas and Suarez down to Maritain and Berdyaev; and the speculations of Jewish and other thinkers of the modern world must be used with discrimination to fortify and re-shape Islamic theological principles. . . .

Subsidiary Principles. When a rule is laid down in the Qur'ān or *Sharī'a* it is necessary to determine whether it is a rule of law or a rule of ethics. If it is a rule of law, the state should enforce it; if it is a rule of ethics, the state cannot enforce it. Once it is determined in accordance with the foregoing principles that there is a *clear rule of law laid down in the Qur'ān,* the question assumes importance. The law of God, it is said, cannot be disobeyed. This statement, it is respectfully submitted, requires careful re-examination. The Qur'ān may lay down a *fundamental* rule governing the actions of man; or it may speak of a *particular* by-law, restricted by time and circumstance, not laying down an eternal verity, or it may speak in the language of poetry, metaphor, myth or legend: *He it is Who hath revealed unto thee (Muhammad) the Scripture wherein are clear revelations* (muhkamāt)—*They are the substance of the Book—and others (which are) allegorical* (mutashābihāt), Qur'ān 3:7.

In such a case, we may come to the conclusion that it is a question of interpretation and that law can be changed, but religion is more permanent and need not be altered.

In order to examine a clear dictate of the Qur'ān . . . we must follow a certain procedure. The procedure submitted is as follows:

1. *What was the rule or custom before Islam?* . . .

2. *How did the Prophet try to reform it?* . . .

3. *What were the results of such reform?* The case of *women* may be taken as an illustration. The law of marriage in Islam, with certain important reservations, is beneficial to women; and so is the law of inheritance. Why is it that almost everywhere in Islamic countries women have been denied rights by custom over immovable property? That is so in India, Indonesia, Egypt, Persia, and North Africa. And what is more disturbing is that not only is woman denied her Qur'ānic rights but she is considered *inferior* to man and not fit for certain political rights. Travel in Muslim countries demonstrates the painful fact that woman is considered the plaything of man and seldom a life-companion, co-worker, or helpmate. It is not enough to brush this aside by saying that a particular practice is un-Islamic or contrary to the spirit of Islam. It is necessary to face facts, to go to the root of the matter, to give up inequitable interpretations, and to re-educate the people. The Qu'rānic verse: *Men are in charge of women, because God hath made one of them to excel the other* (Qur'ān 4:34) should be reinterpreted as purely local and applicable only for the time being. Its wider application should be reconsidered; and it may be possible to construe it as a rule of social conduct which was restricted to conditions existing in Arabia at the time of the Prophet, and as being no longer applicable in modern life.

4. *How were the rules applied and interpreted in the various schools of law in the succeeding centuries?* The two rules mentioned above are closely connected. Contemporary sources, particularly independent and critical accounts, will have to be scrutinized to discover what the immediate results were, and the historical evolution of the doctrines will have to be examined. Were the commands obeyed in the latter and the spirit in the succeeding centuries? Were they misunderstood or changed or distorted? Were they used for political or personal ends? These are some of the questions that arise.

5. *What is the present state of the personal law? How far does it fall*

short of the highest norms fixed by modern juristic thinking? In what way can the rules be sustained, amended, or repealed, so as to conform to modern concepts of social justice and to promote the social well-being of the Muslim community as an integral part of society in general? This method of interpretation deals with the personal law in India; a similar process can be applied to theological and moral rules.

If the complete fabric of the *Sharī'a* is examined in this critical manner, it is obvious that in addition to the orthodox and stable pattern of religion, a newer "protestant" Islam will be born in conformity with conditions of life in the twentieth century, cutting away the dead wood of the past and looking hopefully at the future. We need not bother about nomenclature, but if some name has to be given to it, let us call *"Liberal Islam."*

Results

The greatest gift of the modern world to man is freedom—freedom to think, freedom to speak, freedom to act. . . .

And what does Islam do, so far as religious doctrine is concerned? It closes the Gate of Interpretation. It lays down that legists and jurisconsults are to be divided into certain categories, and no freedom of thought is allowed. Iqbāl and 'Abdur Rahīm amongst recent Indian writers have rebelled against this doctrine, and yet non ventures to face the wrath of the *'ulamā'*. Some ten years ago, there were disturbances in Pakistan and an inquiry was instituted. The Chief Justice of Pakistan questioned several *'ulamā'* regarding Islam and its essential tenets; and, according to his analysis, some of the *'ulamā'* were, in the opinion of their fellow-*'ulamā'*, unbelievers. Such is the degree to which *fossilization* of thought has taken place in our faith. Islam, in its orthodox interpretation, has lost the resilience needed for adaptation to modern thought and modern life.

It must be realized that religious practices have become soulless ritual; that large numbers of decent Muslims have ceased to find solace or consolation in the traditional forms of prayer and fasting; that good books on religion are not being written for modern times; that women are treated badly, economically and morally, and that political rights are denied to them even in fairly advanced countries by the *fatwās* of reactionary *'ulamā'*; that Muslims, even where they constitute the majority in a country, are often economically poor, educationally backward, spiritually bankrupt and insist on "safeguards"; that the beneficial laws of early Islam have in many instances fallen behind the times; and that the futile attempt to plant an Islamic theocracy in any modern state or fashion life after the pattern of early Islam is doomed to failure.

And finally, that the time for heart-searching has come. Islam must be reinterpreted, or else its traditional form may be lost beyond retrieve. . . .

A fatwā is a formal legal opinion or interpretation given by a jurisconsult (*muftī*) in response to a request from a judge (*qādī*) or an individual. Some modern Muslim governments have obtained *fatwās* to legitimate their reforms.

Family Planning in Islam

In the name of God, the Merciful and The Compassionate. Fears of the world from the increase of population have assumed serious proportions everywhere, and experts have come to regard this as a portent of woe, ruination and dire consequences. In their consideration of how the world can be protected against this towering evil and grave menace, they have been led to think that "restriction of procreation" is one of the greatest measures. They know, however, that most people do not follow this course unless the ruling of religion in this respect has been made clear to them. Therefore, Muslims have looked up to reliable religious divines to state to them the ruling of religion on the subject. Questions converged on us for this purpose, including questions from official sources. This is our statement on this matter.

It is acknowledged that the liberal Islamic law accommodates itself to nature and to human conditions. God says: "Set thou thy face then, as a true convert, towards the faith—the nature made by God in which he has made men; there is no altering of God's creation."

One of the natural things inherent in human beings is marriage. But the purpose of marriage is procreation for the perpetuation of the species. The divine Qur'ānic verse refers to that, and regards it as one of the blessings bestowed upon God's servants. God says, "God, too, has given you wives from among yourselves and has given you sons and grandsons from your wives, and supplied you with good things." Therefore, marriage has been one of the Islamic religious ways and procreation has been one of its desirable and gratifying aims. Even the law-giver views multiplicity with favour, for multiplicity implies power, influence and invulnerability. This is why, in one of the traditions of the Prophet, marriage with an affectionate prolific woman is strongly urged. The tradition says: "Marry the affectionate prolific woman, for I shall be proud of you among the nations."

From *Muslim Attitudes Toward Family Planning,* comp. and ed. Olivia Schieffelin (New York: The Population Council, 1967), pp. 3-5.

Nevertheless, the law-giver made marriage with a prolific woman and marriage for procreation conditional upon the availability of means and the ability to bear the costs of marriage and meet the expenses of child education and training, so that children may not go to the bad and develop anti-social ways. And according to the Islamic religious rule (laws change as conditions change), marriage should be disallowed if the would-be husband is incapable of meeting the expenses of married life. To this, reference is clear in the Qur'ān and in the Traditions. The Qur'ān says: "And let those who do not find a match live in continence until God makes them free from want out of his bounty." The Tradition says: "O young men, whoever of you is capable financially let him marry, and whoever is not capable let him fast, for fasting is preventive." From the foregoing verse and the tradition, the definite inference is that "restriction of procreation" is legal *a fortieri* [sic] because to stop procreation altogether is more serious than to limit it. It is a cause for much wonder that those who urge celibacy should at the same time hesitate to allow family planning.

Moreover, there are genuine traditions which allow methods for restricting procreation, such as coitus interruptus. For instance, in the two most reliable collections of traditions, Abū-Sa'īd is reported to have said that in one of the raids, he and others captured a number of women, and they used to practise coitus interruptus. He also said that they asked the Prophet about that and the Prophet said: "Indeed, do that," and repeated it three times, and continued: "No creature to be created from now till the Day of Judgment will not but be created." Another report has it that a man said to the Prophet: "I have a young wife, I hate that she should be pregnant, and I want what men want; but the Jews claim that coitus interruptus is minor infanticide." The Prophet replied, "The Jews lie. If God wishes to create the child, you will not be able to divert him from that." In the two reliable collections of traditions, it is stated that Muslims used to practise coitus interruptus during the life-time of the Prophet and during the period of the Qur'ānic revelation. It is also reliably reported that Muslims used to practise coitus interruptus during the life-time of the Prophet; the Prophet knew of this, but he did not prohibit it.

In these genuine traditions there is definitely permission for the practise of coitus interruptus which is one of the ways of contraception or for restricting procreation, even without excuse. Permission for this practice was reported by a number of the Prophet's Companions and companions of the Companions, as laid down in the Four Orthodox Ways. A corollary of this is the dispensation for the use of medicine for contraception, or even for abortion before the embryo or the foetus is animated. The Hanafi allow that, if for an excuse.

The jurists gave examples to illustrate the meaning of the excuse for abortion, as in Ibn'Abidīn who says: "Like the mother who has a baby still unweaned and who becomes pregnant and thus her milk ceases, and the father is unable to hire a wet nurse to save the life of his baby."

The jurists also state that it is permissible to take medicine for abortion so long as the embryo is still unformed in the human shape. The period of this unformed state is given as 120 days. The jurists think that during this period the embryo or the foetus is not yet a human being. A report says that 'Umar (The Second Caliph) does not regard abortion as infanticide unless the foetus is already past the limit.

Mālik, the founder of the Mālikī Orthodox Way, says that the husband should not practise coitus interruptus with his wife unless she permits it. Al-Zarqānī, in his comment on this, says that the practice is lawful if the wife allows it. Permission or prohibition of coitus interruptus may serve as a guide in deciding the question of abortion before the foetus is animated.

All this shows that there is agreement among the founders of the four Orthodox Ways that coitus interruptus is allowed as a means of contraception. Religious savants inferred from this that contraceptives might be used, and even medicines might be used for abortion.

Accordingly, we hereby give our judgment with confidence in favour of family planning.

Shaykh 'Abdullāh al-Qalqilī

The Grand Muftī of Jordan
December, 1964

FATWĀS

Land Reform

Question: Some of my fellow citizens have asked me whether, as was broadcast by some Islamic States, the socialist laws issued by the United Arab Republic in July 1961 are adverse to the spirit of Islam?

Answer: To tell the truth, I was surprised to hear such allegations broadcast by an Islamic state. All matters related to religion should never have been dismissed so lightly. Any one taking the responsibility of seeking the judgement of God in any religious question should be equipped with definite proofs from the Holy Book, the Prophetic Traditions (Sunna) and the spirit of Islamic jurisprudence. The general rule is that which is allowed by religion is clear, that which is forbidden is also clear but in between there are dubious matters. In view of all this I had to spend a long time studying these laws in the light of what I know of Islamic rulings on similar matters. I have been led to the following:

1. Islamic jurisprudence respects private property which is obtained by lawful means and prohibits any infringement of it; whoever spoils the property of another should pay him either in kind or in terms of real value.

2. Islamic jurisprudence ordains that the proprietors should recognize in their property certain rights for others by which it seeks to attain social adjustment and realize a sense of brotherhood which binds all Muslims. Thus *zakāt* [the poor due] is one of the essentials of Islam. It is imposed on all able Muslims who must pay it in money, goods or crops out of their own accord. If not, the ruler is to exact it and spend it in the ways prescribed by Islam. . . .

3. Private ownership is legitimate in the eyes of Islamic jurisprudence as long as the owner observes the ordinances of Allah concerning his wealth. But if he does not abide by them, the ruler is entitled to devise the laws and regulations which force him to adhere to the commandments of God. For instance, if a father refuses to spend on his children or his grown-up sons who are poor and unable to earn their living the ruler has the right to force him to do so even and if it means confiscating enough of his money to cover their expenses. . . .

4. Money, according to Islamic jurisprudence, is good and a Muslim should acquire it by work and through legitimate means. A Muslim should not secure it by means prohibited by God such as usury, misappropriation of other's property, bribery or larceny. God says: "And do not eat up your property among yourselves for vanities, nor use it as bait for the judges,

From "The Muftī Answers Your Questions," *Minbar Al-Islām* (Cairo: English Edition, July 1962), pp. 56, 58–60.

197

with intent that ye may eat up wrongfully and knowingly a little of (other) people's property."

5. In the eyes of God money is God's property. For God—glorified and blessed be His name—is the creator of everything, and it is he who enables man to gain money. He has made him his vicegerent on earth to exploit it for his benefit and the benefit of others. . . .

6. Ownership in Islam is permissible only as long as the owner alone will bear the consequences. Thus Islamic jurisprudence prohibits the monopoly of food and suchlike materials necessary for the sustenance of people. Books of the Sunna state that the Prophet said: "All people partake in three things: water, fodder [or pasture], and fire." Some other texts add: "and salt." This is so because these elements are fundamental to all people. Hence these fundamentals should not be owned by a single person or a group of persons lest they should bar access to other people on the pretext that these things belong to them exclusively and should not be used by others without their authority and approval. Private ownership in such essentials should be banned in order to guarantee the necessities of life for all people. Fuqahā'—jurists—have unanimously prohibited the monopoly of people's food and the necessities of their daily life. The prohibition safeguards the interests of the people and is in accordance with the afore-mentioned tradition (hadīth).

Thus we can sanction the nationalization of public institutions indispensable to everyday life such as the institution established to secure water, electricity and easy transport.

In the light of these rulings supported by proofs from the Qur'ān, the Sunna and the behavior of the Prophet and his companions, we can proceed to study the contents of the socialist laws issued by the United Arab Republic in July 1961. We came out with the following conclusions:

These laws have not abolished private ownership which Islamic jurisprudence has allowed and which it has made the cornerstone of many individual interrelations. They did not aim at robbing the owner of his property, but rather at amending the law of agrarian reform issued in 1953, making one hundred feddans—acres—the maximum of land-ownership instead of two hundred as was specified in the 1953 law. Moreover the proprietor is to be compensated for whatever land he loses and will be paid by the Government the value of his land within an appointed time. He is to be given also a certain percentage of interest to compensate for his exploitation of land while it remained in his possession. Restriction of land-ownership has been initiated by the desire to enable cultivators and farmworkers to own land, because much of the cultivable area was in the possession of a small, select group of people who would never sell a finger's breadth of it except to other proprietors. Even if they sold it, it would be at prices beyond the paying capacity of most farmers. This act is undoubtedly sanctioned by Islamic jurisprudence. Early Muslims recognized this, al-Awzā'ī said that Caliph'Umar and the Prophet's companions agreed to let the cultivators of Syria and Iraq continue to possess their land and pay its *kharāj* tax—and prohibited anyone to buy it either by the will of its original owner or by coercion. The reason was that the land should remain in the hands of its proper cultivators and should never pass to any one else no matter who. Restriction of land ownership has no other objective than to realize public good through allowing small farmers who own nothing [the] chance to own something. Moreover, for the land to remain in the possession of a few people whose only concern is to exploit efforts of those who till the land, to secure profits only for themselves, never to sell except at highly exaggerated prices—this shows an attitude which runs contrary to social justice. Can anyone then assume that the restriction of land ownership is adverse to Islam, or opposed to its commandments? Surely it is not. Surely it accords with the spirit of Islamic jurisprudence and with what 'Umar and his companions have ruled. For 'Umar did not consent that land should be taken from its owners who cultivated it and be given to the invaders who had nothing to do with husbandry. Add to this argument the fact that the socialist law of agrarian reform stipulated a fair compensation for the land confiscated by law.

The law of agrarian reform has yielded its fruits. It raised the standard of living of farmers and peasants and assured them of a decent way of earning their living from land owned by them which they can cultivate. They are no longer brutally exploited to satisfy the avarice and greed of others. This act has a precedence in what the Prophet has done with the wealth of Beni al-Nadir when he took it from the Jews. In this connection God says: "What God has bestowed on His Apostle (and taken away) from the people of the townships, belongs to God, to His Apostle and to kindred and orphans, the needy and the wayfarer; in order that it may not (merely) make a circuit between the wealthy among you. So take what the Apostle assigns to you, and deny yourselves that which he withholds from you. And fear God; for God is strict in Punishment. . . . "

Thus the distribution of wealth between the poor and the rich so that it may not be circulated among the rich only, is a procedure approved of by Islamic jurisprudence; because it ensures justice among individuals. . . .

REFORM OF ISLAMIC LAW:
THE CHANGING STATUS OF WOMEN AND THE FAMILY

Muslim family law (laws governing marriage, divorce, and inheritance) is the heart of the *Sharī'a* and thus reflects the importance of the family in Islam. As noted in the previous sections, although modern legal reform began in the nineteenth century, Muslim family law remained unchanged.

Reform in family law did not occur until the twentieth century. The process of legal adaptation employed differed from that which had previously occurred in other areas of Islamic law. With few exceptions Muslim family law reform has been characterized not by the replacement of Islamic law with Western-based codes, but by the incorporation of selective changes based upon reform through a process of reinterpretation which drew on the Islamic legal tradition for its rationale and its new provisions. In this way Muslim family law from North Africa to Southeast Asia has undergone change.

The two major purposes of Muslim family law reforms have been 1) to improve the status of women and 2) to strengthen the rights of nuclear family members vis-à-vis those of the more distant male members of the extended family. Reforms have occurred in three areas: marriage, divorce, and inheritance.

Among the more significant changes in marriage laws are the discouragement of child marriages and the restriction of polygamy. The latter has been effected by such measures as requiring that a husband obtain judicial permission to take an additional wife and permitting a woman to include a stipulation in her marriage contract that gives her the right to divorce should her husband subsequently take another wife.

Divorce was perhaps the most crucial area of legal reform. Among the principal changes legislated were an expansion of the grounds upon which a woman may obtain a divorce and the restriction of the male's unilateral right of divorce.

However, family law reform has not occurred without a great deal of debate between conservatives and modernists on both methodological and substantive legal questions. The conflict over family law reform was graphically portrayed in the debate which surrounded Pakistan's *Muslim Family Laws Ordinance* of 1961. The Commission on Marriage and Family Laws was established in 1955. The majority (lay persons) and minority (the sole member of the *'ulamā'*) reports reflected the deep-seated questions which all reform encounters: who shall do it, how shall it be accomplished, what may or may not be changed?

In 1955, the Commission on Marriage and Family Laws, consisting of six lay members and one representative of the 'ulamā', was established. A majority report calling for reforms in marriage, divorce and inheritance was issued in 1956. However, Mawlana Ihstishām-ul-Haq wrote a vigorous dissenting opinion. The majority and minority reports provided the basis for a debate between modernists and traditionists. Finally, in 1961, Pakistan enacted *The Muslim Family Laws Ordinance*.

The Modernist Majority Report

We shall state briefly the reasons for the formation of this Commission. It is an indisputable article of Muslim creed professed by every Muslim that so far as the basic principles and fundamental attitudes are concerned, Islamic teaching is comprehensive and all-embracing, and Islamic law either actually derives its principles and sanctions from divine authority as revealed in the Holy Qur'ān or clear injunctions based on the Sunna. It is this belief which has been affirmed in the Objectives Resolution and the Constitution of Pakistan. It might be objected that if a well-defined code about Marriage and Family Laws already existed, where was the necessity of appointing a Commission for the purposes of any revision or modification? This question can be easily answered both by reference to the history of Muslim jurisprudence and the present-day circumstances. So far as the Holy Book is concerned, the laws and injunctions promulgated therein deal mostly with basic principles and vital problems and consist of answers to the questions that arose while the Book was being revealed. The entire set of injunctions in the Holy Qur'ān covers only a few pages. It was the privilege of the Holy Prophet to explain, clarify, amplify and adapt the basic principles to the changing circumstances and the occasions that arose during his lifetime. His precepts, his example and his interpretation or amplification constitute what is called Sunna. As nobody can comprehend the infinite variety of human relations for all occasions and for all epochs, the Prophet of Islam left a very large sphere free for legislative enactments and judicial decisions even for his contemporaries who had the Holy Qur'ān and the Sunna before their eyes. This is the principle of *ijtihād* or

From *The Gazette of Pakistan* (June 20, 1956), pp. 1198–99, 1202–03, 1230.

interpretative intelligence working within the broad framework of the
Qur'ān and the Sunna.

Ijtihād

Although there was primitive simplicity in the life of Arabia during the
time of the Holy Prophet, his prophetic wisdom was conscious of the fact
that there may be situations and problems not clearly envisaged in the
Qur'ān, and that in such cases the Qur'ān could only lay down basic
principles which could offer light and guidance even in unpredictable circumstances. He knew that his own explanations and amplifications too
could not be expected to cover all details or encompass the novelty of
situations and circumstances. He enjoined on his companions, to whom
important duties were entrusted, to exercise their own rational judgment
with a pure conscience if the Holy Qur'ān and the Sunna did not provide
any precise guidance in any particular situation.

The great *Khalīfas* [Caliphs] and others endowed with wisdom and
imbued with the spirit of Islam exercised *ijtihād* when the Muslim State
and Society were developing. This is what Iqbāl, the great Philosopher and
revivalist of Islam, calls the dynamic principle which according to him is a
distinguishing characteristic of Islam. . . . No Muslim can believe that Islam is an outworn creed incapable of meeting the challenge of evolutionary forces. Its basic principles of justice and equity, its urge for universal
knowledge, its acceptance of life in all its aspects, its world-view, its view
of human relations and human destiny, and its demand for an all-round
and harmonious development, stand firmly like a rock in the tempestuous
sea of life.

Not a clergy state

Many a nation of the West, after centuries of bitter conflict between the
Church and the State, resorted to Secularism having despaired of divine
guidance in the matter of law. Islam was never theocratic in the sense in
which this term is used in the history of Western politics. For Islam life is
an indivisible unity in which the spiritual and the mundane are not
sundered. Religion, according to Islam, means life in the world lived with a
spiritual attitude which sublimates all that it touches. For this very reason
Islam never developed a church with ordained priests as a class separate
from the laity. According to the Holy Qur'ān, the demands of God and the
demands of Caesar are not to be satisfied separately because of mutual
contradictions and conflicts as Islam recognizes no Caesars. As it counte-
nances no kings who can do no wrong and who stand above the law, so it
recognizes no priests. Some may be more learned in the Muslim law than

others, but that does not constitute them as a separate class; they are not vested with any special authority and enjoy no special privileges.

Pakistan and legal reform

Pakistan was carved out of the Indian subcontinent by leaders of Muslim thought beginning with Sayyid Ahmad Khān and culminating in the person of Qaid-i-Azam Muhammed 'Alī Jinnāh. Islamic ideology was expounded by Iqbāl, with the firm conviction that Islam, properly understood and rationally interpreted, is not only capable of moving along with the progressive and evolutionary forces of life but also of directing them into new and healthy channels in every epoch. The creation of Pakistan was a revolutionary step, and all revolutions demand primary remolding of the educational system and the recasting of laws and the judicial system to fulfill the aspirations of a free and expanding life. But Pakistan, at its very inception, was faced with problems of sheer existence and self-preservation. Ugly situations created by the hostility of neighbors and economic chaos, for which Pakistan was not responsible, made the country concentrate its energies on problems of sheer subsistence, leaving little mental or material resources for educational reconstruction and legal and judicial reform. The work of legal and judicial reform requires intensive and extensive efforts over a period of time, and can be undertaken fruitfully only by a team of scholars and legal experts who possess a vast experience in the legal field, are conversant with Muslim law and jurisprudence and are progressive enough to believe that reconstruction and fresh adaptation of the basic injunctions of Islam are urgently needed to remedy the evils and remove the hurdles created by unsalutary traditions and customs masquerading in the garb of religion. The task entrusted to this Commission is of vital importance as legislation relating to human relationships cannot brook any further delay. The entire revision of our Procedural Law is likely to take a considerable time, and it is only right that a beginning should be made in this respect by tackling Family Laws first of all.

With respect to polygamy, which has become a hotly debated issue in every Muslim society, the commission has adhered to the Qur'ānic view. Polygamy is neither enjoined nor permitted unconditionally nor encouraged by the Holy Book, which has considered this permission to be full of risks for social justice and the happiness of the family unit, which is the nucleus of all culture and civilization. It is a sad experience for those who have practiced it and for those who have watched its tragic consequences that in most cases no rational justification exists and the practice of it is prompted by the lower self of men who are devoid of refined sentiments and are unregardful of the demands of even elementary justice. The Qur'ānic permission about polygamy was a conditional permission to meet grave social emergencies, and heavy responsibilities were attached to it, with the warning that the common man will find it extremely difficult, if not impossible, to fulfill the conditions of equal justice attached to it. The members of the Commission, therefore, are convinced that the practice cannot be left to the sweet will of the individual. It is thoroughly irrational to allow individuals to enter into second marriages whenever they please and then demand *post facto* that if they are unjust to the first wife and children, the wife and children should seek a remedy in a court of law. This is like allowing a preventible epidemic to devastate human health and existence and offering advice to human beings to resort to the medical profession for attempting a cure. Great evils must be nipped in the bud, and prevention is always more rational and more advisable than cure. The Commission is conscious of the fact that in rare cases taking of a second wife may be a justifiable act. Therefore it recommends that it should be enacted that anyone desirous of taking a second wife should not be allowed to do it without first applying to a Matrimonial Court for permission. If the court sees any rational justification in the demand of such a husband he may be allowed only if he is judged to be capable of doing justice in every respect to more than one wife and the children. To ask the first wife and her children to resort to a court for the demands of justice is unjust and impracticable in the present state of our society where women, due to poverty, helplessness, social pressure and suppression are not in a position to seek legal assistance. The function of the court is not merely to remove injustice when it is done. In our opinion a more vital function of the legal and the judicial system is to adopt measures that minimize the practice of injustice. Therefore permission of the Matrimonial Court for a contemplated second marriage, so that the demands of justice are fulfilled and guaranteed, is the fundamental reform proposed by the Commission. . . .

The Minority Report

But the selection of members of the Commission, made for the purpose of achieving this objective, is most disappointing and surprising. What greater injustice could be done to Islamic *Sharī'a* than entrusting the work of bringing the marriage laws into conformity with Islamic *Sharī'a* to a Commission the majority of whose members have neither the detailed knowledge of the Islamic teachings and injunctions nor are they versed in the interpretation and application of those laws. In this connection I was told that in constituting the Commission some of the members were included purely for the reason of their possessing legal and judicial experience, the women members were taken in on the ground that they were conversant with family problems and conditions more than men, and only one member was added to advise on *Sharī'a*. There was no apparent harm in utilizing diverse talents but in the meetings of the Commission every member, save myself, assumed the position of an expert authority on *Sharī'a* and an absolute *mujtahid*. Hence they all remained one and united in contravening the Holy Qur'ān and the Sunna and in ridiculing Muslim jurisprudence, and by calling their action an *ijma'* [Consensus] in the Report, they have debased this technical term of *Sharī'a* . . .

The members of our Commission, who hasten to declare, so sweetly, the Holy Qur'ān and the Sunna as their source and fount, are neither prepared to perform the feat of codifying a new set of laws of jurisprudence in supersession of the existing one by generalizing from specific provisions, nor are they willing to be guided by the established laws of jurisprudence as their guiding star and beacon light. It is obvious, therefore, that to take personal and individual whims as the basis for the derivation of laws and principles is neither *fiqh* nor *ijtihād* but amounts to distorting the religion of God and the worst type of heresy. In spite of their blatant departure from the view of the Muslim commentators and jurists, no member of the Commission could take the place of Fakhruddīn Rāzī or Abū Hanīfa. This is the reason that certain recommendations, which reflect subservience to the West of some of the members and their displeasure with Islam, constitute an odious attempt to distort the Holy Qur'ān and the Sunna with a view to giving them a western slant and bias. . . .

In order to seek a justification for the arbitrary *ijtihād* of the Commission, the Introduction of the Report says this about the Holy Qur'ān and the Sunna:

From *The Gazette of Pakistan* (Aug. 30, 1956), pp. 1561–62, 1564–65, 1572–73, 1591–92.

The Holy Qur'ān and the Sunna depict events and contain answers to the questions as they took place and arose while the Book was being revealed. As nobody can comprehend the infinite variety of human relations and situations for all occasions and for all epochs, the Prophet of Islam left a very large sphere free for legislative enactments and judicial decisions even for his contemporaries who had the Holy Qur'ān and the Sunna before their eyes. This is that principle of *ijtihād* or interpretative intelligence working within the broad framework of the Qur'ān and the Sunna.

It is a matter of surprise that persons utterly ignorant of elementary propositions concerning God, His Glory, the Prophethood, and the comprehensiveness and universality of religion, should have the temerity to write on such subjects. Perhaps our Introduction-writer does not know that the Qur'ān is the sacred Word of God and embodies His Divine Guidance, who has the fullest knowledge and embodies prescience of every minor event of every period and every epoch from the beginning of Time to its end. He knows all the infinite varieties of human relationship which can happen in any period for epoch in all futurity. Hence His revealed Book and His appointed Prophet with prophetic wisdom, all are based on the truth that until doomsday all teachings and injunctions of the Holy Qur'ān and the Sunna shall be the authoritative guidance and final work for all the infinity of events that may take place in this Universe. This is the basic and fundamental article of faith in Islam owing to which Islam is a religion for all times. If the scope of the Qur'ān and the Sunna were limited to the circumstances and events that arose during the Prophet's lifetime or while the Qur'ān was being revealed, then it would be meaningless to call the Holy Qur'ān and the Sunna as the revealed Word of God, and Islam as His Revealed Religion. It would then be more correct to dub the Qur'ān and the Sunna as the work and compilation of an individual who could not see beyond the limited horizon of his own time.

Their sole motive to malign the *'ulamā'* was that Muslims should ignore the *'ulamā'* and these so-called progressives should install themselves in the place of Ghazālī and Rāzī themselves. But in spite of the destructive propaganda Muslims had enough religious consciousness and feeling for faith to turn for religious guidance to the pious *'ulamā'* who possess the knowledge of *Sharī'a* and act upon it. It is an obvious fact that in all technical matters only experts and specialists are consulted. This prerogative of the specialist is not based on any racial or tribal ground but is rooted in reason. When people did not take any notice of the nontechnical *ijtihād* and opinions of these anglicized, West-ridden Sahibs, they started propaganda against the *'ulamā'* that they have created priesthood in Islam, so that their own opinion may have the right to encroach upon their domain. They should know that the *'ulamā'* have not got a special privilege of interpreting and quoting the Holy Qur'ān and the Sunna on the basis of any racial distinction. '*Ulamā*' is not the name of any race or tribe but everyone who has devoted the greater part of his life to the acquisition of knowledge on religious subjects is an '*ālim*. This right of theirs is based on their erudition and experience in exactly the same way in which the right of explaining and interpreting the provisions of the Pakistan Penal Code vests in lawyers and barristers only. It is obvious that the lawyers are not a tribe but they have studied law. The right of prescription and treatment belongs only to a doctor. As anyone who studies law is a lawyer or barrister, in the same way anyone who studies *Sharī'a* and religion is an '*ālim* no matter to what race or tribe he belongs.

The main cause of raising this question [of polygamy] is inferiority complex against the West and the desire to copy it blindly. Our young men and women, who happen to visit Europe, often find themselves in situations in which their country is ridiculed for permitting polygamy. Unable to think out for themselves, these young things readily take to the course of condemning polygamy as the greatest evil in society. It is in fact this class of persons who have, on their return from abroad, taken up arms against polygamy permitted by Islam in an attempt to copy the West and to uphold the condemnation to which they have pledged themselves while in foreign lands. In fact polygamy is not a matter for any human society to be ashamed of, nor does its abolition constitute any achievement of Europe that may be worth emulation by others. Moreover, if we cannot put Europe to shame for permitting free indulgence in adultery, we have no cause to blush at the permission granted by *Sharī'a* for lawfully marrying a second wife. The real comparison in this regard is that of contentment with one woman and this contentment is equally absent in Europe as well as in our own society. The difference is that we proceed to take a second wife by entering into a solemn agreement with her and accepting certain bona fide responsibilities in the form of *nikāh* [marriage], while they choose the unworthy and irresponsible course of playing with the chastity of women in return for a few coins. Thus it is clear that marrying a second wife in the lifetime of the first is nothing discreditable; the sin and the shame of it lies in indulging in adultery while living with a lawfully wedded wife—a practice which has not been declared a penal offense in any European country if it is committed with the consent of the woman involved. It is nothing but a sad demonstration of our own shortsightedness and inferiority complex that we feel shy of a just and reasonable injunction of our religion and do not venture to put others to shame for their glaring fault.

In short, we do not have the slightest excuse for imitating the ways of a people with a social setup and a legal system which tolerates sexual satisfaction by means other than marriage. It is indeed hard to imagine a worse type of blind imitation than the one we find in the present case wherein the women who have kicked up so much dust on the question of polygamy and the Commission which has supported their views have not chosen to utter a word against adultery or recommended it to be declared a penal offense, although this form of vice not only means a flagrant violation of the rights of the lawfully wedded wife but also constitutes a deprecation committed on the chastity of others. The question of adultery in this way becomes purely a question of matrimonial and family life in its bearing. The institutions so vociferously advocating the rights of women and the leaders who dub polygamy as the greatest bane on womanhood, would do well to take the trouble of going round the bazaars in Pakistan and cast a glance on the legions of prostitutes who are daily corrupting unmarried as well as married men in the thousands and breaking up many a happy home by sowing the seeds of hatred in the minds of young men against their innocent wives. In this background the conclusion is inescapable that polygamy is to be penalized while adultery is to be left to flourish free of all legal restrictions and that holy alliance between man and woman, as permitted by *Sharī'a,* is to be declared a crime while moral depravity is to be left unscathed. . . .

ISLAM AND ECONOMICS

In economics as in politics and law, most modern Muslim states have followed the West. However, the Qur'ān and the *Sharī'a* do address themselves to economic questions of ownership, taxation, banking, distribution of wealth, and so on. The question of the relationship of modern economic systems to the Islamic tradition has taken on increased emphasis among those who call for more Islamic systems of government.

In our first selection, Āyatullāh Mahmūd Tāliqānī, a leader in Iran's (Islamic) revolution, discusses the major characteristics of Islamic economics. Khurshid Ahmad addresses a fundamental consideration facing developing Muslim nations: is the direction of economic development to be based simply upon the adoption of western models? Or should Muslim nations seek to reconstruct their societies upon more indigenously rooted models of economic development? Is there an Islamic concept of development?

If Jamāl 'Abd al-Nāsir and the Ba'th Party advocated and used Islam to legitimate some form of state socialism as essential to bring about serious socio-economic reform, Muslim economists such as M. 'Umar Chapra and Abūl Hasan Banī-Sadr espouse alternative viewpoints. Chapra discusses the Islamic state and its resources for assuring the social welfare of its citizens. Bani-Sadr differs with many of those who have advocated socialism for he views the fundamental question not so much as private property versus government intervention and control but rather that of balancing individual ownership and community ownership both of which have their origin and destiny in God.

ĀYATULLĀH MAHMŪD TĀLIQĀNĪ
d. 1979

At his death he was the leader of Teheran's clergy. Long a voice for reform, Āyatullāh Tāliqānī was closely allied with the more intellectual and activist elements of Iranian society throughout the 1960's and 70's.

He was a founding member in 1961 of the Freedom Movement (*Nihdat-i Āzādī*) along with lay Islamic leaders such as Mehdī Bāzargān (a former engineering professor at Teheran University and the first Prime Minister appointed by Āyatullāh Khumaynī). Counted among the politically active clergy, he suffered repeated imprisonment. With the Āyatullāhs Khumaynī and Sharī'atmadārī, he was among the principal religious leaders in the revolution.

The Characteristics of Islamic Economics

When one considers the body of Islamic economic principles and laws and compares them with modern economic schools, the indisputable result is that Islamic economics cannot be compared with any of these scientific or practical schools in any way. Islamic economics have special features which can be summarized in the following principles.

First, Islamic economics recognizes individuals as the rightful owner of whatever is the result of their labor in the widest sense, and as the authorized possessor in exchange, within the limits of the special laws of Islam. . . . In this respect Islamic economics are not based on the foundation of the unlimited freedom of individual ownership, the result of which is uncontrolled capitalism. They are also not based upon common ownership the result of which might be the complete deprivation of ownership and of individual freedom, or like mixed or con-joined economies in which limits are confused and unknown. Rather the limits and conditions that characterize Islamic economics are compatible with human nature and with an equitable system and with the rights of all participants. Individual ownership is based on the innate and natural freedom of individuals, and cooperation is based on common needs and interests.

Now the theory of capitalism and the theory of collectivism, when actu-

From Sayyid Mahmūd Tāliqānī, *Islām wa Mālikiyat* [Islam and ownership], trans. William Darrow (Houston, Texas: Islamic Distribution Center, n.d.), pp. 225–275.

ally practiced, dispenses with all their theoretical principles. Capitalist countries, which are based on the principle of free and unlimited owner-ship, inevitably go down the road of unbridled capitalism, and as a result the nationalization of the means of production and of the large industries follows. On the other hand, the principles of collectivism, in spite of their rigidity, make individual ownership possible in practice to a limited extent in the areas of necessities such as housing and farm production, either by law or by tradition. These obvious violations show that these two views are not views actually applicable to real life, but are rather the products of the fluctuations of industrial economics in the past century in Western countries. They must, after the period of fluctuation, be judged according to the absolute scale of truth and natural rights.

Second, from the Islamic point of view, material attachments and eco-nomic relations are intertwined with modes of thought, innate characteris-tics, emotions and human instincts. . . .

Islam posits the connection between an organized system of limits on rights and attachments and the critical assessment of views, the strengthen-ing of faith, the cultivation of consciences and human values. It has ex-plained economic laws and rules according to this principle. . . .

Third, Islam has organized and systematized the limits of ownership and economic relations in terms of three characters: 1. individuals; 2. laws; and 3. government. As in other affairs, individuals are free to enjoy mate-rial things to the limit of their maturity and according to the dictates of their faith and the responsibility of their consciences. They can benefit and enjoy property as long as it does not belong to someone else. This freedom in the area of economic exchanges is limited to the right of ownership of things which are the product of one's labor. This sets the limits of the laws and the conditions of legitimacy in a transaction.

Islamic government is to be defined as the rule of the Imām, or his deputy, or the viceroy of God or someone He has sent. Islamic government has the right to limit the enjoyment and ownership of an individual even more than the rules permit, in the event that there is an opposition be-tween the right of an individual and the right of society because the right-ful rulers give precedence to and seek to ensure that social benefits prevail over individual benefits. . . .

Fourth, distribution like production, in the view of Islam, is the natural and innate right of the one who performs the labor, with the qualification that the individual is free in choosing such labor. Labor is the basis of the right of ownership. As a result of this the owner is free in the enjoyment and distribution of his possessions. The limitations and laws circumscrib-ing the enjoyment and right of ownership, and the general supervision of the sage governor, is the guarantor of the systematization and limitation of distribution and preventor of unreasonable profit. Given this limitation and supervision, why is this right not given to the one who is the original laborer? As has been said before, it is against nature that the results of labor and the product of the effort of individuals who are created free should be at the will of capitlists or the government. Both the capitalists and government take away the independence and freedom and personality of individuals which are more valuable than anything, by giving food and limited means of livelihood in the same way they give machinery oil so that machines are prepared to produce more. If the laborer (i.e. the one who is the one authorized to enjoy and to distribute what he has) is not free and distribution (within necessary boundaries) is limited, then both the rightful owner is deprived of his right and human values go unrealized. These two are the principle motivations for good action and the appearance of talents. . . .

Fifth, based on the principles of Islamic economics, the right of possession and distribution of natural products, is based on the right of possesson and distribution of natural resources, with the stipulation that the land and all natural products belong to everyone. Government which is the guardian and representative of the common good possesses the right of oversight and distribution. At a later stage the cultivation of the land and extraction from it in underground mines and making natural items productive such as rocks on the earth and running water and water and desert animals, all give the right to each individual who does these things, as long as these claims and relations obtain, to enjoy and distribute these products.

These rights, to the extent that there is no injury to the common good, are preserved, because resources and common things in nature belong to the public and their enjoyment is limited by the rights of the public. Therefore, if someone owns more than the average, and has more possibilities, the law of common ownership and the power of the government limits him and prevents him from misusing what is commonly held either in cultivation, extraction or making something productive. . . .

Given this form of limited freedom in transactions and the supervision of the government over commodities, the simple law of supply and demand in the usual capitalist understanding cannot direct transactions. This is because demand in the usual capitalist usage and in actuality depends upon the ability to buy things and on having money. But demand, on the basis of Islamic jurisprudence, arises out of what is actually required by necessity. Therefore supply and the actual making available of goods will be limited to what is actually required by necessity. The marketplace thus cannot become the toy of the greed of capitalists by which they open the way to false demand and oppressive profits.

Therefore these rights that arise out of natural resources and things, as a result of cultivation, discovery, or making something productive, are the prime source for the distribution of these resources and products. But these rights that are entailed are not sufficient basis for the right of absolute ownership of natural resources. The absolute right of ownership applies only to things that are agricultural products which are the actual result of labor and represent human effort . . . The result of labor whether in the form of commodities or exchanged for money is the basis of and motive for new activities. It leads to new activities, and the later labor is the result of the earlier and the earlier has a share in it. The share of those who work later on a product is limited to the labor they actually do or that is attached to the product. The laws of Islam have direct oversight in each affair and transaction and can intervene to negate what is inappropriate so that the protection of freedom prevents unlawful profit and stops unlawful methods.

These rights which are entailed in connection with the enjoyment and distribution that arise from natural resources are the special feature of Islamic economic principles. In practice, capitalism does not have a just and right means to have and distribute natural products. Because no matter how natural resources come into the possession of a capitalist, provided they do not belong to someone else, the capitalist has an absolute right of ownership (not a right which limits profits). . . .

Marxism adds the qualification that it entrusts the possession of natural resources by human beings to evolution, means of production and the course of history so that according to those conditions, the relations of men to those resources are conditioned or limited. Therefore the differences between capitalism and communism mainly concern industrial production, and natural resources are of minor concern in both these systems.

Islam has based the foundation and center of human life on natural resources and has not entrusted them either to the hands of powerful capitalists or to power of the evolution of the means of production. From the Islamic point of view the one who must have the natural resources which are the basis of human life is the worker, to the limit of his labor and always preserving the right of the society. . . .

Sixth, since natural resources, earth, water, forests, woods, lakes and mines are the foundation of life for human beings and all other animals, if the limitations on the rights and benefits derived from them are organized in a clear and just manner, then all other issues connected with the means of livelihood must also be systematized. Then the problems connected with economic relations would be greatly alleviated. Economists of the age of industrialization have devoted most of their attention to the problems of industrializaton and thus have not provided a just and clearcut manner of organizing and systematizing natural resources. . . .

Seventh, the right of ownership is based upon labor and arises from the right of using and holding natural resources. It is determined by Islamic laws in the context of transactions and exchanges. In the course of time death ends the right. Therefore after death no one still continues to have the right to enjoy one's possessions. . . .

At death the dying person has the right of determining the disposition of one-third of his wealth. It can be used for the rights of his relatives or by the way of charity. It is designed to take care of the right of society so that if his heirs do not have sufficient means or are not in the direct lines of inheritance, although they are entitled or if public needs make it desirable, the person who is on the verge of death can dispose of one third of his wealth as he sees fit according to these needs. The Qur'ānic law is that he has only right to make a will concerning one-third of his possessions. . . .

Eighth, Islamic law has also limited the ways in which possessions can be used after it has provided limits on ownership and benefits and on the rights of transaction and limited even the given rights by such means as required alms, setting aside a fifth of your income for religious purposes and charity. These limitations by necessity increase the production of useful commodities and also put wealth to work for the sake of economic progress and increasing employment. In the end it would prevent the use of factories and productive capacities in ways which are harmful and dangerous to individuals and society. . . .

Ninth, in the realm of Islam and under the supervision of its laws, workers and wage earners are not dominated by the capitalist layer of society and by the power of the government. This group has both personal freedom and freedom in their work. Their means of livelihood are supplied according to their own free work and given according to their needs.

Tenth, among the distinguishing features of the Islamic economic system is the protection of independence in financial exchanges and the cultivation of the personality of the individual within society. If we agree that the actual form of a society is nothing but the collection of the legal relationships of individuals and that social classes do not have any external reality and that individuals possess independence and personality while respecting the rights of others and finally that the establishment 'of communal rights and good relations is for the preservation of the individuals' independence (and not individuals for society), then we must agree that since individuals possess two personalities, an individual one and a social one, with regard to the individual personality, he has freedom of action and of enjoying the results of his labor. With regard to his social personality, such enjoyments and profits must be limited by the social good. But the idea of the social good does not mean that society possesses an independent legal personality and is somehow separate from the collectivity of individual rights. Government, in this view, must be like the representative and deputy of individuals and not the representative of a special class nor the possessor of a separate personality. Its purpose is nothing but the preservation of individual rights and of the collectivity of individuals. In this regard government does not have the right to deprive or limit the freedom and independence of individuals or the rights of some classes for the profit of another class in the name of the higher good of the government. . . .

Eleventh, Islam in the economic sphere, just as in the area of spiritual relations and social interactions, has fixed principles and dynamic rules and laws. The fixed principles are the foundation and basis of the dynamic rules and underpin communal interaction. The rules concerning specific issues and affairs which might come up must be applied according to the fixed and beneficial principles. On this basis, the rules of Islam are at once fixed and dynamic. The society which is administered by these principles and rules does not become static, outmoded or dependent. Old and new do not split asunder or separate in it. . . . This subjugation, and feeling of inferiority and of being at a loss that Muslims feel towards foreigners and the governments connected with them, which now appears among Muslims in all areas of action, is what has made them static and blocked the functioning of the Islamic economic system as it has everything else. . . .

Twelfth, thus according to what has been said, Islamic economics are founded on the principles of right and justice, and are not based on any special group or class. In fact, from the point of view of Islam the appearance of the features of classes is not a necessary inevitable thing or a irremediable social necessity. The appearance of classes is the result of the defect of individuals and society [due to their] not following right and just principles. It is the byproduct of transgression, oppression and colonialism. The form of society is only the reflection of individual relationships and individual relationships externalize the thoughts, minds and morals of persons. Let the thoughts and spirits of individuals change into any other form and the communal relations and social form must also change. *Indeed God does not change the condition of a people, until they have changed it for themselves* (Qur'ān 13: 11). Thus in history and in different areas in both large and small manifestations we can observe the appearance of societies bound together without class. This is a decisive proof that the appearance of classes is not an historical necessity. . . .

Thirteenth, the Qur'ān, before explaining the rules and laws about the organization and limitations on relations and financial attachments, turns the mind and ideology of the monotheist toward the foundation and original source of all rights and possessions which manifest themselves out of natural powers. This view, which is the conviction that all existence is created and belongs to the origin and creator and director of the world, is the principle of faith in *tawhīd*. Therefore He who possess the whole world has created man with the power of reason and the capacity for enjoyment, so that he can use his understanding and thought and limbs to investigate mysteries and to put to use whatever exists. In this regard the Qur'ān has introduced this thinking and powerful phenomenon that is

man as the "viceroy" of God before giving man any other name or
title. . . .

Therefore, every Muslim   ɪd monotheist, before his responsibilities of
faith and those related to serving and preserving the rights of others,
communal security and obeying rules, must do the will and commands of
Him who is the rightful possessor. Man is both his possession and also his
viceroy and deputy.

Fourteenth, since the monotheist recognizes himself as the representative
of Him who possesses the world and the agent of His will and executor of
His command and realizes that he is not entirely free and independent in
his possessions, he cannot view what material and attachments he has
independently of this. In this view what wealth and possessions he has are
nothing but a means to reach humane aims and goals and a place in the
other world.

The aim of acquiring wealth in economic relations or using it as a means
for satisfying lust and animal desires is the result of the mental defects and
dull-mindedness and the corruption of human beings. This defective mind-
set is the most significant cause which gives to classes and groups which
follow individuals of the same view in accumulating wealth in whatever
way possible. This causes individuals to become merely the means for the
production and profit and the accumulation of wealth. Any kind of tyranny and transgression in reaching this goal is approved of. Consequently
the way toward progress and just production and distribution is blocked.
These two views, that of acquiring wealth for its own sake and of using
wealth for base purposes, have had an effect in all areas of spiritual and
material life of man, and have been the special topic of discussion by
prophets and the great benefactors of mankind and especially in the
cultivation of the laws of Islam. One should not only see the struggle of
religious leaders for such an evolution of thought and expansion of views
as a topic for spiritual and ethical sermons, but should also realize the
importance of developing towards such an attitude and of its effects in all
aspects of human life. . . .

KHURSHID AHMAD
1934–

He was formerly associate professor of economics at the University of Karachi, a founder and Director-General of the Islamic Foundation (Leicester U.K.), and Federal Minister of Planning and Development, Government of Pakistan. He is currently director of the Institute for Policy Studies, Islamabad, Pakistan.

Islam and the Challenge of Economic Development

A major challenge confronts the world of Islam: the challenge of reconstructing its economy in a way that is commensurate with its world role: ideological, political and economical. What does this demand: economic development with a view to "catch up" with the industrialized countries of the West, Capitalist or Socialist according to one's inclination and sympathy, or politico-economic dependence? Or does it demand total socio-economic reconstruction in the light of a basically different model, with its own set of assumptions, ideals and growth-path, something that would be unique and value-specific?

The Muslim countries suffer from widespread economic underdevelopment, i.e. non-utilisation and or under-utilisation of human and physical resources with consequent poverty, stagnation and backwardness.

The paradox of the Muslim world is that it is resource-rich, but economically poor and weak. Development planning has been introduced in a number of Muslim countries. In some, the art is now at a fairly advanced level. Nigeria, Egypt, Syria, Algeria, Iran, Pakistan, Malaysia, Indonesia are some of the instances in view. But in almost all these countries developmental effort is modelled after the prototypes of growth developed by the Western theorists and practitioners of planning and "sold" to the planners in the Muslim countries via international diplomacy, economic pressurization, intellectual mobilization and a number of other overt and covert means. Whatever be the source of inspiration—the Capitalist economies of the West or the Socialist models of Russia and China—no effort worth the name seems to have been made to re-think the basic issues of

From *The Challenge of Islam*, ed. Altaf Gauhar (London: Islamic Council of Europe, 1978), pp. 339–49.

development economies in the light of the ideals and values of Islam and its world strategy.

How does this policy and the actual developments stand in relation to Islam? It would be correct to say that developmental policies have been, more or less, Islam-neutral. As against this unfortunate "fact," it is our submission that as far as Islam is concerned, it cannot be neutral *vis-à-vis* economic development. But there is no evidence to support that generally speaking, the policy makers derived any inspiration worth the name from Islam and tried to translate its economic ideals into development policies, some lip-service here and there notwithstanding. Actual policies have had no or little relation to Islam with the result that the economies of the Muslim world have failed to be transformed towards Islam and the deformities and inequities inherited from the colonial period and beyond have been generally aggravated. Muslim thinkers have criticised this state of affairs and have emphasised that Islam should be the main inspiration in their development thinking.

The primary task of any theory of development is to examine and explain the nature of the processes of development and factors responsible for it, to identify and analyse principal obstacles to development in a given situation, and to try to prescribe the most desirable and the most efficient ways and means to remove those obstacles and achieve various dimensions of economic development.

A major contribution of Islam lies in making human life and effort purposive and value-oriented. The transformation it seeks to bring about in human attitudes and *pari passu* in that of the social sciences is to move them from a stance of pseudo-value-neutrality towards open and manifest value-commitment and value-fulfilment. As such the first premises which we want to emphasise is that economic development in an Islamic framework as also Islamic development economics are rooted in the value pattern embodied in the Qur'ān and Sunna. This is our basic frame of reference.

Our second premise is that this approach clearly rules out a strategy of imitation. The Capitalist and the Socialist models cannot be adopted as our ideal-types, although we would like to avail ourselves of all those experiences of mankind which can be gainfully assimilated and integrated within the Islamic framework and can serve our own purposes without in any way impairing our values and norms.

But we must reject the archetypes of capitalism and socialism. Both these models of development are incompatible with our value system. Both are exploitative and unjust and fail to treat man as man, as God's vicegerent (*khalīfa*) on earth. Both have been unable to meet in their own realms the basic economic, social, political and moral challenges of our time and the real needs of a humane society and a just economy. Both are irrelevant to our situation, not merely because of the differences in ideological and moral attitudes and in socio-political frameworks, but also for a host of more mundane and economic reasons, like differences in relative resource bases, changed international economic situations, bench-mark differences in the levels of the respective economies, socio-economic costs of development, and above all, for the fundamental fact that the crucial developmental strategy of both the systems—industrialisation primarily through maximisation of investible surplus—is not suited to the conditions of the Muslim world and the demands of the Islamic social ideals.

Development economics is presently passing through a period of crisis and re-evaluation. It is coming under attack from a number of directions. An increasing number of economists and planners are becoming sceptical about the whole approach of contemporary development economics.

A much more critical approach deserves to be adopted towards the panaceas that have been "sold" to the Muslim countries.

On the positive side we submit that our approach should be ideological and value-oriented. In development economics, as in economics—or in any branch of human activity, there is an area which deals with technological relationships. But such technological relationships *per se* are not the be-all and end-all of a social discipline.

Technological relationships are important, and they should be decided according to their own rules. But technological decisions are made in the context of value-relations. Our effort is to weld these two areas and to make our values explicit and to assign to them the role of effective guide and controller for the entire system. This means that as against an imitative stance, our approach must be original and creative. It is only through a thorough understanding of the social ideals and values of the Qur'ān and Sunna and a realistic assessment of our socio-economic situation—resources, problems and constraints—that we can adopt a creative and innovative strategy for change. As such, our approach would be ideological as well as empirical and somewhat pragmatic—pragmatic not in the sense that ideals and values can be trimmed to suit the exigencies of the situation, but pragmatic in the sense that ideals and values are to be translated into reality in a practical and realistic way.

Islam stands for effort, struggle, movement and reconstruction—elements of social change. It is not merely a set of beliefs. it also provides a definite outlook on life and a programme for action, in a word, a comprehensive milieu for social reconstruction. We would, therefore, conclude this section by submitting some basic propositions about the dynamics of social change as they reveal themselves by reflection on the Qur'ān and Sunna. They also provide some indicators for goals of socio-economic policy.

a. Social change is not a result of totally pre-determined historical forces. The existence of a number of obstacles and constraints is a fact of life and history, but man is not subject to any historical determinism. Change has to be planned and engineered. And this change should be purposive—that is, sustained movement towards the norm or the ideal.

b. Man is the most active agent for change. All other forces have been subordinated to him in his capacity as God's vicegerent (*khalīfa*). Within the framework of the divine arrangement for this universe and its laws, it is man himself who is responsible for making or marring his destiny.

c. Change consists in environmental change and change within the heart and soul of man—his attitudes, his motivation, his commitment, his resolve to mobilize all that is within him and around him for the fulfilment of his objectives.

d. Life consists of a network of inter-relationships. Change means some disruption in some relationships somewhere. As such there is a danger of change becoming an instrument of disequilibrium within man and in society. Islamically oriented social change would aim at the least friction and disequilibria, and planned and co-ordinated movement from one state of equilibrium to a higher one, or from a state of disequilibrium towards equilibrium. As such, change has to be balanced and gradual and evolutionary. Innovation is to be coupled with integration. It is this unique Islamic approach which leads to revolutionary changes through an evolutionary trajectory.

These are some of the major elements of healthy social change through which Islam wants man and society to move from one height to another. The task before the Islamic leadership, intellectual as well as politico-economic, is clearly to formulate the objectives and strategy of change along with the ways of achieving it and also to establish institutions and inaugurate processes through which these policies could be actually implemented.

Islamic Concept of Development

Now we would like to elaborate on some of the essential elements of the Islamic concept of development.

Islam is deeply concerned with the problem of economic development, but treats this as an important part of a wider problem, that of total human development. The primary function of Islam is to guide human development on correct lines and in the right direction. It deals with all aspects of economic development but always in the framework of total human development and never in a form divorced from this perspective. That is why the focus, even in the economic sector, is on human development, with the result that economic development remains an integrated and indivisible element of moral and socio-economic development of human society.

The philosophic foundations of the Islamic approach to development, . . . are as follows:

1. *Tawhīd* (God's unity and sovereignty). This lays down the rules of God-man and man-man relationship.
2. *Rububiyya* (Divine arrangements for nourishment, sustenance and directing things towards their perfection). This is the fundamental law of the universe which throws light on the divine model for the useful development of resources and their mutual support and sharing. It is in the context of this divine arrangement that human efforts take place.
3. *Khilāfa* (man's role as God's vicegerent on earth). This defines man's status and role, specifying the responsibilities of man as such, of a Muslim, and of the Muslim *umma* as the repository of this *khilāfa*. From this follows the unique Islamic concept of man's trusteeship, moral, political and economic, and the principles of social organisation.
4. *Tazkiyah* (purification *plus* growth). The mission of all the prophets of God was to perform the *tazkiyah* of man in all his relationships with God, with man, with natural environment, and with the society and state.

We would submit that the Islamic concept of development is to be derived from its concept of *tazkiyah,* as it addresses itself to the problem of human development in all its dimensions and is concerned with growth and expansion towards perfection through purification of attitudes and relationships. The result of *tazkiyah* is *falah*—prosperity in this world and the hereafter.

In the light of these foundational principles, different elements of the concept of development can be derived. We would submit the following as its essential features:

A. Islamic concept of development is comprehensive in character and includes moral, spiritual and material aspects. Development becomes a goal- and value-oriented activity, devoted to the optimisation of human well-being in all these dimensions. The moral and the material, the economic and the social, the spiritual and the physical are inseparable. It is not merely welfare in this world that is the objective; it is also the welfare that Islam seeks to extend to the life hereafter—and there is no conflict between the two. This dimension is missing in the contemporary concept of development.

B. The focus for developmental effort and the heart of the development process is man. Development, therefore, means development of man and his physical and socio-cultural environment. According to the contemporary concept, it is the physical environment—natural and institutional—that provides the real area for developmental activities. Islam insists that the area of operation relates to man, within *and* without.

C. Economic development is a multi-dimensional activity, more so in an Islamic framework. As efforts would have to be made simultaneously in a number of directions, the methodology of isolating one key factor and almost exclusive concentration on that would be theoretically untenable. Islam seeks to establish balance between the different factors and forces.

D. Economic development involves a number of changes, quantitative as well as qualitative. Involvement with the quantitative, justified and necessary in its own right, has unfortunately led to the neglect of the qualitative aspects of development in particular and of life in general. Islam would try to rectify this imbalance.

E. Among the dynamic principles of social life, Islam has particularly emphasized two: First, the optimal utilisation of resources that God has endowed to man and his physical environment and, secondly, their equitable use and distribution and promotion of all human relationships on the basis of Right and Justice. Islam commends the value of *shukr* (thankfulness to God by availing oneself of His blessings) and *'adl* (justice) and condemns the disvalues of *kufr* (denial of God and His blessings) and *zulm* (injustice).

In the light of this analysis, development process is mobilized and activated through *shukr* and *'adl* and is disrupted and distorted by *kufr* and *zulm*.

This is basically different from the approach of those who look upon production and distribution in an either/or relationship with the development process and is a much wider and more dynamic concept than that of the role of production and distribution in development. The developmental effort, in an Islamic framework, is directed towards the development of a God-conscious human being, a balanced personality committed to and capable of acting as the witness of Truth to mankind.

We may, therefore, submit that in an Islamic framework economic development is a goal-oriented and value-realising activity, involving a confident and all-pervading participation of man and directed towards the maximisation of human well-being in all its aspects and building the strength of the *umma* so as to discharge in the world its role as God's vicegerent on earth and as "the mid-most people." Development would mean moral, spiritual and material development of the individual and the society leading to maximum socio-economic welfare and the ultimate good of mankind.

M. 'UMAR CHAPRA
1933–

Born and raised in Pakistan, Dr. Chapra earned a doctorate in economics from the University of Minnesota. He has held academic posts in America and Pakistan, served as Senior Economist for the Pakistan Institute of Development Economics, and is currently Economic Advisor to the Saudi Monetary Agency.

The Islamic Welfare State

Social Security and Equitable Distribution of Income and Wealth

It is the duty of the Islamic state to ensure a respectable standard of living for every individual, who is unable to take care of his own needs and hence requires assistance. The Prophet clearly declared that: "He whom God has made an administrator over the affairs of Muslims but remains indifferent to their needs and their poverty, God will also be indifferent to his needs and poverty."[1] He also said that: "He who leaves behind him dependants, they are our responsibility"[2] and that "the ruler [state] is the supporter of him who has no supporter."[3] These and other similar *hadīths* lay down the gist of Islamic teachings in the realm of social security.

'Umar, the second Caliph, explaining distributive justice in Islam, emphasized in one of his public addresses that everyone had an equal right in the wealth of the community, that none, not even he himself, enjoyed a greater right in it than anyone else, and that if he were to live longer, he would see to it that even a shepherd on Mount Sinai received his share from this wealth. . . .

The Islamic concept of justice in the distribution of income and wealth does not require equal reward for everyone irrespective of his contribution to society. Islam tolerates some inequalities of income because all men are not equal in their character, ability, and service to society (Qur'ān 6: 165, 61: 71, and 43: 32). Therefore, distributive justice in the Islamic society,

1. Abū-Dāwūd al-Sijistani, *Sunan Abū-Dāwūd* (Cairo: 'Isā al-Bābī al-Halabī, 1952), vol. 2, p. 122.
2. Ibid., p. 124.
3. Ibid., vol. 1, p. 481.

From: "The Islamic Welfare State and Its Role in the Economy" in *Islamic Perspectives*, ed. Khurshid Ahmad and Zafar Ishāq Ansārī (Leicester: The Islamic Foundation, 1979), pp. 208–17.

after (i) guaranteeing a humane standard of living to all members through proper training, suitable job, "just" wages, social security and financial assistance to the needy through the institution of zakāt, and (ii) intensifying the distribution of wealth through its system of dispersal of the estate of a deceased person, allows such differentials in earning as are in keeping with the differences in the value of the contribution made or services rendered to society.

The Islamic stress on distributive justice is so emphatic that there have been some Muslims who have been led to believe in absolute equality of wealth. Abū-Dharr, a companion of the Prophet, was of the opinion that it is unlawful for a Muslim to possess wealth beyond the essential needs of his family. However, most of the Prophet's companions did not agree with him in this extreme view and tried to prevail upon him to change his position. . . .

The Wherewithal

To live up to all the above obligations, the Islamic state would naturally stand in need of adequate financial resources. . . .

One principle which is clearly recognised by all jurists is that the state has no right to acquire resources by *confiscating* property duly possessed by individuals or groups. . . .

If the acquisition of resources through either confiscation or nationalisation without just compensation is to be ruled out then the primary sources left would be the following *in addition to the sale of relevant services.*

  i. Zakāt;
 ii. Income from natural resources;
iii. Taxation; and
 iv. Borrowing.

i. Zakāt

To enable Muslims to bring to fulfilment a society which is like a single nuclear family, where wealth is equitably distributed and where the essential needs of all deserving individuals are met primarily by mutual help with the planning and organisational assistance of the state, Islam has instituted a powerful social security system giving it a religious sanctity which it enjoys nowhere else in the world. It is a part of the religious obligations of a Muslim to pay zakāt at a prescribed rate on his net worth or specified income flows to the zakāt fund. Of such great significance is the institution of zakāt in Islam that whenever the Qur'ān speaks of the obligation to establish prayers it also simultaneously stresses the obligation of Muslims to pay *zakāt*. The Prophet went so far as to declare that "whoever offers prayers but does not pay *zakāt*, his prayers are in vain."[4]

There is a general consensus among jurists that collection and disbursement of *zakāt* is essentially the responsibility of the Islamic state. This was the practice during the days of the Prophet and of the first two Caliphs, Abū-Bakr and 'Umar. Abū Bakr even used coercion against those who refused to pay *zakāt* to the state. . . .

However, even if the state collects *zakāt*, the proceeds are likely to be limited. Moreover, the expenditure heads for *zakāt* are clearly enumerated in the Qur'ān. Even though some jurists have widened somewhat the coverage of the expression *fī sabīl Allāh* (in the way of Allah), it can hardly be made to include all expenditure heads of the Islamic state. Thus, if the Islamic state is to live up to its obligations it must have access to the resources beyond the *zakāt* collection. . . .

ii. Income from Natural Resources

It has already been established that natural resources have been provided by God for the welfare of all people. The monetary benefit derived from these resources should, therefore, permeate to all people and should not under any circumstances be allowed to be diverted solely to certain individuals or groups. The acceptance of this principle does not necessarily restrict the management of these resources to the state alone. Whether the state or private enterprise should manage the exploitation of these resources should be determined by the criterion of efficiency. However, even if private enterprise is to manage and operate these resources the profit derived by it should not be more than what is justified by the services rendered and the efficiency attained.

In countries with abundant natural resources to contribute an adequate income to the state treasury to finance public expenditure (as is the case in some major oil-producing Muslim countries) there may be little need for additional sources of revenues. However, countries where income from this source is either not available, or if available, is not sufficient, the state would have to supplement its income by resorting to taxation and/or borrowing if necessary.

iii. Taxation

The right of the Islamic state to raise resources through taxes cannot be challenged provided that taxes are raised in a just manner and are within a certain "bearable" limit. This right is defended on the basis of the Pro-

---

4. Abū-'Ubayd Qāsim ibn Sallām, *Kitāb al-Amwāl* (Cairo: at-Maktabah al-Tijāriyah al-Kubra, A.H. 1353), p. 354:919.

phetic saying that "in your wealth there are also obligations beyond the *zakāt,*" and one of the fundamental principles of Islamic jurisprudence that "a small benefit may be sacrificed to attain a larger benefit and a smaller sacrifice may be imposed in order to avoid a larger sacrifice."

Most jurists have upheld the right of the state to tax. According to Marghīnānī, if the resources of the state are not sufficient, the state should collect funds from the people to serve the public interest because if the benefit accrues to the people it is their obligation to bear the cost. Abū Yūsuf also supports the right of the ruler to increase or decrease taxes depending on the ability of the people to bear the burden. However, only a just tax system has been held to be in harmony with the spirit of Islam. A tax system which is oppressive and too onerous as compared with the ability of the people to bear has been unanimously condemned. All rightly-guided caliphs, particularly "Umar, 'Ali, and 'Umar ibn 'Abd al-'Azīz, are reported to have stressed that taxes should be collected with justice and kindness, that they should not be beyond the ability of the people to bear, and should not deprive the people of the basic necessities of life. . . .

In view of the goals of social justice and equitable distribution of income a progressive tax system seems to be perfectly in harmony with the goals of Islam. It must, however, be emphasized that from the discussion of the jurists what is relevant from the point of view of modern times is the right of the Islamic state to tax with justice. It would not be proper to conclude that taxation should be strictly confined to the items mentioned by the jurists. Circumstances have changed, and there seems to be the need for devising a tax system which is in harmony with the goals of Islam and yields sufficient revenue to allow a modern Islamic state to discharge its functions as a welfare state.

iv. Borrowing

If total revenue from all the above sources (including sale of services) is not sufficient, the Islamic state would stand in need of borrowing. In this case because of the Islamic injunction against interest, the borrowing would need to be free of interest.

For certain sound income-yielding projects amenable to sale of services and distribution of dividends it may be possible to raise funds on the basis of profit-sharing. However, the scope for this is limited in the case of most public projects. In case profit-sharing is not possible or feasible, the Islamic state may have to borrow funds, and this would be possible only if the private sector of the Muslim society is so highly inspired by the ideals of Islam that it is willing to forego the return. In modern acquisitive Muslim societies imbued perhaps more with hedonistic ideals of the economic man as conceived by Adam Smith rather than by the altruistic teachings of Islam, and with continuous erosion of the real value of savings because of the high rate of inflation, it may be expected that borrowing without any return may tend to be unproductive unless it is made compulsory.

"Richest" or "Ideal"

It may be contended here that all Islamic states may not have access to "adequate" resources to finance the functions discussed above and could not hence become "ideal." Here it is important to clarify that the "ideal" Islamic state should not be confused with the "richest" one. The ideal is to be construed in the light of general spiritual and material welfare attained for God's vicegerents within the framework of resources. Hence an Islamic state may be considered to have attained the position of "ideal" if it has at least (i) elevated the spiritual level of the Muslim society and minimised moral laxity and corruption; (ii) fulfilled its obligations for general economic welfare within the limits of its resources; and (iii) ensured distributive justice and has weeded out exploitation. Adequacy of resources is a relative term and is to be judged against attainable standards in the light of the stage of economic development.

Nature and Identity

The above discussion indicates that the Islamic state is essentially a welfare state and is duty-bound to play an important role in the economy for the fulfilment of the goals of the *Sharī'a* in the economic field as briefly specified above. This welfare role is, however, to be played within the framework of individual freedom which Islam values greatly. The most important pillar of the Islamic faith is the belief that man has been created by God and is subservient to none but Him (Qur'ān 13:36) and that one of the primary objectives of the prophetic mission of Muhammad (peace be on him) is to release mankind from all burdens and chains enslaving it (7:157). This provides not only the essence of the Islamic charter for individual freedom from all bondage but also subjects man to the sovereignty of God in all aspects of life which essentially implies subordination of man to the moral law as specified in the Qur'ān and the Sunna.

Because man is born free, no one, not even the state, has the right to abrogate this freedom and to subject him to regimentation . . .

It is to realise this norm of individual freedom that Islam has incorporated in its economic system the essential elements of free enterprise after conditioning it to its own norms and values. The institution of private property along with the market mechanism has been integrated into the Islamic system in such a manner that an "appropriate" part of the production and distribution of goods and services is left to individuals and voluntarily constituted groups enjoying freedom in their dealings and transactions. The profit motive has also been upheld as, besides being consistent with human nature, it provides the necessary incentive for efficiency in the use of resources which God has provided to mankind.

However, since social welfare has a place of absolute importance in Islam, individual freedom—though of considerable significance—does not enjoy a place independent of its social consequences. It is sacred only as long as it does not conflict with the larger social interest or the overall spiritual and material goals of Muslim society, or as long as the individual does not transgress the rights of others. Property can be owned privately but is to be considered a *trust* from God and is to be acquired and spent in accordance with the terms of the trust. The profit motive has also been subjected to certain moral constraints so that it serves individual interest within a social context and does not lead to economic and social ills or violate the Islamic goals of social justice and equitable distribution of income and wealth.

Mixed Capitalism? Socialism?

All these various considerations make the Islamic state completely distinct from both the socialist and the capitalist systems. First of all, socialism, as conceived by Marx, is basically amoral and based on the concept of dialectical materialism; while capitalism, being a secular ideology is, at best, morally neutral. In contrast Islam lays emphasis on both the moral and the material aspects of life and erects the edifice of economic well-being on the foundation of moral values. The foundation being different, the superstructure is bound to be different too.

Moreover, Islam is also fully committed to human brotherhood with social and economic justice, to equitable distribution of income, and to individual freedom within the context of social welfare. Although both socialism and mixed capitalism also claim to pay allegiance to social justice, the concept of justice in socialism or mixed capitalism is not based on human brotherhood reinforced by inviolable spiritual criteria for social and economic justice. In fact, Marxist socialism under the influence of dialectics condones injustice done by one group to the other and even the annihilation of one group by the other. In *laissez faire* capitalism with its slogan of "Don't interfere, the world will take care of itself" there was no innate ideal of social justice to be attained through conscious state effort, while in mixed capitalism the roots of social justice lie in group pressures rather than in an intrinsic belief in human brotherhood.

Although capitalism also recognises freedom of the individual there are no spiritual constraints on this freedom. The constraints that do exist are determined primarily by the pressures of competition or the coercive power of the state, and secondarily by changing social norms without any spiritual sanctity. In the Islamic system, however, the individual is subject to inviolable spiritual values in all aspects of life, including the acquisition, spending and distribution of wealth. Islam normally recognises, like capitalism, the freedom of enterprise with the institution of private property, the market system and the profit motive, but it differs from capitalism because, as already indicated, property in Islam is a trust from God and man as trustee and vicegerent of God is responsible to Him and subject to His guiding principles.

Although both socialism and capitalism recognise equitable distribution of income, in capitalism this recognition is again an outcome of group pressure while in socialism it is accompanied by negation of individual freedom. Islam achieves this equitable distribution within the framework of individual freedom but with spiritual and legal imperatives to safeguard public interest, moral constraints against unearned income, and social obligations to ensure a just distribution of income and wealth.

The Islamic welfare state is hence neither capitalist nor socialist. It is based on its own values and guided by its own goals. It has its own identity and bears no resemblance to any other form of state.

ABŪL HASAN BANĪ-SADR
1933–

In exile from 1963, he earned a doctorate in economics from
the Sorbonne and was part of the anti-Shah movement outside
Iran and a close advisor to the Āyatullāh Khumaynī in Paris.
He returned to Iran with Khumaynī and after holding several
cabinet portfolios was elected the first president of the Islamic
Republic of Iran until June 1981 when he was ousted by the
fundamentalist-dominated Parliament with the approval of the
Āyatullāh Khumaynī.

Islamic Economics:
Ownership and Tawhīd

Ownership—The Relationship Between the Individual and His/Her Work

Any relation between an individual and his/her earnings which is incompatible with the principle of tawhīd[1] is an unIslamic relationship. Therefore the reality of absolute ownership is not acceptable in Islam because it
would imply acceptance of the concept of absolute ownership which
would be a denial of tawhīd.

Absolute ownership is God's alone; to reflect the principle of tawhīd,
human ownership must be relative only. Everyone's work in reality belongs to God; only to the extent that the individual can be God's vicegerent upon earth can s/he have ownership.

In order for relative ownership of the individual over his/her work and
its fruits to be continuously realized, there must be a relation between the
individual, society, and God which is at once the cause and embodiment of
this principle, and which reveals the possibility of ownership at all. It is
this relation which must now be explored.

---

1. Tawhīd—the unity of God. Bani-Sadr in his introduction describes tawhīd as the Islamic
worldview which regards the universe as a unity whose intelligence, will and purpose is
God. (Ed.)

Excerpted from Tauhidi Economics in Tell the American People, ed. David H. Albert (Phila.:
Movement for a New Society, 1980), pp. 157–63.

The Relationship Between the Individual, Society, and God

In all vital affairs, the relations between the individual and God is established only through the relationship between the society as a whole and God. Thus, ownership by the community as the primary vicegerent of God always takes precedence to that of the individual and the vicegerency by the community is retained for all affairs in which community ownership is the condition for the individual's ownership of his/her own labor and its fruits. The origin of all relations is thus:

$$\text{God} \rightarrow \text{society} \rightarrow \text{individual}$$

Based on this relation, individual ownership is rejected for some things and community ownership is rejected for others. The community can determine the extent of individual ownership but is not allowed to prohibit an individual from working or owning the fruits of that work.

Is also follows that no one is permitted to own another's labor or its results. This limitation on ownership must be continued from generation to generation, ensuring that every able-bodied person is able to exercise his or her abilities without any restriction.

Having declared this principle, we are confronted with three questions:
1. Whether individual ownership of labor and its fruits is transferable?
2. If so, what is the direction of this transfer?
3. Is ownership continuous or not?

According to the principle of *tawhīd*, the movement and activity of all things is from relativity to absoluteness—that is, toward God. Transfer of ownership is a case of this movement from relative to the absolute, and thus the common direction of transfer must be from the personal to the social. When conditions for the transfer from the personal to the social realm exist, it should be accomplished. But because the role of the individual as the vicegerent of God is a continuous phenomenon, the individual's ownership of his/her work must also have a constant and stable character.

Until the time when the possibilities of centralization and accumulation of wealth have been removed, until firm borders are established so that the centralization of productive surpluses of the society within one or a few centers becomes impossible, until these centers of accumulation can no longer be transformed by representatives of the society into centers of power, the social relations of dominant/dominated will continue. Past history and the current human situation are evidence of this fact. Therefore, just because the society makes its facilities accessible to the individual for use, it does not follow that it has the right to take away the people's reserves and put them in the hands of the government. Until the society is released from domination relationships, and there are ways to prevent the centralization of wealth and power, the taking away of the people's reserves will merely concentrate all the produced wealth into the hands of the bureaucrat. Rulers will thus be transformed into tyrants over the people's fate, for which there are already too many examples. But because Islam wants, by solving this "accumulation complex," to reach a *tawhīdī* society, it tries to establish alternative kinds of relations for the distribution of the fruits of labor and residual of the individual's activity within the community and within a "natural" territory. This distribution must follow the path of the relation between God, society, and individual and thus move from individual ownership to social ownership.

The stability of ownership in the hands of workers from generation to generation marks the continuity of the community's relation as vicegerent. The reserves built up only from the fruits of labor will not trigger a complex of capital accumulation. But the method of distribution from the Islamic point of view must also be a method of reaching toward community ownership. Thus the distribution of inherited wealth according to Islamic principles is a system for eliminating the accumulation complex, not for promoting it or for placing a boundary between individual and community ownership.

Indeed, if the picture which we draw from the society of the Twelfth Imām (ed. note: in Shī'īte Islam, it is believed that the Twelfth Imām will appear someday to usher in the ideal society) is realizable, it must be that a truly Islamic policy could lead toward it. It would not be reasonable to assume that a system would be presented to the people and its objectives be defined but that legal foundations be set up which would make it impossible for the society to move toward those objectives.

Even if the picture of the ideal society (that of the Twelfth Imām) had not been presented, the *tawhīd* principle itself would be enough for a healthy mind not to countenance the accumulation and centralization of power as the basis for an Islamic society. It is simply not reasonable to be striving toward the objective of a *tawhīdī* society, but like capitalist societies or those which have different productive systems possessing centralized centers of political and economic power, to make it possible for the labor of all the people to be placed in the pockets of the few.

Therefore, until the time that an economically prosperous society is set up within which scarcity and the possibility of accumulation and centralization is removed, Islam prefers the transfer of the fruits of labor after the deduction of "God's share" to be distributed according to Qur'ānic principles. The result of each person's work, tools, and land should thus be placed in the hands of descendants. Principal is returned to the society which is the place of *tawhīd*.

To sum up, both the society and individual can own, according to the vicegerency principle, and to the extent that this ownership of labor and its fruits help remove accumulation of capital and centralization of power forever. And with regard to the tools of labor, ownership must ultimately belong to the society, and the direction of transfer of ownership should make the fulfillment of this principle possible.

Islamic Theory and the Fraudulent Attitudes Engendered by the Powerful

Under a system of private ownership, absolute ownership is assumed. Someone puts a barbed wire fence around a piece of property and then claims ownership. What happens then? What happens if the owners let no one inside to work on it? The masses of people will be obliged to put themselves in the hands of the owners and thus, in a position of submissiveness, saying, "Whatever you say, boss." Or they will be obliged to go to the factories and be ground up in the gears of the machinery or to the construction sites where they will work until they fall. This occurs because it is in the interest of these owners for it to occur. Are not these masses "obliged" to obey the orders of the absolute owners, who have forgotten God, because the owners have "saved" them from death by starvation?

These relations, which are the dominant relations of the *shirk* (atheistic and discordant) world, are not Islamic relations and must be rejected by Islam. The common supposition that the above situation is normal or even Islamic has no relation to the truly Islamic view. The basis of this system is force. It is based on the *shirk* economy, and is incompatible with the Islamic point of view based on *tawhīd*, in which common ownership is the kind of ownership which allows all the people to own their own labor. It is obvious that this is not realizable under a system which legalizes the grabbing of land, resources, and tools from the people.

A society which is true to its own nature as a society has its members do common work together in protecting them from dangers, providing for the needs of each, and ensuring that nobody robs someone else's fruits of labor through cheating or force. A society will reach its objectives of ensuring the needs of all and equalizing opportunities for everyone to the extent that everyone owns his/her own labor; no one uses his/her own labor for destructive activities; individuals do not engage in activity without relation to the total activity of the community or against the interest of the community; and people work as members of the society as a whole. This is *tawhīd,* and possesses the components for unity.

Tawhīd and Stability of Ownership Over Time

Over time, generations after generations have relative ownership of land and resources and the fruits of labor. When it is said that "You are the owner of the land you are working," it means that you and the human community and future generations and past generations are partners in this ownership. The maintenance of *tawhīd* through time is one of the most important elements in the legislating of Islamic law. All rules must be established in accordance with *tawhīd*. This is true even with respect to the individual's own person. The *tawhīd* principle requires a prohibition on suicide because an individual does not have absolute ownership even over him/herself, but belongs to God and through the vicegerent principle belongs to the society, to future and past generations which have labored and are still working and will work for him/her and for which the individual has a responsibility to work.

Governments are not forever and cannot make decisions which lead to the deprivation of future generations. For example, it cannot choose to exhaust the oil and leave the well dry during the lifetime of a single generation, or dry the land and empty the mines for future generations. To make the present time absolute is a kind of domination relation and represents an exploitative point of view. It leads to the forgetting of the principle that every individual and every society is part of the totality of being. Neither individuals nor governments have the right to exploit for the sake of their own wants. Islam does not have a class perspective—it doesn't look from the top to the bottom, or from the point of view of the oppressed upward. The Islamic view is based on *tawhīd*. God exists and all are equal in God's sight. Preference is given according to virtue. There is not a single sub-role or class which is not included in the Islamic view. And it cannot be otherwise, and couldn't be.

The meaning of this is that Islam is a system in which every rule and law and condition reflects the guiding principles. If it were not so, Islam would not be a system. And the reason that Islam has gotten into the present situation is that rules and conditions have become bankrupt of these guiding principles.

Furthermore, in Islamic theory the origin of ownership and its results and the validity of its extensions must be established in such a way so that the objective face of human society reflects the guiding principles. That means ownership is limited to constructive purposes; destructive ends are prohibited. Constructive purposes are those which add to the store of human opportunities in such a way that does not tend to the future destruction of opportunities. If labor is not constructive and creative, how could the Qur'ānic verse, "The ascension of things is toward God," acquire its meaning? If the individual does not add to the store of human opportunities and does not consciously seek evolution, how can s/he ascend to God? By working with nature and with the community, the individual can forget him/herself and ascend through evolution. If people do not use their labor for the extension and growth of the human dimension, they cannot reach toward a *tawhīdī* society or ascend towards God.

Conclusions

In the Islamic theory of ownership, absolute ownership is reserved for God alone. As human relativity and activity is not realized except in relation to God's absoluteness, individual ownership over labor cannot be realized except in relation to God's absolute ownership. Otherwise, force would be the basis of all relations; both dominating and dominated would lose their own freedom and their authority and become estranged from themselves. To the extent that the human race upholds the principle of vicegerency, and maintains the right of labor and the right of innovation for all people without exception and without discrimination in all times and places, and as long as ownership is maintained relatively, humans are the heirs of God. This relation between the community and the individual is to be organized by the Imam.

Accordingly, ownership is one aspect of the God-human relationship. The relation has two directions: that of origin—God → society → individual, and that of ultimate end—individual → society → God. Absolute ownership is that of God and the nearest ownership to absoluteness over the earth and resources is that of the community. Next is that of the individual who, however, maintains relative ownership over his/her own labor. Therefore in transfer with respect to destination, ownership should move from individual to the community, from the community to the society-at-large, and then to the Imam, God's active representative. Until then, all tools of labor should be placed in the hands of those who can make constructive use of them, according to capacity. Work opportunities are to be increased. And the differences between individual abilities should be reduced through the just distribution of opportunities.

Alas that the problem has not been faced this way among the religious community of Islam. The Islamic religious community has always adjusted itself to the economic relations of the time. The truly Islamic view which holds the possibilities for the final freedom of humankind, the view which has been made known in the Qur'ān and described in the religious traditions and sayings, has been forgotten when the political power of tyrants has been established.

The reason for these details and even repetition is that the commonly held ideology based on *shirk*—atheistic contradictions—must be rejected. Once we have done so, we can ask, according to this paradigm of ownership based on the principle of *tawhīd*, how such ownership can be realized and how Islam can organize itself in this vital realm. And in answering these questions, we must study the adjustments of ownership for consistency with the way Islam must fight accumulation of capital and the centralization of power.

IV

THE RE-EMERGENCE OF ISLAM:
THREE CASE STUDIES

The latter half of the 1970's saw a strong re-emergence of Islam in the politics of many Muslim countries. This phenomenon, rooted in a broader Islamic religious revival that has embraced both the private and public spheres of Muslim life, has taken many forms: increased mosque attendance, wearing of more traditional dress, a proliferation of religious literature, growth of Islamic organizations, as well as calls for more Islamic governments. Three case studies—Egypt, Iran, and Pakistan—will be presented to provide some sense of the range of concerns and positions.

EGYPT

Given the centrality of the *Sharī'a* in the traditional Islamic theory of state and society, a major concern of resurgent Islam is the introduction of more *Sharī'a* law in order to clearly establish the Islamic character of the state. The debate on the application of the *Sharī'a* in Egypt provides an instructive example. Najīb Mahfūz speaks of the split personality of many modern Egyptians caught between traditional belief and practice and the demands of contemporary life. 'Abd al-Halīm Mahmūd, Rector (Shaykh) of al-Azhar, provides the perspective of a prominent religious scholar on the contemporary need for Islamic law and the contribution of a leading Islamic center to this process. Finally, Zakī Najīb Mahmūd addresses a central concern of modern Islam: how to root an Islamic renaissance in an historically rich cultural heritage, i.e., how to establish a link between change and tradition.

University students, as in many other Muslim countries, have played an important role in Egypt's Islamic revival. The final selection, from the Islamic (Student) Association of Cairo University, reflects the effect of the Iranian revolution on Muslim youth outside Iran as well as their beliefs regarding the relationship of religion to the state.

NAJĪB MAHFŪZ
1911–

He studied at Cairo University. After writing historical novels, Najīb Mahfūz began in the mid-forties to produce a series of novels that reflected modern Egyptian life. He is currently a director in the Ministry of Education and a leading novelist in the Arab world.

Debate on the Application of the Sharī'a in Egypt

The Islamic *Sharī'a* is an integral whole, the punishments contained in it are nothing more than its outermost fence. Positive thinking demands constructive readjustments. Moreover, in many of its transactions our society cannot be called an Islamic society. If we begin with applying the *Sharī'a* punishments, then we are protecting a non-Islamic government by Islamic punishments. . . .

To begin with, the application of the *hudūd*[1] punishments will uncover contradictions and differences. We make wine and sell it to the people, we set up gambling centers in tourist areas; we recognize furnished apartments and put taxes on them—wouldn't it be wiser to take another look at these things we admit before we apply the *hudūd* punishments? . . .

The problem of youth and sex should be solved before we apply the punishment for adultery. Early marriage was easy in former times . . . but today it is rare that a young man can marry before thirty years of age, and the situation for the girl is no better. How difficult the problem, but how easy the punishment.

We would do much better to direct our zeal to rooting out the causes which lead men to sin, following the historical Islamic model. We can reduce the causes—with the exception of sickness—to two essential vices. They are debilitating poverty and excessive wealth. The state is seriously trying to treat the two by productivity and taxes, but the door is still open for more effort. I fear dire consequences if we resort to Islamic *hudūd* punishments to protect conditions unworthy of Islamic protection.

1. *hudūd:* (sing. *hadd*) Qur'ānically mandated fixed punishments for specific crimes: fornication, adultery, false accusation of illicit sexual relations, wine drinking, theft, armed robbery, and apostasy.

From *al-Ahrām*, May 17, 1977.

But there is some general research concerning a full application of the *Sharī'a;* I believe that every Muslim welcomes this and considers that its execution will accomplish his most cherished dream. This true Muslim persevering in his duties often finds himself perplexed. He leads a contemporary life. He obeys civil and penal laws of Western origin and is involved in a complex tangle of social and economic transactions and is never certain to what extent these agree with or contradict his Islamic creed. Life carries him along in its current, and he forgets his misgivings for a time until one Friday he hears the *imām* or reads the religion page in one of the papers, and the old misgivings come back with a certain fear. He realizes that in this new society he has been afflicted with a split personality: half of him believes, prays, fasts and makes the pilgrimage. The other half renders his values void in banks and courts and in the streets, even in the cinemas and theatres, perhaps even at home among his family before the television set. He listens to an announcement that the application of the *Sharī'a* is near at hand. He is happy and rejoices . . . however his concerns are not removed completely because the matter is not as simple as it first appeared. It is not merely a question of formulating a decree and applying it; but, in fact, it requires an attack on an integral system to demolish it and rebuild it on divine bases. It may be easy for us to close bars and impose a new dress code for women, but what about the banking system and current economic practices. They are closely tied to their counterparts in the international system. We may be able to dominate action but it is absolutely out of the question that we control the reaction. Moreover, we are continuously dealing with international institutions like the United Nations, its committees and the security council. All this requires exact research and serious thought before we can realize our dream without causing a general convulsion. Perhaps also a Muslim's concerns are not completely absorbed by this because he is not only a true Muslim, he is also a true citizen. His ancient ancestors lived in the Islamic kingdom and had no allegiance save to God and the kingdom. That is past history. Nationalism appeared and nations multiplied to the point that the Arabs fought under the banner of nationalism against the abode of the Caliph in the First World War. Thus allegiance was limited to the fatherland. Religion was left to God; the fatherland was for all. The concerns of the true Muslim determined to be both a true Muslim and a true citizen increase. The wise solution is easy for the wise. God has given us the best of gifts— the human intellect. The wise men entrusted with looking into the application of Islamic legislation must 1) produce a thorough interpretation of how these principles should be understood (today); 2) provide a profound interpretation which will help us to understand the reality of our present lives; and 3) maintain wholehearted respect for the principles to which political organizations are bound, namely, the inevitability of the socialist solution, social peace and national unity. . . .

'ABD AL-HALĪM MAHMŪD
d. 1978.

After obtaining degrees from al-Azhar University (1932), and the Sorbonne (Ph.D., 1940) he taught at the College of Arabic Language and Usūl al-Dīn in Cairo. From 1968 onwards he served in a number of academic and government posts, among them General Secretary of the Academy of Islamic Research and Wakīl (Rector) of al-Azhar University. In 1973 he was appointed Shaykh of al-Azhar.

Debate on the Application of the Sharī'a in Egypt

Application of the *hudūd* punishments is the only cure for the spread of crime which we see today. Stealing will be ended once and for all if we cut off the hand of one thief.

The efforts of al-Azhar are beginning to fructify. Al-Azhar has struggled and continues to struggle for the application of the *Sharī'a* and now the fruit is almost ripe. The signs of that are that Dr. Isma'īl Ma'tūq, member of the national assembly for the region of Qana has presented a draft law to the People's Assembly for the application of the rules of the *Sharī'a*, and Engineer Sayyid Mar'ī, president of the People's Assembly, announced that the assembly will proceed according to the directions of President Sadat to make the Islamic *Sharī'a* the chief source of governance.

The Ministry of Justice has created committees to draw up a project which is almost finished, and the Minister of Information has announced more than once that the information media have been directed to spread moral values which will prepare the way for making the *Sharī'a* the source of laws.

More than seven years ago al-Azhar formed committees for putting the *Sharīa* into law. It finished the part on civil law, based on all schools, and published books on this. Now it is working on penal law and has almost finished. . . .

Some people are planning to water down the affair, saying: we must reform the individual first, then apply the law. This is an obvious deception because the law itself is the most powerful means for reforming the

From *al-Ahrām,* May 7, 1976.

241

individual. This is putting things upside down and reversing the desires of believers. . . .

They try to justify the presence of wine, for example, although it brings nothing but filth and although God sends plagues: the boll weevil, for instance and the clover worm . . . worms have destroyed in one year crops valued at much more than all the profits on wine for several years. . . .

Colonialism is responsible for changing Islamic laws and for creating schools and colleges of law teaching European laws. After a while this was taken for granted, and the separation of Muslims from their *Sharī'a* became normal . . . but God forsook colonialism. The colonialists were defeated and returned to their country. . . . There is no longer any justification for colleges of law to devote twenty hours per week to European law and only two hours to the Islamic *Sharī'a*.

These colleges explain our backwardness in legislation because they forced us to be subservient to Western legists, we are pulled into their orbit. Islamic legislation is one of the glories of Islamic civilization, and its adepts are the most famous thinkers in the world. But we have become followers and slavish imitators. . . .

ZAKĪ NAJĪB MAHMŪD
1905–

He has a Ph.D. from London University (1947) and is former editor-in-chief of the Egyptian reviews, *al-Thaqāfah* and *al-Fikr al-Muʿāsir*. He is currently professor of philosophy at Kuwait University.

Debate on the Application of the Sharīʿa in Egypt

We will experience no real renaissance in our life unless this renaissance is firmly tied to our past heritage. The question is: how do we establish this tie between past and present. . . .

If the tie which is sought were limited to a return to texts we have which are understood in one sense only with no differences of opinion, then the matter would be easy. We would merely look at our present position then compare it with the text from which the rules governing this position derive. But it is enough for me to say that the source about which faith has no doubt, I mean the Qurʾān and the Sunna, is itself subject to differences in understanding, exegesis and interpretation. If this were not so then how could we explain the multiplicity of legal schools and the several exegeses so numerous that Qurʾānic exegesis sometimes becomes interpretation, i.e., an attempt to extract meanings other than the obvious meaning of the text.

If differences in understanding the text exist, then why not allow ourselves the right to explain the source of Islamic legislation in our turn by an exegesis which will be for the good of society?

The principle of common good (*maslaha*) is admitted by jurists; it is this principle which states that "necessity makes the forbidden licit" . . .

What I want to say is that our intellectual effort must be directed to searching for a place for ourselves in God's Sharīʿa. We will not contravene it in any sense of the word, but, at the same time, we must do what the first Muslims did, i.e. we must explain it in a way that accords with the new age.

The ancient exegetes formed their exegeses to fit their schools of thought; the Sunnites have their exegesis, the Muʿtazilites have theirs, the

From *al-Ahrām*, March 14, 1976.

Shī'ites have theirs and the Sūfis have theirs, and yet this plurality did not bother Muslims during the first five centuries of our history. Why should it bother us today?

I want to reaffirm my strong faith in the necessity of maintaining a tie between ourselves and our ancestors. This tie must be based on the way we look at things, not on maintaining the letter and the content as they were. . . .

Divine legislation is free from passion, about this there is no doubt. It is the unique legislation for mankind; this needs no commentary. The Muslims themselves, once civilization had broadened them and created new problems for them, were forced to add two other sources (for divine legislation), namely, analogy and consensus. There is no doubt that these two sources contain a human element because they involve judgment and judgment may err. You may rely on analogy and be in error; you may adopt a consensus with which another age may not agree. . . .

It would perhaps be correct to say that one of our sources of error today is the opinion that divine legislation covers all the details of life. . . .

It is true that the Qur'ān and the Sunna defined certain punishments for certain crimes, but who would say that these are the only crimes humans commit? Who would say that these crimes take only one form in all social circumstances and in different periods of time? A robber, for example, may not use his hand in stealing but may obtain millions while sitting in his office.

The saying of God: "Then we put you on the path (Sharī'a), so follow it," may mean the path (Sharī'a) of the intellect, and in this sense it is our duty to use our intellect when there is no text or where something occurs not covered by the text.

I single out what characterizes Islam alone among religions: the call for the governance of intellect. Without this its call lacks true balance. If the present text contains everything, then where is there room for the governance of intellect? Because of this appeal to the governance of intellect, the Islamic message was the last (divine) message since man no longer had need to appeal to anything but his intellect when he saw the form of civilization changing before his eyes.

Those who say that the Islamic world must be freed from subservience to capitalism or Marxism because Islam is all sufficient and because God left nothing to be completed by Adam Smith, Saint-Simon, Hegel or Marx, should realize that the question is not one of technical terms like capitalism, Marxism, etc. What concerns me is the system and the thought contained in certain technical terms. What is called capitalism or Marxism may contain something which is also found in Islam. Before we reject the technical terms we should look at the systems behind them regardless of the names they are given. Perhaps we will find things that do not conflict with our creed.

There is an intellectual terrorism which allows no freedom for open expression. The media open their doors to men of religion who say what they want because they usually present things in a form acceptable to viewers and listeners. But suppose that the speaker wants to express another point of view not in accord with what the masses think, he may want to change the opinion of the masses. Then, most likely, he will not be allowed to speak. The opportunity given those who say what people want to hear is much greater than that given to speakers who may contradict the people while calling on them to change.

THE ISLAMIC (STUDENT) ASSOCIATION
OF CAIRO UNIVERSITY

Lessons from Iran

In the name of God the all-merciful
Cairo University
The Islamic (Student) Association (*al-jamā'a al-islāmiyya*)

"Say, O God, possessor of all sovereignty, you give sovereignty to whom you wish and take sovereignty from whom you wish; you enable whom you wish and you debase whom you wish by your bounteous hand. Verily you are powerful over all things. (Qur'ān 3:26)

The revolution of the Iranian people which shook the world from end to end and forced everyone to follow its events moment by moment in bewilderment, surpassed in its violence and restraint all calculations and even the wildest imaginings. This revolution is worthy of our deep study so that we may extract the lesson, learn from it, derive incentives and benefit from the study.

This is a concise attempt which is certainly not complete; it is exploratory. Possibly it will be followed by serious studies of broader scope which are more appropriate to the importance of this unique and amazing revolution and better designed to awaken Muslims and to restore their confidence in their religion and their adherence to it, so that they may assume the reins of world leadership of mankind once again and place the world under the protection of the esteemed Islamic civilization. "You are the best *umma* given to mankind; you prescribe the good and prohibit evil and you believe in God." (Qur'ān 3:110)

The Creed Is the Motive Force and Point of Departure

The first lesson is the influence of the creed on the Islamic people. What spirit that was which moved in the being of this people who had appeared servile and submissive to injustice and tyranny. They exploded like a volcano, not fearing death and not concerned about life. They dictated their will, though they were unarmed; flesh conquered steel. This spirit is the spirit of faith which fashioned the character of Bilāl and Yāsir and Salmān

From *Lessons from Iran*, mimeo flyer issued by the Islamic (Student) Association (*al-jamā'a al-islāmiyya*) of Cairo University, 1979.

246

al-Fārsī, which made Khālid and Saʿd and AbūʿUbaydah[1] and which produced al-Sadīq (Abū-Bakr) and al-Farūq (ʿUmar)[2] and which allowed the
little bands at Badr, Hatīn and ʿAyn Jalūt to triumph.[3] This very spirit is
capable of creating Islamic society today and it is capable at all times of
moving the Islamic peoples, bringing out their hidden strength, not only in
revolution and battle but in every situation of life. This *umma* is led by
nothing except Islam.

Islam Is the Religion of Strength and Dignity

This revolution indicates the nature of this religion which refuses to let
injustice befall its followers and guarantees strength and dignity for them
just as it guarantees them life because there is no life without strength.
"Strength is God's and his apostles' and all believers'." (Qur'ān 63:8) This
is the way Islam has educated Muslims and this is why a woman, Ismāʿ
bint Abū-Bakr, could say: "By God, the blow of a sword in honor is better
than the stroke of a lash in ignominy." . . . Taking this event as a model
led the Commander of the Faithful, Muʿtasim, to rescue a Muslim woman
who was slapped by a Byzantine thousands of miles away.

Islam is covetous not only of the dignity of Muslims but of everyone
wronged by any government. ʿUmar ibn al-Khattāb came to the aid of a
Copt from Egypt and shouted at his governor ʿAmr ibn al-ʿĀs, "Since
when do you enslave people whose mothers begot free men?"

Islam Is Religion and State

The revolution also indicates the nature of this religion from another
perspective, namely it is a comprehensive religion which legislates for this
world and the next and organizes all of life. It is concerned with the justice
of government just as it is concerned with assuring that prayer is performed. It sets up a system for economy of which *zakāt* is a part. It
establishes its society on the bases of creed and equality among the people
and the brotherhood of faith. It sets forth in detail rules for dealings
between people just as it details the rules of worship. It organizes relations
between the Islamic state and other states. It is religion and state, governance and politics, economics and social organization, education and morals, worship and holy war.

1. Early followers of the Prophet Muhammad.
2. The first two caliphs (successors) of Muhammad were Abū-Bakr and ʿUmar ibn al-
   Khattāb.
3. Historic Muslim victories over the Meccans, the Crusaders and the Mongols.

Separation Between Religion and State (Secularism)
Is an Imported Error

Based on the foregoing, the Iranian revolution represents the first breach in the wall of secularism. It is confirmed that the Islamic peoples have uncovered the spuriousness of this pretension and the extent of its contradiction with Islam. They rejected it and began to set up the rule of God. "Who is better than God in governance for a people who are convinced." (Qur'ān 5:50)

Secularism is a call to separate religion from the state and to prohibit Islam from interfering in politics or in the affairs of government. It is the perpetual resort of those idolatrous rulers who transgress God's limits, paralyze his *Sharī'a* and give free rein to their passions and their relatives to plunder the wealth of the peoples and defile their blood and honor.

The Sharī'a of God Is the Ruler

This revolution confirmed for us that as long as laws and constitutions are not derived from the *Sharī'a* of Islam, they form a counterfeit *Sharī'a* no matter what specious haloes of sanctity may be attributed to them because man-made constitutions and laws are an expression of the real balance of forces between the government and the people; that is the government for the most part is the stronger. They do not enjoy the respect of any of the people because they are the fabrication of man and, in addition, their status is no greater than the place of the goddess of pastry which the Arabs of the *jāhiliyya* used to make and worship. If they got hungry, they ate her. So these authors change their laws when they conflict with their interests. But the *Sharī'a* of Islam is a *Sharī'a* of permanence, justice, wisdom and perfection because it is the *Sharī'a* of God.

The Sincere Learned Men of Religion Are the True Leaders

This revolution indicates to us the truth of leadership in this *umma;* the sincere learned men (*'ulamā'*) of the Muslims have always been the shelter where the people sought refuge when external danger took them by surprise or when the injustice of rulers hemmed them in. The biographies of Saʿīd ibn al-Musayb and Saʿīd ibn Jubayr . . . decorate our history. The liberation movements in the countries of Islam in the modern age were Islamic movements led by the *'ulamā'*. The source of this leadership was faith and love; they were not driven by an appetite for power or fear. As for those *'ulamā'* who make a travesty of learning to justify injustice and seem to say: "Islam is in the service of rulers even if they are ruling by norms other than those revealed by God and make war on those working for Islam," they prefer this world to the next and sell religion to buy position. They are not [true] *'ulamā'*, and their reckoning with God will be harsh.

Injustice Is Darkness

The consequence of injustice becomes clear in this revolution. Here is the tyrant Shah betraying his *umma* and bringing down on it the most repulsive forms of injustice for forty years.

He forgot that God takes his time with the wrongdoer but when He takes him there is no escaping. He forgot that injustice is darkness on the day of final judgement. What then is his destiny? His evil banishes him and he is sought for investigation and judgement. He starts divulging views of disdain which reveal his contempt for all his people in all he did, despite the civility of some of his governors.

We Refuse Subservience to the East or the West

Perhaps the most profound lesson which this revolution embodied was the fruit of working for countries of the East or the West. Rulers sold their countries and hastened to serve the East or the West and repressed their people in the interest of their masters. They showed the courage of lions against their own people but knelt before enemies and were transformed into puppets in the hands of the rulers of East or West. No matter what titles of friendship or descriptions of cooperation they may use to describe this brokerage, no one of them, no matter how he exaggerates his friendship and submissiveness, will be worth more than the Shah who was considered the first agent of the West in this region and the guardian of its interests but the prodigal where the rights of his people and nation were concerned. What happened? The West disowned him and abandoned him just like any one of them discards his shoes when they wear out. After that neither his army, nor his guards nor his secret police were of any help to him, not even American intelligence. Has the time come for others to acknowledge him?. . . .

Two Existing Dangers

There are however two dangers we must clearly take notice of because the enemies of Islam will try to exploit them to the limit. The first is represented by the exploitation of sectarian differences between Shīʿites and Sunnites to tear the Islamic *umma* apart and drain its energies in internal battles, antagonisms and quarrels.

The second is the utilization of the Iranian revolution to instigate local governments to strike out at Islamic movements. We also appeal to rulers to profit from this event by realizing that their strength is in the strength of their peoples and the strength of their peoples is in Islam. Their allegiance must be to God, his Apostle and the believers, "Your only supporters are God, his Apostle and those who believe," (Qur'añ 5:55) and that they rule according to what God has revealed, "May they be strengthened by what God revealed," (Qur'ān 5:49)

We say to those instigators: "God suffices for us; he is the perfect mandatory." (Qur'ān 3:173)

Finally we remind Muslims of God's true promise: "God promised those of you who believe and perform good works that he would make you viceroys on earth as he did with those before you and will make it possible for you to follow the religion which pleases you and will change your fear into safety. You will worship me, associating nothing else with me." (Qur'an 24:55)

PAKISTAN

Pakistan, more than any other Muslim nation, provides the most instructive example of the problems and issues in the struggle for Islamic identity. Since its establishment as a Muslim homeland in 1947, Pakistanis have sought to clarify its meaning. The first two selections provide two models of a modern Islamic state. Mawlānā Abū-l-'Alā' Mawdūdī, the founder of the Jamā'at-i-Islāmī, advocated a more traditional theocratic state while Fazlur Rahmān, Cambridge-educated director of the government-sponsored Islamic Research Institute, delineated a more modernist Islamic state based upon popular sovereignty. However, although she declared herself an Islamic Republic, no systematic program was adopted.

During the 1970's, Islam re-emerged in the politics of Pakistan and led to calls for an Islamic system of government (Nizām-i-Islām). General M. Zia ul-Haq, who seized power from Zulfikar'Alī Bhutto in 1977, has sought to legitimate his coup and subsequent rule through appeals to Islam. Among his major reforms were a series of Islamic laws and regulations announced in his "Introduction of an Islamic System."

Pakistan's failure to effectively implement its Islamic *raison d'être* was raised in the courts by retired Justice B.Z. Kaikaus who in 1976 filed a petition which challenged the Islamic character of Pakistan's political and legal system. When in 1978 Zia ul-Haq introduced a system of "*Sharī'a* Courts", appeals courts that determine whether or not any law is Islamic, Justice Kaikaus resubmitted his petition in a case which attracted national attention. And so the debate continues.

Political Theory of Islam

With certain people it has become a sort of fashion to somehow identify Islam with one or the other system of life in vogue at the time. So at this time also there are people who say that Islam is a democracy, and by this they mean to imply that there is no difference between Islam and the democracy as in vogue in the West. Some others suggest that Communism is but the latest and revised version of Islam and it is in the fitness of things that Muslims imitate the Communist experiment of Soviet Russia. Still some others whisper that Islam has the elements of dictatorship in it and we should revive the cult of "obedience to the *Amīr*" (the leader). All these people, in their misinformed and misguided zeal to serve what they hold to be the cause of Islam, are always at great pains to prove that Islam contains within itself the elements of all types of contemporary social and political thought and action. Most of the people who indulge in this prattle have no clear idea of the Islamic way of life. They have never made nor try to make a systematic study of the Islamic political order—the place and nature of democracy, social justice, and equality in it. . . . some people have begun to present apologies on Islam's behalf. As a matter of fact, this attitude emerges from an inferiority complex, from the belief that we as Muslims can earn no honour or respect unless we are able to show that our religion resembles the modern creeds and it is in agreement with most of the contemporary ideologies. These people have done a great disservice to Islam; they have reduced the political theory of Islam to a puzzle, a hotchpotch. They have turned Islam into a juggler's bag out of which can be produced anything that holds a demand! Such is the intellectual plight in which we are engulfed. . . .

First Principle of Islamic Political Theory

The belief in the Unity [*tawhīd*] and the sovereignty of Allah is the foundation of the social and moral system propounded by the Prophets. It is the very starting-point of the Islamic political philosophy. The basic principle of Islam is that human beings must, individually and collectively, surrender all rights of overlordship, legislation and exercizing of authority over others. No one should be allowed to pass orders or make commands *in his own right* and no one ought to accept the obligation to carry out such commands and obey such orders. None is entitled to make laws on his

From *Islam: Its Meaning and Message,* ed. Khurshid Ahmad (London: Islamic Council of Europe, 1976), pp. 147–48, 158–61, 163–70.

own authority and none is obliged to abide by them. This right vests in
Allah alone:

> "The Authority rests with none but Allah. He commands you not to
> surrender to any one save Him. This is the right way (of life)." (Qur'ān
> 12:40)
> 'They ask: "have we also got some authority?" Say: "all authority
> belongs to God alone"', (Qur'ān 3:154). . . .

According to this theory, sovereignty belongs to Allah. He alone is the
law-giver. No man, even if he be a Prophet, has the right to order others *in
his own right* to do or not to do certain things. The Prophet himself is
subject to God's commands:

> 'I do not follow anything except what is revealed to me.' (Qur'ān
> 6:50)

Other people are required to obey the Prophet because he enunciates not
his own but God's commands:

> 'We sent no messenger save that he should be obeyed by Allah's
> command.' (Qur'ān 4:64). . . .

Thus the main characteristics of an Islamic state that can be deduced
from these express statements of the Holy Qur'ān are as follows:

1. No person, class or group, not even the entire population of the state
as a whole, can lay claim to sovereignty. God alone is the real sovereign;
all others are merely His subjects;

2. God is the real law-giver and the authority of absolute legislation
vests in Him. The believers cannot resort to totally independent legislation
nor can they modify any law which God has laid down, even if the desire
to effect such legislation or change in Divine laws is unanimous;[1] and

3. An Islamic state must, in all respects, be founded upon the law laid
down by God through His Prophet. The government which runs such a
state will be entitled to obedience in its capacity as a political agency set up
to enforce the laws of God and only in so far as it acts in that capacity. If
it disregards the law revealed by God, its commands will not be binding on
the believers.

The Islamic State: Its Nature and Characteristics

The preceding discussion makes it quite clear that Islam, speaking from the
view-point of political philosophy, is the very antithesis of secular Western

---

1. Here the *absolute right of legislation* is being discussed. In the Islamic political theory this
right vests in Allah alone. As to the scope and extent of human legislation provided by the
Sharī'a itself please see Mawdūdī, A.A., *Islamic Law and Constitution*, Chapter II: "Legislation and Ijtihād in Islam" and chapter VI: "First Principles of Islamic State."

democracy. The philosophical foundation of Western democracy is the sovereignty of the people. In it, this type of absolute powers of legislation—of the determination of values and of the norms of behaviour—rest in the hands of the people. Law-making is their prerogative and legislation must correspond to the mood and temper of their opinion. If a particular piece of legislation is desired by the masses, howsoever ill-conceived it may be from a religious and moral viewpoint, steps have to be taken to place it on the statute book; if the people dislike any law and demand its abrogation, howsoever just and rightful it might be, it has to be expunged forthwith. This is not the case in Islam. On this count, Islam has no trace of Western democracy. Islam, as already explained, altogether repudiates the philosophy of popular sovereignty and rears its polity on the foundations of the sovereignty of God and the vicegerency (*khilāfa*) of man.

A more apt name for the Islamic polity would be the "kingdom of God" which is described in English as a "theocracy." But Islamic theocracy is something altogether different from the theocracy of which Europe has had a bitter experience wherein a priestly class, sharply marked off from the rest of the population, exercises unchecked domination and enforces laws of its own making in the name of God, thus virtually imposing its own divinity and godhood upon the common people. Such a system of government is satanic rather than divine. Contrary to this, the theocracy built up by Islam is not ruled by any particular religious class but by the whole community of Muslims including the rank and file. The entire Muslim population runs the state in accordance with the Book of God and the practice of His Prophet. If I were permitted to coin a new term, I would describe this system of government as a "theo-democracy," that is to say a divine democratic government, because under it the Muslims have been given a limited popular sovereignty under the suzerainty of God. The executive under this system of government is constituted by the general will of the Muslims who have also the right to depose it. All administrative matters and all questions about which no explicit injunction is to be found in the *Sharī'a* are settled by the consensus of opinion among the Muslims. Every Muslim who is capable and qualified to give a sound opinion on matters of Islamic law, is entitled to interpret the law of God when such interpretation becomes necessary. In this sense the Islamic polity is a democracy. But, as has been explained above, it is a theocracy in the sense that where an explicit command of God or His Prophet already exists, no Muslim leader or legislature, or any religious scholar can form an independent judgement, not even all the Muslims of the world put together have any right to make the least alteration in it. . . .

God has laid down those limits which, in Islamic phraseology, are termed "divine limits" (*Hudūd-Allāh*). These limits consist of certain principles, checks and balances and specific injunctions in different spheres of life and activity, and they have been prescribed in order that man may be trained to lead a balanced and moderate life. They are intended to lay down the broad framework within which man is free to legislate, decide his own affairs and frame subsidiary laws and regulations for his conduct. These limits he is not permitted to overstep and if he does so, the whole scheme of his life will go awry.

Take for example man's economic life. In this sphere God has placed certain restrictions on human freedom. The right to private property has been recognized, but it is qualified by the obligation to pay *zakāt* (poor dues) and the prohibition of interest, gambling and speculation. A specific law of inheritance for the distribution of property among the largest number of surviving relations on the death of its owner has been laid down and certain forms of acquiring, accumulating and spending wealth have been declared unlawful. If people observe these just limits and regulate their affairs within these boundary walls, on the one hand their personal liberty is adequately safeguarded and, on the other, the possibility of class war and domination of one class over another, which begins with capitalist oppression and ends in working-class dictatorship, is safely and conveniently eliminated.

Similarly in the sphere of family life, God has prohibited the unrestricted intermingling of the sexes and has prescribed *purdah*, recognized man's guardianship of woman, and clearly defined the rights and duties of husband, wife and children. The laws of divorce and separation have been clearly set forth, conditional polygamy has been permitted and penalties for fornication and false accusations of adultery have been prescribed. He has thus laid down limits which, if observed by man, would stabilize his family life and make it a haven of peace and happiness. There would remain neither that tyranny of male over female which makes family life an inferno of cruelty and oppression, nor that satanic flood of female liberty and licence which threatens to destroy human civilization in the West. . . .

The Purpose of the Islamic State

The purpose of the state that may be formed on the basis of the Qur'ān and the Sunna has also been laid down by God. The Qur'ān says:

> We verily sent Our messengers with clear proofs, and revealed with them the Scripture and the Balance, that mankind may observe right measure; and We revealed iron, wherein is mighty power and (many) uses for mankind. [Qur'ān 57:25]

In this verse steel symbolizes political power and the verse also makes it clear that the mission of the Prophets is to create conditions in which the mass of people will be assured of social justice in accordance with the standards enunciated by God in His Book which gives explicit instructions for a well-disciplined mode of life. In another place God has said:

> (Muslims are) those who, if We give them power in the land, establish the system of *salāt* (worship) and *zakāt* (poor dues) and enjoin virtue and forbid evil and inequity. [Qur'ān, 22:41]
>
> You are the best community sent forth to mankind; you enjoin the Right conduct and forbid the wrong; and you believe in Allah. [Qur'ān 3:110]

It will readily become manifest to anyone who reflects upon these verses that the purpose of the state visualized by the Holy Qur'ān is not negative but positive. The object of the state is not merely to prevent people from exploiting each other, to safeguard their liberty and to protect its subjects from foreign invasion. It also aims at evolving and developing that well-balanced system of social justice which has been set forth by God in His Holy Book. Its object is to eradicate all forms of evil and to encourage all types of virtue and excellence expressly mentioned by God in the Holy Qur'ān. For this purpose political power will be made use of as and when the occasion demands; all means of propaganda and peaceful persuasion will be employed; the moral education of the people will also be undertaken; and social influence as well as the force of public opinion will be harnessed to the task.

Islamic State is Universal and All-Embracing

A state of this sort cannot evidently restrict the scope of its activities. Its approach is universal and all-embracing. Its sphere of activity is coextensive with the whole of human life. It seeks to mould every aspect of life and activity in consonance with its moral norms and programme of social reform. In such a state no one can regard any field of his affairs as personal and private. Considered from this aspect the Islamic state bears a kind of resemblance to the Fascist and Communist states. But you will find later on that, despite its all-inclusiveness, it is something vastly and basically different from the modern totalitarian and authoritarian states. Individual liberty is not suppressed under it nor is there any trace of dictatorship in it. It presents the middle course and embodies the best that the human society has ever evolved. . . .

Islamic State is an Ideological State

Another characteristic of the Islamic State is that it is an idelogical state. It is clear from a careful consideration of the Qur'ān and the Sunna that the state in Islam is based on an ideology and its objective is to establish that ideology. The state is an instrument of reform and must act likewise. It is a dictate of this very nature of the Islamic State that such a state should be run only by those who believe in the ideology on which it is based and in the Divine Law which it is assigned to administer. The administrators of the Islamic state must be those whose whole life is devoted to the observance and enforcement of this Law, who not only agree with its reformatory programme and fully believe in it but thoroughly comprehend its spirit and are acquainted with its details. Islam does not recognize any geographical, linguistic or colour bars in this respect. It puts forward its code of guidance and the scheme of its reform before all men. Whoever accepts this programme, no matter to what race, nation or country he may belong, can join the community that runs the Islamic state. But those who do not accept it are not entitled to have any hand in shaping the fundamental policy of the states. They can live within the confines of the State as non-Muslim citizens (*dhimmīs*). Specific rights and privileges have been accorded to them in the Islamic law. A *dhimmī's* life, property and honour will be fully protected, and if he is capable of any service, his services will also be made use of. He will not, however, be allowed to influence the basic policy of this ideological state. The Islamic state is based on a particular ideology and it is the community which believes in the Islamic ideology which pilots it. Here again, we notice some sort of resemblance between the Islamic and the Communist states. But the treatment meted out by the Communist states to persons holding creeds and ideologies other than its own bears no comparison with the attitude of the Islamic state. Unlike the Communist state, Islam does not impose its social principles on others by force, nor does it confiscate their properties or unleash a reign of terror by mass executions of the people and their transportation to the slave camps of Siberia. Islam does not want to eliminate its minorities, it wants to protect them and gives them the freedom to live according to their own culture. The generous and just treatment which Islam has accorded to non-Muslims in an Islamic State and the fine distinction drawn by it between justice and good and evil will convince all those who are not prejudiced against it, that the prophets sent by God accomplish their task in an altogether different manner—something radically different and diametrically opposed to the way of the false reformers who strut about here and there on the stage of history.[2]

2. This paper was written in 1939 and in it the author had dealt with the theoretical aspect of the problem only. In his later articles he has discussed the practical aspect as well. In his article on the "Rights of Non-Muslims in Islamic State" (see *Islamic Law and Constitution*, Chapter VIII, pp. 316–317). he writes:

However, in regard to a parliament or a legislature of the modern conception, which is considerably different from *shūrā* in its traditional sense, this rule could be

The Theory of the Caliphate and the Nature of Democracy in Islam

I will now try to give a brief exposition of the composition and structure of the Islamic state. I have already stated that in Islam, God alone is the real sovereign. Keeping this cardinal principle in mind, if we consider the position of those persons who set out to enforce God's law on earth, it is but natural to say that they should be regarded as representatives of the Supreme Ruler. Islam has assigned precisely this very position to them. Accordingly the Holy Qur'ān says:

> Allah has promised to those among you who believe and do righteous deeds that He will assuredly make them to succeed (the present rulers) and grant them vicegerency in the land just as He made those before them to succeed (others).

The verse illustrates very clearly the Islamic theory of state. Two fundamental points emerge from it.

1. The first point is that Islam uses the term "vicegerency" (*khilāfa*) instead of sovereignty. Since, according to Islam, sovereignty belongs to God alone, anyone who holds power and rules in accordance with the laws of God would undoubtedly be the vicegerent of the Supreme Ruler and would not be authorised to exercise any powers other than those delegated to him.

2. The second point stated in the verse is that the power ro rule over the earth has been promised to *the whole community of believers;* it has not been stated that any particular person or class among them will be raised to that position. From this it follows that all believers are repositories of the Caliphate. The Caliphate granted by God to the faithful is the popular vicegerency and not a limited one. There is no reservation in favour of any family, class or race. Every believer is a Caliph of God in his individual capacity. By virtue of this position he is individually responsible to God. The Holy Prophet has said: "Everyone of you is a ruler and everyone is

---

relaxed to allow non-Muslims to become its members provided that it has been fully ensured in the Constitution that:

i. It would be *ultra vires* of the parliament or the legislature to enact any law which is repugnant to the Qur'ān and the *Sunna.*

ii. The Qur'ān and the *Sunna* would be the chief source of the public law of the land.

iii. The head of the state or the assenting authority would necessarily be a Muslim. With these provisions ensured, the sphere of influence of non-Muslims would be limited to matters relating to the general problems of the country or to the interests of minorities concerned and their participation would not damage the fundamental requirements of Islam.

The non-Muslims cannot occupy key-posts—posts from where the ideological policy of the state can be influenced—but they can occupy general administrative posts and can act in the services of the state.

answerable for his subjects." Thus one Caliph is in no way inferior to another.

This is the real foundation of democracy in Islam. The following points emerge from an analysis of this conception of popular vicegerency:

A. A society in which everyone is a caliph of God and an equal participant in this caliphate, cannot tolerate any class divisions based on distinctions of birth and social position. All men enjoy equal status and position in such a society. The only criterion of superiority in this social order is personal ability and character. This is what has been repeatedly and explicitly asserted by the Holy Prophet:

> No one is superior to another except in point of faith and piety. All men are descended from Adam and Adam was made of clay.
>
> An Arab has no superiority over a non-Arab nor a non-Arab over an Arab; neither does a white man possess any superiority over a black man nor a black man over a white one, except in point of piety. . . .

B. In such a society no individual or group of individuals will suffer any disability on account of birth, social status, or profession that may in any way impede the growth of his faculties or hamper the development of his personality. . . .

> Listen and obey even if a negro is appointed as a ruler over you.

C. There is no room in such a society for the dictatorship of any person or group of persons since everyone is a caliph of God herein. No person or group of persons in entitled to become an absolute ruler by depriving the rank and file of their inherent right of caliphate. The position of a man who is selected to conduct the affairs of the state is no more than this; that all Muslims (or, technically speaking, all caliphs of God) delegate their caliphate to him for administrative purposes. *He is answerable to God on the one hand and on the other to his fellow "caliphs" who have delegated their authority to him.* Now, if he raises himself to the position of an irresponsible absolute ruler, that is to say a dictator, he assumes the character of a usurper rather than a Caliph, because dictatorship is the negation of popular vicegerency. No doubt the Islamic state is an all-embracing state and comprises within its sphere all departments of life, but this all-inclusiveness and universality are based upon the universality of Divine Law which an Islamic ruler has to observe and enforce. The guidance given by God about every aspect of life will certainly be enforced in its entirety. But an Islamic ruler cannot depart from these instructions and adopt a policy of regimentation on his own. He cannot force people to follow or not to follow a particular profession; to learn or not to learn a special art; to use or not to use a certain script; to wear or not to wear a certain dress and to educate or not to educate their children in a certain manner. The powers which the dictators of Russia, Germany and Italy have appropriated or which Ataturk has exercized in Turkey have not been granted by Islam to its *Amīr* (leader). Besides this, another important point is that in Islam *every individual is held personally answerable to God*. This personal resonsibility cannot be shared by anyone else. Hence, an individual enjoys full liberty to choose whichever path he likes and to develop his faculties in any direction that suits his natural gifts. If the leader obstructs him or obstructs the growth of his personality, he will himself be punished by God for this tyranny. That is precisely the reason why there is not the slightest trace of regimentation in the rule of the Holy Prophet and of his Rightly-Guided Caliphs; and

D. In such a society every sane and adult Muslim, male or female, is entitled to express his or her opinion, for each one of them is the repository of the caliphate. God has made this caliphate conditional, not upon any particular standard of wealth or competence but only upon faith and good conduct. Therefore all Muslims have equal freedom to express their opinions.

FAZLUR RAHMĀN
1919–

He graduated from the Punjab University and received his Ph.D. from Oxford University. After teaching at the University of Durham and the Institute of Islamic Studies, McGill University, he returned to Pakistan as Director of the Islamic Research Institute and as a member of the Advisory Council of Islamic Ideology, Government of Pakistan. He is currently Professor of Islamic Studies at the University of Chicago.

The Islamic Concept of State

The State organization in Islam receives its mandate from the people, i.e., the Muslim Community, and is, therefore, necessarily democratic. The Islamic theory is that there exists a group of people which has accepted to implement the will of God as revealed in the Qur'ān and whose model in history was created by the Prophet. By this acceptance such a group is constituted into a Muslim *umma*. The State is the organization to which this *umma* entrusts the task of executing its will. There is, therefore, no doubt that the Islamic State obtains its warrant from the people.

What is necessary is to ascertain what the people's *real* wants and purposes are. This procedure can be a tricky business even in developed societies because of the working of pressure groups; but in the case of developing societies where huge masses are illiterate and only a tiny minority enjoys the benefits of education, it becomes extremely difficult to ascertain what the real will of the people is through normal electoral procedures as followed in Western democracies. This is because the vested interests of various educated classes almost invariably intervene and tend to conceal the mind of the dumb masses from being correctly exressed. Under such circumstances, and particularly so long as the masses remain largely uneducated, the only direct method of giving participation to the people in the running of their own affairs is a system which starts from the grassroots like the Basic Democracies.

The all-important objectives of an Islamic State are to safeguard the safety and integrity of the State, to maintain law and order and to develop the country so that every individual in it may be able to realise his full

From Fazlur Rahmān, "Implementation of the Islamic Concept of State in the Pakistani Milieu," *Islamic Studies* 6 (1967), pp. 205–24.

potentialities and contribute to the well-being of the whole. This requires a strong central authority, capable of taking decisions and enforcing them in the interests of the progress of the country even if they may be temporarily unpopular. It is requisite that at the helm of affairs there be a strong leader with vision, capability and power of decision, as the executive head. He is to be elected by the people and must command their general confidence. An adequate administrative structure should aid him to carry out his decisions. It is of the prime importance that the administration be competent and able to identify itself with the aspirations of the people. It should be imbued with the genuine spirit of service rather than rule.

Islam commands that the affairs of the Muslims should be run by *shūrā* or mutual consultation. It is necessary, therefore, that the Head of the State be aided by a Legislative Assembly which should represent the will of the people. In our view, the Islamic concept of *shūrā-ijmā'* is not quite compatible with a multi-party system as it is practiced in modern democracies. Whereas Islam allows freedom of expression and constructive criticism in the fullest possible sense—and indeed, casts it as a religious duty— it appears to us to be averse to the creation of parties simply for the sake of opposition. It is true that one-party system has certain pitfalls, but the multi-party system seems to be beset with greater pitfalls, particularly in a developing society, since it tends to weaken responsible thought and action among many politicians. But in a state where only one party is allowed, that single party must be a dynamic party fully representing the masses. It must be a mass movement as Islam was in its early days.

Legislation in Islam is the business of the Community *as a whole*. It is, therefore, the function of the representatives of the people who sit in the Legislative Assembly to make laws. The claims of many '*ulamā*' that Islamic legislation is a function properly belonging to the '*ulamā*', is not only patently wrong but is equally falsified by the formative phase of the development of Muslim law in history. The fact is that it is the administrators who created Muslim laws and not the *fuqahā*'. It is also a fact that the *ijmā'* was regarded as the *ijmā'* of the community and not of the '*ulamā*' alone until well after the second century of the Hijrah when the concept of the *ijmā'* of the '*ulamā*' replaced that of the Community. However, it is to be admitted that expert advice will be needed on some technical aspects of legislation, religious, administrative and legal, for which adequate institutions are to be provided.

The task of the '*ulamā*' is, in fact, not to legislate or veto legislation (since no such right exists in Islam), but to constitute religious leadership for the Community. This religious leadership will help create and formulate ideas (*ijtihād*); these ideas will be discussed widely in the Community through the various media of mass-communication and when a general public opinion, i.e., *ijmā'*, has crystallized, this will be embodied in the form of law by the representatives of the people. Such law will be perfectly Islamic law. Of course, one law can be repealed or amended by another, more adequate, law and one *ijmā'* can be replaced by another. It is, thus, the twin pillars of personal thought (*ijtihād*) and collective thought (*ijmā'*) upon which the structure of Islamic legislation will rest.

Islam and Democracy

Before Islam, the Arabs had an institution called the "Assembly (*nādī*)," where the elders of the tribe or the city (for example, of Mecca) chose the head of the tribal or city government and which ran the affairs by mutual consultation. It is this institution which was further democratized by the Qur'ān, which uses for it the term "*nādī*" or "*shūrā*." The ultimate power of decision among the Arabs, who were not under any kingly, absolute or autocratic rule, rested in the elders of a tribe or a city. The change wrought by the Islamic revolution was that at the expense of the tribes, a central government was established with all the authority vested in the centre, which fully reflected the consensus of the community at large. The choice of the first Caliph Abū-Bakr, was also carried out by the elders both from the Meccan immigrants and the Medinese *Ansār* and endorsed by the whole community. In his first speech, Abū-Bakr categorically stated that he had received his mandate from the people who had asked him to implement the Qur'ān and the *Sunna,* that so long as he did their behest, he should be retained but that when they found that he was going grievously wrong, he should be deposed.

This clearly establishes that the Islamic State derives its sanction from the Islamic community and that, therefore, it is *completely* democratic. Democracy can, of course, take different forms according to the conditions prevailing in a society. In an Islamic society, particularly, with its highly centralized governmental institution, it would be quite wrong to insist that only a certain procedure is advisable or that the government must be on the pattern of a parliamentary system. In fact, the parliamentary system is obviously unsuitable for such a strong executive as is envisaged by the Qur'ān. But elections may be direct or indirect, depending on prevailing conditions. Since a developing country is likely to be faced with delicate and subtle capital issues arising out of a socio-economic development programme, the masses are in a great danger of being exploited by sectional interest and, in fact, it is the duty of the government to safeguard the larger interests of the public and not to succumb to the protestations of the educated minority groups. Once people in general become enlightened with the spread of education and with the development of industry, direct elections may well be introduced at that stage. . . .

This analysis also brings out the absurdity of the position of those who have, in recent decades, created a great deal of confusion over the concept of "the sovereignty of God." According to this contention, Muslim people are not sovereign but God is sovereign in a Muslim State. On this ground, Sayyid Abū-l-'Alā' Mawdūdī rejects democracy on principle, and in fact, has equated it with *Shirk*! His argument is that whereas in a democracy people can legislate and thus realise any aspiration they may have, Muslim people cannot do so, but their freedom is limited by God.[1] This argument has caused much confusion in recent Muslim thinking and even some educated Muslims have fallen a prey to it. . . .

But the greatest mischief wrought by this kind of stand is to confuse the religio-moral and political issues. This talk implies and sometimes it is even stated explicitly that God is politically sovereign. Any student of political history knows that the term "sovereign" as a political term is of a relatively recent coinage and denotes that definite and defined factor (or factors) in a society to which rightfully belongs *coercive force* in order to obtain obedience to its will. It is absolutely obvious that God is not sovereign in this sense and that only people can be and are sovereign, since only to them belongs ultimate coercive force, i.e., only their "Word is law" in the politically ultimate sense. It is, of course, patently true that the Qur'ān often makes statements to the effect that God is the most Supreme Judge and that His alone is the power over the heavens and the earth.[2] But it is equally true that this has no reference to political sovereignty whatever. It does not even refer to legal sovereignty. What the Qur'ān is saying is that God has bestowed a certain constitution both to this universe and to man. . . . The Qur'ān sometimes asks Muslims that when they decide matters, they should do so in accordance with the Qur'ān, and at other times, that Muslims should decide matters in accordance with justice and equity.[3] What follows from this is that the Muslims should follow the dictates of justice, whose principles have been enunciated and illustrated in the Holy Book and the practice of the Prophet.

Thus the principles enunciated in the Qur'ān are justice and fair play. This is precisely the meaning of accepting the "sovereignty of God," since the standards of justice are objective and do not depend on or even necessarily conform to, the subjective wishes of a people. People must always *aspire* to find and do justice. This obligation is accepted by the Muslim State naturally as delegated from the Muslim society, which is in the first instance constituted by the acceptance of the will of God in this sense. Once a group accepts the principles of justice as enunciated in the Qur'ān and as illustrated in the glorious example of the Prophet, the Muslim

1. Abū-l-'Alā' Mawdūdī, *The Political Theory of Islam*, (Maktaba-e-Jamā'at-e-Islāmī, Pathankot, n.d.), 29–30.
2. Qur'ān 57: 6; 114:3, etc.
3. Qur'ān 4:58 and 5:51.

society stands constituted thereby. The Muslim State is an organization set up by the Muslim society in order to implement the will of the society and no more. . . .

But, as we stated earlier, the *shūrā* institution allows full scope for criticism, provided it is purposeful and constructive. "Government by consultation" does not imply by any means that there shall be no criticism of the Government policies or of their execution. Indeed, no voice is to be stilled and no expression of opinion is to be suppressed—the only overriding condition being that this criticism or opposition is within the framework of the basic mutual confidence we have spoken of above and is, therefore, directed towards a constructive and helpful end. What is not to be tolerated is an attitude of subversion or disaffection or inviting people to unconstitutional means to overthrow a government or instilling in them a spirit of hopelessness and despair.[4] These crimes are to be regarded as cardinal crimes against the State. . . . all human rights, universally recognised, are automatically vouchsafed and guaranteed by a Government based on *shūrā*, i.e., mutual confidence. Indeed, in such a Government, even the "granting of human rights to people" sounds somewhat peculiar even if only it becomes superfluous. For, mutual confidence entails respect for each other's rights of a free conscience, life, property, honour, etc. Indeed, the "granting or guaranteeing of human rights" is a relatively modern phenomenon and has appeared in the West as a reaction to the *total* despotism obtaining in the medieval West. Like "secularism," guaranteeing of human rights also has a historical context within a segment of history and in that context it takes on full meaning. It is also because of this historical background that Western Constitutions talk of "human rights," but not of citizens' obligations. For an Islamic State, rights and obligations are the two sides of the same coin and entail each other; neither can be understood without involving the other. . . .

Administration

The administration of the state should be headed by a person who is capable of effectively running the affairs of the state. He is to be elected by the will of the people as defined and described in the preceding Section. . . .

The Head of State in Islam is a concentration of all executive powers, civil, military and what are technically called "religious." Thus, he is the Chief Administrator, both in civil and religious matters, and is also the Supreme Commander of the Armed Forces. His being head of "religious" matters does not imply that he is a kind of Islamic Pope. He does not lay

4. Qur'ān 4:83.

down or define the theological dogma by himself as is done by the Pope in Christianity. Rather this function vests in the community as a whole, thanks to the institution of *ijmā'*, under the leadership of the *'ulamā'* and other creative thinkers. But what it does mean is that the ultimate control and direction of the practical religious life of the community vests in the Head. For example, how the mosques are to be manned and run, how the religious schooling is to be done and what religious curricula are to be taught, etc., is his responsibility. If this is not done, the state cannot avoid a bifurcation of functions into secular and religious, which is the essence of a secular state. Many Muslim societies, in general, and Pakistan, in particular, have inherited this dichotomy of society into the religious and the political authority, which, in the case of a country like Pakistan, has been accentuated by over a century of foreign rule. This ugly un-Islamic legacy of medieval-cum-foreign rule has to be eliminated and the Head of the State, i.e., government machinery, must take over full reins of total, indivisible, rule.

It has been a matter of some difference of opinion whether a Head of State in Islam may exercise fullfledged and complete powers of legislation. In the second century of the Hijrah, Ibn al-Muqaffa' strongly advised the 'Abbāsid Caliph al-Mansūr to exercise powers of *ijtihād* in matters of legislation with a view to ending the conflict of legal opinion among the Muslims, which was causing a great deal of confusion. The Caliph, however, did not do so. The Mughal Emperor Akbar, acting on the advice of his confidants, declared himself an absolute *Mujtahid*, but this did not work. The Amīr of the Jamā'at-i-Islāmī, Sayyid Abū-l-'Alā' Mawdūdī, advocates the same in his tractate, and gives to the head of State, the right of absolute veto in legislation over the "council of advisers" which he envisages.[5] However, the practice of the community throughout the centuries has been against it. It is true that later rulers, notably the Ottoman Sultans, promulgated *Farmāns*, but this was either due to administrative needs—which is always allowed in Islam—or because the *'ulamā'* did not allow a rethinking of the *Sharī'a* Law, which forced the rulers to make their own enactments and it is this process which ultimately resulted in the secularism of Mustafā Kemāl, the Atatürk. There was, of course, no effective *ijmā'* or *shūrā* institution in existence.

The practice of the *Khulafā' Rāshidūn* seems to have been that on all questions of major import they used to consult the effective leaders of Muslim opinion who were endowed with practical wisdom. This was the form *shūrā* took and usually this was enforced. Sometimes, however, as has been pointed out earlier on, when, e.g. the Caliph 'Umar or Abū-Bakr felt strongly that the opinion tendered by the majority of the

---

5. *Political Theory of Islam*, op. cit., 58.

shūrā-members would result in a capital mistake of policy, they enforced
their own opinion supported even by a small minority; but they always
went on trying to convince the majority of the soundness of their stand.
Some process like this seems necessary and should be applied now but, of
course, the form has changed. Since a *shūrā* or *ijmā‘* institution, i.e., a
national legislature, has come into existence, which represents the will of
the people, and since the Head of the State also has in the legislature
members who can put forward and explain his views effectively, the decision of the legislature in law-making should be final. If, however, a split
occurs between the stand of the Head of the State and the legislature as a
whole on a capital issue affecting the nation, a reference may be made to
the people in the way described in the preceding Section. When the legislature is not in session, the Head of the State can always issue orders carrying full legal force until they are confirmed or dropped by the legislature in
their meeting at the proper time. At times of national emergency, of
course, the Head assumes total powers of legislation in the interests of
safeguarding security and integrity of the State and the territories of Pakistan. This is in keeping with the pronouncement of the *fuqahā’* who even
go so far as to say that temporarily, i.e. for an indefinite period, the Head
of the State has the power to suspend the operation of the *Sharī‘a* if he
deems this necessary. This principle has been given effect systematically in
Morocco for some time.

Since the Head of an Islamic State is the concentrate of such colossal
powers, which are vested in him Islamically to safeguard the interests of
the Muslim community, he is directly responsible to them. For this reason,
this power can be wielded only by a person who is capable, hard-working,
and at whose centre of interests lies the interest of the community and the
country. He should be a person who generally commands the respect of
the people on this account. It should be noted that sincerity and efficacy
are both equally important for this office. For any major breach of public
confidence, the Head may be deposed after an overwhelming vote of the
legislature against him on that score. The issue, however, which is to be
the subject of such a vote, must be concerned with some capital breach of
trust affecting the life of the country. This is because, since the Head is
elected for a given number of years and is not there for his whole life as
was the case with rulers in old days, he cannot be harassed by controver-
sies over small issues. For this reason also the Head of the State may not
be sued in any court while he is in office.

The Head of the State will work with a Council of Ministers, who
should be men capable, sound of judgement, of good character and in
whose hearts the interest of the nation lies supreme. They must be effective
in their spheres of responsibility. To assist the Head of the State, and
under the Ministers, there shall be various departments or ministries

staffed by capable and sincere personnel dedicated to the task of nation-building and imbued with the spirit of Islamic ideology. . . .

It is the primary duty of the state to safeguard public law and order and internal security. All those forces which have the potentiality for disturbing the law and order situation or endangering security have to be severely curbed. We have had occasions to refer to the Qur'ān earlier to the effect that even the broadcasting of such news may be curbed as is likely to endanger the public morale. In our country, particularly, religious sectarianism and communal issues always threaten to flare up. Various journals issued by various groups and sects publish articles which tend to inflame their opponents. Worse still, many of these so-called religious journals write maliciously against the government and endeavour to undermine the public confidence in the state machinery. People must be saved from their mischief; they are an insidious poison.

Above all, it is the duty of the State to effectively guard the frontiers of the country and guarantee the integrity of the territories of the Muslim State. In fact, this is the first charge laid upon a Muslim State. An effective Armed Force, equipped with the most modern and powerful weapons, has always to be kept as a stand-by. It should be borne in mind that, according to Islam, devoted public service is a genuine form of 'ibādāt [worship]. This spirit has to be fully instilled in the public servants and the proper morale infused into them. But to serve the nation in guarding its integrity i.e., to work selflessly in the Armed Services of the State, is a paramount form of 'ibādāt. Whereas the Qur'ān speaks of fasting only in one passage, almost one-third of the entire Qur'ān is devoted to the building up of an effective power-machine to safeguard the Muslim interests and territories and the Qur'ān insistently says that God is theirs who are prepared to lay down their lives for the sake of the defence of the Muslim territories. . . .

We have already noted that the people in a Muslim State are the sovereign power in law-making. We have assigned the correct meaning to the term "sovereignty of God," which in no way hinders, but on the contrary, provides the necessary frame-work of moral principles for the exercise of the legislative right of the people. Within the frame-work of these moral principles, which may not be transgressed—and which are, indeed, universally recognized by all humanity to be valid—the community has the absolute right to make laws. The Qur'ān itself is not a book of laws but is the Divine teaching and guidance for humanity. Such quasi-laws as do occur in the Qur'ān are not meant to be *literally* applied in all times and climes; the principles on which these legal or quasi-legal pronouncements rest have to be given fresh embodiments in legislative terms. In this process of legislation the twin principles of *ijtihād* and *ijmā'* play the most crucial role. They bestow upon law whatever necessary permanence it requires and also the necessary elements of change and dynamism that it always needs in order to realize the ideals of a changing, progressing and developing society. *Ijtihād* means that individuals "exercise themselves" to think out new solutions of problems on the basis of Islamic principles. This activity will naturally be principally participated in by those who are both learned and have insight in the teachings of Islam. It is sometimes asserted by those who call themselves " *'ulamā'* " that a peculiar unknown kind of capacity is required for exercising *ijtihād,* including, so it is said, the study of a certain prescribed course of books and materials. This assertion is not only historically groundless but patently false. What is required is a good acquaintance with Islam—the closer the acquaintance, of course, the better—and a power of thinking. There is no definite point at which some mysterious "*ijtihād*-capacity" arises; indeed, skill in the Islamic field is just like skill in any other field. This quality can be recognized by the Community at large and requires no occult or obscurantist tests on the part of self-styled *'ulamā'* to judge the qualities of a *mujtahid.* It follows that *ijtihād* of people will vary on different subjects according to their thoughts, points of view, educational equipment and natural endowments. This fact has always been recognized by the classical *mujtahids* themselves. The results of these individual efforts at *ijtihād* will naturally be put at the disposal of the community at large and particularly the educated section of the community in varying degrees, through the various media of information and publicity. The more an issue is important and fundamental, the more it is likely to involve the entire community—like the issue of the creation of Pakistan itself. That issue affords a striking illustration of how the over-powering will of the community can overrule the almost united voice of those who call themselves *'ulamā'.* These issues will then be widely discussed and over a period of time a well-informed body of public opinion will emerge with certain different shades. This crystallization is called *ijmā',* i.e., the consensus of the voice of the community. It is this voice of the community which shall determine legislation.

The situation we have envisaged requires an enlightened class of religious leaders. We must repeat that our present religious leadership is unable to fulfil this function by any stretch of imagination. The intolerable insufficiency and out-moddedness of their curriculum must necessarily condemn them to this position. But besides such a class, if and when it does come into existence, *ijtihād* may be performed by any competent person or persons, whether their vocation is "religious" or not, since *ijtihād,* as has been defined above, is not the prerogative of any class. The question of the creation of Pakistan we have cited as an example. The question of modern education and, indeed, of the education of women is another example which may be cited and so on. *Ijtihād* is really an attempt at thinking and nobody ever either "gave" any one the right to think or "confiscated" this right from him. Man is a thinking machine, and if he is properly fed and educated, he will inevitably think, The *'ulamā'*, however, represent *ijtihād* as something highly technical, which is patently false in the sense we have described. However, there will always be certain technical points in legislation involving various other technicalities—socio-economic, technological, etc. There is also, of course, the fact that the more learned a person is in Islam on correct lines and, consequently, the more insight he has, the better *ijtihād* he will perform. This aspect also at points may need expert advice, e.g. when one tries to trace the historical development of a legal notion in Islam and when one tries to find out as to what, for example, the Holy Prophet intended to perform by a certain measure, etc., etc. There is, therefore, need for a body of experts to which recourse should be had on technical and Islamic questions of legislation in the narrow sense of the term. But even after the experts' advice, the final decision remains with the community and its representatives in the legislature.

The body of opinion, as crystallized in public in the way we have just described, shall be embodied in legislative form by persons who have been elected by the community as their representatives to discharge this function. It is this legislative body which is the supreme law-maker. The only force which conditions it and which contains it absolutely, is the will of the community which is the only sovereign power so far as the legislation is concerned.

It will be seen that the will of the people, which we have termed *ijmā'*, will not be monolithic, but will always allow shades of difference of opinion. It is naturally the generally prevailing opinion which will be formulated as law. It is quite possible, nevertheless, that a minority view on a certain issue is the better opinion and nearer to the truth. But so long as the law remains in force, it will be regarded as the *ijmā'* of the people and as such commanding obedience from every citizen. In the meantime, it will be open for the holders of the minority opinion to propagate their views in the public at large and in the legislative body itself so that it becomes the majority opinion. Thus, one *ijmā'* can be replaced by another, more adequate, *ijmā'* and one law amended or repealed by another. The doctrine held by many of our religious doctors that the *ijmā'* of bye-gone times cannot be repealed or replaced is a merest dogma without any foundation. Neither the Qur'ān nor the Sunna has anything at all to this effect. Indeed, the "closing of the door of *ijtihād*" and the irrepealability of earlier *ijmā'* were the twin doctrines whereby Islamic progress committed suicide.

The law, as enacted by the legislatures, together with the moral basis on which it is enacted, shall be administered through a judicial system which shall be independent of the executive. The Qur'ān and the Prophet on numerous occasions and in many different contexts have emphasized the paramount necessity of the dispensation of unadulterated justice. Perhaps no other ailment of human society has been denounced by Islam in such emphatic terms as corruption of the judicial machinery. . . .

International Relations

Islam enjoins positive peace and goodwill towards all peoples and nations of the world. Indeed, it says addressing the entire humanity, "Enter ye all into peace, O, mankind."[6] This is because Islam envisages the entire world inhabited by the human race as a peaceful order devoted to the well-being of man. In persuance of this over-all objective, Islam asks the Muslims to keep their pacts and the international obligations flowing from those pacts. Indeed, the Qur'ān goes so far as to say that the Muslims should keep the sanctity of international pacts even against their potential enemies.[7] The Qur'ān insists that Muslims should not break pacts unless others have broken them unilaterally.[8]

The other side of this picture, however, is that Islam calls upon Muslims to back up their pacts with physical might so that other peoples may be deterred from breaking these pacts and may not fall into the cheap temptation of unilaterally setting them at naught. In such cases the Muslims must take immediate action which shall be an example to others. . . .

The Muslims must contribute adequately to the promotion and establishment of a sane, progressive and viable world-order. In this sphere, Islam with its message of universal equality, brotherhood and cooperation on a moral plan rather than political expediency, has something vital to contribute which neither the West is in a position to do nor yet the Communist World, since both of these are caught up in a desperate struggle of power-politics. It is, however, obvious that Muslim States must come together in some significant sense before their voice can tell upon the world situation. The import of the preceding pages makes it abundantly clear that a Muslim out of unison with other Muslims is not really a Muslim at all according to the Qur'ān and the Sunna of the Prophet. It is, therefore, imperatively necessary that a Muslim State addresses itself to the task of cementing inter-Muslim unity, not in order to exclude the rest of the world, but simply in order to contribute positively to the rest of the world.

It is only in this way, viz., through the leavening of the emerging world-order with Islamic ideals and aspirations that Islam can really and effectively spread in the world. . . .

6. Qur'ān 2:207.
7. Qur'ān 5:13; IX:7.
8. Qur'ān 9:7, 12–13.

MUHAMMAD ZIA UL-HAQ
1924–

After attending St. Stephen's College of Delhi University (1940–44), he embarked upon a military career, serving with the British Indian Army in Southeast Asia, and from 1945 on as an officer in the armored corps. In 1969, he was promoted to brigadier general and assigned as an advisor to the Jordan Arab Army for two years. In 1976, President Zulfikar 'Alī Bhutto appointed him Chief of Staff, and in 1977, Zia ul-Haq led a successful *coup d'état* to take over leadership of Pakistan.

Introduction of an Islamic System

Today is 'Id-i-Milad al-Nabi, birthday of the Holy Prophet (peace be upon him), which is an important milestone in our religious and national life. Although this day is celebrated by the nation every year, it is for the first time that its celebrations on a gigantic scale have been organized officially.

We owe so much to that great personality, whose birthday we are celebrating today, that we cannot repay the debt of his teachings even if we were to devote our entire life-time giving expression to our gratitude. The greatest act of benevolence which we owe to this benefactor of humanity is that he brought about a peaceful and enlightened revolution, which not only reformed both the individual and the society but also provided them a guarantee for their eternal deliverance. It is a miracle of Prophet Muhammad (peace be upon him) that his own life provided a practical demonstration of this revolution. Not only that he and his family ordered their lives according to the Islamic teachings but he also established an ideological society whose glad tidings had been given in divine revelations.

We claim to be the followers of this great personality, but if we look at our practical life and our social milieu we have to admit with regret that we have gone astray from the path prescribed for us by Islam. We have among us people who have turned their backs even on such obligatory duties as prayer, fasting, *zakāt* and *hajj* (pilgrimage) and are leading a life wedded to materialism instead of devoting it to social welfare, justice and fairplay.

Today we stand at the cross-road of our life. God forbid that we should

From *Introduction of the Islamic System in Pakistan* (Islamabad: Government of Pakistan, 1979), pp. 1–7, 16–19.

take to the path of misguidance and thus end up in disaster. The second course open to us is that we recant forthwith, ask forgiveness of Allah for our sins and spend the rest of our lives according to the teachings of Islam and attain bliss both in this world and the life hereafter.

The people of this country have already determined the path they have to take. It is obligatory on every Muslim to lead an Islamic way of life. Collectively also we had resolved even before the birth of Pakistan that we shall establish a separate homeland where we could live according to our own faith. That generation is still alive among us, whose voices reverberated through every nook and corner of South Asia with the slogan:

What is the meaning of Pakistan?
There is no god but one God.

Objective Resolution

Islam occupied a pivotal position in the Objectives Resolution adopted by the first Constituent Assembly after the establishment of Pakistan. The twenty-two points prepared by the 'ulamā' (religious scholars) of various schools of thought also correctly determined our goal. The constitutions of 1956 and 1962 also recognised the basic relationship between Islam and Pakistan. Again in the 1973 constitution the same relationship has been preserved. All major political parties despite their other differences are agreed that the Islamic system should be introduced in this country. This makes it amply clear that the ideology for which this nation had achieved Pakistan is intact and our people are determined to see this ideology permeate their day-to-day life.

It is Allah's beneficence that the present Government has been able to fulfil these aspirations of the people. In the short period of one and a half years so much work has been done that I am today formally announcing the introduction of the Islamic system in the country. May Allah bless our efforts!

In this connection, a few measures have already been adopted about which I would like to speak briefly. It is our misfortune that we did not acquaint our new generation with the ideology that formed the basis of the establishment of Pakistan. Our text-books and curriculum only drifted us away from our orbit. Consequently, we had to devise a new educational policy to keep us within our intellectual orbit. The basic aim of this policy is to prepare a new generation wedded to the ideology of Pakistan and Islam.

The first step that had to be taken to achieve this end was the revision of the text-books which has already been completed. The revised books will be taught from April 1 this year, while books written afresh will, *Insha' Allāh*,[1] be introduced from the next year. Not only that, the English me-

---

1. *Insha' Allāh:* If God wills.

dium schools will also be switching over gradually to the national language, that is, Urdu, as their medium of instruction from the next year.
Simultaneously, appropriate changes have been made in the programmes
of our media of mass communication especially Radio and T.V. so as to
project our national identity.

Sharī'a Benches

The second important step is the establishment of *Sharī'a* Benches, which I
announced at the beginning of the present Islamic year. In the light of the
views and suggestions received about the *Sharī'a* Benches, the relevant law
has been amended and enforced as part of the Constitution. It means that
every citizen can now move the judiciary to declare a law either wholly or
partially un-Islamic. In other words, the supremacy of *Sharī'a* (Islamic
Law) has been established over the law of the land.

It will not suffice merely to reframe laws according to Islam, but it is
also essential that everybody should be able to get justice without delay
and difficulty. . . .

Another step taken was the setting up of a Post-Graduate Faculty of
Sharī'a at the Islamabad University about which I have spoken earlier
also. This faculty has been established because along with the enforcement
of Islamic laws, a need was being felt of experts who besides being familiar
with the existing laws should have a thorough grounding in Islamic jurisprudence and *Sharī'a*. . . .

New Measures

The measures that I am announcing today relate to certain aspects of
socio-economic welfare. Before going into them in detail, I would like to
stress that Islam is basically welfare-oriented, progressive and enlightened
religion which establishes justice. It has the capacity to meet the changing
needs and requirements of every age. More than the rich and the strong, it
protects the poor and the weak and as between man and woman, an
employer and an employee, and a Muslim and a non-Muslim it safeguards
their rights. It establishes a balance in matters temporal and spiritual.

Research has proved that today's so-called modern and developed societies have in fact borrowed a lot from the teachings of Islam, which were
enforced as a complete code of life some fourteen hundred years ago. It
shows that Islam's principles are eternal and its laws immortal. With the
passage of time, their universality and immutability becomes manifest.

It is not easy to reform a degenerate society. It requires courage, time and
continuous struggle. Those who think that this work can be done in a day or
a week are ignoring the reality perhaps due to some expediency. I do not

wish to go into the details of these difficulties but suffice it to say that it is after a year's hard work that the Islamic Ideology Council, religious scholars both within and outside the country, experts of the Ministries of Law and Religious Affairs, and members of the Cabinet, have been able to finalise certain selected measures, which I am announcing today.

I know there are many other measures on which work is continuing with diligence and devotion. In some fields encouraging progress has been made while in others certain difficulties are being encountered for the present. Efforts are being made to find their solutions through research and inter-petation of Islamic laws. For instance, everyone is agreed on changing the present economic system but this is possible only when an alternative system which meets the needs of Islam is evolved. Experts engaged on this work are of the view that an interest-free Islamic economic system can be introduced by stages. *Insha' Allāh* [If God Wills] this work will be com-pleted in three years.

To begin with, we have picked up *zakāt* and *'ushr*. The main considera-tion for selecting *zakāt* is that it is one of the important pillars of Islam and is related to the economic and welfare aspects of society. The draft order on *zakāt* and *'ushr* is being issued today.

Their main features are:

> Wealth and financial assets on which *zakāt* is leviable, the rate of *zakāt* and the purposes for which *zakāt* collections can be expended. Under the *Sharī'a*, it is obligatory on the Government of the day to make arrangements for total or partial collection of *zakāt* and *'ushr* (tax on agricultural produce) from those Muslims whose financial position warrants payment of *zakāt*. The same obligation has been prescribed for the Government in the Constitution of Pakistan. Two steps are necessary for fulfilling this obligation: a. that a *zakāt* Fund should be created; and,b. a system should be instituted under which arrangements are made for the assessment, collection and expending of *zakāt*. . . .

National Economy

I have spoken on several occasions about the bad state of our national economy. There were many factors responsible for the wrecking of na-tional economy. The policy of nationalisation which was applied indis-criminately also played a major role in it. Islam confers the right to possess property both on the citizen and the state. The public and the private sectors are wheels of the same cart. Unless the two wheels move in unison, the nation cannot move towards progress and development. . . .

Another significant aspect of the Islamic economic system is to rid the society of the curse of interest. We wish to pursue this objective in right earnestness but it should be appreciated that it can be attained only gradually. I feel happy to announce that from the next financial year, the House Building Finance Corporation will provide financial assistance on the basis of sharing of income accruing from rent. . . .

This procedure will lessen the burden of people who build houses with financial assistance from the Government. . . . The Ministry of Finance had been directed to work out a procedure whereby the National Investment Trust and the Investment Corporation of Pakistan could operate on equity basis instead of interest. The Ministry has drawn up a plan which has been approved by the Government. . . .

Punitive Aspects

So far I have devoted myself to the welfare aspects of Islam. I will now briefly touch on the punitive aspects which form part of the Islamic Code of Life.

The extreme limit of punishment prescribed in the Qur'ān and the Sunna for various crimes is called *hadd*. There are only four *hudūd*, namely, drinking, adultery, theft, and imputation of adultery (*qadhf*).

1. Drinking:
   a. Drinking is an evil which breeds many other vices. To wipe it out, prohibition is being enforced from today for all Pakistanis throughout the country. This restriction will not apply to non-Muslim Pakistanis for purposes of their religious ceremonies and the foreigners within the confines of their embassies, and residences.
   b. Together with the use of liquor and other intoxicants, their manufacture, possession, purchase and sale and their import and export are also prohibited. However, permission can be obtained from the Government for the manufacture of intoxicating chemicals for medical and scientific purposes.

2. Adultery:
   Adultery is an evil which has been condemned by all world religions. From today, the Islamic punishment for this crime has been enforced. It will be applicable to all forms of adultery, whether the offence is committed with or without the consent of the parties.

3. Theft and Robbery:
   Punishments for theft and robbery are laid down in every society, but Islam has fixed relatively harsher punishments which are designed to act as a deterrent and also aim at reforming the criminals as far as possible. These crimes have been eliminated to a very large extent in countries where these Islamic punishments are in force.

4. Qadhf (False Allegation):
Islam protects not only life and property but also human dignity and honour. The purpose of this law is to safeguard the people from unfounded allegations and imputations.

The punishments laid down for the four offences are known as *hudūd*. And this extreme punishment is imposed only when to prove the guilt the conditions laid down by *Sharī'a* are duly fulfilled. . . .

B. Z. KAIKAUS

In September 1979, retired Supreme Court Justice B. Z. Kaikaus filed a petition before the Sharīʿa Bench of the Lahore High Court in which he maintained that Pakistan's political system was "repugnant to Islam." The petition and the protracted judicial hearings that followed drew national attention and highlighted the myriad issues related to Islamization in Pakistan. However, in December 1980, the Sharīʿa Bench Court dismissed the case.

Kaikaus vs. the Government of Pakistan

Petition Invoking

1. The jurisdiction of this Court as the judicial *Ululamr* [authority] for the Province of the Punjab,

2. Article 199 of the Constitution of Pakistan,

3. All other jurisdiction vested in this Court,

    for (i) a declaration that Pakistan is a sacred Kingdom of Allah and the Holy Prophet Muhammad (Peace and blessings of Allah be on him) whose sole sovereign and law-giver is Allah, whose only law is Allah's will as it apears from the Holy Qur'ān and Sunna which are the eternal and immutable law governing the Muslim *umma* till the Day of Judgment,

    (ii) for an injunction to all persons exercising any authority in Pakistan to act in accordance with Allah's will as it appears from the Holy Qur'ān and Sunna and not to take any action which conflicts with the Holy Qur'ān and Sunna in the slighest degree:
AND

    (iii) for various reliefs flowing from the Holy Qur'ān and Sunna being in force.

    1. Pakistan is an ideological State whose sole sovereign is Allah, and whose law called the *Sharīʿa* is contained in the Holy Qur'ān and Sunna. But the *Sharīʿa* has not been recognized as law and Allah is not being

From *Writ Petition No. 42 of 1976* (Lahore: Lahore High Court), pp. 2–7, 25–33, 60–66.

obeyed. The sole object of this proceeding is that Allah be obeyed by those in authority in the country. Should those in authority accept that the Holy Qur'ān and Sunna are in force all that the court has to do is to determine the consequences of this admission,

2. About fourteen hundred years ago was revealed the Holy Qur'ān, the pure word of Allah; to worship and obey Whom, is the passion and the sole object of our lives.

> "And I did not create Jinn and man except for this that they worship and obey Me."   (Qur'ān 51:56)

And from the moment of its revelation the Holy Qur'ān became the supreme and the unalterable law governing the whole of the Muslim *umma* till the Day of Judgment and it became the duty of every Muslim individual, every Muslim society and Muslim State, not only to obey that law, but to propagate, defend and enforce that law, to enjoin right and forbid wrong in accordance with that law, and to carry on *jihād* against injustice and evil to the extent possible.

> "You are the best of *ummas* created for mankind. You enjoin right, you forbid wrong, and you believe in Allah."   (Qur'ān 3:110). . . .

3. Every State where political power is with the Muslims has to be an ideological Islamic State and a Kingdom of Allah, because on account of *lā illāha ilallāh* [there is no God but God] and on account of clear commands in the Holy Qur'ān, the Muslim is debarred from obeying any but Allah. For the Muslims there is no option whatsoever in the matter unless they choose to be non-Muslims. So far as Pakistan is concerned there were special reasons too why it had to be an Allah's kingdom, for Pakistan had been created with the avowed object of enabling the Muslims to order their lives in accordance with the injuctions and traditions or their faith and immense were the sacrifices made by the Muslim masses for the achievement of the Pakistan that they dearly loved. Pakistan is admittedly an ideological Islamic State. Article 2 of its Constitution says the religion of the State is Islam.

4. (1) It is the duty of the Government of every ideological State to make all effort to realize the ideology of the State. In the case of Islamic ideology the substance of which it *tawhīd* [unity] and implicit obedience of Allah, it will appear when that ideology is examined, that the Government is legally bound to make all effort:

> (a) for the enforcement of the injunctions of the Holy Qur'ān and sunna which embody the divine law of the State:
> (b) for the attainment of the Islamic object of human life that is a passion for His worship and complete submission to Him;

(c) for strengthening in the Muslim mind faith in the unseen that is, in Allah and the hereafter. . . .

(e) for creating in the society on the one hand a spirit of complete submission to Allah and on the other hand a spirit of absolute freedom from any restraint proceeding from man, a spirit of self-respect and of regard for rights of all human beings. . . .

(i) for the strengthening of the brotherhood and for the practice of absolute equality and respect for the believers.

(2) The duty of the government is the right of the Muslims of this State. It goes without saying that in an ideological State and particularly in an Islamic State no person in authority is entitled to function unless he is capable on account of his mental make-up and otherwise to discharge his duty of realizing the ideology of the State and he does actually strive for it. In case of his failure to discharge his duties properly there is a right in every Muslim to approach the Court for appropriate relief.

5. Had those who were in charge of the affairs of Pakistan done their duty we would today be on the top of the world. We would today have in Pakistan a society of truth and justice and piety, versed in science and technology, a society the members of which were determined to perform the function which Allah has assigned to the Muslim *umma*, and which will presently be explained, a society whose success has been guaranteed by Allah.

6. When we examine how the governments of this country have acted in relation to their duty to realize the ideology of the State we are faced with an amazing situation. In the whole of human history it will not be possible to find an example of such divergence between word and deed. This country had been created for the specific purpose that Muslims may order their lives in accordance with the injunctions and the spirit of their faith, and there is no end to the public declarations that have been made from the day Pakistan came into existence up to this day to the effect that Pakistan is an Islamic State whose ideology is contained in the Holy Qur'ān and Sunna, and that there can be no law in this country which is not consistent with the Holy Qur'ān and Sunna. The objectives resolution which declared that this country was to be governed in accordance with Islamic ideology was passed in 1949, and this resolution was incorporated in the preamble of every one of the our Constitutions framed for Pakistan. In the body of every Constitution too the principle that all laws must conform to the Holy Qur'ān and Sunna was accepted. The *'ulamā'* of this country met together to frame points of Islamic law as to which there was no disagreement and they framed as many as 22 points. . . . Article 2 of the present Constitution says the religion of the State is Islam The oaths of the office of the President, the Governors, the Central Ministers and Provincial Ministers, Speakers, Deputy Speakers, and members of National and Provin-

cial Assemblies, every one of these oaths says that Islamic ideology is the basis of the creation of Pakistan and its preservation is the duty of the functionary taking the oath. On the top of all this are two judgments of the Supreme Court of Pakistan confirming Islamic ideology. Is it not surprising then that the actual conditions prevailing in Pakistan are that twenty eight years have passed since Pakistan came into existence but not even one of the injunctions of the Holy Qur'ān and Sunna has as yet been recognised as part of the law of the land and in accordance with the present Constitution a consideration of Islamic law may take seven or eight years. This is the State of the law. The other obligation of the governments was to try to establish here an ideal Islamic Society. Not only was no step taken in that direction but we have been moving away from Islam. Today we are facing in this country disunity, bitter hostility between political parties, parochialism, irreligiousness, impiety, obscenity, corruption and lack of respect for law and order. Wealth, power, ostentation, luxury and pleasure-pursuits are our life values and our great failing is falsehood which pervades every aspect of life. There is a general feeling of frustration, that it is impossible to remain honest in this country.

7. The main cause of all this is secular politics. Between Islam and secular politics there is a direct contradiction. The life values of the one are directly the opposite of the other. No government of this country ever accepted the Islamic goal or ideal which it regarded as too puritanic. As it did not accept the ideal, it did not accept the law which was only a means of attaining the ideal. This society having thus been left without an ideal its moral basis slipped and when the moral basis disappears the society must be destroyed.

8. The submission of the petitioners is that Pakistan being an ideological state and the Holy Qur'ān and Sunna being in force in Pakistan, the law of this State is in fact entirely different from what it is at present assumed to be. The Supreme Court of Pakistan had in two judgments declared that Allah was the only source of law but no one tried to work out of the logical results of this pronouncement. It will be quite correct to say that the reliefs asked for in this proceeding are the natural and necessary consequence of the pronouncement of the Supreme Court of Pakistan. . . .

> There is no such thing as a man-made law in an Islamic state. Even the Holy Prophet (peace and blessings of Allah be on him) possessed no powers of legislation proper though whatever he said was binding. . . .
>
> All law is based ultimately on moral considerations and so far as morality is concerned the Holy Qur'ān is a complete Code. . . . If then the Holy Qur'ān has fully covered the field of what is right and what is wrong then any so-called legislation will only be implementation of what has been stated in the Holy Qur'ān and at least every so-called legislation will be subordinate to the Holy Qur'ān and Sunna and its validity will be determined by the Holy Qur'ān. . . .

The Muslim is only bound by *Sharī'a* the divine law. . . . there are only four sources of Islamic law as will appear from any treatise dealing with Islamic law. They are the Holy Qur'ān, Sunna, *ijmā'* and *qiyas*. *Ijmā'* is the consensus of the learned, and *qiyas* is a form of reasoning. Both are concerned with the interpretation of the Holy Qur'ān and Sunna and not with any legislation. The members of legislatures are neither learned men nor are they from their objectives, their life values and their attitudes, qualified to be entrusted with the task of discovering Allah's will and they are claiming to have authority which even the Holy Prophet did not possess. It is quite obvious that the *Sharī'a* cannot be produced by legislation. That is divine law contained in the Holy Qur'ān and Sunna and is eternal. It cannot be claimed that any eternal law can be produced by the so-called process of legislation, and whatever general orders be passed they must have some inferior status. The idea of legislation is really the result of the Muslims becoming slaves of the westerners and is foreign to Islam. The plea that Allah delegated His authority to the people and the people appointed their representative is wholly misconceived. There is no warrant for the proposition that Allah ever delegated any legislative authority to the people when He delegated none to the Holy Prophet. Logically as well as historically there is no basis for this doctrine. . . .

Historically there never has been any legislation in Islam, not even in our best period when our civilization was at its height. . . . When we gave democratic principles to Europe, we ruled only with the Holy Qur'ān and Sunna and with no other law. Even now there is no legislation in Saudi Arabia.

It is the impact of Western democracy that has made us accept legislatures. . . .

It is pertinent to point out that the petitioner is asking for nothing more than the removal of an inconsistency. This State does by its words accept that it is an Islamic State and there is no end to the repetition of this declaration and insistence on it. Yet there is a total refusal to work out of the consequences of this state being an Islamic State and to put them into practice. This has been done for more than 27 years. This inconsistency must end. Another aspect of the inconsistency is, that in two judgments already the Supreme Court of Pakistan has held that the only source of law in this State is the Almighty. His commands are contained in the Qur'ān and Sunna and they certainly are in force. An inconsistency is like saying two and two make five. . . .

The following reliefs are prayed for:

1. A declaration that Pakistan is the sacred Kingdom of Allah and the Holy Prophet Muhammad (peace and blessings of Allah be on him) whose sole sovereign and law-giver is Allah, whose law is only Allah's will, to be determined from the Holy Qur'ān and Sunna, every word of

which is binding, and which together constitute the *Sharī'a*, the divine immutable law, that the government of this sacred state is to be carried on only on behalf of Allah, in the name of Allah, and in accordance with the commands of Allah and that every person in authority, in order to decide what action he has to take, puts only one question to himself, what is the will of Allah, and an injunction in terms of the above declaration to all the respondents to act in accordance with the Holy Qur'ān and Sunna, and not to take any action which conflicts with the Holy Qur'ān and Sunna in the slightest degree.

2. A declaration coupled with an appropriate injunction that the Muslim being bound only by the divine law, i.e. the *Sharī'a*, the *Sharī'a* is the only law in this State, the status of the remaining so-called laws including the Constitution being only that of orders whose validity depends on their acceptance as Allah's will by the judicial *ululamr* or the judiciary, and that any order or any so-called law including the Constitution, which is in conflict with any part of the Holy Qur'ān and Sunna including the directions relating to justice and righteousness is null and void.

3. A declaration that the basic principle of Conduct being *tawhīd*, all Muslims of Pakistan are absolutely free persons except that they are to obey the Holy Qur'ān and Sunna and any order passed in execution of the will of Allah as it appears therein, and that they are entitled to resist by all means in their power including the use of force, any order which it is clear to them is not Allah's will and in case of doubt to have the matter settled by a recourse to a Court.

4. A declaration that Article 2 of the Constitution is the only article which represents the true basis of this State and that all those articles of the Constitution which are in conflict with the Holy Qur'ān and Sunna are null and void, and no citizen is to be loyal to the Constitution to the extent that it conflicts with the Holy Qur'ān and Sunna, that the present Constitution is an infidel Constitution in as much as it confers on human beings absolute authority to make any law they like and it does not accept that any provision in conflict with the Holy Qur'ān and Sunna is void, because it permits all the members of the Senate and Assemblies to be non-Muslims, and an injunction to all respondents directing them to act in accordance with what is stated above. . . .

6. A declaration coupled with an appropriate injunction that all provisions which take away the jurisdiction of the courts in respect of any action taken by the executive or in respect of any legal dispute whatsoever and any provision which directs the courts to determine matters except in accordance with the Holy Qur'ān and Sunna are null and void and that all matters have to be decided in accordance with the Holy Qur'ān and Sunna.

7. A declaration that all provision which confer any privileges on any person that his action shall not be called in question or that he shall not be bound to answer to any charge or would not be amenable to any process of court of could be tried only on a complaint or other proceed-

ings by the Government or some officer and any provision whatsoever which confers a privilege on any person on account of his office or status or similar reason, are all null and void.

8. A declaration that all persons governing Pakistan are disqualified for holding office whether as President, Governor, Ministers or members of any Assembly or the Senate or as Speaker and they are not lawfully in possession of their offices and an injunction to the President, the Prime Minister, Ministers, Speakers and members of the Senate and Assemblies prohibiting them from acting as such

9. A declaration that there can be no political parties in Pakistan nor can any person offer himself for election or make effort for success of his election, and an injunction himself to the governments reject the election of any person belonging to a political party or offering or making efforts for the success of his election.

10. A declaration by the Court that in future all elections to the Assemblies shall be held under the supervision of the High Court.

11. A declaration that all Muslims of Pakistan have the right to act in obedience to the directions of the Holy Qur'ān and Sunna and in particular to enjoin right and forbid wrong by staying of hand, by word of mouth, in public speeches and otherwise, by publishing writings as newspapers, journals or otherwise and by processions and gatherings and no obstacle whatsoever can be placed by any person in the way of the performance of their duties, and an injunction to all persons prohibiting them from interfering with the exercise of such right.

12. A declaration that the property, person and honour of all Muslims are sacrosanct and cannot be interfered with except in execution of Allah's will as appearing in the Holy Qur'ān and Sunna, and an appropriate injunction to the Governments prohibiting any such interference.

13. A declaration that all provisions enabling the executive to arrest any person without trial or without proof of the circumstances on which any action is based against him before a court are null and void.

14. An injunction to the governments strictly to observe the prohibition in the Holy Qur'ān relating to liquor to stop all licences of liquor and all making money in relation to its manufacture or consumption and/or in any way dealing with it in violation of the directions in the Holy Qur'ān and Sunna.

15. An injunction to the governments to observe the prohibition relating to gambling in the Holy Qur'ān and Sunna, to stop all gambling in the country and on the horse races, and the stock exchange and to stop the building of the Casino at Karachi, and to stop all lotteries held by the governments or by other persons.

16. An injunction to the governments to observe the provision in the Holy Qur'ān and Sunna relating to *ribā*,[1] to stop all dealing with *ribā*, either paying it, or receiving it, or permitting others to receive it and to stop licencing any person to carry on the profession of a money lender.

---

1. *ribā:* (increase) the taking of interest is prohibited by the Qur'ān as usurious.

17. A injunction to the government to collect *zakāt*

18. An injunction to the governments to stop importing or exhibiting or permitting exhibition of abscenety [*sic*] films and to take all action against abscenety and nudity available to them.

19. An injunction to the governments to implement the provision relating to penalties (*hudūd*) in the Holy Qur'ān by appointing officers to award those penalties and by all steps whatsoever needed in order that the courts may be in a position to inflict the penalities as and when they regard it proper to do so. . . .

b. An injunction to the governments to comply with the verse of the Holy Qur'ān, "those who if we granted them power in the earth established prayer, gave *zakāt*, enjoined right and forbade wrong."

20. An injunction to the governments to stop teaching girls dancing.

21. An injunction to the governments to take all steps for providing to all persons in Pakistan the necessities of life, i.e. food, clothing, residence, education and medical aid. . . .

23. A declaration coupled with an appropriate injunction that the governments are entitled only to such amount of taxes for which they can prove necessity and no more.

24. A declaration that all public records belong to the people and they are entitled to inspect them except when they relate to affairs of State and an injunction to the governments to provide all reasonable facilities to the citizens of Pakistan for examining the records, copying them or taking photo-stats of them.

25. To give all able-bodied Muslims military training.

26. An injunction to the District Magistrate, Lahore, not to stop either now or in future the meetings which the petitioners want to hold for propagation of Allah's faith.

27. An injunction to the Deputy Commissioner, Lahore, to place no obstacles in the way of the publishing by the petitioners of the Weekly Tanzeem Islah.

28. An injunction to the governments to delete music from educational courses. . . .

31. That all such declarations be made and all such injunctions issued as after considering the material before it the Court may deem proper. Dated: 21-12-75

IRAN

The Iranian revolution provides the most dramatic and best-known political expression of resurgent Islam. However, the Iranian debate over the place of Islam in politics has had a long history. The Constitutional movement (1905–1911) provided a major confrontation over how best to express Iran's Islamic character. Leading 'ulamā' were divided on both sides of the issue. While Shaykh Muhammad Husayn Nā'īnī advocated constitutionalism, Shaykh Fadlullāh Nūrī revised his early supportive position and denounced the Constitution as un-Islamic.

Because of the role that Islam played in the Iranian revolution under the leadership of the Āyatullāh Rūhullāh Khumaynī, an Islamic government has been established. However, there have been many and varied Islamic voices speaking to the necessity of Islamic movements and the adoption of a more Islamic form of government. . . . Dr. 'Alī Sharī'atī and the Āyatullāh Murtada Mutahharī were both major Islamic leader-activists who throughout the 1960's and 70's advocated Islamic reform and the renewal of Iranian society. While they shared a common purpose, their vision was often quite different, especially as regards the role of the 'ulamā'.

If one is to understand the actual direction of post-revolutionary Iran under the Āyatullāh Khumaynī there is no better place to begin than his *Islamic Government,* delivered almost a decade before the revolution.

SHAYKH MUHAMMAD HUSAYN NĀ'ĪNĪ
(1860–1936)

He was one of the leading *mujtahids*[1] of his age. Trained in Isfahan and Iraq, he spent most of his years in Iraq, except for a brief exile in Qum (1923–24). He was active in both the Constitutional revolution in Iran, in response to which this work was written in 1909, and in the uprisings in Iraq in the 1920's. In the later part of his life he became less involved in politics, tending to compromise more with existing rulers. His defense of Constitutionalism was and remains a highly influential work.

Islam and Constitutional Government

This work is an introduction describing the essence of tyranny and constitutional government, investigating the fundamental law and the consultative national assembly and describing the meaning of freedom and equality.

Know that nearly all the Muslim nations and all reasonable people throughout the world are agreed that the preservation of world order and the livelihood of humankind depends on rulership and politics. This is so whether rulership is entrusted to one person or to a general council and whether it is acquired by right, by usurpation, by violence, by inheritance or by election. By the same token it is also axiomatic that the preservation of the honor, idependence and nationality of every people, both with regard to their religious and national prerogatives, depends on the placing of the actual ruling power with the people according to their will. Otherwise their privileges and laws, the greatness of their religion and religious group, the honor and independence of the fatherland and their nationality would be annihilated, even if they were to reach the highest level of wealth, power and prosperity. Therefore the holy Islamic law holds that the preservation of the core of Islam is the most important of all duties and has proclaimed Islamic rulership as one of the duties of the Imām.[2] . . . It is

1. *mujtahid:* one who exercises *ijtihād* (reasoning) to interpret Islamic law. In Shī'ī Islam *mujtahids* enjoy special status as interpreters of Islam during the occultation of the Imām.
2. Imām: (leader) for Twelver (Ithnā 'Asharī) Shī'ī or Shī'a Muslims, the religio-political leader of the Islamic community. One of the twelve legitimate successors of the Prophet Muhammad, descended through the family of 'Alī, the Prophet's son-in-law from whom the Shī'a (party of 'Alī) take their name.

From Shaykh Muhammad Husayn Nā' īnī, *Tanbih al-ummah wa tanzīh al-millah* [The admonition to the community and the purification of the nation], 5th ed. (Tehran: Shirkat-i sahāmī intishār 1358 s./1979 c.e.), pp. 6–15, 41, 46–47, 69, transl. by William Darrow.

clear that in all respects the establishment of a system in the world according to the principle of rulership and for the preservation of the honor and nationality of each people is their own affair. It has two principles:

1. Preservation of the internal order of the country, the education of the people, the respecting of each other's rights, the prevention of tyranny and the oppression of any portion of the country by another and such other duties as are related to the internal interests of the country and the people.

2. Preventing the interference of foreigners and stopping their typical cunning and preparing defensive forces and other military needs and the like. This principle in the language of the keepers of the holy law is called preserving the core of Islam and in the language of other nations, preserving the fatherland.

The provisions in the holy law for establishing these two duties are known respectively as political and civil laws and the wisdom of prudence. . . .

The characteristic of authority and the possession of a country by a ruler is either by the virtue of having a complete monopoly over it or by having supervision over it. There is no alternative to these two forms.

In the first type (which is tyranny) the one who rules considers the country and its people as his personal property and imagines everything in the country as his own and the people as his slaves, or at least his attendants and retainers, created and compelled to serve his wishes and lusts. Anyone who devotes himself completely to serving the desires of the ruler is rewarded by him. Anyone who is repulsed by this considering of his country as someone's personal possession is exiled or destroyed. . . .

The actual degree of oppression in this sort of rule depends on the actual amount of corrupt characteristics the rulers have, and on the wisdom and insight of the rulers and their assistants. It also depends on the insights and knowledge of the people of a country concerning the duties of rulership and its rights. The highest degree of such rulership is the claim to divinity and the intellectual power of the people of the country must resist this degree and each one leading to it. Of necessity in such a country the interaction of the people will be according to the religion of their kings and they will injure those below them as does the king. The reasons for this wicked system are twofold: 1) the ignorance of the nation concerning the duties of rulership and common and specific rights and the justice they embody and 2) the absence of responsibility on the part of the ones in charge and their not being subject to check and observation.

In the second form of government the basis of rulership should not be ownership subjugation, arbitrary despotism and dictatorship. The basis of rulership is the performance of the duties for the sake of public benefit. The establishment of a rulership and the authority of a ruler are limited to that extent and he is bound and conditioned from transgressing those rights.

These two types of rulership are in actuality different. The conditions and the effects of the two differ. The first is based upon power and subjugation of the country and of keeping the people under the whims of the ruler and using his power, financial and otherwise, to satisfy his own desires and not being responsible for whatever evil deeds are committed. Whatever such a ruler doesn't do one should be thankful for! . . . The second type in reality is based upon supervision of what are set as duties for the organization and protection of the country. It is not based on ownership. It is like a trusteeship that has been put at the disposal of the country. This power is to be used for the benefit of the people, not for personal desire. In this respect the measure of authority of the ruler accords with the proportion of supervision (*wilāyat*) in the above mentioned affairs and is limited, and his occupation of the office, whether by right or by usurpation, will be circumscribed by the conditions and not be oppressive. Every citizen of the nation is a partner with the ruler in financial and other affairs and is equal in this partnership, and those who are government officials are curators for the people. There is not a relation of owner and servant. Like members of a family who are responsible and obliged to each other, they have responsibility for the whole nation and should be reprimanded for the slightest trespass.

All the individuals in the country as a result of this partnership and equality have the right and power to criticize and question and oppose. They have such power and security and are free in the expression of their opposition. They should not yield to derision and power that arise out of the wishes of the ruler and government officials. This sort of rulership is called bound, limited, just, conditioned, responsible and authoritative. . . .

[The establishment of such a government] is based upon two principles. First, there must be the establishment of a constitution limited to what has been mentioned. . . . It must be free from all interference and tampering. It must be perfectly composed and set out clearly the duties and level of authority of the king and the freedom of the nation. It specifies all the rights of the classes of the people according to the requirement of their religion officially and definitely. Not performing these duties of protection and curatorship and going either to the extreme of too little or too much would be considered treason, and would be, like any betrayal of a trust, grounds for removal from office and other punishments as necessary. This is because the constitution sets the form in the political and social realm which must be actualized and followed in all affairs. The basis for the preservation of the limitations it establishes is preventing the trespassing of those limits. It is called a charter and fundamental law. The soundness and completeness of the constitution arises from its dealing with all aspects that are relevant to the limits it sets and its endeavoring to deal with all affairs that are necessary for the society, with the proviso that none of its provisions are in contradiction with the holy law of Islam. . . .

Second, there must be reliance on the elements of perfect guardianship, calculation and responsibility and the entrusting of a group of people gathered (in a consultative assembly) which is composed of those who are wise ones of the country and the good intentioned. They must know the details of international law and be acquainted with the general political situation of the times. They should be assigned the oversight and guardianship and the organization and establishment of the duties that are necessary. They should prevent all forms of oppression. Thus the whole intellectual power of the country is put into service within the official setting of national consultative assembly. . . .

[The question arises as to] whether in this age when the Imām is absent and the community falls far short of purity and of being under the supervision of an Imām or his regular deputies and the above-mentioned duties are trampled upon and disregarded, is there any reason to turn from the path of extreme tyranny and oppression on top of oppression towards a second path in which the authority (of the ruler) is limited to what is appropriate? . . .

. . . Three topics should be discussed in answer to this question. First, in the case of the responsibility to forbid what is evil (that is incumbent on all Muslims), it is well known that when a person does a number of things which are prohibited, he bears responsibility for each thing that he does. The person who seeks to forbid what is evil, should seek to stop each one of them to the extent it is possible.

Second, one of the prerequisites for those of us who are Twelver Shī'ītes is that in the time of the absence of the Imām, . . . our religion has established the essential duty that is indispensable in the area of supervision: that is that there be the deputyship of the jurisprudents in the age of the absence of the Imām. The proof the deputyship of the jurisprudents and his assistants in the period of absence is the most important issue in the period of absence in order to establish the above-mentioned duties as the central features of our religion.

Third, in the area of Islamic law that deals with the supervision of pious foundations, both special and general, in whatever is written about the area of such supervision, the following is clear and agreed upon. If someone seizes something by force and deprives someone of something and we are unable to take it back, in any way, then a group should be assigned who would be able to take back what has been illegally seized, for example to be used in the pursuit of lusts. This assigning of a group to take back what has been illegally seized is the prime goal of the Shī'īte wisemen. What else would be expected by the least intelligent of people?

When these three points are explained, there can be no doubt about the necessity of taking rulership from the hands of the tyrant, which is the first path and entrusting it to the second path. When you know that the first path is a direct insult to the name of God and that a tyrant's taking of the position of supervisor and clothing tyranny in the garb of religion is an insult to the position of the Imām and that doing so is a seizing of the rights of individuals, which involves all of mankind, then (it is clear one should prefer the second form of government). . . .

The law of equality is among the most noble of the blessed derived laws of Islamic polity. It is the basis and foundation of justice and the spirit of all the laws. . . . The essence of the holy law consists in this. Every law which is meant to apply in all fields and conditions legally in all circumstances is executed equally with respect to individuals and without discrimination. Personal and special connections are not considered. Choice in disposition and suppression, deceit and pardon are closed to everyone. Violation of the law, bribery, and arbitrariness in legal issues is blocked to all. Regarding basic rights, which are common to all people and should be enforced, such as security of life, honor, possessions, dwelling, the absence of harassment without cause, no unreasonable search, no imprisonment or exile without cause, no hindering of religious assembly and the like, these are common to all and are not attached to any one special group. They should be put into effect for all. In the case of special rights among individuals who are entitled to them, within that group there is no arbitrariness or differences. For instance, a defendant is called for trial whether he is lower class or noble, ignorant or learned, ubeliever or Muslim. . . . The special laws for Muslims, and those which apply to the protected religious minorities, are applied uniformly among the members of each of these groups.

SHAYKH FADLULLĀH NŪRĪ
1842–1909

After study in Najaf and Samarra under the noted *mujtahid* Hājī Mīrzā Hasan Shīrāzī, Shaykh Fadlullāh served as a *mujtahid* in Tehran. An early supporter of the constitutional movement (1905), after 1907 he led a number of *mujtahids* in active opposition to the adopted constitution, since it did not acknowledge the *Sharī'a* as the law of the state.

Refutation of the Idea of Constitutionalism

The sources of this calamity (the Persian constitutional revolution) were the new sects and the naturalists who received the idea of constitutionalism from [our] neighbors, [i.e. Russia and Ottoman Turkey] and presented it in a very appealing manner. Obviously, anyone who was fascinated by this [pleasant] presentation and was a lover of [justice and saw a number of people] seeking justice automatically made an effort to earn it as soon as he heard this agreeable word; he did not refrain from giving his life and wealth as such as he could. This writer, for example, took part in this affair and experienced a lot of trouble while traveling or at home. [There were] also [some] means which were agreeable. When we began to put the matter into effect, I noticed that a group of people who had always been accused of deviations [from the right path] involved themselves in the affairs. Little by little I heard some equivocal words from them, but I interpreted them as [sound] ideas. Then they unveiled the matter to an extent and established the [fact] that the representatives [of parliament] should be elected and the majority of the votes relied upon. Again I ignored [these things] interpreting that these [measures might have been taken] to establish order and to promote justice.

Gradually it was decided to make a constitution and to write a [fundamental] law. At times the [matters] were being discussed with some [of the people involved, and the question would arise]: "What is the meaning of this system?"[I would tell them]: "It seems that the constitutionalists want to forge an innovation and to lead [people] astray." Otherwise, what is the

From Shaykh Fazl Allāh Nūrī's "Refutation of the Idea of Constitutionalism," trans. 'Abdul Hadi Ha'iri, *Middle Eastern Studies* 13:3 (Oct. 1977), 327–39.

meaning of a representative system (wikālat)? Who is the elector and for what is the representative elected? If the problems concern secular affairs, there is no need for these religious arrangements. If general religious matters are to be treated, then these matters are related to wilāyat [i.e. the rulership which is authorized by God through His Prophet and the Imāms, that is to say the 'ulamā'] not wikālat. During the [Greater] Occultation of the [Twelfth] Imām, may God hasten his happy ending [i.e. his return], wilāyat is within the capacity [only] of the specialists in fiqh and of the mujtahids, not of a certain grocer or draper. Also relying on the opinions of the majority is wrong according to the Twelver Shī'ī religion. What does it mean to write a law? The law for us Muslims is only Islam which, thanks to God, the exalted traditionists and the mujtahids generation after generation have taken pains to protect and keep in order. Thanks to God, the exalted, there are also many protectors of Islamic law at the present time. . . .

It may not be hidden that there are many reasons for the unlawfulness of constitutionalism and for its repugnance to Islamic provisions and to the Prophetic path; peace may be upon their executors in [all] the aforementioned stages. First of all, [both the writing of] a constitutional law and the following of the opinion of the majority [are against Islam. The idea of depending on the majority] even though it is originally allowed in permissible affairs is an unlawful legislation; it is an innovation in religion because it is made as a law to be obeyed. [And of course] every innovation is a straying from the right path. Also, it is unlawful to make a permissible action as a person's duty to be obligatorily performed and to punish the person for his refusal of performing that duty. "Say: Hath Allah permitted you or do ye invent a lie concerning Allah?" [Qur'ān 10:60]

Governmental matters and orders have always existed, but it has been obvious that those were irreligious principles. But [in our age] everyone witnessed that adherence to the lawful nonsense and absurd opinions of the [national] assembly [were] considered by all Muslims as one of the most obligatory duties, and opposition to the assembly was seen as worse than apostasy. What innovation can be more serious than this?. . . .

One of the articles [No. 8] of that book of errors [i.e. the constitution] rules that all the individuals in this country have equal rights. In its latest edition this phrase is given as: The inhabitants of the country of Iran will have equal rights before the state law. The word "equality" spread and was circulated until it perforated [all] ears. Equality is one of the pillars of constitutionalism, [the latter] would vanish without equality. I remember when this article was being under discussion, one of the few distinguished members of the assembly said to me that this article was extremely important. [He added]: If this article is included in the constitution, foreign states will recognize it even if we change all other articles. If this article disappears [from the constitution] but the rest remains our constitutional system will not be recognised. I answered immediately: then it is all over with Islam and stood up and said: Oh! People who are sitting, you should know that the Islamic country [of Iran] will not accept a constitutional government because it is impossible to have equality in Islam.

Oh! my religious brothers, now think attentively over the Islamic provisions and see how many differences they established among the subjects concerning the persons obligated to observe the precepts of Islam. [In Islam there are differences . . .] in religious observances, trades and policies. [There are differences between] minors and those who are mature, the rational and the irrational, the sane and the insane, the healthy and the ill, the one who has free will and he who is compelled, the satisfied and the dissatisfied, the authentic [client] and the lawyer [or representative] and the guardian, the slave and the free, the father and the son, the wife and the husband, the rich and the poor, the learned and the ignorant, the doubting person and the convinced, the imitator [of a *mujtahid*] and the *mujtahid*, the descendant of the Prophet (*sayyid*) and the non-sayyid, the distressed and those at ease, the Muslim and the infidel, the infidel under [Muslim] protection (*dhimmīs*) and the infidel who is at war [with the Muslims], the originally non-Muslim person and the apostate, the national (sic) apostate and the apostate by nature, and so on, none of which is hidden to the expert *faqīh*. . . .

Oh, heretics! If this state law is in conformity with Islam, it is not possible to include equality in it and if it is at variance with Islam, it would be against what is written in the previous part [of the constitution] that is: whatever is against Islam cannot be lawful.

Oh, Knavish and [individuals] devoid of zeal! See how the master of the *Sharī'a* has granted you honors because you have been embellished with Islam. He has granted you privileges, but you deny them by saying that you must be equal brothers with Zoroastrians, Armenians and Jews: God's curse may be upon those who approve this [equality]!. . . .

Know that heaven and earth depend on justice, the necessity of which is obvious according to both reason and the *Sharī'a*. The question, however, is to find its applicability. . . . Oh Muslims! Islam which is our religion and the religion of [all] adherents of the Prophet is more complete than all other religions. It is based on perfect justice as God the exalted says:

Lo! Allah enjoineth justice and kindness [Qur'ān 16:90]. Thanks to God the exalted that in Islam there is but justice. Prophecy and kingship among preceding prophets were different: sometimes the two authorities were centered [in one person] or were divided. [The two authorities were centered] in the blessed person of the most honorable Prophet, the last of the prophets. [God's] blessing may be upon him and his family as long as the universe lasts. Such was also the case with the caliphs of that magnanimous [personality, i.e. Muhammad], either lawfully or unlawfully. But several months after the occurrence of accidents, these two affairs, namely the assumption of religious affairs and the using of power and glory and alertness over the security [of the state] centered in two [separate] authorities.

In fact, these two authorities are complementary and supplementary to each other, that is to say, the foundation of Islam is laid upon these two [sets] of affairs: deputyship in the affairs of prophecy and kingship. Without these two, Islamic provisions would be inactive. As a matter of fact, kingship is the executive power of Islamic provisions and doing justice depends on executing them. . . .

Yes, in our epoch currency has been given to a subject which [falsely] sounds like justice. Thus, a number of naturalists who deny the origin and return [of creation] and consider [our] life limited only to this world saw that with anarchy and without setting up a law they would not be able to achieve their benefits of life. Therefore, they made [a mixture of] sacred heavenly laws, as well as [the devices created by their own] defective minds and called it law. They accepted this law in order to satisfy their desires. With this arrangement they established order [but] the commander and prohibitor in this order are the same law, plus the punishment which has been considered in the law. It does not create any commander and prohibitor inside one's heart. It is for this reason that shameful actions are current in keeping with the [established] system and equal oppression given to all has been increased. As soon as they find themselves in security of the law they commit treason and injustice. . . .

So many prophets were appointed by God to persuade the children of Adam to [be concerned with] the world to come and [induce them] to abstain from this ephemeral world. On the contrary, whatever our [constitutionalist] orators have said to the people during the past two years [consists only of the suggestion that] one should go after these worldly [affairs] and earn wealth and have pleasure. At one time one of these devils out of "sympathy" said in private to [some] of our countrymen that the removal of poverty in this country depends on two things: firstly, the decreasing of expenses and secondly, the increasing of incomes. The most important thing which limits expenses is the lifting of veil from women [because] the home dress would be sufficient for outside and inside. [They also argued that] one set of servants is enough, needs would be met with one carriage, one party with both women and men would be enough and other things of this sort. Oh zealous [people]! [Do] deliberate [and see] what [evil] thoughts they had about you. Many examples of these evil thoughts were found [in the writings of] newspaper editors and the speeches of orators. Thank God that they did not reach their aim and [let us] hope that by divine favor, they [also] will not reach [their aim] in the future.

Another article included in that erroneous book [i.e. the constitution] says that no punishment will be ordered and executed except according to the law. This provision is in contrast with the sect of Ja'far,[1] peace may be upon him, because during the [Greater] Occultation of the Imām, peace may be upon him, only the Shī'ī *fuqhā'* are authorized to handle new problems and to control [all] the affairs. They would find the truth and execute [necessary] punishments after ascertaining the principles: [this procedure] does not at all depend on the approval of anyone.

Another article [of the constitution] divides the powers of the state into three, the first of which is the legislative power: this is also an innovation and a downright aberration because in Islam, no one is allowed to legislate or to establish a provision. Islam does not have any shortcomings that require completion. Concerning new incidents [i.e. problems] which may emerge, it would be necessary to refer to the gate of the provisions that is the [General] Agents of the Imām, peace may be upon him. The Agents then would deduce the relevant provision from the Qur'an and the Sunna [of the Prophet] but they cannot make law. Many articles of this type can be found in this erroneous book. . . .

In sum, my aim [in dealing with the above discussion] is that there may remain no uncertainty or doubt that constitutionalism is against the religion of Islam [which was given to us by] the best of mankind, upon him be peace and thousands of salutations. It is not possible to bring this Islamic country under a constitutional regime except by abolishing Islam. Therefore, if any Muslim attempts to impose constitutionalism upon us Muslims, his attempts will be taken as destructive to the religion. Such a person is an apostate, to whom the four provisions regarding the apostate may be applicable regardless of his being knowledgeable or illiterate, strong or weak. . . .

---

1. Ja'far al-Ṣādiq (d. 765), the sixth Imām.

'ALĪ SHARĪ'ATĪ
1933–77

The son of a prominent religious preacher, he was active in the struggle against the Shah. In 1959 he went to Paris where he earned a doctorate in sociology at the Sorbonne and also became heavily involved in Iranian and Third World opposition movements. He later joined the Freedom Movement (*Nihdat-i Āzādī*) along with Āyatullāh Tāliqānī and Mehdī Bāzargān. He lectured at the University of Mashhad and subsequently at the Husayn-iya-i Irshad, a religious center in Teheran, where he drew large crowds and became very popular among the politically and religiously committed youth. The center was closed down, and Sharī'atī was arrested. Finally, after an international campaign, he was released and allowed to go to England, where shortly after his arrival, he died of a heart attack.

Intizar, the Religion of Protest

I wish to make a general statement, not as an individual believer who analyses scientific and historical issues from his religious point of view, but as an impartial teacher of history of religions . . . : in the history of mankind no religion has ever witnessed such a widening gap separating existing reality from its original truth as Islam has. . . . Within Islam itself, of all the various sects, . . . Shī'īsm has witnessed the widest gap separating "what was" from "what is". . . . Original Shī'īsm was an intellectually progressive Islamic movement as well as a militant social force, the most committed, most revolutionary Islamic sect. Of all the doctrines which characterize the sect, belief in the "end of time," in "*ghaybat*,"[1] and in the "promised Saviour," in short the doctrine of *intizar* . . . reflects this gap most. The *raushanfikr*[2] . . . might accuse me of safeguarding superstitions,

1. The period of occultation, or absence of the Imām, begun in 874 and lasting to the present.
2. This term was first coined in the second half of the nineteenth century by Iranian secularists who admired and were influenced by eighteenth-century European Philosophers of the Enlightenment. It literally meant "enlightened thinkers," and was used to identify the modernist liberal intellectual and professional dedicated to social, political and cultural

From *Intizar . . . madhab-i i'tiraz* [Awaiting . . . the religion of protest] (Teheran: Husainiya Irshad Pub., 1350 A.H./1971), pp. 1–4, 6, 8, 12–15, 21, 24, 32, 35–44, 47, 50–51. transl. by Mangol Bayat.

of keeping this generation's attention from thinking of the future, science and social progress, of keeping them in ignorance. The believer ... might accuse me of speaking against their religious principles. . . .

... *Intizar,*[3] that is the belief in the end of time, in the Imām of the Age, and in the final revolution at the end of historical time, has been interpreted in different ways. The non-religious view it as incompatible with science and reason, as an antiquated idea causing social decline, preventing man from assuming full responsibility over his destiny, since it denies him free will. It (allegedly) promotes the belief that social reforms, human awakening, destruction of the unjust and corrupt order, lie not in man's hands but in the hand of the "hidden one" who someday shall appear to rescue man's fate from corruption and decline. . . .

The religious masses, on the other hand, like all religious masses, do not doubt their beliefs. . . . They firmly, categorically, believe in the idea . . . of a living though hidden Imām who, when corruption and injustice universally reign, would arise, sword in hand, to fight the [enemies of religion and], restore the order of justice, the regime of the Imām . . . , the rule of the Qur'ānic laws, and thus set up a universal government . . . and universal peace. . . . They basically do not think that the Imām's long life is unnatural and unscientific, as their opponents do. . . . They have to have faith, and they do have it. God has willed to keep alive an individual for as long as He wished for the execution of a Revelation. And that is that! Nor do they think that this idea, if wrongly interpreted, might contradict many Islamic beliefs and Qur'ānic rules, in particular those regarding individual responsibility towards society and history. They are not even aware of the fact that such an understanding of this idea renders good and justice impossible, (since) to seek one's well-being . . . would lead nowhere. . . . Our religious leaders also believe any idea found in the Qur'ānic and traditional texts to be true. Since the idea of the "promised, rightly guided one" is found in the scriptures it is necessarily rational and acceptable. Whatever is declared Islamic and Shī'ī is also declared true and accept-

---

change, as opposed to the more tradition-bound, religious-minded, clerical or non-clerical, members of society. In the twentieth century the term became synonymous with an intellectual or any other professional, who used his pen to promote modern liberal views. Prior to the 1978–79 revolution, some writers applied the term to some revolutionary clerics as well, though using it next to the name or the title of *'ālim*, religious leader, (*'ālim-i raushanfikr*). With the emergence of the lay Islamic ideologist in the 60's and 70's, the religious-minded who was committed to change was also referred to as *raushanfikr*. Currently the term has reverted to its original, lay modern, liberal meaning, as the clerics, aiming at consolidating their hold over government and society, are waging a fierce battle against the modern educated professionals and itellectuals.

3. *Intizar,* awaiting the expected Twelfth Imām who was declared occulted (alive, everpresent yet hidden from men's view) in 874 A.D., constitutes one of the most fundamental features of Imami Shī'ī doctrine.

able. Thus they have endeavored to solidly plant the root of this idea in people's faith and have them believe in it without seeing the necessity of independent rational, scientific analysis. . . .

As for the religious modernists of our society, whether educated in the traditional sciences or modern sciences or both, they have found a third way: to prove the validity of this religious doctrine through the same method used by the non-religious *raushanfikr* in their refutation, namely, the materialist scientific method . . . They have proven the scientific possibility of the thousand year life of the Imām . . .

In the age of *ghaybat,* that is the indefinite period begun in the third century of the *hijra*[4] which is to last until God wills, Shī'īsm becomes a special political and social philosophy which is at once: the cause of the people's decline, contemptuous of human free will, of liberty and of human thought, negating social responsibilities. . . . and is basically indefensible; as well as progressive, honorable, popular, respectful of human free will, of liberty and of human intellect, enforcing social responsibilities. . . . emanating historical optimism as well as bestowing spiritual and intellectual independence.

With the beginning of the age of *ghaybat* . . . the age of appointment comes to an end, and that of election comes about. That is, the age of *taqlīd.* [the practice of following the guidance of a religious leader. Here the author using the term in its broadest meaning definds *taqlīd* by "those who do not know" of "those who do know", as a logical necessity universally practiced so that the "specialist" in any field of human knowledge guides the less knowledgeable. (Tr.)] Thus we see that in this age of greater *ghaybat* a particular system of election comes into being. It is a democratic election of the leader, yet it is not a free democracy. Though the chosen one is elected by the people, he is responsible to the Imām . . . and his school of thought. Contrary to the democratically elected candidate, he is not responsible to implement the ideas and ideals of those who voted for him. He is responsible to guide people in accordance with the Imām's laws and thought . . . This election is limited, in the sense that not all people vote, nor is anyone who gets the most votes (automatically) elected to the post of the Imām's deputy. Since such an individual is both a social person [activist] and a scholar, the masses who possess no knowledge are not worthy of electing him. Reason dictates that those learned ones ('*ulamā*') who know who is the most learned and best specialist of this school of thought . . . choose. The people who rely on and follow their religious leaders naturally accept their choice of the Imām's deputy . . . The Imām, while in *ghaybat,* grants the enlightened, pure and religiously aware '*ulamā*' the task of guiding the faithful till the advent of his manifestation. . . .

4. Muslim calendar

There exist two Imāms of the Age, two Imamates, two Shī'isms, two Islams. One, Islam the ideology . . . , the other Islam the culture. Islam the Ideology is created by Abu-Dharr;[5] Islam the culture by Ibn Sina;[6] Islam the ideology creates a muɩjāhid;[7] Islam the culture the mujtahid.[8] The raushanfikr creates Islam the ideology; the 'ālim[9] (pl. 'ulamā') creates the culture. Islamic ideology provides responsibility, consciousness and leadership; Islamic studies is a special scholarly branch which an Orientalist, or a confused reactionary thinker, or an evil-thinking self-interested individual could acquire. Thus it is that an uneducated individual could understand Islam better, think in a more Islamic way, and define Islamic responsibility better than a faqīh,[10] or an 'ālim, or a philosopher or a mystic. . . . Islam as an ideology must be studied in the Qur'ān and in the life of the Prophet. [Sharī'atī declares himself not a specialist of the traditional religious sciences; that his perspective and method are sociological, leaving to other specialists the task of studying Islam from their respective perspectives. Deploring the fact that nowadays the religious specialist has given up the traditional multi-disciplinary approach to Islamic sciences, reducing them to the narrow discipline of fiqh; he claims the "Qur'ānic truths" related to sociology, philosophy of history, anthropology, natural sciences, economics, psychology, political science and philosophy, have all remained in the dark, or distorted. All these aspects of a doctrine must be accordingly studied by the educated thinkers and the raushanfikr of the age, and not only by the faqīh. (Tr)]

Thus religious beliefs can follow, step by step, social, cultural and scientific progress. So would our understanding of religion. . . . The issue of the "expected-promised-rightly-guided-One" is one such issue. It is defined and attested in the Shī'ī texts and laws. However, its proper understanding by people of different times; its social analysis . . . the sociological evaluation of the idea, the investigation of its influence upon the social, political and intellectual life of its adepts, change according to time and conditions. . . . [Sharī'atī asserts that intizar is conceived in two different, self-contradicting ways, negative and positive. The negative interpretation sees man's salvation and the establishment of justice as lying solely in the hands of the "Hidden Saviour," and in no one else's. In the time of ghaybat man

5. Abū-Dharr, one of the three original companions of 'Alī, the first Shī'ī Imām, who had chosen to fight for 'Alī's claim to leadership of the Muslim community as the sole legitmate successor to the Prophet.
6. Eleventh-century Muslim philosopher
7. A fighter for the holy cause.
8. High ranking Shī'ī clerical position.
9. Literally, he who is learned in religious sciences or knowledge of the Divine, i.e. clerical leader. (plural: 'ulamā')
10. A theologian specializing in religious jurisprudence. Khumaynī's government is thus called "government of the faqīh."

must submit to the rule of the oppressor, reduced as he is to fighting against evil only morally and spiritually. Such an interpretation guarantees the lasting influence of three interest groups representing three forces of evil: political, economic and religious. The last group especially, ever since the Safavids,[11] have used the doctrine to the point of abuse. In the name of religion and as vicegerents of the Imām, they have imposed their will, and those of their two other collaborating groups, upon the people. Since the Imām is both the religious and the temporal leader of the community, in his absence they have appropriated to themselves his exclusive spiritual and worldly rights. They have enslaved the people's mind and forced them to pay taxes. And yet they are not the Imām's special vicegerent since they are not appointed directly by him. Nor is there any official election. The *faqīh* and the *mujtahid* have suppressed true knowledge of religion and hindered the true understanding of Shī'ī beliefs. Consequently, the people who dutifully submit to their will are not qualified to identify, hence choose, the worthiest, most learned individual to become their leader. (Tr.)] The same belief in *intizar*, in *ghaybat* and in man's certain, predetermined salvation at the end of time, has an opposite meaning. *Intizar* is both a social idea and a natural human (disposition). Basically man is an expecting being. . . . Similarly, human society, be it a class, a nation or a group, is instinctively expectant. Thus belief in the messiah, that is the Saviour, has always existed. . . . All civilizations we know of share two basic characteristics in common: 1. any culture, even the most primitive or backward, . . . possess in their remote past a "golden age" when justice, peace and love reigned. It then disappeared to be replaced by the rule of corruption and injustice. 2. belief in a future great Revolution and in a Saviour, in the return of the Golden Age when justice and equality will triumph once more. . . . Related to the idea of messianism is a humanist and anthropological concept of futurism. . . . It is a school of thought, an ideology, a religion. . . . Futurism is one of the most progressive ways of embracing life. . . . For it opposes conservatism, status quo, classicism, that is, belief in the past; and traditionalism, that is, belief in traditions and "reactionaryism". . . .

Even you, followers of the Prophet, you must not stop with the person. This is not a matter of prophetic cult, but the goal of a school of thought. The value of the Prophet lies in his showing the way to that goal. His task was, like previous prophets, to come, bring a Message, show the way, then go. If he died, or was killed, would you turn on your heels! . . . Reaction! Cult of the past! Go forward. . . . This is a progressive movement: not to stop with the person; not to look back to the past with nostalgia; it is to

---

11. Ruling dynasty of Iran, 1501–1725, responsible for establishing Imāmī Shī'ism as the official State religion.

look forward to the future. Basically, belief in the promised one and the doctrine of *intizar* means futurism, to move forward towards a future that is destined to come. A man who awaits, awaits the future; one cannot await the past. Whoever awaits is hopeful, and the hopeful is alive.

Intizar is the thesis of two antitheses: truth and reality. . . . We believe that the Qur'ān was sent to save man from oppression, force, aristocracy, cult of blood ties, racial ties, pain and wretchedness, exploitation; to fight ignorance and backwardness. We believe 'Alī and his sons, and the Shī'ī leaders are the successors of the Prophet. We believe Shī'ism guarantees man's salvation. Yet reality shows us the opposite of this truth.

We see that the moment the Prophet passed away . . . the same old system resumed its rule over history. Neither truth remained, nor justice; nor did mankind find salvation. Neither was oppression eliminated, nor were deviation, deceit, and lies. In those days they ruled in the name of Khusraw or Caesar; in later days they ruled in the name of the Prophet's Caliph. What is the difference? In those days it was better, since (the ruler) claimed he came to plunder. Thus when Alexander came to Iran, he announced he had come to burn Persepolis, to plunder Iran. . . . He did exactly that. Whereas, in Islamic history, the same Khusraw, the same Caesar, announced they came to wage holy war in order to spread justice in the world, and to implement the practice of the Prophet and the Qur'ānic laws. Yet they plundered. Where was the difference? What victory came about? How did the Qur'ān rescue the masses from the heavy yoke of oppression? How did 'Alī successfully lead his people against oppression and force? He himself suffered defeat and was oppressed. How did the Imāmate, which is the system of infallible leadership legitimately succeeding that of the Prophet, enable man to enjoy its rule. . . . They themselves were eliminated in prison.

Thus we see that the reality occurring in the external world contradicts the Islamic truth we believe in. What do we do? . . . We, deprived people who, in pre-Islamic times, were victims of oppression, exploitation, aristocracy, ignorance and poverty, and who have turned to Islam hoping for liberty, honour and justice; find ourselves in Islamic times plundered, tortured, hungry, oppressed and discriminated against. Naturally a question comes to our mind: was the religion, sent to save mankind and establish world justice, defeated? Was it destroyed? Could one say that God had sent His Prophet, entrusted him with the greatest and superior of all books, commissioned him to save mankind; that (the Prophet) himself had appointed his successors as the people's leaders' and yet, in the midst of it all, He changed His mind? . . . Or could it be that God had not changed His mind, and that the Prophet and the Imāms of His religion had done their duty . . . but to no avail? . . . There is no alternative for the followers of this religion other than to believe that this Truth . . . shall definitely triumph and that justice is destined to be established. . . . We believe in and are expecting such a day and such an event since God had truly promised victory to Islam. He had promised the wretched masses they would become leaders of mankind; He had promised the disinherited they would inherit this earth from the mighty. . . . Only *intizar*, awaiting the final, predetermined triumph of Truth, can solve this disparity between the reigning false reality and the presently condemned redeeming Truth. . . .

Intizar means to say no to what is. . . . Even negative *intizar* implies revolt. . . . Whoever is content with the present, is not awaiting. On the contrary, he is conservative; he fears the future. . . . Contrary to what Beckett says in *Waiting for Godot, intizar* is not a futile idea. . . . For a condemned nation to give up intizar means to accept defeat as its fate forever. . . . Oppression, crime, injustice, all are unfinished stories and events in human history. The story shall end with Justice and Truth triumphing over oppression and corruption. . . . This is what I believe in. *Intizar* is historical determinism. . . . I, in this part of the world and at this moment of history, am expecting, in a future that might be tomorrow or any other time, a sudden world Revolution in favour of Truth and Justice and of the oppressed masses; a Revolution in which I must play a part; a Revolution which does not come about with prayers. . . . but with a banner and a sword, with a true holy war involving all responsible believers. I believe that this movement shall naturally triumph. Thus I believe in historical determinism and not historical random accidents. . . .

It is this belief in determinism, that history shall end up promoting justice, that with time the human species is destined to see the triumph of communal society and communal way of life, which constitutes the greatest source of strength and faith for the oppressed and exploited masses. . . . Belief in *intizar*, far from discouraging those who are crushed beneath the yoke of oppression and who see Truth has become a plaything in the hands of the oppressors and their religion an instrument in the hands of the enemies of religion, gives them confidence in the will of God. The will of God is that very historical determinism which . . . following the same natural law, moves towards the implementation of His thought, His way. Destiny has already condemned all forces running counter to man's historical course to justice. . . . Thus we see that belief in *intizar* is historical determinism. . . .

The struggle for liberty and justice follows a course similar to that of a river. There is Abraham, Moses, Jesus, Muhammad, 'Alī, Hasan, Husayn, and so on until the end of time when this movement triumphs all over the world. Belief in the final Saviour, in the Shī'ī Imāms and the Twelfth Imām, means that this universal Revolution and final victory is the conclusion of one great continual justice-seeking movement of revolt against oppression; a movement which was first led by Prophets then, following the Seal of all prophets [Muhammad], by the Imāms and, in the long period of *ghaybat*, by *'ilm*[12]. . . .

Belief in *intizar* is belief in God's promise to the Muslims, in the final realization of the wretched masses' ideal and hope; in the final triumphant emergence of the classless society, a society freed from tyranny, injustice and deceit. . . .

12. Sharī'atī uses the term *'ilm*, not in its original Muslim meaning of knowledge of the Divine or of the religious science, but in a more secular, universal, modern meaning of science.

"Return to the Self"

I support religion; I support Islam; I support a reformed, revised Islam, specifically leading to an Islamic renaissance movement. I have not reached such a religious view as a result of a systematic study of all religions and sects ending with my professing faith in Islam as the best religion of all. Nay, I have followed a different approach which I wish to explain in order to show that not only the religious believers among the *raushanfikran* can hear my call and accept it. Any *raushanfikr* with an independent consciousness who wished to serve his society, . . . and relate his own enlightened message to the generation of his time, could follow the same path we took. I do not discuss the issue of religion in society on the basis of an idea or a religious sentiment. My support of religion is such that even a non-religious *raushanfikr* can join me and support it. With the difference that, whereas my support is for the sake of a faith and a social obligation, this *raushanfikr* collaborates with me for the sake of a social obligation. At present, the issue of "return to the self" is not being studied by the religious believers of the world. Progressive, non-religious *raushanfikran* have first considered it, such as: Aime Cezaire, Franz Fanon, Sanghor, Kātīb Yassīn, Āl-i Ahmad of Iran. . . . Neither is of the religious type. . . . They are important leaders of a Third World anti-imperialist movement. . . . It is our duty to study this issue here in Iran, in this society, with this generation. When I come to discuss it together with the non-religious who share a common social obligation, when we both reach mutual understanding, then we can change the term "self" into "Islamic culture" and "Islamic ideology." Not Islam the tradition, the legacy, the system or a belief existing in society, but Islam the ideology, the faith that generates consciousness. . . . In truth this view is not based on inherited religious sentiments or on a dried-out spiritual sentiment. It is based on a liberal principle adopted by all *raushanfikran* of the world . . . and which is discussed by the author of *Christ re-crucified,* and which makes me say, here in Iran, "Husayn re-martyred." Ever since the eighteenth century the West, with the help of its sociologists, historians, writers, artists, and even the humanists and the revolutionaries, has tried to enforce the thesis that culture is one and only one: western culture. Anyone who wishes to be civilized must consume the same culture; should one reject it, one remains savage forever. Thus one must buy western culture the same way one buys western products. . . . Either one becomes western-cultured, or one remains savage. Those are the

From *Bazgasht bi khishtan* [Return to the self], trans. Mangol Bayat (Conference at the University of Ahvaz, n.p., n.d.), pp. 13–17, 19–20, 23, 26–27, 36–38, 40–41.

two fates a human being can choose from. Throughout the last two centuries the West has endeavored to spread this faith in the West, and lack of faith in oneself. . . . Chinese, Japanese, Iranian, Arab, Turk, black, white, all must be transformed into . . . consumers buying their greatness, pride, honor, ideals in the West. Thus all national values are negated. . . .

Whoever possesses a cultural personality of his own is an independent productive human being. A productive human being is a person who builds ideas, ideologies and faith as he does machines. . . . A society that produces its values, its ethics, its beliefs, its religious faith, . . . its class structure, . . . is a society which can achieve industrial and political independence as well. . . . What must be done today now that the West has uprooted all human beings from their natural cultural ties, transforming them into needy slaves, into clients, into clinging imitators? The principle considered by the *raushaɑfikran* in the past fifteen years as the latest anti-imperialist cultural experiment is the "return to the self." . . . But return to which self? The one Aime Cezaire talks about? Or that of Iran? When I, an educated Iranian, and Aime Cezaire, an educated African, and Franz Fanon, an educated Caribbean, all come to say "return to the self," then we must part. . . . All three of us are westernized, French-educated, and hence very much alike as imitators. Now that we want to go back to our respective cultural roots, we must part in order to consider, each on his own, his self. . . .

Which self should I return to? Should I return to my racial self, but then this is a reactionary return. . . . Could we return to our ancient self of the Achameanids, the Sasanians and earlier peoples? . . . This self is an old self, recorded in history, discovered by historians, sociologists, scholars and archeologists. But the long centuries have broken our ties to it. . . . The schism of the Islamic culture has created a distance between our pre-Islamic and Islamic selves. Our nation does not feel this self as its own. . . . Our masses do not remember any of it. . . . The return to the past I am talking about . . . is the past that still exists in the midst of our society, and which a *raushanfikr* can extract and revive. . . . Is this self a religious self? An Islamic self? Which Islam? Which Shī'ism? . . . The self which through the past thousand years has displayed a great civilization in our universities, literature, sciences? Is that the Islam that exists now, as presently attained by our people . . . and which is of no use? It is only a cause of their stagnation, a cause of their worshiping traditions and ignorance, the cause of personality cult and of "repetition of the repeated." . . . This religion has nothing to do with this work, does not hold men responsible for this world but only for the next. It is this religion which alienates the socially conscious *raushanfikr*, and makes him run away from it. In brief I say: we support Islamic culture and must return to this self, for it is the self nearest to ourselves; it is the only culture that is now alive. . . . However, we must distinguish the

Islam that generates consciousness, that is progressive and in revolt, the ideology . . . from its traditional aspect which has caused decline. The return to the self, the duty of the *raushanfikr* be he religious or non-religious, is the starting point. . . . The image of Islam must therefore be changed: the socially traditional to be transformed into an ideology; the collection of mystical studies currently being taught to be replaced by self-conscious faith; the centuries-long decline into a resurgence. . . . With this shape, the *raushanfikr*, religious and non-religious, would return to his self. He would confront the cultural imperialism of the West and, with the force of religion, awaken his own society stupefied with religion. He would thus mobilize society. . . .

ĀYATULLĀH MURTADĀ MUTAHHARĪ
d. 1979

He was a professor in the School of Theology at Tehran University and a leading figure in religious reform movements in the 60's and early 70's. He played a leading role in the revolution and in the post-revolutionary period until his assassination in 1979. That assassination was said to have been committed by an underground group called Furqān which is religiously based but opposed the role of the clergy in the actual governance of the country. Matahharī wrote a number of books on social and political philosophy.

The Iranian Islamic Movement

The question arises why have the Sunni religious leader's been unable to carry on a movement, although they have vigorously talked of reformation and struggle against colonialism and exploitation? Why against this situation, has the Shī'ā orthodoxy initiated and successfully led great revolutions but has seldom cared to think of the prevailing ills, to opine on the ills, to suggest the remedial measures and to enter into a discussion on the political philosophy of Islam.

This aspect has to be carefully examined in the systems of Shī'a and Sunni orthodoxy. The Sunni ecclesiastical system is of such fashion that it becomes farcical in the hands of its rulers whom it introduces as the supreme [political authority] to issue commands.... We find that the Sunni ecclesiastical institution as a system aligned to the political is not strong enough to rise against its rival and to win over to its side the masses of the people.

But the Shī'ī ecclesiastical order is an independent institution, drawing strength (from the spiritual point of view) from God alone and (from social point of view) from the power of the masses. It will be, therefore, noted that the whole institution has, during the long course of its history, emerged as a rival force to the oppressors of their age. It has already been said that in the Islamic countries with the Sunni majority of the population, Sayyid Jamāl al-Dīn al-Afghānī approached the masses of the people

From the English translation by Maktab-i Qur'ān, Keshmir, India, entitled *Islamic Movements in the Twentieth Century* by Murtaza Muhtahhari (Tehran: Great Islamic Library, 1979), pp. 52–67.

308

but in Iran where the majority are the Shī'as, he approached the religious leaders. In Sunni countries he wanted the masses to be galvanized into action, but in Shī'a countries, he expected the religious leaders ('ulamā') to initiate the revolution. This is because the Shī'a church was independent of the institution of the ruling authorities. It is from this phenomena that the Shī'ā church has had the potential of bringing about a revolution whereas the Sunni church did not enjoy that strength. The Shī'ā religious leaders have, in practice, rejected the thesis of Karl Marx that the triangle of religion, government and the capital has been throughout the course of history, interactive and the factors have been in collusion with one another; that they have shaped a class against the masses and that the three factors mentioned above are the result of the self-estrangement of the people.

Iranian Islamic Movement

Scholars and knowledgeable persons in contemporary history concede that in the second half of our century in almost all or at least in a large number of Islamic countries Islamic movements have been in ascent openly or secretly. These are practically directed against despotism, capitalist colonialism or materialistic ideologies subscribing to colonialism in its new shape. Experts on political affairs acknowledge that after having passed through a period of mental crisis the Muslims are once again struggling to reestablish their "Islamic identity" against the challenges of capitalist West and the communist East. But in no Islamic country has this type of movement gained as much of depth and extent as in Iran since the year 1960. Nor is there a parallel to the proportions which the Iranian movement has obtained. It, therefore, becomes necessary to analyze this remarkably significant event of history.

The Nature

Like all natural occurrences, social and political events also tend to differ from one another in their behaviours. All historical movements cannot be considered identical in their nature. The nature of the Islamic movement is in no case similar to the French revolution or to the great October revolution of Russia.

The current Iranian movement is not restricted to any particular class or trade union. It is not only a labour, an agrarian, a student, an intellectual or a bourgeois movement. Within its scope fall one and all in Iran, the rich and the poor, the man and the woman, the school boy and the scholar, the warehouse man and the factory labourer, the artisan and the peasant, the clergy and the teacher, the literate and the illiterate, one and all. An announcement made by the preceptor of the highest station guiding the movement is received in the length and breadth of the country with equal enthusiasm by all classes of the people. . . .

This movement is one of the glaring historical proofs which falsifies the concept of materialistic interpretation of history and that of the dialectics of materialism according to which economy is recognised as the cornerstone of social structure and a social movement is considered a reflection of class struggle. . . .

The awakened Islamic conscience of our society has induced it to search for Islamic values. This is the conscience of the cumulative enthusiasms of all classes of people, including perhaps some of the hereby dissident groups, which has galvanized them into one concerted upsurge.

The roots of this movement shall have to be traced in the events that occurred during the last half century in our country and the way these events came into conflict with the Islamic spirit of our society.

It is evident that during the last half century, there have been events which adopted a diametrically opposite direction as far as the nobler objectives of Islam were concerned and which aimed at nullifying the aspirations of the well-meaning reformers for the last century. This state of affairs could not continue for long without reaction.

What happened in Iran during the last half century may be summed up as under:

1. Absolute and barbaric despotism.
2. Denial of freedom of every kind.
3. A new type of colonialism meaning an invisible and dangerous colonialism embracing political, economic and cultural aspects of life.
4. Maintaining distance between religion and politics. Rather, divorcing politics from religion.
5. An attempt at leading Iran back to the age of ignorance of pre-Islamic days. Also the attempt of reviving the pre-Islamic culture of Iran—the Magian culture—as is manifest from the change of the Hijri era to the Magian era.
6. Effecting a change and corrupting the rich Islamic culture and replacing it with the ambiguous Iranian culture.
7. Gruesome killing of Iranian Muslims, imprisonment and orture of the alleged political prisoners.
8. Ever increasing descrimination and cleavage among th. classes of society despite so-called reforms.
9. Domination of non-Muslim elements over the Muslim elements in the government and other institutions.
10. Flagrant violation of Islamic laws either directly or by perpetrating corruption in the cultural and social life of the people.

11. Propaganda against Persian literature (which has always been the protector and upholder of Islamic spirit) under the pretext of purifying the Persian language of foreign terminology.
12. Severing relations with Islamic countries and flirting with non-Islamic and obviously with anti-Islamic countries like Israel.

The Various Roles of Orthodoxy
in Bringing About the Revolution

The Shī'ī divines have performed various roles in bringing about this pious Islamic revolution. Their efforts have, at last, culminated in success.

Some of the divines embarked on an open struggle against the regime of the Shah. They gave the cry for revolt and infused the masses with the spirit of an anti-Shah revolt. As a result they had to suffer privations like extirpation, incarceration, torture and martyrdom. Some persisted with the struggle openly as well as secretly mobilizing mass opinion, and at times, they had to seal their lips for the sake of expediency.

There were some of the fighters who apparently desisted from making utterances and did not betray any sign of being the die-hards. Their attitude has been, unfortunately, misunderstood by a number of short-sighted persons as something anti-revolutionary. But the truth is that they were among the most zealous, the most sincere and the most humane of the revolutionaries. Their task was to infiltrate into the various sections of the society; choose the persons with capacity and infuse in them the spirit of revolution. For this purpose, the first thing was to strengthen in them faith and belief; to establish in their minds the fact that their duty was divine and that they had to lay their lives in the path of God. Their role was to expose the fact that the regime of the Shah was an anti-Islamic regime and if allowed to continue as it did, true Islam would appear in the shape of Pahlavi Islam. Hence a struggle against such a regime was the will of God, and one meeting death in the struggle would be a martyr. It hardly needs to be emphasized what singular role those people (who had been indoctrinated by the divines) performed in this great struggle. In the course of their struggle, these persons, like their preceptors, trained and educated another generation, in a wider field of activity. They infiltrated into all such places as were not attended by the divines in person and carried on the propaganda incognito.

Struggle for the Sake of God or the World?

One who joins a struggle with the objective of achieving material gains and worldly position without any realization of duty towards God and religion, cannot be supposed to be sincere to the movement. If he is offered material benefits or a worldly position, he will readily accept it and will withdraw from the struggle. He had joined the struggle for this purpose, otherwise he would not. We have seen that some of those materialists ceased to persist with their opposition to the regime of the Shah when they received material benefits and finally succumbed to the position of servitude to the absolutism of the regime.

But he who reckons his participation in the revolutionary struggle as a divine and religious duty is least concerned when, in the course of struggle, his material position and property are lost altogether. He continues with the struggle even when he is conscious of the fact that his life is in peril. He does not, therefore, attach much significance to a life which ultimately must come to an end. But an honourable death, death for the religious cause, would bestow upon him the everlasting life. . . .

The Objective

What is the objective pursued by the movement and what does it want? Does it aim at democracy? Does it want to liquidate colonialism from our country? Does it rise to defend what is called in modern terminology as human rights? Does it want to do away with discrimination, inequality? Does it want to uproot oppression? Does it want to undo materialism and so forth and so on.

In view of the nature of the movement and its roots as already brought under consideration and also in view of the statements and announcements given out by the leaders of the movement, what one may gather as an answer to these questions is "Yes" as well as "No."

"Yes" because all the objectives mentioned above form the very crux of it. And "No" because the movement is not limited to only these or any one of these objectives. An Islamic movement cannot, from the point of its objective, remain a restricted affair, because Islam, in its very nature, is "an indivisible whole" and with the realization of any of the objectives set before it, its role does not cease to be.

However, it does not mean that from a tactical point of view, a particular set of objectives does not enjoy priority over another set and that the stages of realization of these objectives are not needed to be taken into consideration. Did not Islam pass through a tactical evolution? Today the movement is passing through the stage of rejection and disregard (of the ruling authority) and of striking hard at despotism and colonialism. Having emerged victorious out of this struggle, it shall address itself to stability and reconstruction and other objectives shall then demand its attention.

. . . Imām Husayn during the times of Mu'āwiyah and in the presence of a distinguished Islamic gathering on the eve of the holy pilgrimage [summed] up the core of the philosophy of reformation in Islam. He has said it in four sentences:

1. "The effaced signs on the path leading to God be reinstated." It refers to the original principles of Islam and return to those very principles. Innovations be done away with and their place be filled by true and original customs. In other words it means reform in the very thought, the very conscience and the very spirit of Islam.

2. Fundamental, actual and far-reaching reforms which would invite the attention of every observer and would be carrying in them seeds of welfare for the people at large, in urban and in rural areas and the society as a whole be brought about. It means the most radical reforms in the living conditions of the masses of the people.

3. God's humanity under victimisation be given security against the oppressor. The tyranny of the oppressor be eliminated. It means reform in the social relations of human beings.

4. God's commands hitherto suspended and the Islamic laws hitherto ignored be revived so as to establish their supremacy in the social life of the people.

Leadership

No movement can be led successfully without leadership. But who should be the leader or the group of leaders when the movement is an Islamic one in its nature and when its objective is exclusively Islam?

Evidently the leadership should, in the first place, fulfill the general conditions of the task before it. Then the leaders must be deeply Islamic, fully conversant with the ethical, social, political and spiritual philosophy of Islam. They must have the knowledge of Islam's universal vision, its insight about empirical matters like the creation, the origin, the creator of the universe, the need for creation of the universe, etc. They must have the deep knowledge of Islam's views and stipulations on man and his society. It is of great importance that the leaders must have a clear picture of the Islamic ideology of man's relations with his society; his manner and method of framing the social order; his abilities of defending and pursuing certain things and resisting others; his ultimate objectives and the means of attaining those objectives, etc.

It is obvious that only such persons can lead as have been brought up under the pure Islamic culture having perfectly mastered the branches of religious learning and Islamic sciences, the Qur'ān, tradition, jurisprudence, etc. It is, therefore, only ecclesiastics who qualify for the leadership of such a movement. . . .

ĀYATULLĀH RŪHULLĀH KHUMAYNĪ
(1900–

After completing his studies at Qum, a major center of religious learning in Iran, under Shaykh 'Abd al-Karīm Hā'iri Yazdī, the Āyatullāh Khumaynī taught philosophy, ethics, and law. In 1963, he emerged as a critic of the Shah in his sermons at the Faydīya Madrasa (religious school) in Qum. The Āyatullāh Khumaynī was arrested and from 1964 lived in exile, fifteen years in Iraq and later France. He became a symbol for and leader of the opposition movement. In February 1979, the Āyatullāh Khumaynī returned to Teheran to establish the Islamic Republic of Iran.

Islamic Government

In the name of God, the merciful and the compassionate, whose help we seek. God, lord of the universe, be thanked and God's prayers be upon Muhammad, the best of mankind, and upon all his kinsmen.

Foreword

The Governance of the Jurisprudent is a clear scientific idea that may require no proof in the sense that whoever knows the laws and beliefs can see its axiomatic nature. But the condition of the Muslim society, and the condition of our religious academies in particular, has driven this issue away from the minds and it now needs to be proven again.

Since its inception, the Islamic movement was afflicted with the Jews when they started their counter-activity by distorting the reputation of Islam, by assaulting it and by slandering it. This has continued to our present day. Then came the role of groups that can be considered more evil than the devil and his troops. This role emerged in the colonialist activity which dates back to more than three centuries ago. The colonists found in the Muslim world their long-sought object. To achieve their colonialist ambitions, the colonists sought to create the right conditions leading to the annihilation of Islam. They did not seek to turn the Muslims into Christians after driving them away from Islam because they do not believe in

From *Islamic Government*, trans. Joint Publications Research Service (Arlington, Va.: National Technical Information Service, 1979), pp. 1a–3, 10, 13–14, 17–18, 20–22.

either. They wanted control and domination because they were constantly aware during the Crusades wars that the biggest obstacle preventing them from attaining their goals and putting their political plans on the brink of an abyss was Islam with its law and beliefs and with the influence it exerted on people through their faith. This is why they treated Islam unjustly and harbored ill intentions toward it. The hands of the missionaries, the orientalists and of the information media—all of whom are in the service of the colonialist countries—have cooperated to distort the facts of Islam in a manner that has caused many people, especially the educated among them, to steer away from Islam and to be unable to find a way to reach Islam.

Islam is the religion of the strugglers who want right and justice, the religion of those demanding freedom and independence and those who do not want to allow the infidels to dominate the believers.

But the enemies have portrayed Islam in a different light. They have drawn from the minds of the ordinary people a distorted picture of Islam and implanted this picture even in the religious academies. The enemies' aim behind this was to extinguish the flame of Islam and to cause its vital revolutionary character to be lost, so that the Muslims would not think of seeking to liberate themselves and to implement all the rules of their religion through the creation of a government that guarantees their happiness under the canopy of an honorable human life.

They have said that Islam has no relationship whatsoever with organizing life and society or with creating a government of any kind and that it only concerns itself with the rules of menstruation and childbirth. It may contain some ethics. But beyond this, it has no bearing on issues of life and of organizing society. It is regrettable that all this has had its bad effect not only on the ordinary people but also among college people and the students of theology. They misunderstand Islam and are ignorant of it. Islam has become as strange to them as alien people. It has become difficult for the missionary to familiarize people with Islam. On the other hand, there stands a line of the agents of colonialism to drown Islam with clamor and noise.

So that we may distinguish the reality of Islam from what people have come to know about it, I would like to draw your attention to the disparity between Qur'ān and the *hadīth* books on the one hand and the (theological) theses on the other hand. The Qur'ān and the *hadīth* books, which are the most important sources of legislation, are clearly superior to the theses written by religious interpreters and legists because the Qur'ān and the *hadīth* books are comprehensive and cover all aspects of life. The Qur'ān phrases concerned with society's affairs are many times the phrases concerned with private worship. In any of the detailed *hadīth* books, you can hardly find more than three or four chapters concerned with regulating man's private worship and man's relationship with God and few chapters dealing with ethics. The rest is strongly connected with social and economic affairs, with human rights, with administration and with the policy of societies. . . .

What we are suffering from currently is the consequence of that misleading propaganda whose perpetrators got what they wanted and which has required us to exert a large effort to prove that Islam contains principles and rules for the formation of government.

This is our situation. The enemies have implanted these falsehoods in the minds of people in cooperation with their agents, have ousted Islam's judiciary and political laws from the sphere of application and have replaced them by European laws in contempt of Islam for the purpose of driving it away from society. They have exploited every available opportunity for this end. . . . In the prophet's time, was the church separated from the state? Were there at the time theologians and politicians? At the time of the caliphs and the time of 'Alī, the Amīr of the faithful, was the state separated from the church? Was there an agency for the church and another for the state?

The colonialists and their lackeys have made these statements to isolate religion from the affairs of life and society and to tacitly keep the 'ulamā' of Islam away from the people, and drive people away from the 'ulamā' because the 'ulamā' struggle for the liberation and independence of the Muslims. When their wish of separation and isolation is realized, the colonialists and their lackeys can take away our resources and rule us. I tell you that if our sole concern is to pray, to implore and mention God and never go beyond, colonialism and all the agencies of aggression will never oppose us. Pray as you wish and call for prayer as you wish and let them take what God has given you. The final account is to God and God is the only source of strength and might. When we die our reward will come from God—if this is our thinking, then we have nothing to be concerned with or to fear. . . .

Need for Continued Implementation of Laws.
. . . Because Islam is immortal, it must be implemented and observed forever. If what was permissible by Muhammad is permissible until the day of resurrection and what was forbidden by Muhammad is forbidden to the day of resurrection, then Muhummad's restrictions must not be suspended, his teachings must not be neglected, punishment must not be abandoned, tax collection must not be stopped and defense of the nation of the Muslims and of their lands must not be abandoned. The belief that Islam came for a limited period and for a certain place violates the essentials of the Islamic beliefs. Considering that the implementation forever of laws after the venerable prophet, may God's prayers be upon him, is one

of the essentials of life, then it is necessary for government to exist and for this government to have the qualities of an executive and administrative authority. Without this, social chaos, corruption and ideological and moral deviation would prevail. This can be prevented only through the creation of a just government that runs all aspects of life.

Islamic System of Government

Distinction from Other Political Systems
The Islamic government is not similar to the well-known systems of government. It is not a despotic government in which the head of state dictates his opinion and tampers with the lives and property of the people. The prophet, may God's prayers be upon him, and 'Alī, the Amīr of the faithful, and the other Imāms[1] had no power to tamper with people's property or with their lives. The Islamic government is not despotic but constitutional. However, it is not constitutional in the well-known sense of the word, which is represented in the parliamentary system or in the people's councils. It is constitutional in the sense that those in charge of affairs observe a number of conditions and rules underlined in the Qur'ān and in the Sunna and represented in the necessity of observing the system and of applying the dictates and laws of Islam. This is why the Islamic government is the government of the divine law. The difference between the Islamic government and the constitutional governments, both monarchic and republican, lies in the fact that the people's representatives or the king's representatives are the ones who codify and legislate, whereas the power of legislation is confined to God, may He be praised, and nobody else has the right to legislate and nobody may rule by that which has not been given power by God. This is why Islam replaces the legislative council [branch] by a planning council that works to run the affairs and work of the ministries so that they may offer their services in all spheres.

All that is mentioned in the book (Qur'ān) and in the Sunna is acceptable and obeyed in the view of the Muslims. This obedience facilitates the state's responsibilities, however when the majorities in the constitutional monarchic or republican governments legislate something, the government has to later exert efforts to compel people to obey, even if such obedience requires the use of force.

The Islamic government is the government of the law and God alone is the ruler and the legislator. God's rule is effective among all the people and

1. Imām: For Shī'ītes, the Imām is the successor of the prophet Muhammad and thus the religio-political leader of the Islamic community. Ithanā 'Asharīte (Twelver) Shī'ī Islam recognizes twelve Imāms who are descendants of Muhammad through 'Alī, his son-in-law and first Imām.

in the state itself. All individuals—the prophet, his successors and other people—follow that Islam, which descended through revelation and which God had explained through the Qur'ān and through the words of His prophet, and has legislated for them.

The venerable prophet, may God's peace and prayers be upon him, was appointed ruler on earth by God so that he may rule justly and not follow whims. God addressed the prophet through revelation and told him to convey what was revealed to him to those who would succeed him. The prophet obeyed the dictates of this order and appointed ʿAlī, the Amīr of the faithful, as his successor. He was not motivated in this appointment by the fact that ʿAlī was his son-in-law and the fact that ʿAlī had performed weighty and unforgettable services but because God ordered the prophet to do so.

Yes, government in Islam means obeying the law and making it the judge. The powers given to the prophet, may God's peace and prayers be upon him, and to the legitimate rulers after him are powers derived from God. God ordered that the prophet and the rulers after him be obeyed: "Obey the prophet and those in charge among you." There is no place for opinions and whims in the government of Islam. The prophet, the Imāms and the people obey God's will and Sharīʿa.

The Sharīʿa and reason require us not to let governments have a free hand. The proof of this is evident. The persistence of these governments in their transgressions means obstructing the system and laws of Islam whereas there are numerous provisions that describe every non-Islamic system as a form of idolatry and a ruler or an authority in such a system as a false god. We are responsible for eliminating the traces of idolatry from our Muslim society and for keeping it away from our life. At the same time, we are responsible for preparing the right atmosphere for bringing up a faithful generation that destroys the thrones of false gods and destroys their illegal powers because corruption and deviation grow on their hands. This corruption must be wiped out and erased and the severest punishment must be inflicted upon those who cause it. In his venerable book, God describes Pharaoh as "a corrupter." Under the canopy of a pharonic rule that dominates and corrupts society rather than reform it, no faithful and pious person can live abiding by and preserving his faith and piety. Such a person has before him two paths, and no third to them: either be forced to commit sinful acts or rebel against and fight the rule of false gods, try to wipe out or at least reduce the impact of such a rule. We only have the second path open to us. We have no alternative but to work for destroying the corrupt and corrupting systems and to destroy the symbol of treason and the unjust among the rulers of peoples.

This is a duty that all Muslims wherever they may be are entrusted—a duty to create a victorious and triumphant Islamic political revolution.

Need for Islamic Unity.
On the other hand, colonialism has partitioned our homeland and has turned the Muslims into peoples. When the Ottoman State appeared as a united state, the colonialist sought to fragment it. The Russians, the British and their allies united and fought the Ottomans and then shared the loot, as you all know. We do not deny that most rulers of the Ottoman State lacked ability, competence and qualifications and many of them ruled the people in a despotic monarchic manner. However, the colonialists were afraid that some pious and qualified persons would, with the help of the people, assume leadership of the Ottoman State and (would safeguard) its unity, ability, strength and resources, thus dispersing the hopes and aspirations of the colonialists. This is why as soon as World War I ended, the colonialists partitioned the country into mini-states and made each of these mini-states their agent. Despite this, a number of these mini-states later escaped the grip of colonialism and its agents.

The only means that we possess to unite the Muslim nation, to liberate its lands from the grip of the colonialist and to topple the agent governments of colonialism, is to seek to establish our Islamic government. The efforts of this government will be crowned with success when we become able to destroy the heads of treason, the idols, the human images and the false gods who disseminate injustice and corruption on earth.

The formation of a government is then for the purpose of preserving the unity of the Muslims after it is achieved. . . .

Need for Rescuing Wronged and Deprived.
To achieve their unjust economic goals, the colonialists employed the help of their agents in our countries. As a result of this, there are hundreds of millions of starving people who lack the simplest health and educational means. On the other side, there are individuals with excessive wealth and broad corruption. The starving people are in a constant struggle to improve their conditions and to free themselves from the tyranny of the aggressive rulers. But the ruling minorities and their government agencies are also seeking to extinguish this struggle. On our part, we are entrusted to rescue the deprived and the wronged. We are instructed to help the wronged and to fight the oppressors, as the Amīr of the faithful ('Alī) instructed his two sons in his will: "Fight the tyrant and aid the wronged."

The Muslim '*ulamā*' are entrusted to fight the greedy exploiters so that society may not have a deprived beggar and, on the other side, someone living in comfort and luxury and suffering from gluttony. . . .

The opinion of the Shī'ī concerning the one who is entitled to lead the people is known since the death of the prophet and until the time of the disappearance (of the Shī'īte leader). To the Shī'ī the Imām is a virtuous man who knows the laws and implements them justly and who fears nobody's censure in serving God.

Ruler in Time of Absence.

If we believe that the laws concerning the establishment of the Islamic government are still present and that the *Sharī'a* denounces chaos, then we must form the government. Reason dictates that this is necessary, especially if an enemy surprises us or if an aggressor who must be fought and repelled attacks us. The *Sharī'a* has ordered us to prepare for them all the force that we can muster to scare God's enemy and our enemy, and it encourages us to retaliate against those who attack us with whatever they attack us. Islam also calls for doing the wronged justice, for wrenching his rights and for deterring the unjust. All this requires strong agencies. As for the expenses of the government that is to be formed for the service of the people—the entire people—these expenses come from the treasury house, whose revenues consist of the land tax, the one-fifth tax and the tax levied on Jews and Christians and other resources.

Now, in the time of absence, there is no provision for a certain person to manage the state affairs. So what is the opinion? Should we allow the laws of Islam to continue to be idle? Do we persuade ourselves to turn away from Islam or do we say that Islam came to rule people for a couple of centuries and then to neglect them? Or do we say that Islam has neglected to organize the state? We know that the absence of the government means the loss and violation of the bastions of the Moslems and means our failure to gain our right and our land. Is this permitted in our religion? Isn't the government one of the necessities of life? Despite the absence of a provision designating an individual to act on behalf of the Imām in the case of his absence, the presence of the qualities of the religious ruler in any individual still qualify him to rule the people. These qualities, which are knowledge of the law and justice, are available in most of our jurisprudents in this age. If they decide, it will be easy for them to create and establish a just government unequalled in the world.

Rule of Jurisprudent.

If a knowledgeable and just jurisprudent undertakes the task of forming the government, then he will run the social affairs that the prophet used to run and it is the duty of the people to listen to him and obey him.

This ruler will have as much control over running the people's administration, welfare and policy as the prophet and Amīr of the faithful had despite the special virtues and the traits that distinguished the prophet and the Imām. Their virtues did not entitle them to contradict the instructions of the *Sharī'a* or to dominate people with disregard to God's order. God has given the actual Islamic government that is supposed to be formed in the time of absence (of Caliph 'Alī ibn Abi Tālib) the same powers that he gave the prophet and the Amīr of the faithful in regard to ruling, justice and the settlement of disputes, the appointment of provincial rulers and officers, the collection of taxes and the development of the country. All that there is to the matter is that the appointment of the ruler at present depends on (finding) someone who has both knowledge and justice.

The Rule of the Jurisprudent (wilāyat i-faqīh)[1]
The above-mentioned must not be misunderstood and nobody should imagine that the fitness of the jurisprudent for rule raises him to the status of prophecy or of Imāms because our discussion here is not concerned with status and rank but with the actual task. The rule here means governing the people, running the state and applying the laws of the *Sharī'a*. This is a hard task under which those qualified for it buckle without being raised above the level of men. In other words, rule means the government, the administration and the country's policy and not, as some people imagine, a privilege or a favor. It is a practical task of extreme significance.

The rule of the jurisprudent is a subjective matter dictated by the *Sharī'a*, as the *Sharī'a* considers one of us a trustee over minors. The task of a trustee over an entire people is not different from that of the trustee over minors, except quantitatively. If we assume that the prophet and the Imām had been trustees over minors, their task in this respect would not have been very different quantitatively and qualitatively from the task of any ordinary person designated as a trustee over those same minors. Their trusteeship over the entire nation is not different practically from the trusteeship of any knowledgeable and just jurisprudent in the time of absence.

If a just jurisprudent capable of establishing the restrictions is appointed, would he establish the restrictions in a manner different from that in which they were established in the days of the prophet or of the Amīr of the faithful? Did the prophet punish the unmarried fornicator more than one hundred lashes? Does the jurisprudent have to reduce the number to prove that there is a difference between them and the prophet? No, because the ruler, be he a prophet, an Imām or a just jurisprudent, is nothing but an executor of God's order and will.

The prophet collected taxes: The one-fifth tax, the alms tax, the tax on the Christians and the Jews and the land tax. Is there a difference between

---

1. *Wilāyat i-faqīh* (Guidance of the jurisprudent): During the absence (*ghaybat*) of the Imām and a formal Islamic government, Shī'ī political theory developed the belief that the jurisprudent(s) should provide guidance (*wilāyat*) for the Islamic community. Shī'ī religious leaders differ significantly in their interpretations. For Āyatullāh Sharī'atmadārī *et al.*, the jurisprudents provide moral guidance. For Āyatullāh Khumaynī *wilāyat* means governance itself by an individual *faqīh* who assures Sharī'ah rule.

what the prophet and the Imām collected and what the present-day jurisprudent should collect?

God made the prophet the ruler of all the faithful and his rule included even the individual who was to succeed him. After the prophet, the Imām became the ruler. The significance of their rule is that their legal orders applied to all and that the appointment of, control over and, when necessary, dismissal of judges and provincial rulers was in their hands.

The jurisprudent has this same rule and governance with one difference—namely that the rule of the jurisprudent over other jurisprudents is not so that he can dismiss them because the jurisprudents in the state are equal in terms of competence.

Therefore, the jurisprudents must work separately or collectively to set up a legitimate government that establishes the strictures, protects the borders and establishes order. If competence for this task is confined to one person, then this would be his duty to do so corporeally, otherwise the duty is shared equally. In case it is impossible to form that government, the rule does not disappear.

The jurisprudents have been appointed by God to rule and the jurisprudent must act as much as possible and in accordance with his assignment. He must collect the alms tax, the one-fifth tax, the land tax and the tax from Christians and Jews, if he can, so that he may spend all this in the interest of the Muslims. If he can, he must implement the divine strictures. The temporary inability to form a strong and complete government does not at all mean that we should retreat. Dealing with the needs of the Muslims and implementing among them whatever laws are possible to implement is a duty as much as possible.